Landscape Architecture at **TSINGHUA** University

APPLIED
RESEARCH
+DESIGN
PUBLISHING

Published by Applied Research and Design Publishing. An Imprint of ORO Editions
Gordon Goff: Publisher

www.appliedresearchanddesign.com
info@appliedresearchanddesign.com

10 9 8 7 6 5 4 3 2 1 First Edition

ISBN: 978-1-939621-62-7

Color Separations and Printing: ORO Group Ltd.
Printed in China.

International Distribution: www.appliedresearchanddesign.com/distribution

AR+D Publishing makes a continuous effort to minimize the overall carbon footprint of its publications. As part of this goal, AR+D, in association with Global ReLeaf, arranges to plant trees to replace those used in the manufacturing of the paper produced for its books. Global ReLeaf is an international campaign run by American Forests, one of the world's oldest nonprofit conservation organizations. Global ReLeaf is American Forests' education and action program that helps individuals, organizations, agencies, and corporations improve the local and global environment by planting and caring for trees.

Department of Landscape Architecture
School of Architecture **TSINGHUA** University

Landscape Architecture at **TSINGHUA** University

66 Years of Excellence

Edited by Yang Rui and Zheng Xiaodi
Department of Landscape Architecture
School of Architecture, TSINGHUA University

Contents

FOREWORD
66 Years of Excellence and Beyond

The landscape education at Tsinghua University has grown from a burgeoning idea into a world-renowned program, and this book is a compiled retrospect of the evolution of the Department of Landscape Architecture at Tsinghua University over the last 66 years. It is a document and homage to the growth and flourishing of the institution, and all the individuals who have participated, contributed, and shaped its growth along the way.

In 1945 Professor Liang Sicheng sent a written proposal to the president of Tsinghua University, Mei Yiqi, calling for the establishment of the Department of Architecture. "Once the war is over, it is time to study the situations and establish the School of Architecture, and gradually adding to it the Departments of Civil Engineering, Urban Planning, Courtyard Design, Interior Decoration, etc." In 1949, Professor Liang again petitioned for landscape architecture content in his curriculum framework for the Department of Architecture and Urban Planning at Tsinghua, however, it wasn't until 1951 that Professor Wu Liangyong and Wang Juyuan established the first ever landscape architecture program at Tsinghua. In 2002, Professor Qin Youguo, former dean of the School of Architecture, formally put forward the proposal to establish the Department of Landscape Architecture in his report entitled, "Tsinghua Architectural Education Looking into the 21st Century." The proposal was reviewed and passed at the 20th convocation of Tsinghua University, in July, 2003, and the Department of Landscape Architecture was officially established in October with Professor Laurie Olin as the first chair.

Over the course of the years, there has been gradual growth through the proposals and work of those faithful to the ideals and goals of developing, not only a department of Landscape Architecture at Tsinghua University, but a method for landscape planning and design for China's future that is culturally sensitive and diverse, and ecologically responsible. Set within Tsinghua School of Architecture, the Landscape Architecture program works hand-in-hand with other related disciplines of Architecture and City Planning in order to create a harmonious environment through collaboration.

The three sections in this book show the historical record, educational achievements, and academic research of the department as it has been shaped into the department it is today, and to remember where we have come from as it continues to evolve to address the needs of the future. With records of key events and developments, faculty and students, and projects that have shaped the course of the department, this book celebrates the work and lives of over 50 faculty members that have guided the program, and the 257 students who have graduated from the department.

The mission statement, "Thorough knowledge of East and West and of past and present," has guided the department to "being dedicated to foster Chinese professional landscape architects and tomorrow's leaders in landscape planning, design, management, and research." Each assignment in the undergraduate and graduate courses is centered on this philosophy and the courses are detailed within this book along with selected students' work and theses and dissertations from 1951 to the present. Key research and practice projects in the field of landscape architecture undertaken by faculty members at Tsinghua University, past and present, are introduced. They have made a big impact in various aspects to shape the landscape of Chinese cities and to contribute to the development of the discipline in China, leading frontier works in the field, such as national park system, brownfields regeneration, therapeutic gardens, and more.

During the Chinese National Discipline Evaluation in 2017, the Department of Landscape Architecture at Tsinghua School of Architecture received a score of "A+" and ranked as one of the two top-programs in China. In the same year, the Chinese Ministry of Education, the Ministry of Finance, and the National Development and Reform Commission jointly released the "Double-First Class" initiative, which aims to ultimately build a number of world class universities and disciplines by the end of 2050, in an effort to make China an international higher education power. All three first-level disciplines at Tsinghua School of Architecture were selected into this initiative, including the discipline of architecture, urban and rural planning, and landscape architecture. This is a very impressive achievement for the Department of Landscape Architecture with a limited number of faculty members and students. It surely will provide a good platform for the department to continually develop and grow.

Under the current context of ecological civilization development in China, along with the urgent need to improve the quality of ecological and living environment threatened by the fast urbanization process, there are challenges and opportunities for the profession of landscape architecture in China. With the dedication and diligence of its members, the Department of Landscape Architecture at Tsinghua University can be expected to make a profound difference in shaping a better environment that we all live in.

–Zhuang Weimin, *dean of the School of Architecture at Tsinghua University*

INTRODUCTION
Celebrating Growth

The year 2013 marked the 10th anniversary of the Department of Landscape Architecture, School of Architecture, Tsinghua University, the 60th anniversary of the commencement of first batch of graduates from the 1951 Landscape program, and the 100th anniversary of the birth of Wang Juyuan, co-founder of the Landscape Architecture (LA) Program. To mark the special year, teachers and students at the Department of Landscape Architecture have published a series of three books in Chinese to introduce research and practice at Tsinghua, and to record the physical and philosophical development and history of the Landscape Architecture program. The essence of these three books are translated and reorganized into this publication. The history of Tsinghua's LA Program can be divided into three stages: initiation, continuation, and actualization. The initiation stage spanned eight years, from 1945 to 1953. In 1945 Liang Sicheng planned to establish the Department of Gardening, one of four departments he envisioned for the School of Architecture, of which the LA program would grow from. In 1951 Wu Liangyong and Wang Juyuan co-founded the LA Program at Tsinghua, which was a monumental achievement in collaboration between the architecture, agriculture, and forestry institutions. In 1953, the department celebrated the graduation of the first eight students, among whom, Li Zhiruo, Zhu Junzhen, Liu Shaozong, and Wang Sui, went on to become important members of the landscape architecture community in China. That year also marked the end of the LA Program due to adjustments in the national institutions of higher learning.

This was not the end though. The five decades from 1953 to 2003 mark the continuation stage of Tsinghua's Landscape Architecture research and practice. Liang Sicheng, Wu Liangyong, Mo Zongjiang, Zhu Changzhong, Wang Guoyu, Zhu Zixuan, Zhou Weiquan, Chen Zhihua, Lou Qingxi, Zhang Binshi, Liu Chenxian, Zhu Junzhen, Yao Tongzhen, Zheng Guangzhong, Feng Zhongping, Guo Daiheng, Shan Deqi, Sun Fengqi, Zuo Chuan, Ji Huailu, Wang Lifang, and Zhang Junhua faithfully guarded and passed the torch of the landscape architecture program through different periods and by different means, leaving behind remarkable achievements in academic research and publications, graduate education, and engineering practices. Wu Liangyong set the parameters for the development of LA at Tsinghua with his *Introduction to the Sciences of human Settlements*; Zhu Changzhong has special contribution in the institutional construction and planning practice of scenic areas in China; Zhou Weiquan's *A History of Classical Chinese Gardens*, Zhu Junzhen's *A History of Modern Chinese Gardens*, Chen Zhihua's *Foreign Garden Crafts*, and Feng Zhongping's *China's Landscape Architecture* are all hallmarks of Tsinghua's LA historical and theoretical research; and the development of the Institute of Landscape and Gardening and the Institute of Natural Resource Preservation and Tourism respectively led by Sun Fengqi and Zheng Guangzhong laid a foundation for the eventual establishment of the Department of Landscape

Above: The logo of the Department of Landscape Architecture.(Records from the Archive of the School of Architecture, Tsinghua University).

Architecture in 2003. There were three failed attempts to start a Department of Landscape Architecture at Tsinghua University during this period, which culminated in the successful establishment of the department on October 8, 2003—the actualization—during Qin Youguo's tenure as dean of the school.

The establishment of the Department of Landscape Architecture marks the formation of a systematic, formal, and sustainable LA education program at Tsinghua with growing enrollments. Laurie Olin, the first chair of the Department together with his chair professor team made great efforts and contributions to the department from 2003 to 2006. The department now offers five master degree programs and a doctoral program, as well as a bachelor program starting in 2017. As of September 2017, there are 257 graduates, including 22 doctors and 235 masters. Currently, 132 students are enrolled in LA programs, of which 22 are in the doctoral program and 110 are in the master's degree program. The program has a studio based curriculum with three specialization options in landscape design, landscape planning, and synthetic project planning. A joint master's degree in collaboration with Chiba University in Japan has been offered since 2009.

The titles of the three sections in this publication, Invigorating Growth: Historical Overview; Nurturing Excellence: Education Programs; and Crossing Boundaries: Research and Practice, epitomize the pedagogical philosophy of landscape architecture education at Tsinghua University which strives for the nurturing of excellence in landscape architecture with a global perspective, bridging the east and west and the past and present. The logo of the Department of Landscape Architecture which I designed myself is a vivid display of this philosophy. It shows a semicircular tree pattern on ancient eave tiles found in the Chinese State of Qi during the Warring States period. The left and right halves represent the unity of Yin and Yang – the complementary and harmonious relationship between two opposites: history and present, east and west, humankind and nature, theory and practice, science and arts, technology and humanities, logic and vision. A Chinese proverb says that it takes 10 years to grow a tree, but 100 years to educate people. The central graphic element not only symbolizes a vibrant, large tree, but also engaged and thriving students. The persons are kneeling down to express their reverence for nature, respect for culture, and devotion to education. The light green of early spring in the logo conveys infinite energy and vitality while the reflective white space indicates endless hope and possibilities.

楊鋭

–Yang Rui, *chair of the Department of Landscape Architecture.,School of Architecture at Tsinghua University*

SECTION 1
Invigorating Growth: Historical Overview

借古開今

The dusty records, kept in the old-fashioned filing cabinets, ranged from the student assignments from the 1950s to the graduate theses in the 1960s, to the planning projects of decades of bachelor and graduate design and landscape architecture studios and research projects provided precious information to form a historical overview of the development of landscape architecture program at Tsinghua University. Adding on more vivid memories, some of the teachers and students of the 1951 Landscape Architecture Program —Wu Liangyong, Chen Youmin, Li Zhiruo, Zhu Junzhen, and Liu Shaozong—were invited to sit together again and look back on 60 years in a roundtable discussion that provided us with stories reminiscent of the changing times, struggles, and joys that led to the development of the Department we have today. In the days after the dissolution of the program and before the establishment of the Department of Landscape Architecture, Tsinghua scholars had not ceased LA-related teachings, research, and practice, and continued to push for the addition of courses to the Department that would grow and benefit the University and country for decades to come. Landscape Architecture was introduced as one of the three pillars of the Sciences of Human Settlement put forward by Professor Wu Liangyong, and this theory has become a backbone of Tsinghua University School of Architecture. Along with the interviews of former graduates, former teachers were also interviewed including Zhu Zixuan, Zhu Junzhen, Lou Qingxi, Zheng Guangzhong, Feng Zhongping, Guo Daiheng, Ji Huailu, as well as Zhu Changzhong's student Gan Weilin and his friend Xie Ninggao. Professor Zhou Weiquan's manuscripts were donated by his descendants, and document his training programs from the past six decades.

The combination of all these sources culminated in a rough picture of the early days of the Landscape Architecture discipline in Tsinghua University and its development thereafter. The discoveries we made in researching the evolution of the Department are a testament to us, by generations of forerunners, of the Tsinghua motto "Self Discipline and Social Commitment." The devotion of the School of Architecture to talent cultivation, research, and the professional pursuit of "good architects serving to make a great nation," has created a legacy of brilliant professionals full of vigor and warm memories.

Left: In 1950 Mr. Liang Sicheng proposed to restructure Beijing city walls into a "loop park" (Records from the Archive of the School of Architecture, Tsinghua University).

1.1 Reflections
The Evolution of an Idea

Wu Liangyong, *rofessor of Tsinghua School of Architecture; academician of the Chinese Academy of Sciences, and academician of the Chinese Academy of Engineering; a famous architect, city planner, and educator, and the founder of Sciences of Human Settlements in China.*

A landscape architecture program had been envisioned at the time Liang Sicheng established the Department of Architecture at Tsinghua University in 1945. Later, he advised a change to the name of the Department of Architecture to the Department of Architecture and Urban Planning (changed 1949), to encompass and establish a "landscape program," which was adopted by the founding principles into the syllabus. The entire article was published by Wen Wei Po. Even though I was in the United States at that time, one of my friends sent me a copy of the revised syllabus and I was impressed. I returned from my studies abroad and resumed my teaching post at Tsinghua in 1951. Liang Sicheng and Chen Zhanxiang's proposal for the capital city of New China in Bejing was put aside, though the discussion of the city design was still on the table. Wang Mingzhi, director of the Beijing Municipal Construction Bureau, organized three committees in support of the planning: the master plan committee, the transportation committee, and the landscape gardening committee. All three committees were active at that time and had representatives from various professional fields. I was on all three committees and on the landscape gardening committee with Wang Juyuan from the Beijing Agriculture University and Liu Hongbin from Beijing University. The Landscape Gardening Committee met several times and we all felt it necessary to start a program to train individuals in the field since landscape gardening was pivotal to urban development. After one of the meetings, Wang Juyuan and I agreed to create a cooperative landscape architecture program between the two universities we represented. Within days, Wang was able to obtain approval for the program from his university and, I, after discussing the idea with Professor Liang who brought it to Director Ye Qisun of the University Board was also able to gain approval. The program was launched in Tsinghua shortly after. The first batch of eight students was chosen from juniors at the Department of Horticulture at Beijing Agriculture University. Wang Juyuan moved to Tsinghua and established his studio in the I-shaped Hall. Tsinghua assigned teachers and developed a cariculum for these students. When, in 1952, adjustments to the national institutions of higher learning were made, I was acting as supervisor of the Department of Architecture and the landscape architecture program was well established with a strong faculty.

Things moved ahead smoothly. The Ministry of Education located similar programs that had been placed under "forestry" in universities in the Soviet Union. At the time, all national universities were required to follow the Soviet pattern. Wei Que, Vice Minister of Education, called for a meeting with President Sun Xiaocun of the Beijing Agriculture University and President Qian Weichang of Tsinghua University to discuss the matter. Wang Juyuan and I were both present. The final decision was to continue the co-founded program but to base it out of the Beijing Agriculture University. So teachers from the Beijing Agriculture University returned and Tsinghua arranged for its faculty to teach architecture-related courses there. There was one teacher from Tsinghua who chose to transfer to the Agriculture

University in order to continue teaching gardening courses. During the 10 years of "Cultural Revolution," the development of the discipline was at a standstill. In 1978, I was made head of the Department of Architecture at Tsinghua, determined to restart the landscape architecture program. With the many hassles we had been through, including efforts to transfer Zhu Junzhen—one of the first graduates of the landscape architecture program at Tsinghua—back to teach at Tsinghua. We failed to re-establish the program though.

In the early 1980s, Tsinghua sent teachers out to study landscape architecture with the plan of returning to develop a Landscape Architecture department at Tsinghua, however, upon return they were unable to continue their work. In 1984 the School of Architecture was established with Li Daozeng as the dean. The School developed a joint landscape architecture curriculum in cooperation with the University of Pennsylvania (Penn). Some professors from Penn visited to teach courses, but, again, Tsinghua University failed to structure this cooperation into a department. It wasn't until Qin Youguo served as dean that Tsinghua was able to finally establish an LA department promising of a wider curriculum of courses.

I can only attribute the past failures to a lack of proper understanding of, and attention to, the program. Despite all the ups and downs, landscape architecture teaching and research at Tsinghua have remained active over the past six decades with amendments to the disciplinary foundation along the way.

Early in the 21st century, under the influence of curriculum design in the United States, I traveled to San Francisco to engage with landscape architects. I was moved by the tremendous impact the city beautification and national park movements were having upon urban development. I met with Wang Juyuan upon my return, who had shifted his professional interest from plants and flowers to landscape architecture and urban development. Together, we blended the Bejing Agriculture University's stength in botany and Tsinghua's strength in architecture to lay down the multi-disciplinary foundation.

Laurie D. Olin came on as the chair professor and head of the Department from 2003 to 2006. He and his team introduced Tsinghua to western landscape architecture education and helped Tsinghua keep pace with the international academic world, while integrating modern western learning into the foundation at the LA Department of Tsinghua University.

In 2007 (until present), Yang Rui became the head of the LA Department. Under his guidance, the department has blended and added theoretical and practical research into the LA curriculum. He continues to build on the foundations of the department.

The 62nd anniversary of the launch of landscape architecture education at Tsinghua University was in 2013, and also marked the 60th anniversary of the commencement of the first batch of students, and the 10th anniversary of the founding of the contemporary LA Department under Laurie D. Olin. The 18th National Congress of the Communist Party of China has given ecological progress an unprecedented and prominent position by incorporating it into the country's overall development plan along with economic, political, cultural, and social progress. Today's landscape architecture program is based on the integration and development of Chinese and Western science, humanities, and the arts, and will play an extremely important role in alleviating ecological crises, rehabilitating the natural environment, and building a beautiful China while aiding in the rejuvenation of the Chinese culture.

Billion: Reflections Upon the 10th Anniversary of the Department of Landscape Architecture, Tsinghua University

Laurie D. Olin, *first chair of the Department of Landscape Architecture at Tsinghua University. Practicing professor of Landscape Architecture at the University of Pennsylvania, former chair of the Department of Landscape Architecture at Harvard University, a Fellow of the American Academy of Arts and Sciences, and a Fellow of the American Society of Landscape Architects.*

Marco Polo entitled his account of his travel and experiences in China *Millione*. In Italian it means thousands, and to his readers in Renaissance Europe it suggested a vast quantity, whether of humans, regions, cities, or experiences. If he went today, he would have to change the title to *Billione* or *Trillion* to evoke the nature and extent of China, the nation, its people, their remarkable achievements, their cities, activities, issues, and problems.

Everyone knows that China is the most populous country in the world and that it has a long history of great accomplishment in art, literature, science, philosophy, agriculture, urban development, technology, national politics, and international relations. For many thousands of years people have lived and worked in the vast and varied terrain of this portion of the earth, in some periods engaged with other regions and cultures and at other times isolated. The 19th and 20th centuries brought enormous change and disruption, often violent and unfortunate, but change that has for the moment brought China back onto the world stage as a major economic, technological, political, and cultural force. In the course of the changes of the past century, hundreds of millions of people have had their physical and social lives improved from a condition of agricultural servitude to one of urban life and work. While other portions of the world's population, primarily in Western Europe and North America, have previously undergone a transformation from ancient agricultural societies to urban industrial ones, with considerable disruption and social turmoil as well, such changes took place in smaller territories and occurred over longer periods of time. In China it has been (and still is) occurring in a much more accelerated period and at a scale unprecedented in world history.

In the West this transformation was and continues to be disruptive of natural environments, historic landscapes, and cities, and has generated considerable social turmoil to disparities in wealth and amenities. This is due, in part, directly to the capitalist, free enterprise economic system, and in part to numerous experiments in governance and political organization. For all the enormous, obvious benefits of the institutions, industries, and organization of western societies, for all of the unquestionable creativity and energy present in America and Europe over the past 200 years, there is no question that there are serious problems as well. Wars, poverty, crime, pollution, and ill health persist. The great universities have continued to study these problems and to send brilliant young people out into the world to grapple with these issues through planning, design, law, science, and technology, both in government and in the private sector. As a result, remarkable park systems have been created, great architecture and urban spaces built, vast tracts of wilderness and habitat have been protected and preserved, industries have been regulated, air and water quality standards have been raised, and the health and lives of millions have been improved. Yet still, the West struggles with issues of inequities in wealth and housing, pollution and contamination, of energy consumption and waste, of loss of wetlands combined with diminished sources and needed volumes of clean water, of clean energy, emissions, climate change, and sea level rise – a more useful and accurate term for the effect of global warming.

It was knowing all of this that the situation of China seemed to me as challenging and critical as it was interesting when I first came to assist the World Monument Fund in their work on the restoration of the private retirement garden of the Qiang Leong Emperor in the northwest quarter of the Forbidden City in 2002. While working on this project I began to explore Beijing, visited Tsinghua and its Architecture School, and met several faculty members and officials in the Beijing Municipal, Institute for City Planning & Design. I was impressed by their ambition, knowledge, and candid assessment of the daunting problems facing the nation regarding its environment and cities, and therefore the situation of the populace. In the spring of 2004, Professor Tony Atkin and I brought graduate architecture and landscape architecture students from the University of Pennsylvania to Beijing for a joint planning and design studio. One evening, Dean Qin and several other faculty members took Professor Atkin and I out to dinner within the Summer Palace. It was a lovely moonlit night, and at one point the Dean turned and asked if I would help – specifically if I would help him to start a graduate level Department of Landscape Architeture at Tsinghua University. It seemed ridiculous to me at first. How could I possibly help? I didn't even speak the language and couldn't read a sign, let alone a professional paper or a student essay. I dismissed the idea. Qin then went on to explain how two famous graduates of the University of Pennsylvania, Liang Sicheng and his wife had largely started Tsinghua's School of Architecture and Planning. They had been part of a group of Chinese scholars and designers who had attended Penn in the 1930s, had returned to China, and had helped to establish the modern fields of architecture, planning, and architectural history and research. After World War II and the Communist Revolution, he had done considerable planning for the nation and the City of Beijing, and also created the design for China's national emblem. Part of his plan, according to Dean Qin, was to produce a school modeled upon Harvard and the University of Pennsylvania that had three key departments: Architecture, Planning, and Landscape Architecture. He managed to get the first two in place, but for several reasons, landscape architecture was prevented from being established. Like many intellectuals and those in the arts and humanities, he was denounced by the Red Guard, and, as an elderly person, when he became ill his health declined and he died without completing his ambition for the school. Dean Qin was determined to do so, and felt that the model of Penn, Harvard, Berkeley, and other American Universities was essential. He urged me to consider how important this would be for China and the School.

Later, back in America I began to reflect upon the situation. Landscape Architecture is a field that has developed in the past 100 years in America, and then in Europe, that specifically addresses many of the issues regarding planning for health and well being of both people and their environment. It is a messy and at times unsuitably broad field that attempts to plan for regional ecological and resource management as well as for urban and district plans for cities down to the scale of parks and campuses, infrastructure that engages transportation and natural systems, and to gardens large and small. In both America and Europe the modern academic and professional fields of City Planning and Urban Design both began and grew out of Landscape Architecture. As Planning has become more and more involved in public policy and economic and social modeling, and less engaged in physical planning, the field of Landscape Architecture in America, having made enormous strides in large scale resource management and park planning, once again has turned a significant amount of focus and attention upon cities and the urban situation – some aspects of which have come to be referred to as Landscape Urbanism or Urban Ecological Landscape. In part, this has been a result of the development of GIS and other digital mapping processes that occurred within the field several decades ago and are now widely disseminated and used by others as well. In part, it is a response to the fact that for all the architects, engineers, economists, and planners that have been engaged in recent decades in the planning, design, and production of cities around the world, resulting environments have been deficient in quality, and in fact have often become unhealthy, inefficient, dangerous, and undesirable places in which to live, work, and have families.

I thought about this and about how our small department of Landscape Architecture at the University of Pennsylvania had made an enormous contribution to America under the leadership of Ian McHarg. His book *Design With Nature*, and the tireless work of a generation of his students, conferences, and personal connections—in conjunction with a broader environmental movement—influenced government policy at both the local and national level regarding water and its management: the capture, cleansing, detention, and reuse of water that is now standard; as well as land use and ecological planning for development, conservation, and preservation. I thought about how in my 30-plus years at Penn we had sent a generation of graduates out all over the country and world who had taken positions in government and private practice, in development, planning, and design, and had supplied teachers for colleges and universities around the globe. And then I thought about China's headlong rush toward a market economy, its rampant construction boom, and the mess I'd seen in Shanghai and Beijing—the traffic tangles, the polluted skies and rivers, the miles of housing standing in unsuitable and unusable land, in conjunction with the vast terrain of mountains, forests, and agriculture as one flies over it—and how on earth it could be helped; how such energy and momentum to copy all the most disappointing and destructive aspects of Western history could be redirected. One possible answer might be to help create a Department of Landscape Architecture that was not large, but nimble and intelligent; a place that could study the situation and train a generation of leaders that would be able to redirect agencies and developers, corporations and politicians, architects and planners toward methods and results that are more sustainable and humane, more ecological and economical – in the long term, not short term. It seemed to me that it would be preferable rather than sending a cohort of bright young Chinese graduate students abroad each year to learn our (often bad) habits and methods. Possibly, at Tsinghua one might share as much technology, science, and methods prevalent in the better schools in America, along with an ecological point of view that leads to stewardship and a land ethic, without the unfortunate baggage of our rapacious real estate and development management practices.

I returned to Beijing with students from the University of Pennsylvania and while working on a studio project with them had further discussions with faculty members. I concluded that there were a number of wonderful people—students, faculty, government officials—and that it was a difficult situation in terms of politics and economics. A number of universities had begun offering degrees of varying quality and nature under the heading of landscape architecture, but all seemed to be in the mold of European or American undergraduate schools with an emphasis either upon site design or quasi-scientific planning and restoration. The work that their graduates were doing was largely in service of preordained plans by orthodox planners and politicians or architects who shouldn't be doing large site planning, with the results being more of the same environmentally poor sprawling mess that had been spreading out from the historic center of all the cities in the country. I concluded that it would be worth trying to help Tsinghua create a department that would be different from "business as usual," one that would challenge the status quo quietly and professionally, producing a group of idealistic and well trained landscape architects who could see the problems of their country clearly and would seek to find new and better alternative ways to shape policy, and to plan and design landscape at any of several scales: from physiographic regions and watersheds, to urban districts and communities, to national and urban parks and gardens.

I accepted Dean Qin's offer of the chairmanship on the basis that I would visit and be in residence for periods of time each semester for a number of years, as it was impossible for me to move to China full time due to obligations at the University of Pennsylvania, my office, and with my family. In the fall of 2003 I set about attempting to help create the Department. In what was something of a miracle, a brilliant young professor, Yang Rui, was assigned the task of assisting me. There were several pressing tasks that I knew we needed to do: write a curriculum; find a faculty; and recruit some students. The two of us met frequently in one or another of several coffee houses near campus to discuss and work out the details, one of which I hadn't thought much about was that we needed space for the department: for offices, classrooms, and lectures. For the moment we didn't even have a room to meet at the University. I knew nothing about Chinese economics or those of the University. What happened was both astonishing to me and fortuitous. Professor Yang found an abandoned portion of an upper floor in the Architecture building, managed to persuade the Administration into giving it to us, and then proceeded to prepare a design for offices, a conference space, and a large work space, and found the men and materials to build it, which required masonry, walls, electrical work, some heating, and painting. When I inquired how we were paying for it as the budget I'd received had no funds for architectural renovation. In his most cheerful manner he explained that he'd paid for it with a portion of the operating funds from one of his research funds, and that it was okay, as he would put part of his research team there for a time. It was the beginning of my education about how things were done at the time in China. I learned about the system of institutes set up by faculty and government officials throughout the country prior to more recent commercial market developments to do much of the sort of work that is generally done by private companies and professional firms in the West. All of the faculty were, and I am sure still are, working extensively in various institutes they'd invented to do their research or professional creative work, and importantly to supplement their University salaries, which were often quite small. The result was a fresh and handsome office, ample for our beginning.

After learning about several courses that all graduate students in the school were required to take I proposed a sequence of classes that would cover some of the fundamental ecological and technical topics that I believed to be the minimum any graduate in landscape architecture should study. The one subject that I didn't reach a satisfactory solution for was that of history. Any student coming into the program would have had some history I felt, probably architectural, art, or national history. I felt it was important that they also have a history of landscape and its design and planning, one that dealt with settlement, agriculture, urbanism, and parks and gardens. It should cover, to some degree, an ecological history (human as well as natural). I also felt that it should include India, Thailand, Cambodia, Laos, Indonesia, Vietnam, Korea, and Japan as well as China. I had no idea where to find someone or even several individuals to teach such a course but I thought it would be revolutionary and help to establish a broad perspective that could ground the next generation of scholars and practitioners in a way more helpful for China and Asia, and might allow them to develop their own vision for landscape planning and design that could take a different trajectory from that of the west so they might avoid some of our mistakes and problems, in part because of different historical and philosophical attitudes toward society, nature, and land. After a semester of this I felt that they could then have a semester of Western landscape history that would include the usual narrative from Egypt and classical antiquity through the Renaissance to the enlightenment and the rise of modernism, and, which, in addition to presenting great works and the evolution of ecological planning would honestly present the serious failures of western landscape policies, practices, and values, not the least of which were contributing significantly to global pollution, warming, and climate change.

Where we would find the teachers for the different topics was a bit of a mystery. There were some marvelous individuals on the faculty, several of whom were landscape architects, architects, urban designers, or planners, but a couple were either retired or about to retire, and were already either teaching a full load in the Architecture Department or heavily engaged in projects at one or another institute. One who was sympathetic and encouraging was Professor Wu Liangyong, one of the most distinguished Architect/planners in China, and a gifted artist. Another was Professor Sun, an architect/landscape architect who taught basic design and site planning. Both had travelled widely through Europe and Asia, had studied in America, and were busy with professional practice projects. Another who was encouraging and helpful with advice and collegial support but was tied up in his own research, teaching, and consulting was Professor Zhang Jie. Yang Rui introduced me to him, however, the two young, talented, and energetic men who had been doing some teaching—Hu Jie and Zhu Yufan—both had degrees but were also landscape architects and were actively engaged in practice through one or another of the institutes, but usefully at different scales and with different interests. Zhu was deeply interested in history, both Western and Eastern, and in the poetics and craft of gardens, their meaning, and composition; Hu, working at a large scale on urban plans, public parks, and infrastructure, had recently helped the prominent American firm Sasaki Associates win a competition for a large park that was to create a considerable portion of the Beijing Olympic Games site on the north of the city. There was also Professor Yang Rui, the youngest person ever to become a professor at the School of Architecture, Tsinghua University. He had enormous energy, talent, and intelligence, was well educated, had traveled and studied abroad, and had an extensive professional consulting practice that included cities and vast sensitive ecological regions in diverse parts of the country. He had enormous skills and was developing a network of contacts and politically useful connections at several levels of government and the University. Here were three ideal young teachers if the Department could get enough of their time. Even if we did, these three combined with my periodic visits wouldn't make a full faculty, especially for some of the technical material, number of classes, lectures, and studio critiques needed.

So, I decided that in order to get going we would have to bring several other people from outside China, probably the US, that I knew and might be able to talk into coming for periods of time to teach and help out while the department was preparing its first graduates, one or two of whom if they were good enough could then be brought on as junior faculty to help, thereby gradually growing a cadre of individuals who shared a vision, values, and professional and academic skills. It is my belief that to some significant degree this has actually been and continues to be accomplished. My one significant defeat was that the school was absolutely opposed to my ideas about history. In retrospect I realize that my desire that a history course that placed China in a broader context of ideas and events (without diminishing any of its history or accomplishment), and that attempted to see if in the various people, cultures, philosophies, and built environment of Asia there were sources for different planning and design models that would help to cope with modernization and growth better or differently from those with such deleterious effects as in the West.

Despite this one thing, the Department was approved and launched with a skeleton staff and a first small group of students that Professor Yang and several Tsinghua faculty members selected from entry applications and exams. I was certain that there had to be several individuals in China who would be ideal members for such a faculty as I envisioned, but neither Yang nor I knew them at the time. So, I called upon several colleagues and friends in America to help us start. For Ecology I invited Professor Richard T.T. Forman from Harvard. Richard, who couldn't come on short notice the first year, was and still is the leading landscape ecologist in America whom I had recruited to Harvard for our faculty there in the early 1980s. So for the first year Yang and I managed to teach the rudiments of landscape ecology with the help of various texts, a series of lectures by an ecologist from Beda, and one of his PhD students. The next year Forman came with his wife, and the third year I invited Bart Johnson from Oregon, who has since written a superb book on ecology and landscape planning and design with Kristina Hill, a protégé of Forman's. Their intensive lectures and inspiration helped several young doctoral students move the department toward our intention to give landscape planners and designers a solid belief and grounding in ecology.

For landscape planning, in an attempt to supplement the work of Professor Yang, I invited Professor Frederick Steiner, the dean of the School of Architecture at the University of Texas in Austin. Fritz, as he is known, is a graduate of the Department of Landscape Architecture and Regional Planning at Penn, and I had known him since he was a student of Ian McHarg's and I was a young assistant professor. Having written a number of books, organized conferences, taught and consulted professionally for years in America and Europe, Steiner was a perfect person to bring. I was counting upon his intellectual curiosity and landscape ethic to want to come to China to help, which turned out to be true, as he enthusiastically came and taught effectively several times within the department, forming professional and social contacts that endure.

For site scale design and engineering, as well as an interest in culture and the art of our field I felt I needed for a time to supplement Hue Jie and Zhu Yufang, as they were already nearly overloaded with work. I invited Ron Henderson, one of my former students, who had worked professionally for me briefly before he began successfully teaching at the Rhode Island School of Design and Roger Williams University. While he was rather busy, having opened a small but award-winning firm in Providence, Rhode Island. Knowing of his talents and of his earlier involvement in Asia, I believed he would enjoy the opportunity to come to Tsinghua and would fit in if I could get him to come. Not only did Professor Henderson accept my invitation, but he flourished in the situation, teaching and working in the Institute with Hu Jie on a number of important professional projects that subsequently won design awards, but also commencing upon research and study of his own that has recently led to a superb compact guide to the gardens of Suzhuo published by the University of Pennsylvania Press.

While I could be at Tsinghua for periods of time, I worried about having others there to keep the excitement and work in the studios going when I wasn't there. In addition to my discovery that my view of history wasn't politically acceptable to the school, I also found that there wasn't as much emphasis upon studio projects as I believed to be normal and necessary. One solution was to have the studios we were allowed to schedule into the students' careers be intense, interesting, well taught, and engrossing. To do so it seemed that it would be useful to have a steady rotation of excellent practitioners and problems. In addition to Henderson and Steiner, I invited another gifted architect/landscape architect/planner/designer, Colin Franklin, to assist in studio teaching and to lecture. Franklin, an English trained architect, had been a student in our department at the University of Pennsylvania and had worked for a number of years at Wallace McHarg Roberts and Todd on a number of major projects. With his wife Carol, who I taught with for eight years, Colin was one of the founders of Andropogon Associates, a firm that rapidly became one of the premier firms in the world doing ecological planning and design. Gifted artistically, and professionally superb, I knew he was fond of Asia and would be an excellent teacher, which proved to be the case.

In my first year as chairman I was expected to give an inaugural talk to the school, its students, faculty, and administrators. Among the things I said were the following:

Landscape Architecture, like Architecture, serves many needs, and is a technical and practical art. Like Architecture, it is also an art, and at its best is one of the greatest, encompassing all the elements of the built and natural environment. Beyond utility it can also bring great beauty into our lives. Cultural landscapes created over centuries are among the greatest creations of civilization … The needs of China are great. A nation of 1.4 billion people cannot meet its needs in creating a fitting environment for the future by sending a handful of students abroad to study each year, nor with a few undergraduate programs. Nearly every river in every city is polluted unnecessarily. Thousands of hectares of land adjacent to residential buildings are left over, and are neither useful nor beautiful. Yet, through design, this could all be changed. A generation of students is now in and approaching China's universities and are eager to improve this situation, and with education can and will. China must educate its own landscape architects in its own way. At this exciting moment, Tsinghua can set the direction.

It is common knowledge that there are many problems with environmental policies in America. Large portions of our countryside and urban regions are marvelous, healthy, productive, and beautiful. Much, however, is also badly designed and abused. Unlike buildings and roads, landscapes take years to create and develop fully. This is good. As China rebuilds and transforms itself it must not blindly copy development patterns and processes from elsewhere, but consider carefully what is good for China. This nation has the opportunity to choose the world it wishes to build. My first hand experience of China has been recent and brief, but I have been a friend to China since my childhood. I followed your struggles in World War II, and have followed your course since. This is a great nation with an artistic and environmental tradition of its own stretching back many thousands of years. China today is probably the most dynamic nation on earth. So much is possible. I feel privileged to have been invited to participate in Tsinghua University's new Landscape Architecture program. I look forward to working with your faculty, students, and people.

After three years of commuting back and forth, for weeks at a time, from Philadelphia to Beijing, teaching heavily in two schools, and practicing professionally at an intense level in America and Europe, I had become very tired. While I loved the students and my colleagues in China, I decided that I couldn't continue. By then the Department seemed established and relatively healthy – although financing was and probably always will continue to be an issue, as it is everywhere. A school, department, and profession are only as good as the people within them. It is an old axiom that one should always try to work for and hire people smarter than oneself. I was fortunate in this. I have fond memories of my time in China. It was a period of growth and stimulation for me: sitting on a wilder portion of the Great Wall that Yang Rui took us to one afternoon with Richard Forman and his wife; of taking our students into the mountains west of Beijing to visit the monastery where Genghis Khan's daughter is buried where we saw horse chestnut trees that were 800 years old and ginko trees that were over 900 years old; of dinners beside Ho Hai Lake eating superb food with great company and watching boats and floating candles in the moonlight; of having the students measuring streets in one of the older hutongs and studying how the residents socialized in the public spaces; of drinking beer and having picnics while watching movies about nature and design that we decided should be seen with the students in the evening in their studio; of entering a classroom expecting to find the eight students registered in the class only to find 40 who had turned up from other departments and other universities eager to learn; of long and enjoyable hours with Yang and his family in their home, and many days of sitting together dreaming, working, and laughing giddily, as we tried to figure out how to get all the work done that was needed. Somehow it mostly got done, almost always because of Professor Yang Rui, who I always considered the actual chairman with me as his advisor and friend.

Congratulations to the Department of Landscape Architecture on its 10th birthday.

Eight Notes

Yang Rui, *chair of the Department of Landscape Architecture.,School of Architecture at Tsinghua University*

While growing in both bitterness and joy during the past decade, I have borne in mind many precious memories, and now, I think it is the right time for me to make a collection of them.

Since 1997 I have been an honorary participant in the preparation, establishment, and management of the Landscape Architecture Department, School of Architecture, Tsinghua University in a hands on way. The period was one of the most important times in my life, during which I grew with the growth of Landscape Architecture Department through passion and frustration, ideal and reality, joy and bitterness. From my youth I have experienced the joy of learning, the bitterness of transformation, and the pleasure of perception. I would like to express my deep gratitude to my predecessors, peers, and the younger generation, and also to my teachers, students, and relatives who offer me opportunities, impetus, support, tolerance, and understanding, thus enabling me to explore the meaning of life. As the saying goes, "pick up in the evening flowers fallen in the morning," I hope to share the specifics of my growth with would be readers through this record of my feeling.

I

Before formally getting into things related to the Landscape Architecture Department I would like to talk about the influence Tsinghua teachers and classmates have had on me.

In 1984 I was admitted by the Department of Architecture (evolving into the School of Architecture in 1988) of Tsinghua University from Xi'an Middle School in Shaanxi Province in an unexpected way. The reason I use the word "unexpected" is that my family helped me select the major of Biomedical Electronic Engineering (at that time it was the most popular major) at Tsinghua University based on my scores. However, when taking my college examination scores that year I failed, in fact, it was the worst score on any examinations that I had even received. Although barely passing the enrollment score for Tsinghua University, I would by no means be admitted to the Biomedical Electronic Engineering Department of Tsinghua University. Coincidentally, there was no other student in Shaanxi Province who passed the enrollment score for Tsinghua University that selected architecture as their first or even secondary school of intent. After finding this out I selected architecture as my major from the South China Institute of Technology (changed to South China University of Technology in 1988) as a second field of intent. Mr. Li Zhonghu, a student recruiter in Shaanxi, notified my father to bring me to the recruitment office of Tsinghua in Hu County, Shaanxi Province for an extra examination. He had me draw a sketch of a few things (hot-water bottle and tea cup) prior to the interview. With an obvious northern Shaanxi accent, Li was very amiable and sincere, which was my first impression of Tsinghua teachers. He said that the Department of Architecture of Tsinghua hoped to recruit students with a balance in the arts and sciences. Having served as the representative in a science class in middle school, I qualified for the condition to some degree.

I can still remember my life as an undergraduate: welcoming freshmen with the waving of a red flag in front of the auditorium; tongue-tied and red-faced introductions during the first gathering of our class, revealing my inner cowardice; practicing watercolor on Fragrance Hill with Mr. Zhang Geming evoking my strong interest in painting by saying that, "your purple tones are quite fantastic"; Mr. Lv Zhou warning me not to be impractically ambitious while tutoring me on my villa assignment, which I did not heed staying true to my personality; Mr. Zhuang Weimin adding a tree in my presentation drawing in a natural and unrestrained way, that I couldn't help not envying; chatting happily and freely with Li Hui (another offspring of rightists) in the large, western park under the stars (at a time when you could see the stars); the care and concern of Professor Yuan Bin and Professor Zou Huying during the transition period between spring and summer of 1989; and the serious and responsible expressions of Professor Guan Zhaoye and Professor Gao Yilan during our postgraduate recommendation interview.

After qualifying for direct postgraduate recommendation, I phoned Professor Zhu Zixuan nervously to inquire whether I could join his postgraduate class and he readily agreed. It took me less than two years to earn my masters degree of engineering in urban planning and design in July 1991, following my admission to Tsinghua University in September 1989. I was one of the fastest to do so among all my classmates, which I contribute in part to the painstaking, meticulous, and interlocking instruction of professor Zhu. In my masters thesis titled "Research on Protection and Rehabitation of the Historical Beiyuanmen Area in Xi'an" one of the basic viewpoints was to formulate a specific protection and re-habitation plan starting from and based on the "value analysis," which was quite different from general methods for planning of traditional blocks. Professor Zhu made repetitive reflections on this, during which we had many discussions with me, finally coming to agree with my viewpoint. Professor Zhu's attitude of "academic equality" touched me and I learned a great deal from his rigorous and responsible academic style.

After graduating with my masters degree, I worked in the Department of Urban Planning for 12 years (from 1991 to 2003) prior to the establishment of the Department of Landscape Architecture. The Department of Urban Planning was full of vitality, democracy, and equality. Although there were still disputes (even red-faced ones) therein, we could always openly and frankly discuss various issues, and finally found effective solutions together, and all my colleagues remain friends years later. Professor Zheng Guangzhong (serving as chair of the department then), with an energetic yet straightforward personality, played an important role in the formulation of such an open and effective culture within the Department of Urban Planning. As testament to Professor Zheng's vitality I would like to tell a story about him. While undertaking the planning and design of Yalong Bay National Recreation Area with his team (including Bian Lanchun, Deng Wei, and me) in 1992, Zheng went directly to the National Tourism Administration to seek necessary materials and to build a connection by bike, alone and without calling in advance. His connections from this approach opened the door for continued and direct contact between Tsinghua University and the field of tourism and leisure. During my cooperation with Zheng during my years in the Department of Urban Planning I acquired my doctoral degree while on the job (under the supervision of Professor Zhao Bingshi) and visited Harvard University under his encouragement and support. I am deeply grateful for the instruction, support, and assistance of Zheng and to the precious memories presented to me by my predecessors and colleagues in the Department of Urban Planning.

I was once evaluated by certain middle-school classmates as "a typical Tsinghua person." While I understand the ridicule within the statement, I also know that I was not quite up to the standard of a "basic Tsinghua person" let alone a "typical one." However, I felt immense pride at that moment for having the opportunity to receive an education from Tsinghua and to study and work with "Tsinghua people," true Tsinghua people (Mei Yiqi, Chen Yinke, Wang Guowei, Wen Yiduo, and other teachers and classmates), all who are shining examples of the school motto: "self-discipline and social commitment." Every time when I was under pressure or experienced difficulty in my work at the Department of Landscape Architecture, the sense of pride and responsibility originating from my time at Tsinghua served as the source of strength for me to muster up courage to push ahead once again.

II

In 1997 I passed WSK and acquired the qualification of a visiting scholar based on the national scholarship fund. Professor Qin Youguo (serving as the dean of the School of Architecture then) personally contacted Professor Peter Rowe (the dean of Harvard GSD) and recommended me to pay an academic visit to Harvard University. Professor Wu Liangyong invited me for a conversation at his home located at No. 14 Institute of Tsinghua Campus after dinner on December 15, two days before I set out to the United States. As it was the first one-on-one conversation between Wu and me, it left a deep impression. Wu mainly talked about two things: first, how to make the best use of the one-year trip to Harvard to improve my academic standing; and second, his desire to establish the Department of Landscape Architecture at Tsinghua University. As to the first point, Wu said that there were mainly three tasks in terms of studying abroad, namely, establishment of academic relations, field investigation, and knowledge accumulation by means of note taking and recording which could be brought back home for careful reading, thus saving more time for visiting, investigation, and interpersonal exchanges. Wu thought that establishing academic relation would be the paramount task. As to the second point, Wu introduced the development history of the Tsinghua landscape program, including the conception by Professor Liang Sicheng, the "LA group" jointly formed by Tsinghua University and Beijing Agricultural University in 1951, and successive efforts on department establishment after the reform and opening. After that, Wu said that to establish the Department of Landscape Architecture at Tsinghua we would need to pay attention to large scale rather than small-scale design issues concerning buildings, which could also be done by architects, thus making it unnecessary to cultivate talents through specially establishing a department. The Department of Landscape Architecture at Tsinghua University is mainly designed to resolve certain large-scale problems in China, such as watershed and landscape, in order to cultivate talent on such aspects. Wu's speech left a profound and sustainable impression on me, and, as such, his words have directed the vision for the program for more than a decade. In 2004, while accompanying Professor Richard Forman (member of Laurie D. Olin's chair professor team and a famous landscape ecologist from Harvard University) on his investigation of Fragrance Hill I shared with him the above-mentioned speech by Wu and also expounded on my understanding (of the speech) and relevant practice in the Department of Landscape Architecture at Tsinghua University. Completely agreeing with what I said, he thought that the focus of landscape architecture discipline should be practiced as such around the world.

During my academic visit to Harvard University, Professor Carl Stenitz served as my tutor. The reason why I selected Professor Stenitz was that he was an expert on large-scale landscape planning and had also garnered remarkable achievements in landscape planning theory. On the third day after my arrival at Harvard, Carl invited me to have lunch at the restaurant for teaching staff to understand my plan for this academic visit, during which he also reminded me to apply for credits to GSD when selecting courses and that such credits would be useful should I apply for a doctoral degree at Harvard University in the future. As I had started work towards my on-the-job doctoral degree at Tsinghua University in 1995, and hoping for more flexible time on my visit, I did not apply for credits at Harvard. During the second week I called on Professor Peter Rowe (serving as the dean of Harvard GSD then), and we had a pleasant conversation. Peter spoke highly of China and Tsinghua then. He actively proposed to supply $4,000 to me as a travel fund after finding out my hope to travel around the United States, which was wonderful news to me as I had only a $500 budget towards life expenses. It was thanks to this fund that I was able to travel around the United States, during which time I experienced and learned a lot. The following issues in Harvard University left a deep impression on me: Carl's courses on landscape planning, Richard's courses on landscape ecology science, the arduous efforts of students studying, abundant library resources. Carl and Richard's lectures at the joint fields of "Harvard Forest" are still vivid to me today. Another interesting thing occurred in the landscape planning studio directed by Carl, who invited me to participate in the teaching. The topic was to select a land occupying an area of more than 10 hectares from a region with an area of dozens of square kilometers to plan and design a community for residents with the same religious beliefs. Of the nine groups, four selected religions related to Chinese culture, namely Taoism, Zen, Tibetan Buddhism, and Islam, which surprised me greatly and made me feel that Chinese culture was so charming.

In May 1998, while reading in my office at the GSD, I received the call from professor Zuo Chuan who expected me to return home for a while to participate in the investigation of the project of human settlement in northwest Yunnan in the charge of Professor Wu Liangyong – specifically undertaking research related to national parks. In retrospect, the call from Zuo is undoubtedly of profound importance to me as it allowed me to gain valuable experience in broad academic research and practice, especially concerning national parks and heritage protection. After that, under the support of Zuo, I also participated in practical projects in northwestern Yunnan such as, the nomination for the world heritage foundation, the "three parallel rivers" project, the "master planning of Meri Snow Mountain," the "master plan of Thousand Lake

Mountain," and the "master plan of Laojun Mountain," as well as the "master plan of Mount Huang Scenic Area," thus accumulating a solid research and practice basis. Zuo is a key figures in the establishment of the Department of Landscape Architecture, but when I collected and combed through photos related to the establishment of the Department, I failed to find even a single photo of hers, but when I apologetically called her about it she replied that it's just right to find no photos of hers.

III

The School of Architecture proposed to restart the Landscape Architecture program and established relevant research institutes in January 1997. Around 2002, thanks to his extensive contacts during the visit to America, the current dean, Professor Qin Youguo finally reached a consensus with Professor Laurie D. Olin, the former chair of the Department of Landscape Architecture of Harvard University, and invited him to serve as the first chair of the Department of Landscape Architecture of the School of Architecture at Tsinghua University. In the spring of 2003, Qin took me to Wangfujing Grand Hotel where Laurie resided to negotiate with him on specifics about department establishment, and we also planned to hold a department establishment ceremony as soon as possible. The SARS virus broke out the moment Laurie left, yet the establishment of the Department of Landscape Architecture pushed on and was approved during the 20th university assembly on July 13, 2003 under the powerful promotion of Qin.

Our department establishment celebration was held on October 8, 2003, during which an interesting story occurred: Professor Gu Binglin (serving as the president of Tsinghua University then) had the sentence in his speech manuscript that read "the autumn of Beijing is a beautiful season filled with the hopes of harvest," but which was misstated as, "the spring of Beijing is a beautiful season." I prefer the misstatement of President Gu, as spring is a vital season for cultivation, infinite possibilities, and growth.

IV

Laurie is a tall and lean gentlemen who often wore a blue sweater, coffee-colored corduroy trousers, brown leather shoes, black-framed glasses, and a delicately trimmed gray beard, giving him an air of elegance and nobility. When coming to Tsinghua for the first time, Laurie lived in the apartment for senior visitors located next to Zhaolan Yard. When I drove to receive him in the morning one day, about 7 am, I saw him writing and drawing facing a group of old ladies who were chatting with each other in front of his apartment. He told me in the car that he liked to observe the behaviors of various people and have various figures, landscapes, and trees drawn in his sketchbook every time when he reached a new place, and while drawing, he also tried to figure out what people were chatting about based on their expressions and gestures. Laurie was very diligent. I remember taking him to the Temple of Heaven for an academic tour before dawn and seeing him painting with watercolors at the west dike of the Summer Palace at sunset one day: the glow of golden light, a pool of tiny waves, the erected Temple of Buddhist Incense, and the view of his back while he was sitting on a low stool were quite beautiful and harmonious. One time when we waited for a car in front of the main building, and I asked him why he chose to teach at Tsinghua, he replied that China needed high-level landscape education, and Tsinghua could possibly contribute to that. I told him that what he described was also my dream. Sharing the same dream with a foreign man moved me with sentiment and excitement.

As a famous landscape ecologist in America, a senior professor of Harvard University, and a member of the Laurie D. Olin chair professor team, Richard Forman once came to Tsinghua twice in succession at 70 during a period when his Parkinson's Disease was affecting him less. He is a fantastic teacher. He could lecture on "landscape ecology" for eight hours within a day or give a three-hour lecture in the afternoon after leading students in field practices at Fragrance Hill in the afternoon. Even his students could not keep up with his intensity, but when giving lectures, he was always full of passion while adopting abundant gestures and simple but profound words without any note. Frederick Steiner was another member of the Laurie D. Olin chair professor team who showed great interest in China. Frederick was once the student of McHarg, and his teaching on landscape and ecology planning was quite impressive. Ronald Henderson, another member of Laurie D. Olin's chair professor team, was the longest serving member of the team in China. In 2006, upon finishing his term in Laurie D. Olin chair professor team, Ronald was invited to serve as the associate professor of the Department of Landscape Architecture in the School of Architecture, Tsinghua University until he was appointed as the professor and chair of the Department of Landscape Architecture of Pennsylvania State University in 2011. Ronald was quite popular among his students. Other members of Laurie D. Olin chair professor team include Peter Jacob, Colin Franklin, Bart Johnson, Goge Tesiler, and Bruce Ferguson, all of whom have their own specialties and have made outstanding contributions to the establishment and development of the Department of Landscape Architecture of Tsinghua University.

V

Following the establishment of the Fourth Council of the Chinese

Society of Landscape Architecture (CHSLA) in October 2008, I proposed to the newly elected president, Chen Xiaoli, that Tsinghua University organize the 2009 Annual Meeting of the Chinese Society of Landscape Architecture – the first comprehensive annual meeting of CHSLA.

Under the stewardship of President Chen Xiaoli, the annual meeting was held in the main building of Tsinghua University from September 12 through 13, 2009. Mr. Liu Xiuchen, the then vice-president and secretary-general of CHSLA, told me that the vast sky left a deep impression on him when he stood on the steps in front of the main building after the end of the meeting. The theme of that year's annual meeting was "fusion and growth." In keeping with the theme, I designed an emblem that was engraved by my student Hu Yike (see the picture below). This emblem has now become a permanent emblem of the annual meeting of CHSLA. A description of the emblem was written at the time. It is now recorded as follows: "Chinese landscape architecture is rooted in millennia-old Chinese culture, so the emblem is evolved from the oracle bone script character '囿,' '宀,' '木,' '羊,' and '土' are the radicals of '宅 (house),' '林 (forest),' '美 (beauty),' and '地 (land)' respectively, representing the contribution of architecture, forestry, art, and earth science to landscape architecture. They integrate and grow on the basis of '田(field).' '田' also implies the contribution of agriculture to landscape architecture."

VI

During the annual conference, as the host, I gathered Professor Liu Binyi of Tongji University, Professor Du Chunlan of Chongqing University, Professor Liu Hui of the Xi'an University of Architecture and Technology, and Professor Ye Qiang of Hunan University to chat over a cup of tea near Tsinghua University. We discussed how to cope with the challenges and opportunities brought by a new round of discipline adjustment initiated by the Academic Degree Committee of the State Council in June 2009. It was unanimously agreed that we should strive to promote the upgrading of landscape architecture discipline to a first-level discipline in the engineering category. This was the common aspiration of colleagues with different backgrounds in the field.

Nevertheless, to upgrade landscape architecture from a level-three discipline to a first-level discipline, we had to achieve broad consensus on the discipline name and its category, and secure the understanding and support of the related disciplines such as architecture and forestry. Although this seemed an impossible task at that time, several colleagues at the time decided to do whatever possible. We first reported this idea to Chen Xiaoli and Deputy Department Chief Zhao Qi of the Ministry of Housing and Urban-Rural Development (MOHURD) who was attending a meeting at Wenjin International Hotel near Tsinghua University. Their firm leadership was one of the keys to successfully upgrading the landscape architecture department to a first-level discipline. Later, several "tea buddies," together with Professor Cao Lei from Tianjin University, paid a visit to Liang Guoxiong, the deputy director responsible for this round of discipline adjustment at the Academic Degree Committee of the State Council. Because we had no prior contact, Director Liang thought that we were a group of graduate students who wanted to file a petition when we knocked on the door to his office at 1 pm. Although he had a cold, he still allowed us into his office, heard our thoughts and suggestions patiently, and explained the directions and steps of this round of discipline adjustment. Afterwards, we pressed on and worked separately, making key progress rapidly: on September 23, 2009, the deans of 41 schools of architecture nationwide signed the "Joint Letter by Deans of Universities for Supporting the Establishment of Landscape Architecture as a First-Level Discipline in the Engineering Category"; on October 9, a total of 20 academics in the field of architecture, urban planning, and landscape architecture signed to support the establishment of landscape architecture as a first-level discipline in the engineering category.

On December 21 of the same year, the MOHURD presided over the "Appraisal meeting on the demonstration report on the adjustment of architecture and the establishment of urban and rural planning and landscape architecture as the First-level Discipline." The appraisal involved 24 experts from MOHURD, the State Council's Academic Degree Committee, the Architectural Society of China, the Urban Planning Society of China, the Chinese Society of Landscape Architecture, Tsinghua University, China Agricultural University, Southeast University, Tongji University, Chongqing University, Beijing Forestry University, Nanjing Forestry University, China Urban Construction Design and Research Institute, and China Academy of Urban Planning and Design. On behalf of the demonstration team, I gave the "Demonstration Report on the Establishing of Landscape Architecture as a First-Level Discipline."

In May 2011, the State Council's Academic Degree Committee promulgated the "Catalogue of Disciplines for Degree Award and Talent Cultivation (2011)." Landscape architecture and urban and rural planning became part of the 110 first-level disciplines in China. In October of the same year, landscape architecture officially became a specialty in the catalog of architecture in the "Catalogue of undergraduate programs at general institutes of higher education (2012)" promulgated by the Ministry of Education.

Above: Emblem design for the 2009 annual meeting of the Chinese Society of Landscape Architecture (Designed by Yang Rui and carved by Hu Yike) Chinese Landscape Architecture is deeply rooted in the ancient Chinese culture and so it was decided that the thematic logo was to be derived from the Oracle Bone character for garden, tree, house, earth, and beauty to symbolize that the contributing disciplines of forestry, architecture, geoscience, and arts prosper on the framework of farmland and agronomy.

VII

The year 2010 was a bitterly painful year. My wife, Zhao Wenqi, and son, Yang Zhixuan, lost their lives in a car accident on October 4. My world was turned upside down, sending me into an abyss that I had never imagined before. I was utterly overwhelmed by all manner of negative emotions: pain, sadness, regret, fear, anger, and confusion. I had to address their deaths, which I had tried to avoid. In January 2012, I was exhausted physically and mentally and was on the verge of collapse. I could not get to sleep for several days on end, as if I was in the grip of death. I made my dying wishes to my two elder sisters. However, they refused to give up on me, taking care of me as if I were a child. A few months later, I was finally brought back to the world again.

VIII

Looking back on the development of the Department of Landscape Architecture in the past decade, I think that I have made some achievements in the following aspects: I learned to combine tradition and modernity; integration of the eastern and western knowledge; scale consistency; and balance between knowing and doing. This has guided the Department of Landscape Architecture to focus on absorbing knowledge and viewpoints from around the world, using these skills to build a contemporary landscape architecture theoretical system. It has also driven the Department of Landscape Architecture in the implementation of educational and social practice. The goal of landscape training at Tsinghua University is to educate students who can understand landscape phenomena around the world, with a deep theoretical literacy and strong practical skills in a certain scale or field. Along with the initial Department of Landscape Architecture, a forward-looking masters degree curriculum has been established. It is adjusted and improved based on the curriculum system developed by Professor Laurie D. Olin, adapted for the unique situation of Tsinghua University. The three peripheral sections of "Theory & History," "Natural Science Application," and "Technology," and the core section of "Planning and Design" form a relatively complete and close course structure. Although the landscape department is a small group based on the number of teachers and students, we have now generally formed a vigorous, open, and inclusive cultural atmosphere after only one decade. These guidelines have laid the foundation for the long-term development of the Department of Landscape Architecture. Without the joint efforts of teachers and students these achievements would not have been possible. As the incumbent head of the department, I hereby extend sincere gratitude to my colleagues Zhu Yufan, Li Shuhua, Dang Anrong, Jia Yun, Zhuang Youbo, Liu Hailong, Wu Dongfan, and He Rui; all members of Laurie D. Olin's chair professor team; Wu Liangyong; the chief leaders of the school including Qin Youguo, Zuo Chuan, Zhu Wenyi, Bian Lanchun, and Zhuang Weimin for their support.

I dedicate this essay to the tenth anniversary of the Department of Landscape Architecture of the Tsinghua University School of Architecture that I dearly love. May people live a healthy, happy, and joyful life because of landscape architecture.

1.2 Landscape program period (1940s–1952)

On March 9, 1945 Liang Sicheng wrote from Lizhuang to President Mei Yiqi suggesting that a Department of Architecture be established at Tsinghua University, "to adapt to expanded future demands, it is necessary a School of Architecture be established. However, under the present circumstances, it would be better that a Department of Architecture be built first under the School of School of Engineering ... As soon as the war is over, it will be the time to consider establishing the School of Architecture and gradually adding to it the departments of architectural engineering, urban planning, gardening, interior decoration" (From University of Pennsylvania to Tsinghua University – Liang Sicheng's Educational Philosophy of Architecture [1928–1949] by Qin Youguo).

In his "Draft Plan of School System and Education Program for the Department of Architecture and Urban Planning (nowadays Department of Architectural Engineering) at Tsinghua University" published by Wen Wei Po in series from July 10 to 12, 1949, Professor Liang proposed an educational framework spanning the disciplines of Architecture, Urban and Rural Planning, Gardening, Industrial Arts, and Architectural Engineering, and even incorporated a curriculum he envisioned for the proposed Department of Gardening broken down as follows:

A. Cultural and Social Backgrounds

Chinese, English, Economics, Sociology, Physical and Social

Left: Liang Sicheng, Records from the Archive of the School of Architecture, Tsinghua University.

Environments, European and American Architectural History, Chinese Architectural History, European and American History of Painting and Sculpture, and Chinese History of Painting and Sculpture.

B. Science and Engineering Physics

Biology, Chemistry, Mechanics, Mechanics of Materials, Surveying, Engineering Materials, Gardening Engineering (Ground and Underground Drain, Roads, Drainage, etc.)

C. Presentation Technology

Building Painting, Projection Painting, Sketches, Water Colors, Sculptures

D. Design Theory

Vision and Pattern, Introduction to Gardening, Horticulture, Planting Materials, Presentations

E. Integrated Studies

Architectural Design, Gardening Design, Practices, Papers (Thesis Studies)

In 1951, with the Ministry of Education's approval of the joint initiative of the Department of Horticulture of Beijing Agriculture University and the Department of Architecture and Urban Planning of Tsinghua Universtiy, the Landscape program was launched on a pilot basis (with junior and senior students to be stationed on Tsinghua campus). It stated under the joint facilitation of Professor Wang Juyuan (Beijing Agriculture University) and Professor Wu Liangyong (Tsinghua University), the first ever LA educational organization in China—The Landscape program—established at Tsinghua University to offer full-time trainings for LA professionals, marking the beginning of the modern landscape architecture discipline in China.

During the early days of the Landscape program, Tsinghua University dispatched teachers for the paintings, drawings (preliminary design), urban planning, surveying, architecture, and Chinese architecture courses offered specially to students majoring in gardening in accordance with the teaching program designed by Wang Juyuan and Chen Youmin in reference to the Soviet Union models.

It was Wang Juyuan and Chen Youmin again who took the eight students majoring in gardening on the 1952 summer internship trip to Nanjing, Wuxi, Suzhou, Hangzhou, and Shanghai.

In the autumn of 1952, a second batch of gardening majors, 10 altogether, were sent over from the Beijing Agricultural University to study on the Tsinghua campus, and a projective geometry course was added to the curriculum.

Curriculum for the 1951-1953 landscape program

S.N.	Course Name
1	Urban Planning (including Urban Greenery)
2	Garden Design
3	Architectural Design
4	History of Chinese Gardens
5	History of Western Gardens
6	Introduction to Architecture
7	Cartography Perspective
8	Drawing: Sketches
9	Drawing: Watercolors

S.N.	Course Name
10	Plant Classification
11	Forestry
12	Surveying
13	Architecture
14	Ornamental Trees and Flowers
15	Garden Art
16	Garden Engineering
17	Landscape Management (lecture)
18	Chinese Architecture

Left: This list was derived from Chen Youmin's "In Commemoration of the Fiftieth Anniversary of the Founding of the Landscape program (Landscape Architecture)," Zhu Junzhen's "Recollections about the Landscape program, School of Architecture, Tsinghua University," Dr. Ling Guangsi dissertation "Study of the Chinese Landscape Architecture Discipline and Its Curriculum Design" and related recall interviews.

Faculty for the 1951-1953 landscape architecture program

Program Founder: Wang Juyuan

Program Founder: Wu Liangyong

Liu Zhiping

Hua Yiyu

Li Zongjin

Li Jiale

Wu Guanzhong

Zhang Shouyi

Chen Youmin

Hu Yunjing

Hao Jingsheng

Mo Zongjiang

1.3 Development of Program to Department (1953–2002)

1953–1962

In the summer of 1953, the first batch of gardening majors with official titles graduated. As the discipline entitled gardening was still at the start-up phase with a high demand for "gardening" professionals, half of the eight graduates were assigned to related teaching posts.

Starting with the students (sophomore) of the No. 5 Architecture Class, the History TRG of the Department of Architecture embarked on a yearly survey and mapping of the Summer Palace, which continued for years till the beginning of the "Cultural Revolution."

Since it was discovered in 1953 by the Ministry of Education that Landscape programs were with the forestry institutions in the Soviet Union. The management of the two universities were called up for consultation that resulted in the transfer of the Landscape program to Beijing Agricultural University with continued faculty support from the Architecture School of Tsinghua University.

From 1953 onward, Wu Liangyong made several unsuccessful attempts to resume the Landscape program at Tsinghua (in 1958, 1980, and 1985); despite the failure, LA-related postgraduate trainings, research, and practices have never ceased.

In 1953 Liu Chengxian and Zhu Junzhen was recruited upon graduation by the Architecture Department as assistant teachers and set about translating Soviet publications on landscaping, including the book *Greening Construction* translated and published in collaboration with colleagues studying plants in Beijing with the Chinese Academy of Sciences.

From 1954 to 1956, under the guidance of a guest professor from the Soviet Union, Liu Chengxian accomplished the design of the Yuyuantan Park in Beijing and Zhu Junzhen, City God Hill Cultural and Repose Park in Hangzhou.

In 1954, the Y1952 (No. 8 Architecture Class) and Y1953 (No. 9 Architecture Class) students conducted a detailed survey and mapping of the Qianlong Garden of the Forbidden City and the Summer Palace under the guidance of faculty, with continued follow-ups later on.

Despite the termination of the Landscape program, a small amount of necessary LA related courses were retained in the curriculum of the Department of Architecture and Urban Planning of Tsinghua University, including the "urban greening" course offered by Liu Chengxian to undergraduate architecture majors along with with an on-campus plant internship, the "Ancient Chinese Architectural History" course offered by Zhao Zhengzhi, of which classical gardens (mainly referring to the southern gardens and the imperial gardens in Beijing) form an important part coupled with invited lectures by Chen Congzhou, and the "Foreign Architectural History" taught by Chen Zhihua which addresses foreign classical gardens.

In 1956, graduate student Xiong Ming finished his thesis entitled "Problems Related to Planning and Design of Cultural and Repose Parks," the earliest of its kind on park studies.

In 1961, Wu Liangyong and Zheng Guangzhong supervised the master planning and detailed planning of the Tsinghua campus, which contained an overall functional adjustments and an addition of the Main Building Square.

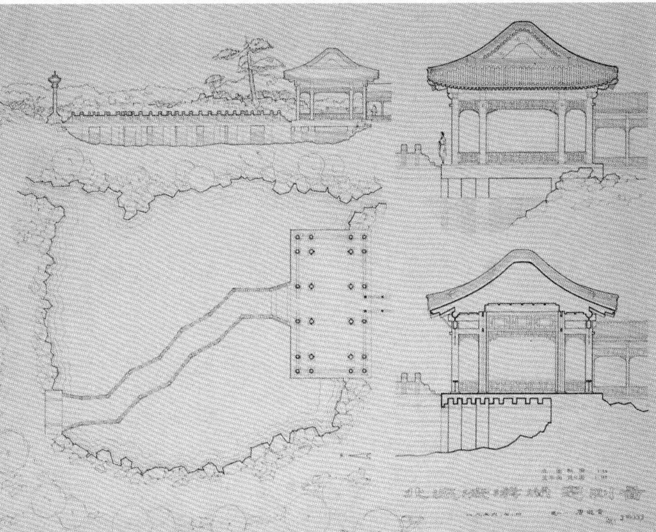

Above left: Ink rendering of the floral-pendant gate in front of the Hall of the First Time in the Qianlong Garden of the Forbidden City by Zheng Guangzhong (Class No. 9 of the Architecture Department), July 1954.

Above right: Survey drawing of the pavilion for quiet meditation in Beihai Park by Jiayin (Class No. 1 of the Architecture Department), July 1956.

Right: Graduate design work of Li Wenbao and Li Duofu in 1961 – aerial-view design plan of the main axis square of Tsinghua University.

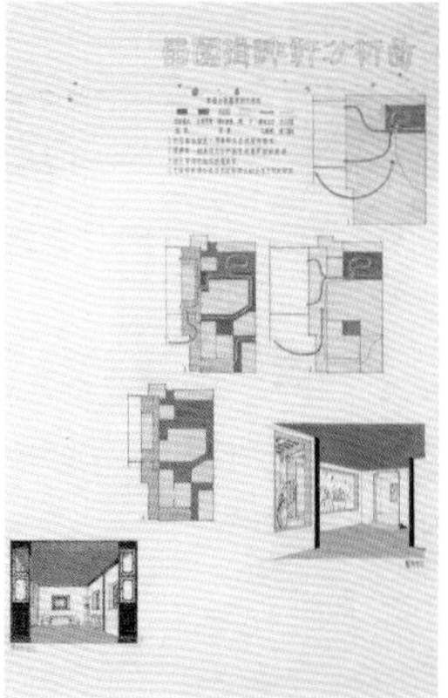
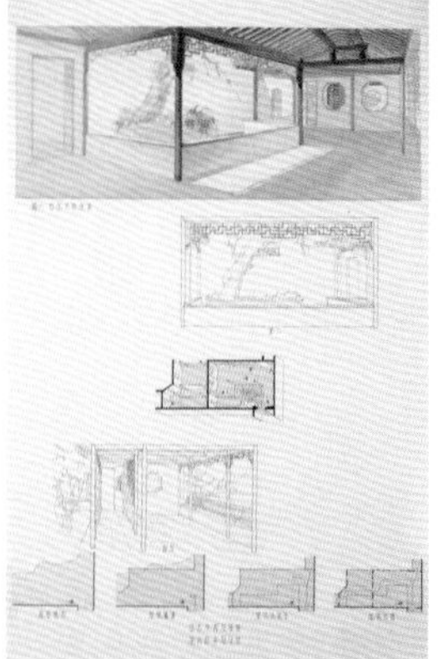
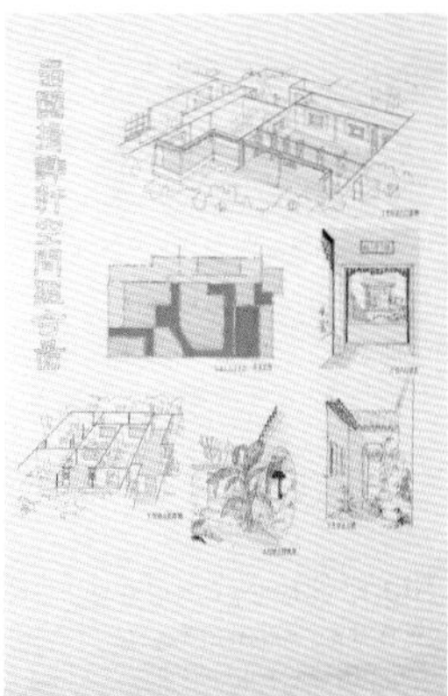

Right: Hand-drawn spatial analysis chart by Zhang Jinqiu during her building space research over the Lingering Garden of Suzhou (which was converted into a sketchup illustration for publication in the *Proceedings of Architectural History, Volume 1*).

1963–1972

In 1963, Survey and Mapping of the Summer Palace was converted from a freshman to a senior project, and was no longer restricted to the surveying and mapping of landscape architecture, but extended to the relationship between architecture and the surrounding environment and regional landscape issues as well. A product of this project was the production and practice drawings, which students found to be very rewarding.

Mo Zongjiang began to study the Summer Palace; and under his guidance, graduate student Zhang Jinqiu completed her thesis entitled, "Original State, Gardening Experience, Utilization and Transformation Challenges of Rear Hill and West Part of Summer Palace," the first Tsinghua master thesis on the study of the Summer Palace.

There are two graduation thesis papers completed by students of the graduate program at the Department of Civil Engineering in 1965 worth mentioning: the "Original State, Gardening Experience, Utilization and Transformation Challenges of Rear Hill and the West Part of Summer Palace," (Tutor: Mo Zongjiang) by Zhang Jinqiu; and "A Probe into the Tian'anmen Square Renovation and Planning Experiences," (Tutor: Wu Liangyong) by Su Zemin.

Right: Survey chart of the Summer Palace by Yuan Ying from July 1963.

1973–1982

In 1977, upon the invitation of Wan Li, the Anhui Provincial Party Secretary, Tsinghua (under Wu Liangyong), Southeast (under Yang Tingbao), and Tongji (under Feng Jizhong) Universities joined hands in the planning of the Hefei-based Science and Technology University. At the planning report meeting, Wan Li commissioned Tsinghua University with the planning of the master plan for Mt. Huangshan and after the meeting, Wu Liangyong, Zhu Changzhong, Zheng Guangzhong, and Zhou Yihu, visited Jiuhua Mountain, Taiping Lake, Mt. Huangshan, and other sites with Feng Jizhong, Deng Shuping, and Zhang Zhenshan from Tongji University in order to lay a sound basis for the plan.

Above: Sketches of the Stalagmite Peak by Zheng Guangzhong during his site visit to Mt. Huangshan. (Taken from Architecture Sketches of Zheng Guangzhong).

In 1978, the Landscape program of Beijing Forestry University was transferred back to Beijing, and Professor Wu Liangyong involved himself to no avail in the preparations for the return of the Landscape Architecture Department to Tsinghua University.

Wu Liangyong, Zhu Changzhong, and Zheng Guangzhong, teachers from the Planning TRG, compiled the "Master Plan for the Protection of the Yuanmingyuan Garden" and printed some reference materials for internal use, which effectively prevented the proposal of turning the garden into a modern royal hotel.

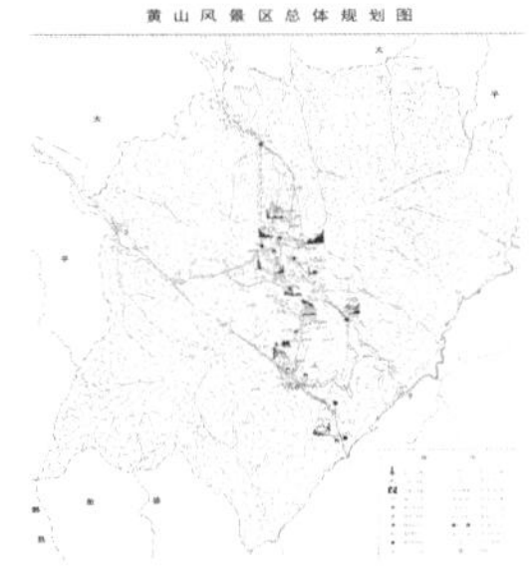

Above: "Master Plan of Mt. Huangshan Scenic Area (1979–1983)" One of the earliest of its kind, this master plan marks the very beginning of the scenic area projects with myriad practices highly commendable and planning principles even relevant today.

In 1979, Comrade Deng Xiaoping visited Mt. Huangshan, accompanied by the First Secretary of Anhui Province Wan Li, and mapped its development and construction (Annals of Mt. Huangshan).

In the same year, Zhu Changzhong, Zhu Zixuan, Zheng Guangzhong, and Xu Yingguang set about compiling the Master Plan of Huangshan Scenic Area (1979–1983) together with the last batch of worker, peasant, and soldier students under their guidance.

In 1979 Wu Liangyong managed to transfer Zhu Junzhen from the Beijing Municipal Research Institute of Environmental Protection back to Tsinghua University to teach the "urban greening" course, to serve as assistant to Professor Wang Juyuan in the preparation of the "Landscaping" section for the "Encyclopedia of China," to resume research on the botanic composition of the Hangzhou parks started before the Cultural Revolution in cooperation with the Hangzhou Parks and Cultural Relics Bureau in order to finalize the publication.

After the "Cultural Revolution," Zhou Weiquan began to study the Summer Palace. In 1979, he directed his graduate student Jin Boling in the preparation of his master's thesis entitled, "Original State and Artistic Achievements of the Rear Hill Section of the Clear Ripples Garden, and Planning Vision for the Rear Hill Construction of the Summer Palace."

Zhu Changzhong turned his research interest to landscape architecture and guided his graduate student Zhao Honghong through her preparation of the master thesis entitled, "Suzhou City Landscape" in 1979.

Zhu Zixuan guided his graduate student Tian Guoying through the

Above: Group photo on the top of Lotus Peak of teachers participating in the planning of Mt. Huangshan. (from Zheng Guangzhong).

preparation of the master thesis entitled, "Past, Present, and Future of the Six-Hai Water Systems in Beijing," which provides the basis for continued research of Shichahai 30 years later.

In 1981, Zhou Weiquan started to offer the "Chinese Classical Garden" course to the undergraduate students majoring in Architecture. Feng Zhongping started on his massive investigation of, and research on, the scenic areas and gardens in China, with survey and mapping, photography and sketches done for the most outstanding specimens, and more than 200 survey charts and sketches added to greatly enrich the research databank. "Agakhan: Atrium Planning," by Zhu Shaozhu, Li Tang and Liu Xiaoming won first prize in the international competition organized by the *MIMAR* magazine.

In 1982 Ji Huailu and Yin Yihe directed "*The Summer Palace: Her Garden Arts and Architecture*," a television teaching film 2.5 hours long targeting architecture schools, and architectural design and research institutions across the country. The Landscape Environmental Planning and Design Group of the China Urban Planning Society was established at the Donghu Hotel of Wuhan on May 19, 1982 and Zhu Changzhong served as the deputy leader of the group.

1983–1992

In the early 1980s, Ji Huailu and Yin Yihe directed and produced the teaching film *Summer Palace: Her Garden Arts and Architecture*, which is two and a half hours long and addresses architectural schools, building design, and research units all over the country.

In 1983, Zhu Changzhong and Xu Yingguang guided Wang Menghui, Meng Weikang, and Li Yong (earliest students following the restart of college entrance examinations after the "Cultural Revolution") through their preparation of the Master Plan for the Seven Star Crags Scenic Area of Zhaoqing, Guangdong Province. They aided in researching specialized details for planning, detailed planning, and application of traditional gardening practices and completion of the studio design as the graduation thesis.

The "Planning of the Shichahai Historical and Cultural Tourist Resort in Beijing" project was supervised by Zhu Zixuan, Zheng Guangzhong, Zhu Junzhen, and Huang Changshan and received Second Prize for the 1986 Outstanding Planning and Design Award of the Ministry of Urban and Rural Construction and Environmental Protection and the honorary recognition of "100 Projects with Outstanding Scientific and Technological Contributions to Beijing in Celebration of the 40th Founding Anniversary of China," in October 1989. Shichahai Historical and Cultural Tourist Resort is an important section of key heritage sites on the north axis of the old city of Beijing, which has long been the hub for scenic and tourist activities. The project, fused with the bachelor graduation design program, covers themed research on the greening, water sceneries, commercial street, amusement activities, and transportation issues within the Shichahai area, which played an important role in the project and for academic purposes.

The planning is of great significance to the vernacular style protection, heritage conservation, and maintenance, environmental management, greening, and beautification of the Shichahai area. In the planning implementation, there was close coordination with the Xicheng District, the 3-Hai Remediation Command, and the Shichahai Administration regarding the guiding principles of integrated protection, renovation, development, and management for gradual enhancements.

In 1985, Zhou Weiquan, Feng Zhongping, Yao Tongzhen, and Lou Qingxi finished the script of Summer Palace, which failed to be published in time due to the restriction of domestic publication conditions. It is the first draft of the script published by the Taiwan Architects Association in 1990 and the edition published by the China Building Industry Publishing House in 2000. The "Landscaping Plants" course was put into the curriculum of Architecture students in 1985.

In 1987, the "Master Plan of the Huangshan Scenic Area" supervised by Zhu Changzhong and other successors, was approved by the State

Council in 1979.

In 1947, Zhu Changzhong, a graduate from the Architecture Department of Chongqing Central University in 1945, and a recipient of the First Prize of the Guizai Scholarship from the Society for the Study of Chinese Architecture was hired to teach at Department of Architecture of Tsinghua University, and rendered great assistance and support to Liang Sicheng in the start-up, development, and burgeoning of the department. From 1952 to 1957 he studied at and received a deputy doctor's degree from the Urban Planning Department of Moscow School of Architecture. In 1957, he resumed his teaching post at Tsinghua, serving successively as associate professor at the Department of Architecture, head of the Urban Planning TRG, professor of the Tsinghua School of Architecture, chairman of the Landscape and Environment Planning and Design Academic Committee under the Urban Planning Society of China (UPSC), and expert consultant to the Ministry of Construction on scenic area problems.

Delegated by Tsinghua University in 1985 to serve as the first dean of the Department of Architecture of Yantai University, Zhu Changzhong laid a solid basis for the founding and development of the department. Zhu Changzhong was a key member of the emblem design team at Tsinghua University when they won the national emblem design contest in 1950.

In 1980, Zhu Changzhong was posted as the supervisor for the project of the Huangshan Scenic Area Master Plan. The "National Scenic Area Declaration" drafted under his supervision during the 1992 Academic Symposium on Landscape Environment and Architecture was later published and became the most important document on the protection of scenic areas in China at the time.

From 1988 to 1990, Chen Zhihua oversaw a project supported by Tsinghua University's Science Foundation entitled, "Overseas Classical Gardening Arts and Comparison with Chinese Gardening Arts," and published the book *Overseas Gardening Arts*.

The "Chinese Landscape Architecture" research project supervised by Feng Zhongping won the Second Prize for the 1988 Science and Technology Progress Award given by the Ministry of Construction. The book *Chinese Landscape Architecture* published by the Tsinghua University Press in May 1988 is a systematic presentation of the evolution of Chinese landscape architecture, its origination from the aesthetic trends, and analyses illustrated with sufficient domestic survey mappings.

In May 1990, the book *Gardens in Hong Kong* compiled by Zhu Junzhen was published by Joint Publishing (Hong Kong), which was acclaimed as a "pioneering work" for filling the Hong Kong landscape research gap. This book systematically introduces the Hong Kong garden types, distribution and basic characteristics with original depiction and analysis of the designs. Zhu Zixuan stressed in the preface of the book "it is also a valuable reference for professionals."

In December the same year, Zhou Weiquan's *A History of Classical Chinese Gardens* was published, which breaks down the evolution of the ancient Chinese gardens into the genesis, transition, heyday, maturity, and post-maturity periods.

Qian Xuesen wrote a letter to Wu Liangyong to exchange views on urban water and mountain landscapes, and in 1992 Zhu Changzhong, Xie Ninggao, and Dong Liming wrote to Qian to further deliberate on the actualization of the urban landscape practice in Tongshi City of the Hainan Province.

From 1990 to 1991, Zhu Zixuan, Zheng Guangzhong, and Deng Wei completed planning studies over the Fragrant Hill area in Beijing; Zheng Guangzhong and Zhuang Ning accomplished the planning of the Sanya Bay Resort of Hainan.

On October 22, 1991 the Landscape and Environment Planning and Design Academic Committee, under the Urban Planning Society of China (UPSC), was established in Guilin (formerly known as the Landscape and Environment Planning and Design Group of the Urban Planning Society of China), with Zhu Changzhong serving as vice chairman.

In 1992 Zheng Guangzhong, Bian Lanchun, Yang Rui, and Deng Wei undertook the planning and design project of the Yalong Bay National Resort District of Sanya, Hainan, one of the earliest cases of its kind in China. In preparation for planning, the team and the management of the Yalong Bay Company took a study tour to Hawaii, Miami, and several international coastal tourist resorts in Southeast Asia as well as some domestic coastal tourist areas, which resulted in the publication of the "Research Report on the Investigation into Coastal Scenic Areas in China" the following year.

Right: Leadership of Tsinghua University including Zhang Xiaowen, Li Chuanxin, Fang Huijian, Huang Shenglun, and Zhang Xutan on an inspection tour to Beijing Shichahai Historical and Cultural Tourist Resort Planned and Designed by the Department of Architecture (Records from the Archive of the School of Architecture, Tsinghua University).

Right: The Planning Project of the Beijing Shichahai Historical and Cultural Tourist Resort was rated as one of "100 Projects with Outstanding Scientific and Technological Contributions to Beijing in Celebration of the 40th Founding Anniversary of China."

清华大学建筑学院城市规划系

在迎接建国四十周年百项科技贡献活动中 什刹海历史文化风景区保护开发规划 被评为优秀贡献项目，特发此状，以兹鼓励。

北京市科学技术委员会
一九八九年 月

Right: The "Protection and Rehabilitation Planning and Study of Beijing Shichahai Historical and Cultural Tourist Resort (1984–2004) (Records from the Archive of the School of Architecture, Tsinghua University) was of great significance to the vernacular, style, protection, heritage, conservation, maintenance, environmental management, and greening and beautification of the Shichahai area. In the planning implementation there had been close coordination with the Xicheng District, the 3-Hai Remediation Command, and the Shichahai Administration in line with the guiding principles of integrated protection, renovation, development, and management for gradual face-lifting and comprehensive benefits in return for sure financial resources to set the overall planning going within a virtuous circle.

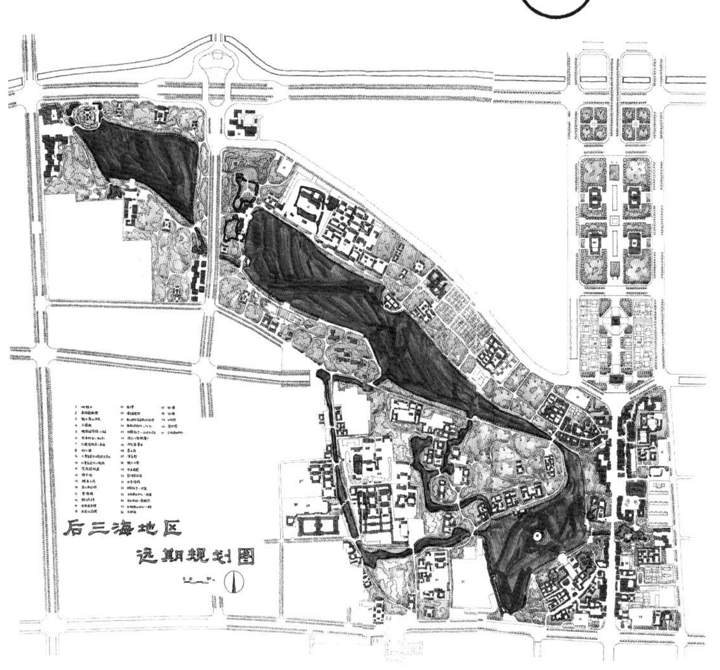

Above: The design plans of the Huitong Temple Island in the western part of Shichahai (Records from the Archive of the School of Architecture, Tsinghua University).

Right: Research of Huangshan planning (Zhu Changzhong, Su Wujiu from Mt. Huangshan administration office is on the left side of the photo; records from the Archive of the School of Architecture, Tsinghua University.

Right: Seal made by Zhu Changzhong for Huangshan planning (extract from "Mr. Zhu Changzhong's seal").

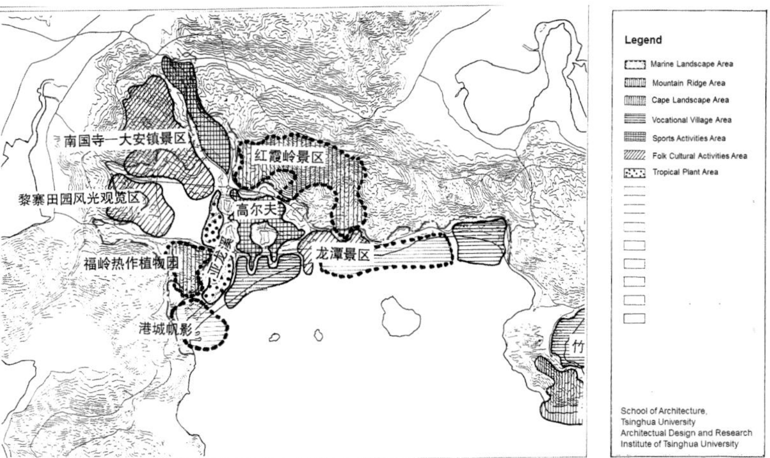

Right: Master planning of Yalong Bay National Tourist Resort of Sanya Yalong Bay was among the 12 earliest national tourist resorts in China and Tsinghua University was entrusted by the Sanya Bureau of Urban Planning with the task of planning for this national tourist resort with the idea of facilitating protection and development at the same time to turn it into a first-class tourist resort in the world.

1993–2002

In 1993, Zheng Guangzhong and Yang Rui undertook and completed a number of projects including the Hainan Jianfeng National Forest Park Planning and Wuzhishan Baihualing Scenic Area Planning.

The Summer Palace Rear Lake Commercial Street (Suzhou Street) reconstruction project designed under the supervision of Xu Boan won third prize for excellent design from the State Education Commission and the Ministry of Construction, as well as an outstanding project award for tourism infrastructure building over the 7th FYP period from the National Tourism Administration.

Sun Fengqi applied for and completed, from 1994 to 1997, the "Research on the Redevelopment of City Squares," a project financed by the National Natural Science Foundation of China and one in which effective countermeasures are proposed for reconstruction and development of typical squares in some large and medium-sized cities in reference to advanced theories and practices at home and abroad in consideration of the national situations.

Zheng Guangzhong, Yang Rui, and others did the feasibility study and master plan for the Three Gorges Dam Scenic and Tourism Project. In 1995, the "Chinese Classical Garden" course offered by Ji Huailu was added to the undergraduate curriculum and ran until 2004 to follow up on the one taught by Zhou Weiquan before his retirement in 1992.

On January 28, 1996, Professor Wang Juyuan, who was the first academician representing landscape architecture in the Chinese Academy of Engineering, a horticulturist, landscape expert, and one of the founders of the Landscape Program, died from illness in Beijing at 83.

On December 1, 1996, *Famous Mountain Scenic Spots in China* written by Zhou Weiquan was published by the Tsinghua University Press, which was the first to put forward the concept, denomination, and meaning of the "famous mountain scenic spots" and to make it a major landscape category with a full explanation of the history, scenic resources, case presentations, and aesthetic appreciation. This is the most intact book on the studies of scenic areas in China to the present and one representing the highest level of study in this field.

In 1996 faculty teacher Ji Huailu began to offer the course, "*Chinese Classical Gardens*," at Tsinghua University.

In addition, the School of Architecture also offered other garden-related courses, including "*History of Ancient Chinese Architecture*," "*Suzhou Garden Internships*," and "*Urban Greening Design*."

On April 25, 1998 the Institute of Landscape and Gardening was established at the Tsinghua School of Architecture with the approval of the Tsinghua University administration and Sun Fengqi, appointed as director. This marked the landscape architecture studies at the Tsinghua School of Architecture being raised to a new level. In the same year, Zhang Junhua joined the Institute of Landscape.

Commissioned by the National Tourism Bureau, Zheng Guangzhong, Yang Rui, and Deng Wei teamed up in the development of the "General Specification for Tourism Planning (GB/T 1897–2003)," which was proposed on February 24, 2003 and came into effect on May 1, 2003.

In 1998, upon his PhD graduation from the Beijing Forestry University, Zhu Yufan entered into the postdoctoral working station of Tsinghua School of Architecture. Under the tutelage of academician Wu Liangyong, he became the first postdoctoral of landscape architecture at the Tsinghua School of Architecture.

On March 8, 1998 Zhu Changzhong, who was at the same time head of the urban planning TRG and professor at the Tsinghua School of Architecture and chairman of the Landscape and Environment Planning and Design Academic Committee under the Urban Planning Society of China (UPSC), passed away at the age of 77.

In June 1999, the Institute of Natural Resource Preservation and Scenery Tourism was set up at the Tsinghua School of Architecture, with Zheng Guangzhong serving as the first director. Zheng Guangzhong, Yang Rui, and Zhuang Youbo undertook the project for preparation of the "Mt. Taishan Scenic Area Master Plan."

The "Northwest Yunnan Human Settlements (including National Parks) Sustainable Development Planning and Research," a project in cooperation with the Yunnan Provincial School under the supervision of Wu Liangyong embarked under severe ecological conditions on regional research, seeking to establish a sustainable development path for human settlements featured by harmony between man and nature, and recommending focused protection over local natural environment, biological diversity, and traditional culture plus prudent and reasonable development of local resources to help free local people from poverty and develop the national park system.

In August 2000, the book *Summer Palace* compiled by the Tsinghua School of Architecture was published by the China Building Industry Press, which contained sufficient detailed case studies and vivid illustrations and greatly pushed forward research on imperial gardens and Chinese classical gardens. Putting together yearly survey mapping outputs from students and faculty of the Tsinghua School of Architecture since 1952, this is the most extensive book of themed research on the Summer Palace to date.

The "Introduction to Landscape Design" course offered by Zhang Junhua was added to the postgraduate curriculum, and the "Introduction to Landscape Architecture" course offered by Yang Rui, was added to the undergraduate curriculum in 2000.

Wu Liangyong's book *Introduction to the Sciences of Human Settlements* was published. Human settlements refer to places where people live together along with the surrounding environments such as villages, townships, cities, and regions. *The Sciences of Human Settlements* takes human settlements as the research object and seeks to study the relationship between human communities and the surrounding environments and the development laws of the same. In response to the contradiction between the demand for human settlement and the limited space resources, it abides by social, ecological, economic, technical, and artistic principles for realization of two objectives: orderly space (i.e., the coordinated order of space and its organizations); and livable environment (i.e., a better living environment that is suitable for living and production). The inception of *The Sciences of Human Settlements*, which later became a most important theoretical basis for LA development at Tsinghua, broadened the vision for further development of the landscape architecture discipline.

In spring 2002, the Hong Kong Government Information Services published the book, Temple and Monastery Gardens in Hong Kong written by Zhu Junzhen.

The master planning of the "Meili Snow Mountains National Park in the Three Parallel Rivers Scenic Area," a project under Yang Rui's supervision with Dang Anrong's and Zhuang Youbo's participation, was accomplished in October 2002. It won the first prize for the Excellent Landscape Architecture Planning and Design Award from the Chinese Society of Landscape Architecture in 2011 and the first prize for the China Building Science and Technology Award in 2012.

In 2002, Zhu Yufan started to offer the postgraduate course of "Introduction to Modern European and American Landscape Architecture."

Left: Group photo of Mt. Huangshan planners on their site study tour. (from Zheng Guangzhong.)

Above: Qin Yougguo, former dean of School of Architecture delivering a speech at the inauguration ceremony of the Research Center for Landscape Architecture Planning (Records from the Archive of the School of Architecture, Tsinghua University).

神农燕天全景

Above: Shen Nong Yan Tian panorama from "Zheng Guangzhong book sketch" (June 2000)..

Above: Landscape design for the centennial of Yangzhou Middle School supervised by Wang Lifang (from Wang Lifang).

Above: Beiyuan Garden and Aspen Plaza (Lovers' Slope). Designed by Wang Lifang. (from Wang Lifang).

1.4 Department of Landscape Architecture (2003–2017)

Above: Laurie D. Olin, first chair of the Department of Landscape Architecture.

Above: Yang Rui, first deputy chair of the Department of Landscape Architecture.

2003

On March 20, 2003 Tsinghua University hired Laurie D. Olin—professor of the Landscape and Planning Department of the School of Art of the University of Pennsylvania, member of the American Academy of Arts and Sciences, former chair of the Landscape Architecture Department of Harvard University, and a well known landscape architect in the United States—as chair professor. On October 8 the founding ceremony and academic symposium of the Department of Landscape Architecture was held in the Wang Zesheng Hall, School of Architecture, which was attended and addressed by President Gu Binlin of Tsinghua University, with keynote speeches delivered by Wu Liangyong and Laurie Olin entitled, "Sciences of human Settlements and Landscape Education" and "Development Trends of International Landscape Education" respectively. It was announced on the occasion that Laurie Olin was appointed as the first chair and Yang Rui as executive vice chair.

The Landscape Planning and Design Program, a secondary discipline set by Tsinghua University as a doctoral degree conferring body within its primary-discipline program in accordance with the provisions of the State Council No. 47 Degree Document of 2002 and the No. 84 Document of Degrees Committee of 2002 and duly endorsed by and documented with the Degrees Committee of the State Council. The founding objective was to build the Department of Landscape Architecture as soon as possible into a first-class, professional landscape architect training base with worldwide influence in key areas by holding fast to regional and urban landscape planning, landscape and garden design, natural and cultural heritage resource protection, and tourism planning as the major academic orientations while following an integrated teaching, research, and research planning and design approach.

Upon the establishment of the Department of Landscape Architecture, Laurie Olin's Chair Professor Team was established, consisting of nine professors with rich teaching and practical experiences including Laurie Olin – they operated, formally, from September 2004 onwards. From 2004 to 2007 the Chair Professor Team undertook the teaching of the landscape history, landscape ecology, landscape hydrology, landscape technology, studios, and other major courses of the program. They introduced the most advanced teaching methods and professional theories and technologies from abroad, and set a high standard and a solid basis for the smooth operation of, and further improvements on, teaching at the Department of LA. Laurie Olin drafted the Graduate Training Program for the Department of Landscape Architecture, Tsinghua University.

In 2003, Hu Jie joined the department faculty. In September, the Landscape Architecture Department of Beijing Tsinghua Urban Planning & Design Institute was established with Hu Jie serving as the director.

Left: Group photo for the inauguration ceremony and Symposium of Department of Landscape Architecture, School of Architecture, Tsinghua University. (Records from the Archive of the School of Architecture, Tsinghua University).

Left: Gu Binglin, president of Tsinghua University (left) next to Laurie Olin (right) presented letters of appointment (records from the Archive of the School of Architecture, Tsinghua University).

Left: Laurie Olin, Wu Liangyong, and Yang Rui in a heated discussion (from Laurie Olin).

2004

In September 2004, the first students enrolled in the graduate program and began their two-year studies. On December 5, Laurie Olin, Chair of the Department of LA, held the LO Talk and delivered a keynote speech, "Tendencies in Contemporary Landscape Architecture at exemplified by work of Olin Partnership."

In June 2004 the Department of Landscape Planning and Tourism was set up under the Beijing Tsinghua Urban Planning & Design Institute, with Yang Rui serving as the director.

Left: Drawings by Laurie Olin: a birthday cake, October 2003 (from Laurie Olin).

Left: Drawings by Laurie Olin: curtains in the Tsinghua apartment, October 2004 (from Laurie Olin).

Left: Taking LA students on an investigation tour to Tanzhe Temple (from Zhao Zhicong).

Left: Built-up landscape of the central area of the Tsinghua Institute of Nuclear and New Energy Technology (from the designer: the unique historical background of the site and the original juniper enclosure led to the designer's final determination to adopt the Le Notre's axial space as the general blueprint for the environmental transformation while resorting to fundamental strategies of consolidating pool series for enhanced space dramaticism and sequence along the central axle and horizontal axle of the landscape for addition to the original axial space) (from Zhu Yufan).

Left: Beijing Yushuzhuang Park, with a total planning area of 768 mu (about 51.2 hectares), designed chiefly by Ji Huailu to be the sole newly-built garden in Beijing to maintain the wetland landscape and a purely classic style (from Ji Huailu).

2005

On December 24 the Department of Landscape Architecture hosted the Fifth Joint "Landscape and Tourism Academic Forum" of Tsinghua, Peking, and Beijing Forestry Universities. Scholars from Peking University, Beijing Forestry University, Tongji University, Zhejiang University, the Chinese Academy of Sciences, National Taiwan University, and Tsinghua University made impressive presentations on the theme of "Imitation of Nature – Natural Factors in Landscape and Tourism Planning and Design." Presenters at the forum included Wu Liangyong; Bart Johnson, associate professor at the University of Oregon and visiting professor of Department of Landscape Architecture, Tsinghua University; and Wang Xin, professor at the National Taiwan University. Wu Liangyong delivered a speech entitled, "From Small Gardens to Regional Landscape Systems," and raised a question for deliberation: "How do we accelerate the development of landscape architecture in the 3-in-1 architecture, urban planning, and landscape architecture system?"

Above: Richard Forman (second from left), Yang Rui (first from left), and LA faculty and students on a study visit (from the Department of Landscape Architecture).

Above: Ron Henderson (fourth from left) instructing a landscape design course (from the Department of Landscape Architecture).

2006

Above: The monument to Lin Huiyin, a joint project of the Hangzhou Municipal Government and the School of Architecture of Tsinghua University designed by Wang Lifang, was accomplished and open to public at Huagang Park of Hangzhou in August 2006.

The 2006 spring semester marked the first formal enrollment of the part-time Master Program of Landscape Architecture. Based on the teaching and practice requirements, Professor Bao Zhiyi from the Zhejiang Agriculture and Forestry University was invited to offer the course, "Plant Landscaping Planning and Design," and Professor Dang Anrong, the course, "Landscape Geo-Science." In June, an integrated graduate landscape ecology, botany, and geology internship program was developed and launched, which continued on and became an important component of the teaching and practices at the Department of LA. Spring 2006 also marked the graduation of students from the first professor's program.

In March, the Department of Landscape Architecture and Design was set up at the Beijing Tsinghua Urban Planning & Design Institute, with Zhu Yufan serving as the director.

Along with Stephen F. McCool, Professor David Gerard Simmons, dean of the Tourism Department of Lincoln University, New Zealand, came for a visit and delivered an academic presentation. In November, students and teachers from the University of Hong Kong came for a visit to conduct the one-week joint studio under the theme of "CBD Landscape Concept Design."

In November, "LA Friday" was officially launched, aiming to facilitate academic development and standing academic exchanges between the students and teachers. The event is held from 11:30 am to 1:00 pm every other Friday as a platform for internal and external presentations followed by a question and answer time. Since 2006, "LA Friday" has become a tradition of the Department of LA.

On December 9, the second Beijing Tourism Forum was held by Tsinghua University in collaboration with Peking University, Beijing International Studies University, the Beijing Tourism Society, and the Chinese Academy of Social Sciences, which engaged a number of top-notch domestic tourism research experts and scholars in extensive and in-depth exchanges on the theme of "Urban Tour vs. Rural Tour."

In August, the monument to Lin Huiyin, a joint project of the Hangzhou Municipal Government and the School of Architecture of Tsinghua University, was completed and open to public at Huagang Park in Hangzhou. The monument, designed by Wang Li Fang of the Tsinghua School of Architecture, won an Excellence Award in the 2008 from the National Public Sculpture Accreditation. In the same month, the residential landscape design of the No. 81 Yard, Fragrant Hill overseen by Zhu Yufan was completed, which later became the first project in China to win an honor award of the general design category for the 2012 ASLA Professional Awards. By adopting the dark gray rubble walls, which respond sensitively to the slope, the design of No. 81 Yard, Fragrant Hill gained the distinct rustic characteristic of Beijing villages. Enhanced by the contemporary landscape design scheme, this project demonstrates easily recognizable integrity. The design style co-exists in harmony with the built environment while demonstrating traditional continuity and locality of hillside residence.

In August, Yang Rui and others finished the master planning of the Mt. Huangshan National Park, and the Tibet Autonomous Region Tourism Development master plan (2005–2020), which had Yin Zhi, Zheng Guangzhong, and others on the design team was finished. In light of the characteristics of the Mt. Huangshan National Park and problems with the traditional planning techniques and skills, the planning included explorations and experiments made on multiple objects and methods, including the target system, zoning, visitor experience management, spatial and temporal distribution model, designated tourism products and marketing, for peak day, monitoring system, and community coordination.

Above: The external landscape design of No. 81 Yard, Fragrant Hill (from Zhu Yufan).

Above: Group photo of the combined Ecology-Botany-Geology internship scheme at Zhoukoudian (Fourth and ninth from the left in the second row: pedologist doctor from Beijing Normal University and petrologist doctor from China University of Geosciences respectively). (From the Department of Landscape Architecture.)

Right Drawings by Laurie Olin: working with Qin Yougguo, 2006 (provided by Laurie Olin). (Records from the Archive of the School of Architecture, Tsinghua University.)

Right: The external landscape design of No. 81 Yard, Fragrant Hill (phase II of Banshan Fenglin Residential Area) was a built project taking on the distinct rustic characteristic of Beijing villages by adopting the dark gray rubble walls, which respond sensitively to the slope forging easily-recognizable integrity via contemporary landscape design schemes to create a style in harmony with the built environment and in continuation of the tradition and locality of the hillside residences (from Zhu Yufan).

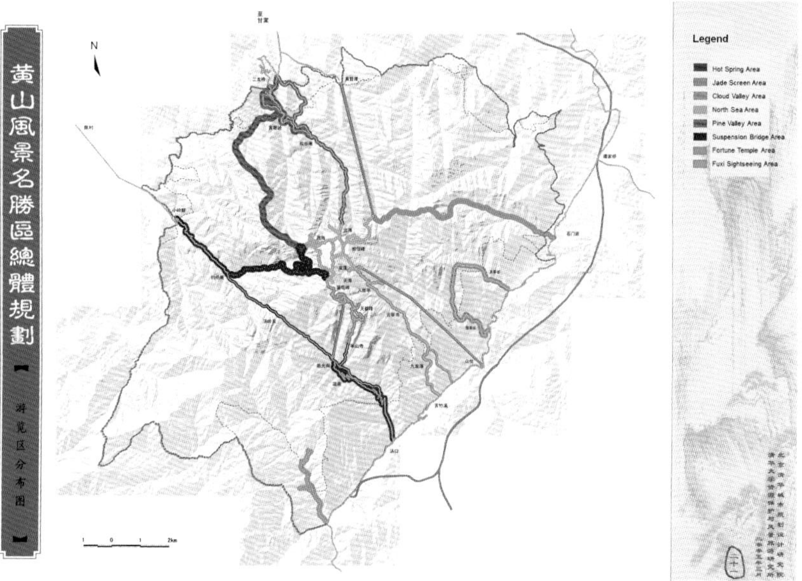

Right: Tourist site distribution map for the master planning of Mount Huangshan Scenic Area (from the Department of Landscape Architecture). This time the planning was targeted at the characteristics of the Mount Huangshan Scenic Area and problems with the traditional scenic area planning techniques and methods. New probes into and experiments on the planning content and methodologies cover: the target system, zoning, visitor experience management, spatial and temporal distribution model, designated tourism products, marketing for peak days, monitoring system, and community coordination.

2007

In October 2007, Ronald Henderson from the Roger Williams University, Rhode Island, USA was officially engaged as associate professor of the Department of Landscape Architecture, School of Architecture, Tsinghua University to teach the Landscape Technology course and undertake other related teaching assignments.

In 2007, Dean Jack Davis, Deputy Dean Patrick A. Miller, and noted landscape architect Peter Latz visited Tsinghua University to give academic presentations from the College of Architecture and Urban Studies at Virginia Polytechnic Institute and State University (Virginia Tech), USA.

On April 26, the Department of Landscape Architecture, School of Architecture, and Tsinghua University hosted a meeting with the *Chinese Landscape Architecture Journal's* chief editors under the theme, "Landscape Architecture and Traditional Culture."

On May 13, Professor Zhou Weiquan of Tsinghua University, the famous architect, a pioneer of China's landscape architecture, adviser to the Beijing Municipal Government, member of the landscape architecture expert committee of the Ministry of Construction, and executive director of the Chinese Society of Landscape Architecture, passed away in Beijing at the age of 80.

Yang Rui oversaw the Beijing Scenic Area System Planning project and completed it in January 2007, and its revision in July 2011.

In April, the reconstruction planning and design of the Daming Lake Jinan was overseen by Zhang Jie and won the first prize of the First Excellent Landscape Architecture Planning and Design Award from the Chinese Society of Landscape Architecture (in 2011).

In May, Zhu Yufan oversaw and completed the landscape design for the Modern Art Park in the Beijing CBD Area, which later won a BALI National Landscape Award (in 2009).

Both Laurie Olin and Hu Jie received the 2007 "Great Wall Friendship Award" for foreign experts conferred by the Beijing Municipal People's Government.

The graduation design work of Que Zhenqing entitled "From the Sewage Canal to the Green Corridor: Riverfront Landscape Transformation of the Xiaojiahe Section of the Qinghe River" (tutor: Yang Rui) won the honor award of the general design category for the 2007 ASLA Student Awards.

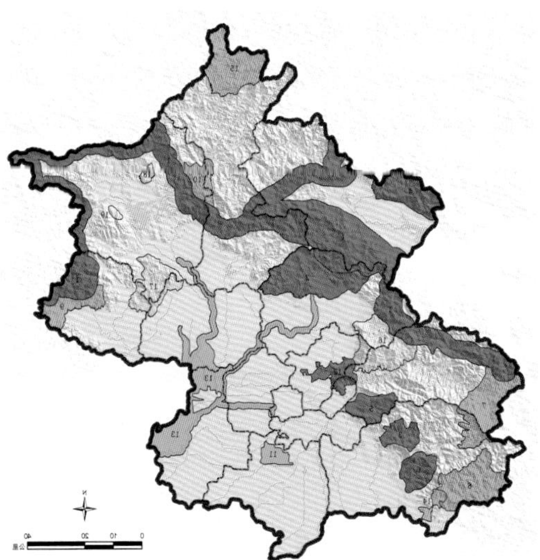

Above: The Beijing scenic area system planning studies were one of of the earliest carried out at the provincial and municipality level, and was therefore original and of demonstration relevance. It has played an important role in guiding the development, positioning, and direction of scenic areas in Beijing and the overall planning of various scenic areas in Beijing (from the Department of Landscape Architecture).

Above: A delegation from Chiba University of Japan visiting the Department of Landscape Architecture (from the Department of Landscape Architecture).

Above: Built-up landscape of the modern art park in the Beijing CBD area. The park is cut into two halves by a road, so the designer devised an eight-meter-high and 80-meter-in-diameter circular green passage platform as the core of the park space, which is no simple connection between the north and south park halves, but a central hub in its actual sense, core to the slope of the landscape of the central park (from Zhu Yufan).

Above: Built-up landscape of the reconstruction planning and design of the daming lake scenic area, Jinan. The design converted the Daming Lake, one of the three most noted spots in Jinan, from a "garden lake" into a "city lake" by linking it to the moat and preserving all historical relics along the original shoreline. While paying attention to the protection of tangible elements of history, great stress was laid on the protection and excavation of intangible cultural heritage spots in a bid to restore the original cultural sites.

2008

The Department of Landscape Architecture held joint studios with the University of Hong Kong and the University of Texas at Austin under the respective design themes of landscape transformation of the wedge green space in the Zhongguancun West District and pocket parks.

In December, Yang Rui took over as the second chair of the department, with Zhu Yufan serving as Vice Chair. In the same year, Yang Rui started to serve as Executive Director and Deputy Secretary General of the China Society of Landscape Architecture.

Under the support of the National Development and Reform Commission, State Administration of Cultural Heritage, Ministry of Housing and Urban-Rural Development, and the Ministry of Education, Tsinghua University had the "National Heritage Research Center" established at the School of Architecture, which is dedicated to the cultural and natural heritage conservation, integration of related resources, and the establishment of a teaching, research, and practice platform for cultural and natural heritage protection. Lv Zhou was made director, and Yang Rui and Zhang Jie became deputy directors of the Center.

With the completion of the Beijing Olympic Forest Park in 2008, the main designers, Hu Jie and Zhu Yufan, won the first prize of the Torsanlorenzo International Awards in Urban Green Space Section (2007), the President's Award of the International Federation of Landscape Architects Asia-Pacific Regional Congress Award in the Design Category (2009), an Honor Award from the ASLA Professional Awards-General Design Category, and first prize in the First Excellent Landscape Architecture Planning and Design Award from Chinese Society of Landscape Architecture (2011).

Earlier, in November 2003, the project proposal by Beijing Tsinghua Urban Planning and Design Institute in cooperation with the SASAKI Office in the United States won the Beijing Olympic Forest Park and the Central District Landscape Planning and Design Competition.

In November 2008, The Department of Landscape Architecture, School of Architecture, Tsinghua University, in cooperation with the National Tourism Administration, completed the compilation of the Grading of Tourist Resorts (National Standards), which was released on January 14, 2011 and took effect on June 1, 2011. Soon after, the *Implementation Guideline for the Grading of Tourist Resorts, Administrative Regulations on the Grading of Tourist Resorts,* and *Tourist Resort Development Status Quo and Outlook*, of which Yang Rui and Wu Dongfan were major contributors on the drafting teams, were released.

In the same year, Hu Jie oversaw and completed the landscape design of the National Wetland Park of Lianhua Lake, Fanhe New District, Tieling City, which won the second prize at the Torsanlorenzo International Awards in the Regional Reconstruction Landscape Design Section (2009), the

President's Award for the International Federation of Landscape Architects of Asia-Pacific Regional Congress Award in Landscape Architectural in the Design Category (2011), and the ASLA Honor Award in the Analysis and Planning Category (2012).

In January 2008, commissioned by the Shanxi Provincial Department of Construction and the Mt. Wutai National Park Administrative Office, faculty and students, led by Yang Rui, Wu Dongfan, and Zhuang Youbo finished the compilation of the World Heritage application document for the Mt. Wutai National Park, together with a conservation and management planning of the nominated property, which were successfully submitted to the UNESCO World Heritage Centre; the work continued until January 2008 when Mt. Wutai was added to the World Heritage List as a cultural landscape at the 33rd session of the World Heritage Committee in August 2009.

In March, Yang Rui recieved the Tsinghua University honorary title of "mentor."

Above: Group photo on the occasion of preliminary research on Mt. Huashan for preparation of the world heritage inscription application documents and management planning for protection of the nominated property (from the Department of Landscape Architecture).

Above: Bird's-eye view of the Beijing Olympic Forest Park (from Hu Jie).

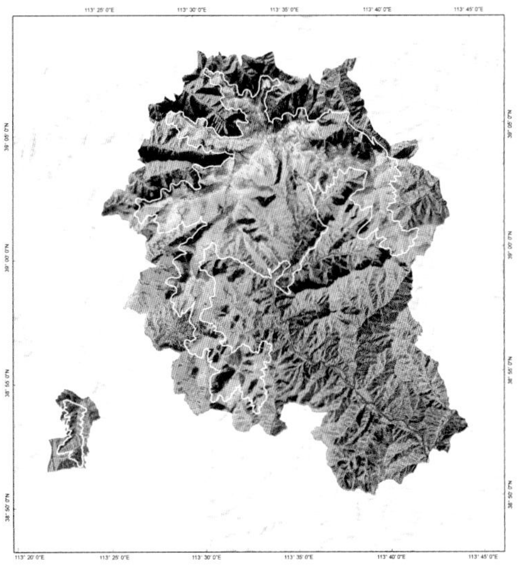

Above: Application documents and protection management planning for nominating Mount Wutai as a World Heritage Property – satellite images of the nominated site and the buffer zone (from the Department of Landscape Architecture).

2009

From the 12th–13th of September 2009 the Chinese Society of Landscape Architecture held its annual meeting at Tsinghua University with the theme, "integration and growth." The Tsinghua-Chiba Dual-Degree program was launched to enable graduate students of the two universities to do a one-year exchange study in the other to obtain a degree from both. Famous landscape designers such as Peter Walker, Martha Schwartz, Colin Franklin, and Charles Waldheim—Chair of Landscape Architecture at Harvard University's Graduate School of Design—visited the department to deliver academic lectures. Li Shu-hua, the former dean of the Department of Ornamental Horticulture and Landscape Architecture, China Agricultural University was appointed as master with the department of Landscape Architecture, School of Architecture, Tsinghua University.

In June, Zhu Yufan oversaw and completed the Memorial Park of National Patriotism Education Base in Qinghai Atomic City project, which received the BALI National Landscape Award (2010), and First Prize of the First Excellent Landscape Architecture Planning and Design Award from the Chinese Society of Landscape Architecture (2011).

Digital Summer Palace, a joint project of Tsinghua School of Architecture and Tsinghua Urban Planning and Design Institute under the supervision of Guo Daiheng, was launched to build a digital bank of the basic historical data of Yuanmingyuan, to create a three-dimensional panoramic digital reconstruction of Yuanmingyuan, and to release the virtual Yuanmingyuan for public use.

In the same year, Ronald Henderson completed the design project of Yingzhou Central Park, which gained the 2009 ASLA Rhode Island Honor Award in November, and Hu Jie managed the survey library construction and digitized analog simulation of the Qianlong Garden, Beijing Forbidden City.

In January, *Olympic Green* and *Landscape Planning and Design*, two books compiled by the Beijing Tsinghua Planning and Design Institute, with Hu Jie as the editor-in-chief and deputy director of the editorial board, were published by the China Building Industry Press, and in April Zheng Guangzhong's *Architectural Sketch* was published by the Tsinghua University Press. In May, *China's Ancient Architecture Popularization and Inheritance* book series, compiled by the School of Architecture, was published by the Tsinghua University Press. It included the *Temple of Heaven* written by Wang Guixiang and the *Summer Palace* written by Jia Jun. In December Jia Jun's book *Private Gardens in Beijing* was published by the Tsinghua University Press and won the honor of "Best Architectural History Book" in the third Chinese Architecture Book Award (2010).

In August Guo Daiheng's book *Past Glory: Yuanmingyuan Architecture and Landscape Research and Protection* was published by the Shanghai Science and Technology Press. The book is derived from research conducted by a project team led by Guo Daiheng, a well-known Chinese architecture history scholar and master with the Tsinghua School of Architecture on Yuanmingyuan's architectural, mountain, and water landscape features and evolution and probes into the heritage landscape protection philosophies and issues concerning the protection of Yuanmingyuan. It is an academic monograph with both theoretical values and practical relevance.

Below: Bird's-eye view of the core zone of the National Wetland Park of Lianhua Lake, Fanhe New District, Tieling City, a project in which water was drawn into the city and linked to the Lotus Lake to form a river (Tianshui River), adding to the new city an axial of vitality and a characteristic lake landscape to which gulls flow in groups, to echo the one in the old city. A hill was then heaped around the lake to enrich the urban space to make perfect the yin-yang symbolization of the landscape. To echo the Longshou (Dragonhead) Mountain in the old town and to bring out the implied symbolization, the newly heaped hill to the south of the Lotus Lake was called the Fengguan (Phoenix Crest) Mountain (from Hu Jie).

2009 Annual Meeting of the Chinese Society of Landscape Architecture (CHSLA) held in Tsinghua University

This meeting, the first plenary annual meeting since CHSLA, officially became a level-one national association in 1989, was hosted by CHSLA and co-organized by Tsinghua School of Architecture, the Beijing Bureau of Landscape and Forestry, and the Beijing Municipal Administration Center of Parks with assistance from the Beijing Tsinghua Urban Planning and Design Institute, *Journal of Chinese Landscape Architecture*, and *Journal of Landscape Architecture*. More than 400 practitioners in the landscape architecture profession from across the country attended the annual meeting where five well-known scholars from home and abroad delivered keynote speeches and sixty-eight scholars, experts, and doctoral candidates made their presentations.

One of the outcomes of the Annual Meeting was the adoption of the Beijing Declaration of Chinese Landscape Architecture, in which it is proposed that the core values of the profession include the harmony between humanity and nature, spirit and matter, science and art, that is, "man is an integral part of nature" in the modern context; the historical mission is to protect the natural ecosystems and natural and cultural heritages, to plan, design, construct, and manage the outdoor human settlement environment. The meeting urged to create a vibrant, healthy, inclusive, and orderly culture, and to explore fully, conscientiously, and constructively the major issues affecting the development of landscape architecture so as to reach consensus conducive to the development of the Chinese landscape architecture industry. Wu Liangyong, academician with the Chinese Academy of Sciences and the Chinese Academy of Engineering, delivered a keynote speech entitled "Deliberations on the Landscape Architecture Restructuring and Professional Education"; Zhou Ganzhi, academician with the Chinese Academy of Sciences and the Chinese Academy of Engineering, and honorary chairman of the Chinese Society of Landscape Architecture delivered the keynote speech entitled "Retrospect and Prospect of Landscape Architecture" at the closing ceremony of the annual meeting; Meng Zhaozhen, academician with the Chinese Academy of Engineering and honorary chairman of the Chinese Society of Landscape Architecture, delivered the keynote speech entitled "Some Thoughts on Borrowing Landscape" at the closing ceremony of the annual meeting.

Above: Built-up landscape designed for the National Patriotism Education Base in Qinghai Atomic City. By setting a zigzag path, the designer restudied and reorganized the status space and the design space in attempt to protect and use the poplars on site as carriers of the genius loci that build an ideal, seamless connection between it and the linear representation of China's epic self-independence in developing atomic and hydrogen bombs (from Zhu Yufan).

2010

In 2010, Takahiro Ohashi and Johannes Matthiessen visited the department to deliver academic lectures. From the 29th of October to the 11th of March, a four week-long joint studio was organized for 26 graduate students of the Landscape Architecture Department and 10 MLA students of the University of Hong Kong on the theme of "Beijing Financial Street Exterior Space Concept Design." On the 24th of December the Landscape Department held the first alumni gathering to celebrate the New Year, the largest of its kind, with a total of 80 participants.

On the 18th of April, a seminar on "Qian Xuesen's Scientific Thoughts: Landscape and Landscape City" was held in Beijing under the sponsorship of the Organizing Committee of the 47th World Congress of the International Federation of Landscape Architects and was organized by the Chinese Society of Landscape Architecture and Beijing Tsinghua Urban Planning and Design Institute. From the 18th to the 19th of September, the "International Forum on Yuanmingyuan (Research and Protection) from the Digital Perspective" was successfully held by Tsinghua Urban Planning and Design Institute, Tsinghua School of Architecture and the Yuanmingyuan Administrative Office at Tsinghua, at which the phase one outcome of the "Digital Yuanmingyuan" project showing digital representations of twenty-two scenics in Yuanmingyuan, overseen by Guo Daiheng, was released, and the website www.Re-relic.com, officially launched. From the 17th to the 18th of November, the Tsinghua University and Technical University of Berlin held a joint doctoral forum called "Designerly Research," which was successfully held at the Jackson Wang Hall at Tsinghua School of Architecture. This was the first international joint research activity held at the doctoral level in history of Tsinghua School of Architecture.

An earthquake measuring magnitude 7.1 struck Yushu on April 14. Zhu Yufan oversaw the Landscape Design of the Gyana Marnyi Stone Mound, New Village in the Yushu reconstruction project.

Hu Jie finished the Tangshan Nanhu Eco-City Central Park Master planning & design project he supervised, which won him the outstanding award of the IFLA Asia Pacific Excellence Awards in the landscape architecture category (2011), the BALI National Landscape – International Project Award (2011), first prize in the Torsanlorenzo International Awards in the Transformation of the Territory Section (2011), and the Green Good Design Award from the European Centre for Architecture Art Design and Urban Studies (2012).

Zhu Yufan accomplished the landscape design project of Quarry Garden in the Chenshan Botanical Garden of Shanghai, which was nominated for the Best Building Award in the Second China Architecture Media Awards, and won the BALI National Landscape Award International Project Award (2011), and the honor award under the General Design Category of the ASLA Professional Awards (2012).

From the 29th of August to the 21st of November the "water seal" installed by Zhu Yufan was exhibited in the China Pavilion at the 12th International Architecture Biennale in Venice in 2010.

In November, Zheng Xiaodi won second prize (first prize vacant) in the World Society for Ekistics (WSE) essay competition held in India.

Above: Zhu Yufan (first from left) on a research tour to the Yushu Reconstruction project site.(from Zhu Yufan).

Above: Spot photo of the "Flow Seal" (from Zhu Yufan). "Flow Seal," a design product of Zhu Yufan, on a show at the China Pavilion for La Biennale di Venezia – The 12th International Architecture Exhibition from 29 August to 21 November, 2010 (from Zhu Yufan).

2011

On February 14, 2011, academician Wu Liangyong received the State Supreme Science and Technology Award at the Great Hall of the People.

According to the "Degree-Granting and Personnel Training Discipline Catalog (2011)," used by the Academic Degrees Committee of the State Council and the Ministry of Education, urban planning, landscape architecture, and architecture are all listed as level-one disciplines and the Tsinghua Department of Landscape Architecture played an important role in the successful inclusion of landscape architecture in the level-one disciplines under the engineering category.

In March, a delegation of professors from the Chiba University of Japan visited the Department of Landscape Architecture to interview and recruit students for the joint program and gave a series of lectures on March 17. On the delegation commitee were professors of environment and horticulture including Makoto Akasaka, Isami Kinoshita, Mitani Toru, and Zhang Junhua.

From the 26th of March to the 6th of April a delegation of 12 students and faculty members travelled to Spain for the joint studio of the Tsinghua University and the Catalonia Polytechnic University. In December the same year, Spanish teachers and undergraduate students paid a return visit for the joint studio. In July, some third-year students of the Tsinghua School of Architecture conducted surveys, mapping the existing modern gardens in Nanxun, Huzhou City, Zhejiang Province.

From the 11th to the 25th of November, Zheng Xiaodi, and Sun Yong-hoon from the Horticulture Department of Chiba University, jointly supervised the China-Japan-Korea Joint Landscape Design Exchange Workshop, which was attended by students from Tsinghua University, Beijing Forestry University, Chiba University, and Seoul National University.

John Macleod, Michael Turner, and Adriaan Geuze—founders of the West 8 Landscape and Urban Design Firm in the Netherlands—Ken Brown, Haruto Kobayashi, Herbert Dreiseitl, and Linda Jewel who was the former dean of the Department of Landscape Architecture and Environmental Planning of the University of California in Berkeley, visited to deliver academic lectures at Tsinghua University.

In April, the Centennial Woods, designed by the Li Shu-hua, were created in celebration of the Centenary of Tsinghua University.

Above: Zheng Xiaodi (second from left) supervising the China-Japan-Korea landscape design exchange workshop (from Zheng Xiaodi). Students from Tsinghua University, Beijing Forestry University, Chiba University, and Seoul National University participated in the workshop entitled "Elderly Community Landscape Update Design." This exchange program was organized by the Department of Environmental Science and Landscape Architecture, Faculty of Horticulture, Chiba University under the supervision of Professor Zhang Junhua.

Above: Group photo taken on the occasion of the first alumni gathering of the Department of Landscape Architecture (from the Department of Landscape Architecture).

2012

In 2012, the Academic Degrees and Graduate Education Development Center, under the Ministry of Education, launched a third round of disciplinary assessment and Tsinghua Department of Landscape Architecture ranked second among universities (together with Tongji University and Southeast University, the first being Beijing Forestry University). In May, the Beijing Municipal Science and Technology Commission announced the list of the 2011 Beijing Key Laboratories, among which was the "Beijing Key Laboratory for Evaluation and Control Technology of Ecological Functions of Green Space" which is based at the Beijing Institute of Landscape Architecture and built in cooperation with the Tsinghua University. A sub-lab of the "Beijing Key Laboratory for Evaluation and Control Technology of Ecological Functions of Green Space" was built at the Tsinghua School of Architecture, with Li Shu-hua as Deputy Director.

Eva Castro was appointed as a senior visiting professor to guide the studio courses. In June, Taiwan's Fu Jen Catholic University visited. Peter Ogden and Peter Petschek visited for academic lectures as well. From the 3rd to the 13th of September, the School of Architecture, Catalonia Polytechnic University of Spain and the Tsinghua Department of Landscape Architecture conducted the joint workshops of landscape design. Ten Spanish students led by Professor Miquel Vidal formed research teams with 17 students from the Tsinghua Department of Landscape Architecture for research design of the Landscape Renewal of the Three Mountains and Five Imperial Gardens Area, as part of the landscape architecture teaching cooperation program series. From the 2nd to the 18th of November the same year 17 students and faculty members from the Tsinghua Department of Landscape Architecture paid the return visit to the Catalonia Polytechnic University of Spain.

Zhu Yufan presided over the Landscape Design Project of the Ruyuan Exhibition Area in Beijing Wukuang Vanke Residential Area and brought it to completion, which won the BALI National Landscape Awards International Award in 2012.

Above: Group photo of LA teachers and students with counterparts from Taiwan's Fu Jen Catholic University (from the Department of Landscape Architecture).

Above: Design studio investigation tour to Spain led by Dang Anrong (fifth form left), Zhu Yufan (sixth from left), and Zheng Xiaodi (eighth from left) with professor Miquel Vidal Pla (seventh from left) from the School of Architecture, Catalonia Polytechnic University of Spain with students from the Department of Landscape Architecture, Tsinghua University, in Spain (from Zheng Xiaodi).

2013

In April, the Department of Landscape Architecture was conferred the honorary title of "2012–2013 Outstanding Group of Tsinghua University." A postdoctoral landscape architecture research station was established at the Department of LA and a doctoral student social practice base was established at Jiuzhaigou in Sichuan Province.

Above: Photo of participants of the "Landscape architecture program" roundtable (from the Department of Landscape Architecture).

Hu Jie presided over the projects for the master plan and design of the Landscape Eco-Rehabilitation of Beidahe River, Jiuquan City, Gansu Province; the landscape design of Yanxiu Garden, Liaoyang, Liaoning Province; the overall green systems of the Beijing Future Science & Technology Park and the landscape planning and design of its waterfront forest park, which won the President's Award in the Planning Category, President's Award in the Design Category, and honor award in the Planning Category of the International Federation of Landscape Architects of Asia-Pacific Regional Congress Award.

On May 18th, the Ninth China International Garden Expo opened in Beijing. Ji Huailu was the chief designer of the landmark buildings of Yongding Tower, Wenchang Pavilion, and Wenyuan Pavilion. The "Water Seal" designed by Zhu Yufan and "Sunken Garden" by Eva Castro were on display during this time.

On May 31st, some teachers and students of the 1951 Landscape Program gathered at Tsinghua Department of Landscape Architecture for an interview about the formation of the Landscape Architecture education in China, and to donate valuable historical records to the School Library.

From October 7th to 13th, Tsinghua LA Department held a series of celebration events for Tsinghua Department of Landscape Architecture 10 Years Anniversary. On October 7th, "Invigorating Growth – the forum of education development on landscape architecture program" was held at School of Architecture, Tsinghua University to celebrate the 60th anniversary for first class of graduates of the Landscape Group initiating the Chinese modern landscape architecture education, and 100th anniversary for Wang Juyuan who is one of the initiators for the Landscape Group, as well as press conference for publication of a series of three books. More than 60 renowned scholars and representatives in the field of landscape architecture from universities across China attended these events.

On October 8th to 9th, the International Conference on Landscape Architecture of Tomorrow was held at Meng Mingwei Concert Hall at Tsinghua University. More than 330 participants from the fields of academia, education, and practice in landscape architecture, as well as graduate students attended the conference. At the same time, a workshop on Frontiers of Landscape Architecture Practice and Research and a series of related exhibitions were held during the celebration. These events provide a retrospect of the history and achievements over the past decades, and also look into the future of the Department of Landscape Architecture.

Right: "Invigorating Growth" the forum of education development on landscape architecture program (from Department of Landscape Architecture).

Right: "International academic conference on landscape architecture of tomorrow" in Meng Mingwei Concert Hall (from Department of Landscape Architecture).

On October 10th, the conference for the establishment of Landscape Architecture Theory and History Specialized Committee – Working Conference 2013 was held at Tsinghua University. More than 60 people including leaders of Chinese Landscape Architecture Association, first generation of consultant committee members and members of Landscape Architecture Theory and History Specialized Committee participated the conference.

From November 15th to December 3rd, part of faculty members and students from Department of Landscape Architecture visited the School of Architecture, Polytechnic University of Catalonia in Spain for a joint design workshop. On November 19th, in order to improve the collaboration between two sides, School of Architecture, Tsinghua University signed the cooperation memorandum with the School of Architecture, Polytechnic University of Catalonia, which means that the joint teaching activities will continue until 2018. Exhibitions on "10 years anniversary for Department of Landscape Architecture at School of Architecture, Tsinghua University" and "Beijing and Barcelona, Comparation of Regional Features and Development Under the Global Perspective" were also held at the School of Architecture, Polytechnic University of Catalonia, which introduced the history, pedagogical philosophy, achievement, and faculty members of Tsinghua LA Department, enhancing the mutual understanding and exchanging, benefiting significantly for further collaboration.

2014

On July 29th, 2014, the founding conference of the professional department of Chinese horticulture therapy was held in Shenyang, China. It marked the new historical stage of the development of horticulture therapy in China. Li Shuhua, professor of landscape architecture at Tsinghua University, deputy director of the Mental Health Work Committee of China Social Worker's Association, and director of the Department of Horticultural Therapy, gave a keynote speech entitled "landscape design of stress reduction garden."

In April 2014, a memorandum of cooperation was signed between Tsinghua University, Lincoln University, and Kunming University of Science and Technology which set forth the cooperative research in the field of national parks and protected areas over the next five years between teh universiteis. From December 4th to the 24th in 2014, the urban construction division of the Ministry of Housing and Urban-Rural development (the management office of the scenic area) organized the "New Zealand National Park Visitor Impact Management Training Program." Tsinghua University and Lincoln University worked together to undertake the training program. Three faculty members from the Department of Landscape Architecture, Tsinghua University attended this event, and were responsible for the work involving: 1) working with Lincoln University for the training program and designing field study route; 2) interpretation, translation, and negotiation during the event from the beginning to the end; and 3) working on training reports. This training program promoted the understanding of the national parks (protected areas) and future scientific research cooperation between the two universities, enhanced the exchanges for institution of the two countries in national parks (protected areas), planning, and practice, and expanded the influence of Tsinghua University in the field of protection and management of scenic spots.

Left: Li Shuhua, deputy director of the CSHT committee, was interviewed by the media.Joint landscape design studio by three universities (from Department of Landscape Architecture).

2015

On October 26th 2015 Jeremy Baker, executive vice president of Lincoln University in New Zealand, with six other visiting members came to Tsinghua University. Gao Hong, vice provost of Tsinghua University, met with Baker and other accompanying personnel. Vice dean of the school of architecture Liu Jian, circctor of landscape architecture program Yang Rui, associate professor of landscape architecture Zhuang Youbo, and international department head Xu Jing attended the meeting. The two sides reviewed the schools' exchanges and collaborations since April 2014, signing the "cooperation agreement of three schools" in the filed of national park and heritage conservation areas, and discussed how to promote the exchanges and cooperation in the field of landscape architecture teaching and research between the two schools. After meeting, Professor Jacky Bowring, chief editor of *Landscape Review Journal* and associate professor Mick Abbott, director of the landscape architecture program at Lincoln University gave multiple lectures: "Landscape and Emotion: The Use of Memory and Grief" and "Creating Social, Cultural, and Commercial Value by Increasing Biodiversity." Professor Abbott also met with faculty members and post-doctoral researchers from the Department of Landscape Architecture, Tsinghua University.

From May 16th to the 17th in 2015, under the organization of the Landscape Department, the International Symposium on Urban Stormwater Management & Landscape Hydrology was held at Tsinghua University. The symposium included five topics: 1) a study on the management of stormwater and the history of human settlement environment; 2) the ecological conservation of lake and water systems; 3) urban water science and stormwater management; 4) stormwater smart city architecture and landscape design; and 5) the standards and implementation of stormwater management. More than 400 scholars from across the world attended the meeting, and 37 domestic and foreign guests made excellent academic reports. The symposium conference proceeding accepted 79 papers with covering the five topics, which were published by Tsinghua Press. Sponge campus design workshop and urban stormwater management project exhibitions were also held during the symposium, which promoted the development of research and practice in the field of stormwater management.

2016

From September 10th to the 11th of 2016, the first International Conference on Brownfield Regeneration & Ecological Restoration (ICBRER) was held at Tsinghua University with the theme of "Brownfield Regeneration and Healthy Cities." As one of the important academic activities of the 70th anniversary of the School of Architecture at Tsinghua University, the conference was co-organized by the School of Architecture of Tsinghua University, the Technology and Environment Center of Harvard Graduate School of Design, and the Foreign Economic Cooperation Office of the Ministry of Environmental Protection, and was hosted by the Department of Landscape Architecture, the School of Architecture, Tsinghua University. Yang Rui of Tsinghua LA and Niall Kirkwood of Harvard University served as co-chairs of the conference, and Zheng Xiaodi served as acting chair and general secretary. The conference included five forums, covering themes on policies and regulations, win-win cooperation, design and technology, ecological restoration, and international experience and exchanges. Twenty-four speakers from the United States, the United Kingdom, Germany, Israel, and China spoke and had lively exchanges with more than 250 delegates on policy, practice, and theoretical issues in the field of brownfield regeneration. Invited government officials from the Ministry of Environmental Protection, the Ministry of Housing and Urban-Rural Development, and other ministries and committees were addressed at the opening ceremony. Conference proceedings accepted 25 papers on topics covering design practice, theoretical research and technology, and management. At the end of the conference, the declaration of the 2016 International Conference on Brownfield Regeneration & Ecological Restoration was read out at the closing ceremony and all participants approved it by acclamation. It put forward six core actions with the hope of providing guidelines and references for scholars and practitioners in the field of brownfield regeneration.

As one of the important components during the conference, 58 students from America, Spain, and China attend the Brownfield Regeneration and Healthy Cities Design Workshop, taking the Beijing Shougang coaking plant as the project site and instructed by Zhu Yufang, Zheng Xiaodi, Mique Vidal, Ron Henderson, and Martin Felsen. The workshop enhanced the communication of theory, concept, representation, and design methods for students from the Illinois Institute of Technology, Polytechnic University of Catalonia, and Tsinghua University. It also promoted two collaboration workshops focusing on brownfield challenges. One was carried out with the Illinois Institute of Technology from November 12th to19th in China Town in Chicago. The other was a collaboration with Polytechnic University of Catalonia in Spain from November 21th to 26th at La papelera Española in Barcelona.

In 2016, faculty members from the Tsinghua LA Department engaged in three important landscape planning projects for the 2022 Winter

Olympic Games to be held in Chongli, a small town 220 kilometers to the northwest of Beijing. These projects include the concept planning of sports and recreation demonstration areas with a design team lead by Yang Rui; landscape planning for the central area of Winter Olympics with a design team lead by Zhu Yufang; and the master plan of the Olympic forest park with a design team lead by Hu Jie. It shows that landscape architecture programs plays an important role in national events.

The "plant and environmental innovation" project jointly applied by Tsinghua University, Zhejiang University, Chiba University, and Yonsei University in South Korea was selected for the new project of "Campus Asia" in 2016. The project was approved by the leaders from China, Japan, and South Korea, aiming to improve collaborations and mutual understanding for student among the three countries, and to promote the competitiveness for schools, cultivating the next generation of outstanding talent in Asian.

Above: International Conference on Brownfield Regeneration & Ecological Restoration (from Department of Landscape Architecture).

Above: Brownfield regeneration and healthy city design workshop, Beijing (from Department of Landscape Architecture).

Above: Filed trip, Shougan coaking plant, Beijing (from Department of Landscape Architecture).

2017

From May 26th to 29th, 2017, the International Conference on Landscape Architecture Education was held in Beijing, China, which was also the joint Annual Conference of the Council of Educators in Landscape Architecture (CELA) and the Chinese Landscape Architecture Education Conference (CLAEC). The organizers were the Chinese Steering Committee of Landscape Architecture Education, the Chinese Steering Committee for the Masters of Landscape Architecture Education, the Education Committee of the Chinese Society of Landscape Architecture, and CELA. It was hosted by the Tsinghua University, School of Architecture, Department of Landscape Architecture; Beijing Forestry University, School of Landscape Architecture; and the Peking University College of Architecture and Landscape Architecture. Professor Yang Rui was one of the co-chairs and associate professor Zheng Xiaodi is the secretary-general of the conference.

The theme was "Bridging," and more than 300 lectures were given at the conference emphasizing the exchange of ideas in landscape architecture across disciplines and cultures, and the sharing of knowledge and experience. There were also workshops, posters, and films on topics such as communication and visualization, design education and pedagogy, and design implementation that encouraged participants to discuss and exchange ideas. Field trips were organized to visit historical sites and other projects in Beijing and surrounding areas. Six hundred and seventy-four scholars from 13 countries attended the conference, among which 189 were from overseas. This was the first time in history that these two major annual meetings were held together, and is the first time that the CELA annual conference has been held in Asia. The conference ushered in a new chapter in international landscape architecture education exchange.

Supported by the "Campus Asia" program, graduate students from the Tsinghua Department of Landscape Architecture attended a joint workshop at Chiba University in Japan in February 2017, and a team of Japanese students, led by Professor Zhang Junhua and Shimoda from Chiba University visited Tsinghua University in March attending design projects advised by associate professors Wu Dongfang, Zheng Xiaodi, and Liu Hailong. The Tsinghua University-Chiba University joint training program has sponsored 10 students from China and Japan, and aims to educate students to confront challenges in landscape planning and design.

Left: International Conference on Landscape Architecture Education, Tsinghua University (from Department of Landscape Architecture).

Faculty of Department of Landscape Architecture 2017

Yang Rui

Zhu Yufan

Li Shuhua

Hu Jie

Liu Hailong

Wu Dongfan

Zhuang Youbo

Zheng Xiaodi

Zhao Zhicong

Guo Yong

• Master Plan

SECTION 2

Nurturing Excellence: Education Programs

Section 2 is a vivid, illustrated representation of the fruitful LA education at Tsinghua, containing not only rare old photos showing how hard the founding scholars and experts had worked for the establishment of the LA discipline during the 1950s and 1960s but also stacks of hand-painted works of early students majoring at the LA department that reflect the great traditions and rigorous academic style started upon the inauguration of the Tsinghua LA programs. As for the projects showcased after 2003, this section only showcases some of the projects that Tsinghua LA, being rooted deeply in the old tradition, has been involved in. The university continues to thrive in the application of theoretical and technological innovations in close response to the needs of national development.

In the preparation for this section, we've received support and information from all founding and forming members of Tsinghua LA education. It is worth particular mention of Professor Zhu Junzhen who contributed all the rare photos of earlier student works to the department, the librarian at the Tsinghua School of Architecture who rendered immeasurable support, and of course, the faculty and students of the Department of LA who worked so hard to bring together all those student works and photos at the early stage. It was a difficult process through the initial collection of materials and history. Many incredible projects and images had to be cut out due to space limitations. This then is only a small piece of the iceberg, in terms of the Tsinghua LA achievement. Of all achievements, it is no exaggeration to say that Tsinghua LA graduates active at the forefront of the profession across the country and around the world are the most precious fruit of Tsinghua LA education.

Left: In-class comments and reviews for the Graduate Studio of Beijing Three Mountains and Five Imperial Gardens Area Regional Landscape Design (Y2006).

2.1 Overview

Pedagogical Philosophy

The pedagogical philosophy of Tsinghua LA is "Thorough Knowledge of East and West and of Past and Present." This philosophy is not only a continuation of the spiritual tradition of Tsinghua, but also the settled wisdom of earlier Tsinghua scholars on the problem of how to borrow from history and learn from western culture.

"Thorough Knowledge of East and West and of Past and Present" emphasizes studying and combining philosophies to obtain a holistic knowledge. If the LA education at Tsinghua is compared to a tree, then the social, economic, and cultural conditions in China are the soil in which the tree grows; the classical gardens and the mountain and water aesthetics of China are the roots of the tree; and modern theories and technologies of Landscape Architecture are the air and water required by the tree for growth. None of the above can be dispensed with. East and West, past and present, are only means to an end, and only a thorough knowledge of all will provide reliable solutions to concrete problems at the proper time and place in the landscape architecture field – whether the problems appear in China or elsewhere.

From the history of the LA education at Tsinghua, "Thorough Knowledge of East and West" marks the basic feature of the evolution of Tsinghua LA for half a century. "Thorough Knowledge of Past and Present" gives more reflection in theoretical research and practice. In recent years, Tsinghua has conducted research on the new dimensions of natural and cultural heritage protection, ecological planning and design, tourism and recreation planning and design, and urban landscape and large urban park planning and design. It is in this regard that "equal emphasis on past and present" marks another feature of the evolution of Tsinghua LA. However, it is worth noting that equal emphasis is not thorough knowledge but can lead to thorough knowledge. Key to the concept of "Thorough Knowledge of Past and Present" is the word "thorough." How to combine the ancient Chinese thinking on Nature with present ecological science and environmental technology; how to inject the essence of the Chinese classical garden arts into the planning and design of the public large-scale urban open spaces; how to incorporate the Chinese mountain and water aesthetics into natural and cultural heritage protection; and how to develop royal ancient meaning and converge with new knowledge still requires constant exploration.[1]

[1] Yang Rui. Integration, Interaction, Multi-scales & Public Concerns – Philosophy & Its Practice of Landscape Architecture Education in Tsinghua University of China. [J]. (Chinese Landscape Architecture, 2008), 01.

Mission

The LA mission of Tsinghua University is to foster Chinese professional landscape architects and tomorrow's leaders in landscape planning, design, management, and research. To this purpose, Tsinghua LA education developed a unique pedagogical philosophy of its own that can be expounded from the perspectives of space and time, academic study, and practice.

Space and time play an important role in the mission of Tsinghua LA education by keeping Chinese landscape architecture in the current global vision. This is the fundamental goal of the department. It suggests that our landscape architecture, targeted at actual problems in China, absorbs and refers to international experiences while finding its roots in the Chinese culture and philosophy. Excellent ideas from Chinese traditional philosophy provide the ground for Tsinghua LA: classical gardens and the mountain and water aesthetics of China are the roots for disciplinary development; modern theories, technologies, and approaches of Landscape Architecture are the air and water. Without the roots, air, or water, the tree will whither, and so would Tsinghua LA.

Landscape architecture is viewed within the framework of the sciences of human settlement and academic study. This is the fundamental goal of the department, which has two implications: to develop the discipline of landscape architecture within the framework of the sciences of human settlement, and to enrich, expand, and deepen the human settlement theories through the study of Chinese landscape architecture in relationship with global context. Integration of multiple disciplines within architecture, landscape architecture, and urban planning is at the core of the fundamental pedagogical approach of the Tsinghua Department of LA. Realizing the cross-disciplinary integration, the Department of LA highlights the diversification of faculty resources, knowledge structure and student resources, and in particular, the combination with geological science, ecology, and environmental science.

Landscape architecture is the process of urban-rural protection and development. This is the core challenge of the department. Close links between theory and practice have been part of the tradition of the School of Architecture of Tsinghua University, and the exterior driving force for the development and burgeoning of the Department of LA. The Department of LA intends to identify, research, and solve key challenges in the process of urban-rural protection and development during the economic and social transitions of the country. It is essential to follow the issue of development closely, and, during this special historical stage, to pay attention to landscape and resource conservation issues.

Developmental Direction and Strategies

The landscape architecture discipline of Tsinghua University is oriented around large-scale landscape planning and small-scale landscape design. Landscape planning can be further divided into the national park and reserve protection and management, natural and cultural landscape protection, planning and design of eco-systems, regional landscape planning, tourism, and recreation site planning. Landscape design focuses more on the design and management of regional culture and human space and can be further divided into the urban public space design, landscape design investigation and analysis, efficient realization of large-scale landscape, medium- and small-scale design deepening, rain garden design, brownfield restoration design, and cultural landscape design.

The development strategies of the LA discipline of the Tsinghua University include: 3-in-1, multi-stakeholder cooperation, integration of teaching, and production, focal breakthroughs.

Three-in-one refers to the architecture-landscape and architecture-urban planning disciplines in one school, which is intended to leverage the current disciplinary strengths of the School of Architecture and the advantages of Tsinghua as a comprehensive university for complementary development with architecture, urban planning, and other related disciplines.

Multi-stakeholder cooperation invites individuals to focus on international cooperation by strengthening the cooperation with well-known LA departments and schools in other countries and relevant international organizations to form an international academic support network. Meanwhile, cooperation with domestic institutions will be intensified to give full play to respective strengths to advance development of the discipline jointly.

Integration of teaching and production refers to the integration of teaching, scientific research, and research-oriented planning and design, integration of theory and practice, that is, to guide practice projects with landscape architecture theories while testing the theories and generating feedback in practice so as to improve and promote the disciplinary system of landscape architecture.

Focal breakthrough means resources are focused on important breakthroughs in the short term in accordance with the needs of the disciplinary development and national development so as to build an image for Tsinghua LA's future in the shortest possible time. For instance, research on key projects such as the urban-rural landscape protection in the urbanization process and natural and cultural heritage protection during the social and economic transitional period. [1]

[1] Yang Rui. Regarding the Detailed Program for Establishment of the Department of Landscape Architecture at the School of Architecture Tsinghua University. March 2003.

2.2 Curriculum

Curriculum System and Features

Above: Four segments of the LA education of Tsinghua University.

The curriculum system of Tsinghua LA are composed of "4 levels—4 segments," developed with expansions on the "Landscape Architecture MLA Program" proposed by the first chair, Professor Laurie D. Olin.

"Four levels" refers to level 1 (Entrance Level) for undergraduates of Architecture, Level 2 (Comprehensive Training) for engineering professors (landscape planning and design program), Tsinghua-Chiba Design Studio professors, and MLA (full-time), Level 3 (Career Advancement) for MLA, and Level 4 (Comprehensive Research) for engineering doctors.

"Four segments" refers to the "*Landscape Planning and Design Studio*," "*History and Theory of Landscape Architecture*," "*Technologies of Landscape Architecture*," and "*Applied Natural Science*" segments, among which the first is a segment focusing on hands-on ability and the other three focus on knowledge.

Of the "4 segments," "*Landscape Planning and Design Studio*" is the core segment, with all the other three centered upon the studio teaching. The studio corresponds to the multiple scales and covers the four dimensions of site design, urban landscape design, regional landscape design, and integrated planning design in its curriculum. The first three dimensions are courses of growing scale with the last one integrating multiple scales. It is intended to offer students comprehensive trainings on the "design amidst planning and planning amidst design" ability (Table 2). Meanwhile, this curriculum system also incorporates natural and social science, "*Landscape Ecology*," "*Landscape Hydrology*," "*Landscape Geo Science,*" and other natural science courses are the first steps; "Landscape Sociology," "*Landscape Economics,*" and other social science courses will be added gradually to the list.

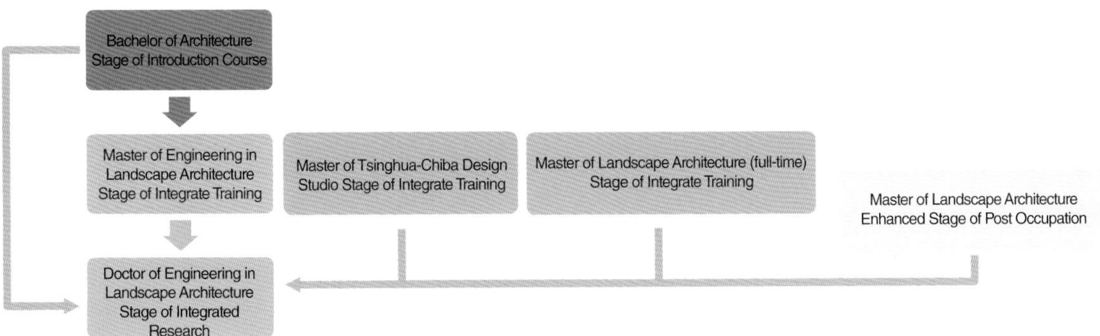

Above: Flow chart of the 4-levels of LA education of Tsinghua University.

Tsinghua Landscape Architecture Education Curriculum

Course Module		Course Name	Stage of Introduction Course						Stage of Integrate Training				Stage of Academic Research	
			Bachelor Grade 2		Bachelor Grade 3		Bachelor Grade 4		Master Grade 1		Master Grade 2		Doctor Grade 1	
			Fall	Spring	Fall	Spring	Fall	Spring	Fall	Spring	Fall	Spring	Fall	Spring
Theory	Landscape History and Theory	introduction to landscape architecture			■									
		site surroundings				■								
		theory of landscape and ecological planning								■				
		landscape architecture research methods											■	
		methods landscape architecture frontier											■	
		history of western classical gardens	■		■		■							
		history outline of Asian landscape									■			
		history of European and American landscape										■		
		history of landscape architecture ideas											■	
		landsacpe architecture professional literature reading							■					
	Applied Natural Science	landsacpe architecture plants							■					
		plants, landscape planning, and design							■					
		ecology basis		■										
		landscape ecology							■					
		landscape hydrology							■					
		landscape geology basis								■				
		field ecology									■			
	Landscape Technology	grading and road							■					
		tourism planning and design									■			
		natural and mixed heritage protection									■			
		industrial wasteland planning and design									■			
Landscape Planning and Design Studio		architecture and landscape drawing							■					
		site design				■								
		urban landscape design							■					
		regional planning and landscape planning								■				
		integrated landscape planning and design									■	■		
		integrated thesis training							■					

Note: Final thesis project is offered during the spring semester of the fifth grade for undergraduate programs.

Selected Topics for the Studios by School Year

Year	Semester	Category	Topics	Remarks
2005-2006	2005 Autumn	Studio1	Urban Landscape Design	
			"Beijing CBD" Urban Landscape Design	
	2005 Spring	Studio 2	Beijing Three Mountains and Five Imperial Gardens Area Regional Landscape Design Landscape Design Regional Landscape Design	For first- and second-year graduate students, 14 in total
2006-2007	2006 Autumn	Studio1	"Beijing CBD" Urban Landscape Design	
	2007 Spring	Studio 2	Beijing Three Mountains and Five Imperial Gardens Area Regional Landscape Design	For first-year graduate students and LA graduate students, ten in total
2007-2008	2007 Autumn	Studio1	Landscape Planning and Design in the Reconstruction of Ertong Machinery Factory of Capital Steel Group	For first-year graduate students and LA graduate students, 16 in total
	2008 Spring	Studio 2		
2008-2009	2008 Autumn	Studio 1	"Western Zhongguancun" Urban Landscape Design	
	2008 Autumn	Studio 1	Dazhongsi POCKETPARK Landscape Park Design	Joint Studio with UT
	2009 Spring	Studio 2	Zhoukoudian Regional Landscape Planning	For first-year graduate students and LA gradWWuate students, 22 in total
2009-2010	2009 Autumn	Studio 1	Outer Altar of Temple of Heaven Renovation Landscape Design	
	2010 Spring	Studio 2	Wudalianchi Regional Landscape Planning	For first-year graduate students and LA graduate students, 24 in total
2010-2011	2010 Autumn	Studio 1	Beijing Financial Street Exterior Space Landscape Design	
	2011 Spring	Studio 2	Beijing Three Mountains and Five Imperial Gardens Area Regional landscape designRegional Landscape Design	
2011-2012	2011 Autumn	Studio 1	Regional Landscape Planning and Design of Summer Palace Southwestern Exterior	Tsinghua University-Barcelona Tech (UPC) Joint Program, 24 in total
	2012 Spring	Studio 2	Zhoukoudian Regional Landscape Planning	A Joint Program with AA School of UK, for first-year graduate students and LA graduate students, 16 in total
2012-2013	2012 Autumn	Studio 1	Regional Landscape Planning and Design of Summer Palace Southwestern Exterior	In two groups: one for the Joint Program with Barcelona Tech (UPC) and the other for the Joint Program with AA School of UK
	2013 Spring	Studio 2	Fuzhou Jiangbei Water System Landscape Planning	A Joint Program with Italy and AA School of UK, for first-year graduate students and LA graduate students, 21 in total

Features

The LA disciplinary development, historically, has addressed the relationship between "Past and Present," "East and West," "Knowledge and Action," "Planning and Design," and "Learning and Teaching." The LA curriculum of the Tsinghua University primarily focuses on "Integration of Multiple Disciplines and Equal Emphasis on Knowledge and Action."

The key focus of "Integration of Multiple Disciplines" was put forward by Professor Wu Liangyiong, with the emphasis on integration rather than cross-discipline in a general sense. The "Integration of Multiple Disciplines" is advocated for because it is the modern trend of development. "While science is constantly breaking down, there is an emerging tendency of science integration." This tendency has become a common practice of scientists today.

The "Equal Emphasis on Knowledge and Action" was borrowed from Ming thinker Wang Tingxiang. The "Equal Emphasis on Knowledge and Action" (or the "Equal Emphasis on Theory and Practice") is advocated because, it goes without saying, knowledge is important, both as theoretical foundation of past "practices" and as theoretical guidance for future practices. The features of the discipline of LA at Tsinghua show the importance of knowledge. LA, in the end, is a practical science on the same footing as planning and design of space and form (of site and environment). The importance of the discipline of LA is determined by what contribution its planning and design practices make to the social and economic development and environment protection in China. In this regard, action is indispensable when guided by theory and sound practice.

The Tsinghua LA curriculum system represents the characteristics of integration between "East and West," "Past and Present," "Knowledge and Action," and multiple disciplines. At Tsinghua, integration is the key feature and goal of the LA discipline. Accommodation, interaction, and integration form a linear process. Interaction with site and client is only possible after accommodation for all variables and without interaction there can be no integration. Interaction is the means by which accommodation becomes integration. Tsinghua LA is a primary practitioner of interactive education starting with the interaction between the Past and Present, East and West, Theory and Practice, among multiple disciplines, and more extensively between learning and teaching, planning and design, and partnership of schools.(1)

The object of LA education is to assemble students with individual differences ranging from personal interests and hobbies to abilities and vision, and even to future career paths. Identical teaching content and method is not the goal. Tsinghua LA values the transfer from "teacher-oriented" to "student-oriented" education and intends to build an interactive LA learning and teaching platform. "LA Friday," launched in the Autumn Semester of 2006, is an attempt at building such a platform.

LA Friday, held every other week, is the inter-department academic exchange platform of the Department of LA, School of Architecture, Tsinghua University. Lectures are given by graduate students and post-doctorate program members of the department, and at times by doctoral students, young scholars, or outstanding member of the profession from other schools. Lecture topics mostly relate to academic papers or recent practices. LA Friday, organized and anchored by on-campus students, has been in operation for seven consecutive years. The objective of LA Friday is to provide a platform for students of different grades and of different programs to observe and learn from each other, to identify their focal points of interest, and to exercise their organization and language skills. LA Friday has achieved some of the desired results and a high regard among students.

[1] Yang Rui. Integration, Interaction, Multi-scales & Public Concerns – Philosophy & Its Practice of Landscape Architecture Education in Tsinghua University of China. (Chinese Landscape Architecture, 2000), 01.

2.3 Undergraduate Courses and Selected Students Work

The undergraduate program at the School of Architecture, Tsinghua University adopts the wide-caliber training method of teaching architecture-oriented courses on *Human Settlement Science* (consisting of the three branches: architectural design, urban planning, and landscape architecture). Students of this five-year program will receive a Bachelor of Architecture degree upon graduation.

The LA undergraduate program features separated studio and theory studies. *The Landscape Planning and Design Studio* has two component parts: the *Site Design studio* for third-year students, and the *Urban Landscape Design* for fifth-year students. LA theory courses, including "*Introduction to Landscape Architecture*," "*History of Western Classical Gardens*," and "*Chinese Classical Gardens*" are interspersed in second to fourth year curricula.

1) Introduction to Landscape Architecture

Instructor: Professor Yang Rui
Course Nature: Compulsory / Professional Elective
Total Hours: 16
Credit Points: 1

Course Description:

This is an introductory course for Landscape Architecture, consisting of four parts: the Evolution from Classical Gardens to Modern Landscape Architecture; Landscape Elements and Landscape Systems; Site Design: Its Subject Matter, Principles, and Approaches; Trends of Modern Landscape Studies; and Incorporating Natural and Cultural Heritage Conservation and Management, GIS Application in Landscape Planning and Design. Students will be appraised through classroom assessment, which is composed of an in-class question and answer session, group case studies, and thesis writing.

2) History of Western Classical Gardens

Instructor: Zhu Yufan
Course Nature: Compulsory / Professional Elective
Total Hours: 16
Credit Points: 1

Course Description:

This is a fundamental course offering systematic introduction into the historical evolution of western classical gardens and traditional garden types ranging from the Middle Egyptian, Ancient Babylonian, Ancient Greek, Ancient Roman, and Medieval gardens to the terraced gardens of the Italian Renaissance, the French Classicism-style gardens, and the English landscape gardens. The characteristics of each, and laws of development and succession, are the primary focus.

3) Site Design for Third-Year Students

As one of the basic training and core subject matters of landscape planning and design, Site Design is the proper arrangement and planning of artificial and natural elements of a design lot. This is the first studio series of three (Site Design, urban landscape design, and landscape planning) at the Department of Landscape Architecture and one of the necessary skills for LA, architecture, and planning professionals.

Through training in transportation organization, and vertical and planting design, students are expected to develop a basic sense for landscape and a general understanding of the LA as a means of coordinating the natural, cultural, and human relations.

It is intended to help students develop the abilities of research-oriented planning and design; of problem identification, analysis, and solution; of working in teams; and of proper communication – verbally in particular. Students receive training in transportation organization, vertical design, and planting design.

2009: Open Space for Business Districts Central Open Space Renovation, Tsinghua Science Park

Course Time: Fall Semester 2009
Instructors: Zhu Yufan, Wu Dongfan

Course Content:

Urban open space in business context is one of the most important subject matter types for site planning. Tsinghua Science Park is the urban business area nearest to Tsinghua University, and as it is relatively familiar to students it has become a helpful training ground for students.

2010, 2011: Tsinghua Centenary Memorial Landscape Design

Course Time: Fall Semester, 2010 and 2011
Instructors: Zhu Yufan, Wu Dongfan, Zheng Xiaodi, Lin Guangsi

Course Content:

Tsinghua centenary is an event followed with great interest and anticipated with zest by people of various walks of life on and off of the Tsinghua campus. What spiritual and cultural tradition can be drawn from the 100-year history of Tsinghua to pass on to the future generations? How can the LA department recapture and represent these legacies in the context of spaces?

Memorial Landscapes, urban open space with profound cultural connotations, are sites that exhibit, display, and educate visitors on historical events. Memorial landscapes are different from others in that context analysis and narrative skills are key factors in space creation that can help students develop the ability to shape outdoor environments and gain the inspiration for the representation of genius loci.

Site I: Tsinghua Swimming Pool

Site II: Space between Tsinghua Xuetang and Centennial Hall

2012: "Under the Bridge" – Activation of Urban Negative Space

Course Time: Fall Semester, 2012
Instructors: Zhu Yufan, Wu Dongfan

Course Content:

Crisscrossing the bustling cities are various bridges, highways, railways, light railways, pipelines, and pedestrian walks. Bridge decks are for passage of people and vehicles and for facilities while the space under the bridge is often the neglected by urban designers. However, these urban negative spaces do not get lost in an actual sense; they are still the social arena where you can find Chinese drama, dressed in red and green doing boisterous square dances, the homeless find shelter from the bad weather, the commuters park their bicycles before hustling for the subway, and the peddlers try to make a buck from the wares they spread. Urban designers often complain about tight control over land use and insufficient public space. Why didn't they turn to urban negative space like this?

Pick out any "under-the-bridge" space and its 1- or 2-hectare surrounding area, and you will find it has the potential to be transformed into a personalized, open space, and that urban functions are densely located in the surrounding area creating a high demand for public space.

2013: Landscape Transformation of Informal Landfills

Course Time: Fall Semester, 2013
Instructors: Zhu Yufan, Guo Yong, Zhang An, Shen Jie

Course Content:

The informal landfill at Xiaobao Village, Songzhuang Town, Tongzhou District, Beijing was picked out as the design object in a bid to guide students through solutions to specific environmental issues towards a better understanding of the meaning of landscape architecture, mastery of certain site design techniques, adaptation to multi-disciplinary collaboration, and forming creative response options.

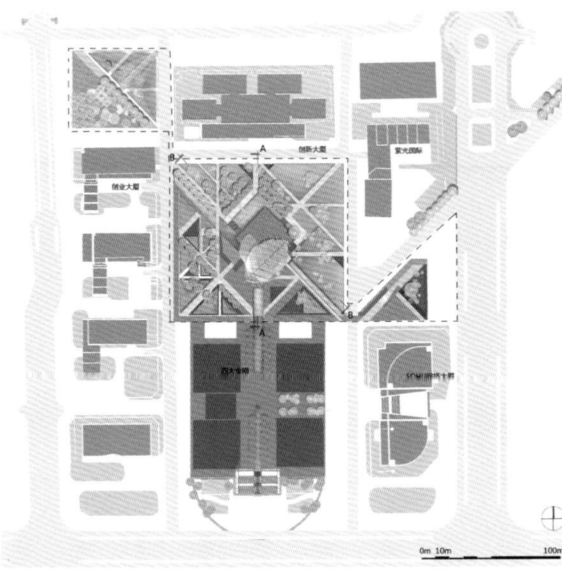

Left and Below: Selected Work: Business Landscape Design for Tsinghua Science Park (Students: Chen Kan, Chen Jingya, Liu Lun, Sun Chenguang).

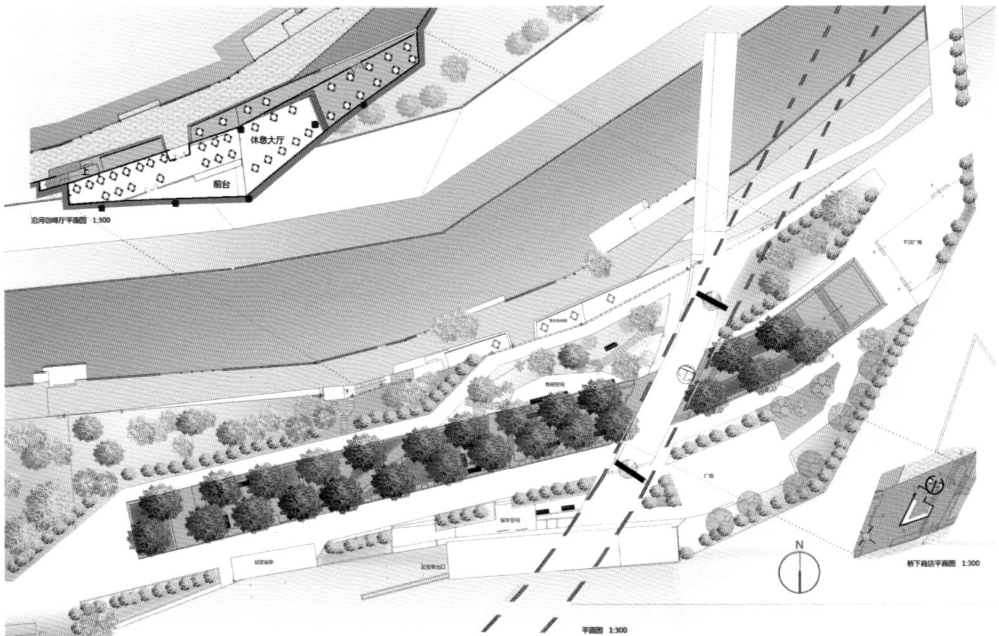

Above: selected work: Deshengmen West Bridge Space Landscape Design (Students: Ao Ran, Zhao Feiqi, Zhang Ningyi, Zhang Gui).

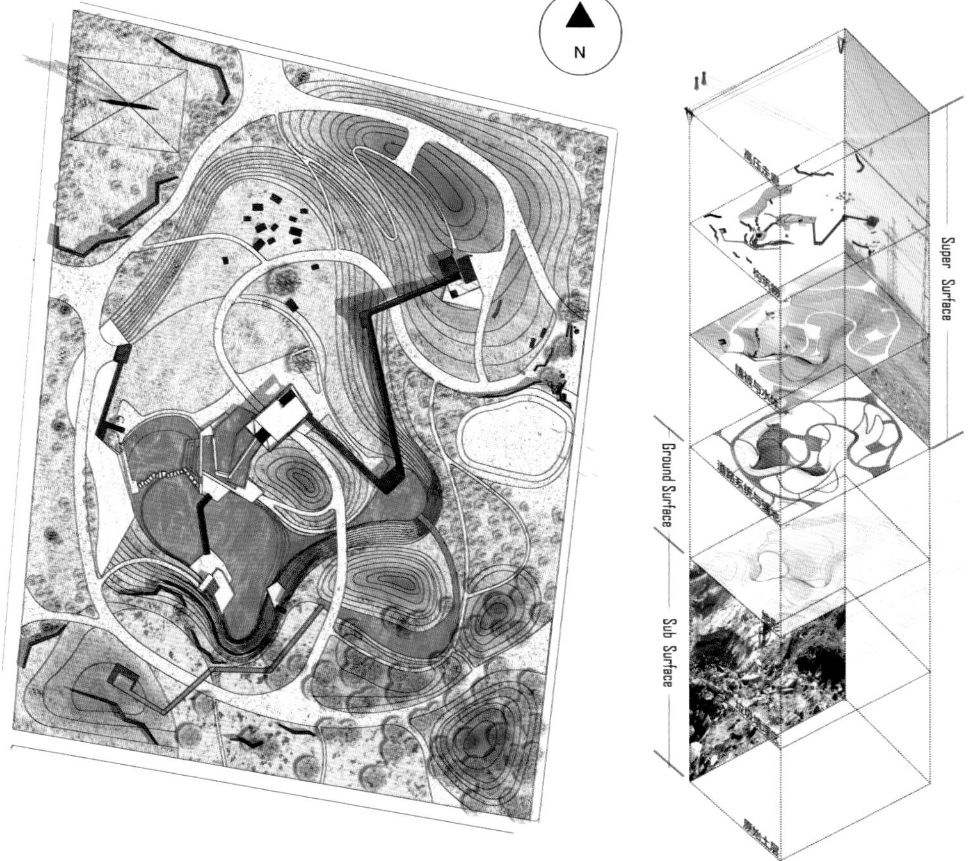

Above: selected work: Wilderness Garden—Xiaobao Village Landfill Reconstruction Design (Students: Zhou Yujing, Chen Ai, Shi Shengsong).

Right: selected work: THE OPPOSITE CITY (Students: Zhu Haoying, Lin Zhitong, Qin Chengzuo).

2.4 Graduate Courses and Selected Students Work

Tsinghua LA education is basically graduate-oriented, with the following degree programs available currently: Doctorate of Philosophy in Engineering: Landscape Architecture; Master of Science in Engineering: Landscape Architecture (Academic); Master of Engineering: Landscape Architecture (Design Studio); Master of Landscape Architecture (MLA); Full-Time Master of Landscape Architecture Degree (FMLA); and (Tsinghua-Chiba Design Studio) Master of Landscape Architecture (see Appendix 1 for details about the degree programs).

Tsinghua LA graduate education covers doctoral and master programs, with the latter serving as the main teaching task of the Department of Landscape Architecture of Tsinghua University within the basic course framework designed by Professor Laurie Olin and adjusted according to the actual circumstances of Tsinghua University. The two-year MLA curriculum system designed by Professor Laurie Olin is composed of four sections: LA history and theory; applied natural sciences; technology; and landscape planning and design (Studio). Each semester there are courses on these four basic sections.

The Landscape Planning and Design Studio series are the core courses for the LA Programs. The two-year graduate training program is composed of three responsive studios: landscape design studio and landscape planning studio and the graduation thesis in the form of Final Studio.

The Final Studio is a teaching model integrating classes, lectures, workshops, design practice, engagements, and presentations. Studio topics are normally set by the tutor for students to work in groups to accomplish the tasks of investigation and research, interaction and exchange, planning and design practice. The students are then responsible to organize workshops and give final reports within a given period of time (a semester, for instance). Currently there are three Studios at the Department of Landscape Architecture:

1. The *Landscape Design Studio* (First Semester), which mainly involves learning the practices of urban landscape design;

2. The *Landscape Planning Studio* (Second Semester), which mainly involves planning and design of relatively large-scale landscapes. The goal is for students to become familiar with the planning procedure of investigation, analysis, resource evaluation, planning, environmental impact assessment, decision-making, implementation, and related planning approaches;

3. The *Final Studio* (Second Year), where students independently go through the whole process from topic selection to final presentation under the guidance of the team instructor, and will finish with a dissertation defense. The purpose of this phase is to apply the knowledge, methods, and skills acquired in the first year within independent research in order to solve practical problems in landscape planning and design and achieve a higher level of theory and practice.

The purpose of Studio teaching is reflected in three aspects: the development of landscape planning and design capabilities; the mastery of the landscape planning and design theories and methods, and a knowledge of current landscape planning and design principles and theoretical trends; and the cultivation of team spirit. Each studio includes a variety of sections: lectures by experts in relevant areas invited over by the instructor, which address ecology, natural resource conservation, the humanities, geography, and other related disciplines; research including literature research and site investigation; teamwork in groups of three to four students for making, interacting, and forming decisions over planning and design proposals; workshops and discussions with the instructor on a semi-weekly or weekly basis for in-depth discussion of information and analyses; sketching and modeling for the best possible representation of the planning and design outcomes by the most efficient means and techniques; dissertation defense with experts and teachers in relevant disciplines; and exhibitions to fully showcase the students' design outcome.

Each Studio has the following four characteristics:

(1) a teaching team composed of domestic and foreign teachers combine international vision with domestic practices;

(2) a comprehensive curriculum focuses on multi-disciplinary cooperation;

(3) topics cover current and practical problems;

(4) flexibility, which encourages teamwork and in-depth exchanges. [1]

The Tsinghua LA doctoral program has a curriculum system built mainly upon that of Graduate School of Architecture to offer broader vision and interdisciplinary methodology for doctoral LA research. At the same time, a seminar on "*LA frontier*" has been offered specially to doctoral candidates as the academic platform for capturing and exploring the frontiers of the discipline. The Tsinghua LA doctoral program is comprised of compulsory qualifying examinations, social practice, themed reports, a literature review, interim reports, a pre-defense, and a formal thesis defense. Doctoral dissertation writing is a key component of Tsinghua LA education. For the moment, completed PhD dissertations relate to urban green space system, historic urban landscape protection, national parks and protected areas, historic gardens, city parks, and cultural landscapes (see Appendix 4.5 for a directory of Tsinghua LA doctoral dissertations and Appendix 6 for a directory of Tsinghua LA postdoctoral research reports).

[1] Zhao Zhicong, Yang Rui. The Studios of MLA Program at Tsinghua University [J]. Chinese Landscape Architecture. 2006 (05).

Current Curriculum of MLA Program

Course Number	Course Title	Credits
1	The Literature of Landscape Architecture	2
2	History of Landscape Architecture	2
3	History of Landscape Architecture	2
4	Landscape Garden Plants	1
5	Landscape Planting Design	2
6	Applied Natural Science I: Landscape Ecology	2
7	Applied Natural Science II: Landscape Geo-Science Basics	2
8	Applied Natural Science III: Landscape Hydrology	1
9	Architecture and Landscape Sketchs	1
10	Landscape Engineering: Grading and Paths	2
11	Landscape Architecture Frontier	1
12	Theory in Landscape Architecture	2
13	Landscape Design Studio	4
14	Landscape Planning Studio	4

1) The Literature of Landscape Architecture

Instructor: Professor Yang Rui
Total Hours: 32
Credit Points: 2

Course Description:

This course is offered to master's candidates at the beginning of the program and is intended to help them gain a basic understanding and awareness of the professional classic literature on landscape architecture at the outset of their study. Students are expected to collect data related to the following 10 professional concepts from their readings, and to create a write-up on each: architectural process, careers, ideas and ethics, methodology, theory and knowledge, technology and arts, purposes, mechanisms, formats, and meaning and culture.

2) History of Landscape Architecture (Part 1: Asia)

Instructor: Professor Jia Jun
Course Nature: Compulsory/Professional Elective
Total Hours: 32
Credit Points: 2

Course Description:

This is a basic theory course on the study of landscape architecture, focusing on the illustration of the development history and classical works of the Asian landscape architecture art from China, Japan, and India, while offering important valuable reference to current architecture and landscape architecture design. Via systematic representation of the course of development, the basic principles, techniques, and cultural connotations of ancient gardens in China, Japan, India, and other Asian countries, this course familiarizes students with the history and specimens of ancient Asian garden art, further enhancing their cultural understanding and thereby increasing their research and creation competence.

3) History of Landscape Architecture (Part 2: Europe and America)

Instructor: Professor Zhu Yufan
Course Nature: Compulsory / Professional Elective
Total Hours: 32
Credit Points: 2

Course Description:

The History of Landscape Architecture (Part 2: Europe and America) is an important part of the curriculum system of the Department of Landscape, and an important component of the basic framework of the history section along with the History of Landscape Architecture (Part 1: Asia). Through a process of dynamic presentation and bilingual teaching, this course enables students to develop a broad understanding of the history of the discipline, and enhances theoretical analysis and logical thinking abilities.

This course reflects the development trajectory of the European and American Landscape Architecture History (from prehistoric times until CE 1900) with the focus on typical gardens, cities, and landscapes in the Western world. The intent is to provide a thorough understanding of the relations between the case sites and their design forms and the way such relations affect their economic and political structures. Four issues should be taken into account when starting each case study: its association with the history; its definition of nature; its interpretation of form; and author and time.

4) Landscape Plants

Instructor: Professor Li Shuhua
Former Instructor: Professor Bao Zhiyi
Course Nature: Compulsory/Professional Elective
Total Hours: 16
Credit Points: 1

Course Description:

Plantings are a subject often regarded as the skeleton of landscape architecture. While addressing the morphology, classification, ecological habits, ornamental characteristics, propagation and cultivation, and environmental factors of landscape plants, this course is intended to help green-hand graduate students gain a basic understanding of relevant botanical knowledge, specifically relating to herbaceous and woody landscape plants native to Beijing. By the end of the course students develop the capability to make independent selections of plants to lay a solid foundation for subsequent studies of plant landscape planning and design.

This course requires an understanding of basic landscape plantings, and professory of the morphology, ecological habits, ornamental characteristics, and landscape applications and knowledge of more than 100 commonly used landscape plants and more than 200 woody plants.

5) Landscape Planting Design

Instructor: Professor Li Shuhua
Course Nature: Compulsory / Professional Elective
Total Hours: 32
Credit Points: 2

Course Description:

This is a course for landscape architecture master's candidates focused on raising students' theoretical level of botanical landscape planning and design through the learning of theoretical knowledge regarding the history and evolution of botanical design, cultural elements of landscape plants, ecological and artistic principles for botanical design, and configuration of garden plants and other landscape elements in order to improve creative and practical ability of landscape planning and design through in class study and various practices in the profession.

Students are required to master the natural and cultural elements of landscape plants as well as the principles of planting design in order to select appropriate landscape plants based on specific environmental characteristics, to conduct scientific planning and design depending on differing types of gardens and landscapes, and to have independent botanical planning and design of various large and medium urban green spaces.

6) Applied Natural Sciences I: Landscape Ecology

Instructor: Lecturer Zhuang Youbo
Former Instructors: Professor Richard Forman, Professor Laurie D. Olin, Professor Frederick Steiner, Professor Bart R. Johnson, Professor Gaugert Sierra, Professor Ronald Henderson
Course Nature: Compulsory/Professional Elective
Total Hours: 32
Credit Points: 2

Course Description:

This is a compulsory course for the landscape architecture program that covers applied natural sciences, one of the four component segments of the Department of LA. Students are expected to acquire basic theories and concepts related to Landscape ecology, learn to use landscape index and related software, know principles and classical cases for the application of landscape ecology in planning and design, and have the ability to follow the latest research developments and application trends.

7) Applied Natural Sciences II: Landscape Geo-Science Basics

Instructor: Professor Dang Anrong
Course Nature: Compulsory / Professional Elective
Total Hours: 32
Credit Points: 2

Course Description:

This is a basic course of the MLA and Professional MLA degree programs, and a precursor of other professional theory and design courses. Taught from the earth sciences point of view, this course covers the basic theories related to the formation and development of landscapes as well as the theories of evolution, which provide the scientific ground for understanding landscape resource characteristics and the conservation of the landscape resource values. This knowledge is to aid in planning, protecting, and using landscape resources in a scientific manner, to create harmony between mankind and the environment.

This course is intended to help students develop a basic understanding of the geoscience elements (geology, geomorphology, and soil) constituting landscapes and landscape formation process. During this course, students will gain a professional acumen for geology, geomorphology, soil, and other natural elements, and will practice the ability to conduct and analyze relevant elements of the natural and cultural settings.

8) Applied Natural Science III: Landscape Hydrology

Instructor: Associate Professor Liu Hailong
Former Instructors: Professor Bart R. Johnson, Professor Gaugert Sierra, Professor Bruce Ferguson
Course Nature: Compulsory / Professional Elective
Total Hours: 16
Credit Points: 1

Course Description:

This is a required course belonging to the segment of the applied natural sciences, one of the four component segments of the Department of LA. It is mainly oriented around planning and design majors under the MLA, urban planning, and architectural programs. Its purpose is to conduct research, planning, design, and management of water and various natural and cultural processes, structures, and functions related, to the perspective that "landscape" is as an integrated ecosystem on the Earth's surface.

Students are required to acquire systematic knowledge in hydrology, water conservation, and related natural sciences, frontline technologies, and cutting-edge research development, while maintaining a proper understanding of the relationship between the hydrological systems and natural and social environments. This is, process-pattern-function approach to analyze various water related landscape phenomena and issues.

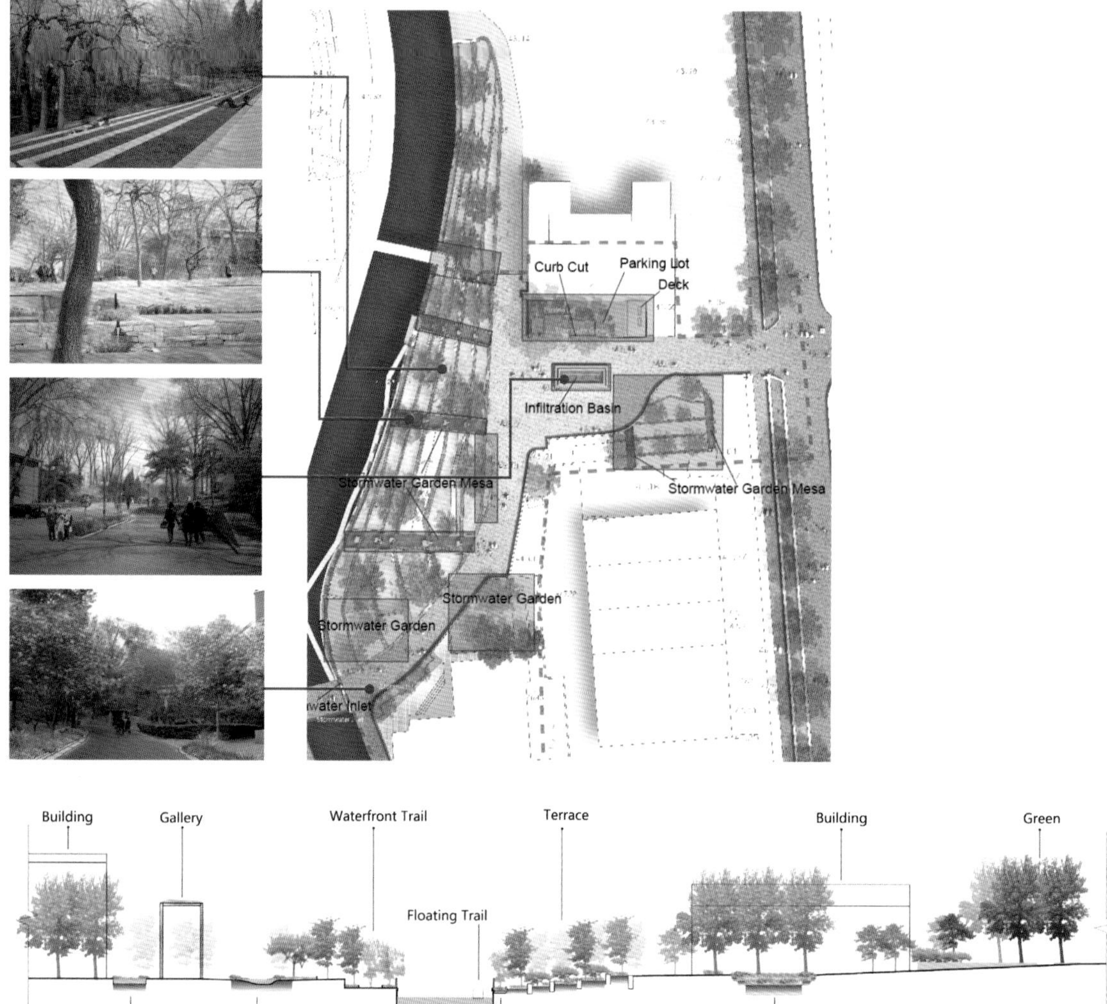

Above: selected work: Storm Water Control Design for Campus River Embankments to the southeast of the Water Pollution Control Laboratory and to the southwest of the Broadcasting Station (Students: Zhang Shuo, Zhu Yijun, Zhang Yanjie, Liu Chang, Liao Lingyun).

9) Architecture and Landscape Sketches

Instructor: Professor Sun Fengqi
Course Nature: Compulsory/Professional Elective
Total Hours: 16
Credit Points: 1

Course Description:

This course is conducted through field observation and first-hand experience, and is supplemented by demonstrations, presentation, in-class discussion, and sketching practice. It is expected that students will have plenty of time to practice and devote sufficient time and efforts to research and study the landscapes in order to improve their painting and presentation skills. It is further expected that efforts be made to help students gain better understanding of art theories that can help improve their painting and presentation skills by enhancing their aesthetic perception. Each week there are four in-class hours and four to six extracurricular hours involved. At the end of the semester a demo exhibition will be set up and followed by oral presentations where students will be appraised on the basis of their overall performance.

Right Selected student work. (from Liu Dan).

Right Selected student work. (from Peng Feng).

10) Landscape Engineering Technologies: Grading & Paths

Instructor: Senior Engineer Hu Jie, Associate Professor Zheng Xiaodi
Former Instructor: Professor Ronald Henderson
Course Nature: Compulsory / Professional Elective
Total Hours: 32
Credit Points: 2

Course Description:

This course is intended to train students on vertical design, site drainage, landscape materials, and engineering practices, with the following criteria:

(1) Course Sketches: Students are required to submit their hand-painted sketches of roads, squares, landscapes, or drainage on a weekly basis, which is intended to deepen the students' knowledge of the course content and to help students accumulate source materials while improving hand-painting skills.

(2) Case Studies: Students will be divided into groups to study a world-famous landscape case focusing on topography and grading design, and will create a model based on known information of the site by reverse engineering the conditions of the original site to infer the pre-construction topography and vertical design, which is intended to help students understand the landscape construction and the decision-making process for modifying the landscape form.

(3) Field Mapping (dynamic analysis of the vertical design): Regular site visits and mapping will be arranged to give students first-hand experience of the material and dimensions of pedestrians, tree-lined roads, motorways, squares, courtyards, and other landscape design elements in authentic settings.

(4) Curriculum Design: Students will be given a topographic map and expected to design roads, squares, and other landscape forms in accordance with different needs to meet the grading and drainage requirements for the hypothetical site.

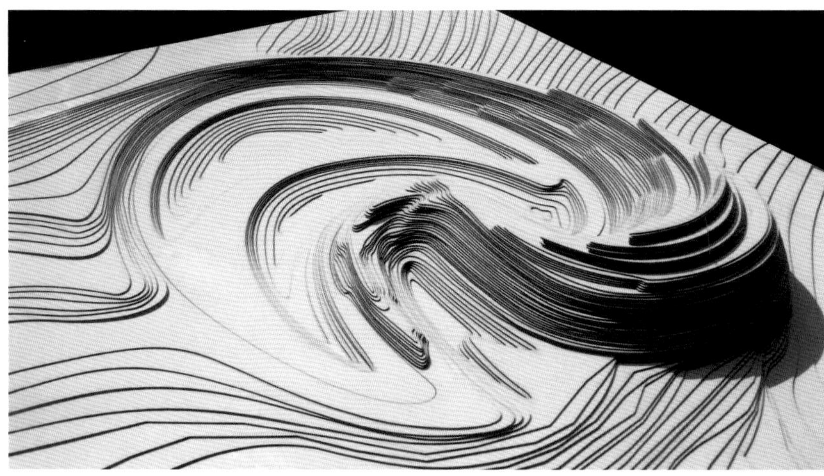

Left: Model making.

11) Landscape Architecture Frontier

Anchor: Professor Zhu Yufan
Course Nature: Compulsory / Professional Elective
Total Hours: 16
Credit Points: 1

Course Description:

The course explores LA related issues from a macro development perspective to help doctoral candidates gain a full perspective of the framework for the discipline and to keep them up-to-date with the latest developments. As a young, comprehensive, and practical discipline, landscape architecture has been making constant improvements and has evolved greatly during the transition of the human society from an industrial civilization to an ecological civilization since its inception in the 19th century, giving rise to a diverse, academic, thoughtful study. How then does the modern landscape architecture evolve? What are its major areas of study? What is the historical context of various sites or traditions? What are their major characteristics and challenges? How should it be interpreted and evaluated? This course is lecture based, and includes guest lectures from relevant, well-known experts and scholars who address the discussions over the above problems. Graduate students taking this course are expected to have a general understanding of the LA discipline through theoretical literature reading, case studies, and discussion, which creates a sound basis for their subsequent doctoral dissertation.

12) Theory in Landscape Architecture

Instructor: Associate Professor Zheng Xiaodi
Course Nature: Compulsory / Professional Elective
Total Hours: 32
Credit Points: 2

Course Description:

What is landscape architecture theory? What is the relationship between theory and practice? These are critical questions for both landscape architecture research and practice. "Transformative Landscapes" could be the course subtitle, with brownfields as the subject of exploration. On the one hand, brownfields have become one of the hot subjects in contemporary landscape architecture research and practice due to their challenge, complexity, and large scale. On the other hand, sustainable development has become the guiding principle for urban development in China, so it is especially important for Chinese students to understand the challenges of remediation and ecological restoration, the various angles of landscape architecture theory, and the intersection between landscape and other disciplines in their future career. The course focuses on a unique topic each week including ethics, laws, stakeholders, remediation strategies, landscape and urbanism, industrial heritage, industrial nature, land art, landscape performance, "Brown Earth-work," and landscape strategies.

13) Landscape Design Studio

Landscape Design Studio is the first studio for the master's programs, which lasts a semester (16 weeks, four hours per week, and a total of four credit points).

The objectives of the course are:

·To master the content and methods of design research and to learn about site mapping methods;

·To learn the content and methods of site analysis, to improve the analytical ability, and to learn about the functional attributes and social and cultural functions of urban public space in depth;

·To improve knowledge of plants, to have first-hand experience with landscaping and renovation technologies, and to focus on soil improvement, ecological restoration, and other specialized landscaping techniques;

·To improve form and space handling capacities and techniques related to the designing purpose, principles, contents, procedures, and analytical methods;

·To acquire the ability to balance interior functions with external relations in site design and to practice landscape design for different functional spaces (such as squares, parks, etc.).

2005: Urban Landscape Design

Course Time: Fall Semester, 2005
Instructors: Laurie Olin, Hu Jie, Ron Henderson, Zhu Yufan

Course Content:

Landscape Design for Shuangqing Road

Campus Design for Tsinghua University from East Gate to Main Building

Design for Haidian Park

2006: Urban Landscape Design for Beijing CBD

Course Time: Spring Semester, 2006; Fall Semester, 2006
Instructors: Laurie Olin, Ron Henderson, Zhu Yufan, Wu Dongfan

Course Content:

Field trip and spatial investigation – 2 weeks

Topic I: Design for Caifu Central Square – 6 weeks

Topic II: Design for CBD Park – 6 weeks

Joint Studio with The University of Hong Kong – 2 days

2008: Urban Landscape Design for the Western Area of Zhongguancun

Course: Fall Semester, 2008
Instructors: Zhu Yufan, Wu Dongfan, Ron Henderson

Course Content:

Field trip and spatial investigation – 3 weeks

Topic I. Landscape design for the pedestrian street of Haidian Tushucheng Book Store – 5 weeks

Topic II: Landscape design for a cuneiform park in the western area of Zhongguancun – 8 weeks

Key Lectures:

Liang Wei/Instruction on the Planning of the Western area, Zhongguancun
Zhang Junhua/Methods for Spatial Investigation
Wang Zuo/Urban Open Space
Li Shuhua/Botany and Basic Principals of Planting
Yin Shuangxi/Public Art
Zhu Yufan/Case Study and Methods for Landscape Design
Ron Henderson/Landscape Technology
Li Dexiang/Landscape Ecology
An Youfeng/Organization of Landscape Construction

2010: Landscape Design of Exterior Space, Beijing Financial Street

Course Time: Fall Semester 2010
Instructors: Zhu Yufan, Wu Dong Fan, Ronald Henderson, Zheng Xiaodi

Course Content:

Topic 1: Site Design of Central Square, Beijing Financial Street – four weeks

The design site has a total area of about two hectares, which may be well adjusted to the neighboring block within the indicated scope based on specific design needs. It is required that traffic (including static traffic) problems be solved based on the functions of the surrounding buildings, and that the site utilization conditions and requirements be investigated and analyzed and that site design be reorganized. The topic included group discussion and independent design, with discussions held in four groups, split into six or seven members each.

Topic 2: Investigation and Analyses of All Exterior Space of Beijing Financial Street – three weeks

The investigation and analyses covered the entire 2.59-square-kilometer Financial Street and urban surroundings, and was conducted in groups on a project issue basis. Each group was composed of four to five people who addressed one of six project issues, namely, urban background (including related planning studies), natural ecology, social economy, history and culture, infrastructure (including transportation), and space (including form, utilization conditions, etc.). In addition, each group was required to choose at least one international and one domestic case for a comparative study,

Topic 3: Master planning and Landscape Design of Exterior Space, Beijing Financial Street – one week

As this was a joint Studio with the MLA program of the University of Hong Kong, participants were mixed into six groups. It was required that overall design planning of the exterior space of the Beijing Financial Street be made on the basis of topic 2 investigations and analyses, with design concepts and overall design structure proposed, and key areas and design intent identified. This topic is intended to train students as chief architects of the regional landscape who identify problems and propose integrated planning proposals from a global perspective. It is equivalent to the formulation of a design mission and intent.

Topic 4: Focused Regional Landscape Design for Beijing Financial Street – eight weeks

The design objects were the key design areas identified in topic 3. It was required that the overall landscape design be accomplished in groups, and in-depth design be conducted on individual basis of any node taken within the design scope.

2012: Regional Landscape Planning and Design of Summer Palace Southwestern Exterior (LASA THU-AA Joint-Studio)

Course Time: Fall Semester 2012
Instructors: Zhu Yufan, Wu Dong Fan, Eva Castro, Zhao Zhicong

Course Content:

The course covers the Three Mountains and Five Imperial Gardens area while the design covers the Summer Palace Southwestern Exterior with a total area of about 320 hectares. The first eight weeks are for mixed-up group work with EPMA students while the second eight weeks are for individual design.

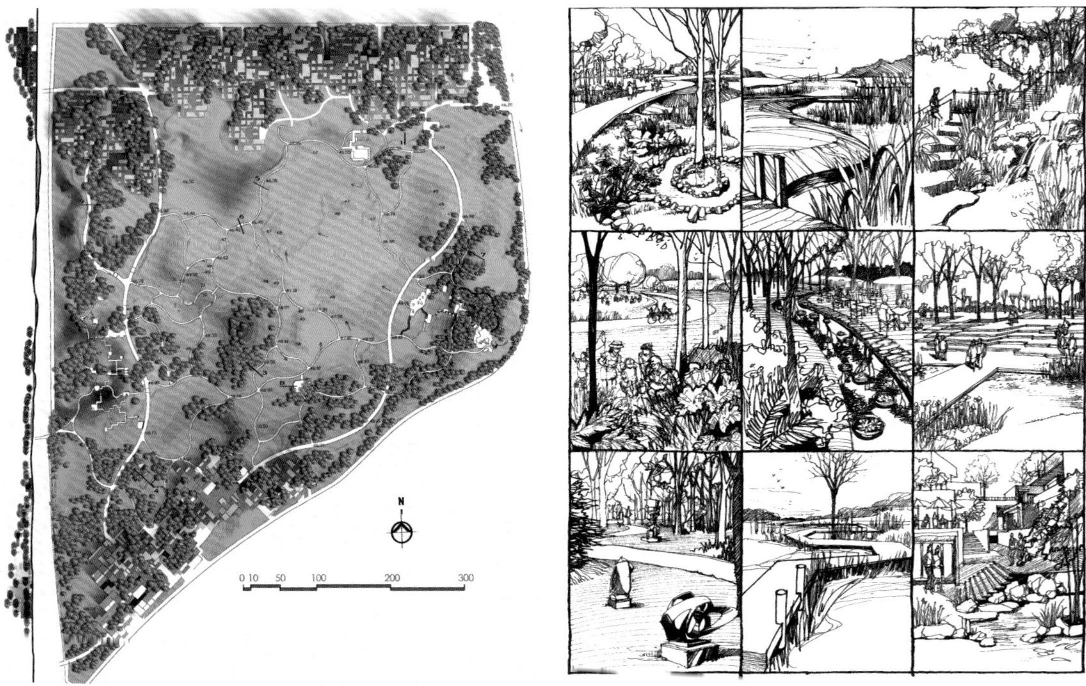

Above: selected work: Haidian Park Landscape Planning and Design (Student: Lv Han).

Above: selected work: Beijing CBD urban landscape designing (Students: Zou Yubo, Wu Hong, Fan Chao, Liu Wen).

Above: selected work: RE-SURFACE LANDSCAPE DESIGN (Students: Yang Mi, Wang Yinglin).

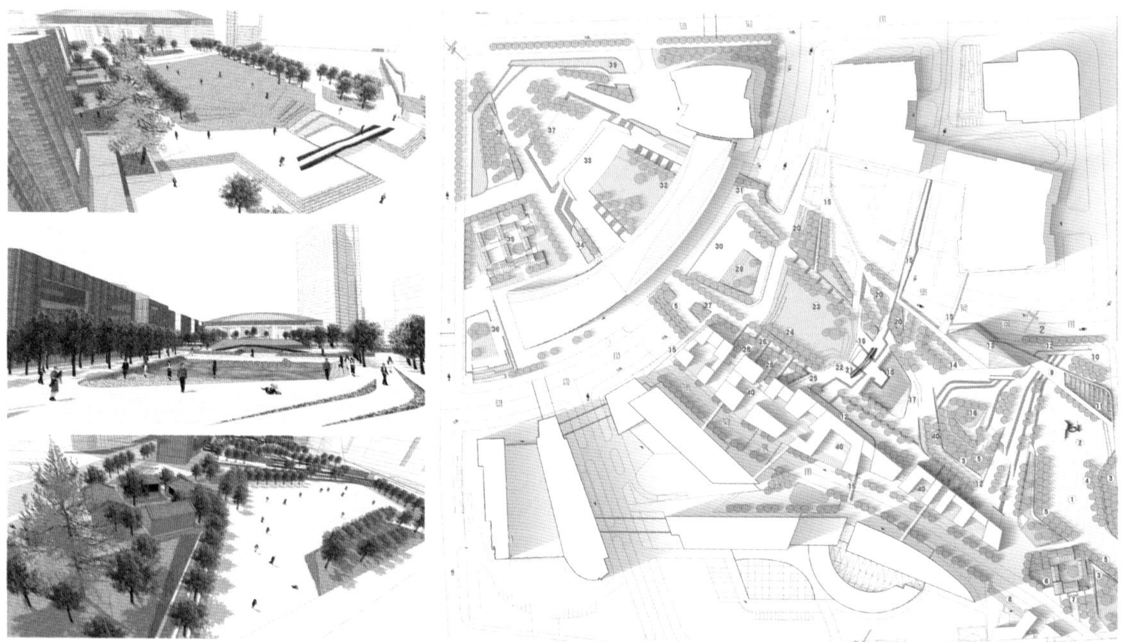

Above: selected work: Aesthetics of the Urban Eden Urban Design and Landscape Design for the Wedge Land Plot in west Zhongguancun (Students: Liang Shangyu, Zhang Jingni, Peng Lin, Wang Jun, Li Runnan).

Above: selected work: The design of surrouding of Tiantan (Students: Xu Diandian, Zhang Juancen, Guo Jianmei, Liu Yaodong, Yan Qinling).

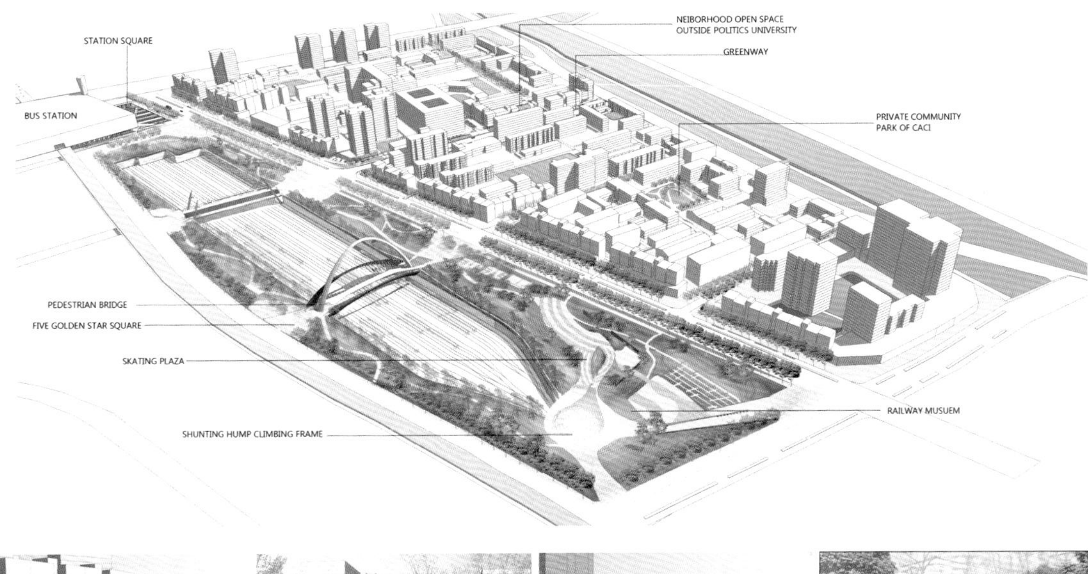

Above: selected work: UNBREAKABLE EDGE, THE CONCERTO FOR SUSTAINABLE BEIJING CITY (Students: Ji Wanjing, Shen Xue, Xu Tinyun, Cheng Guanhua).

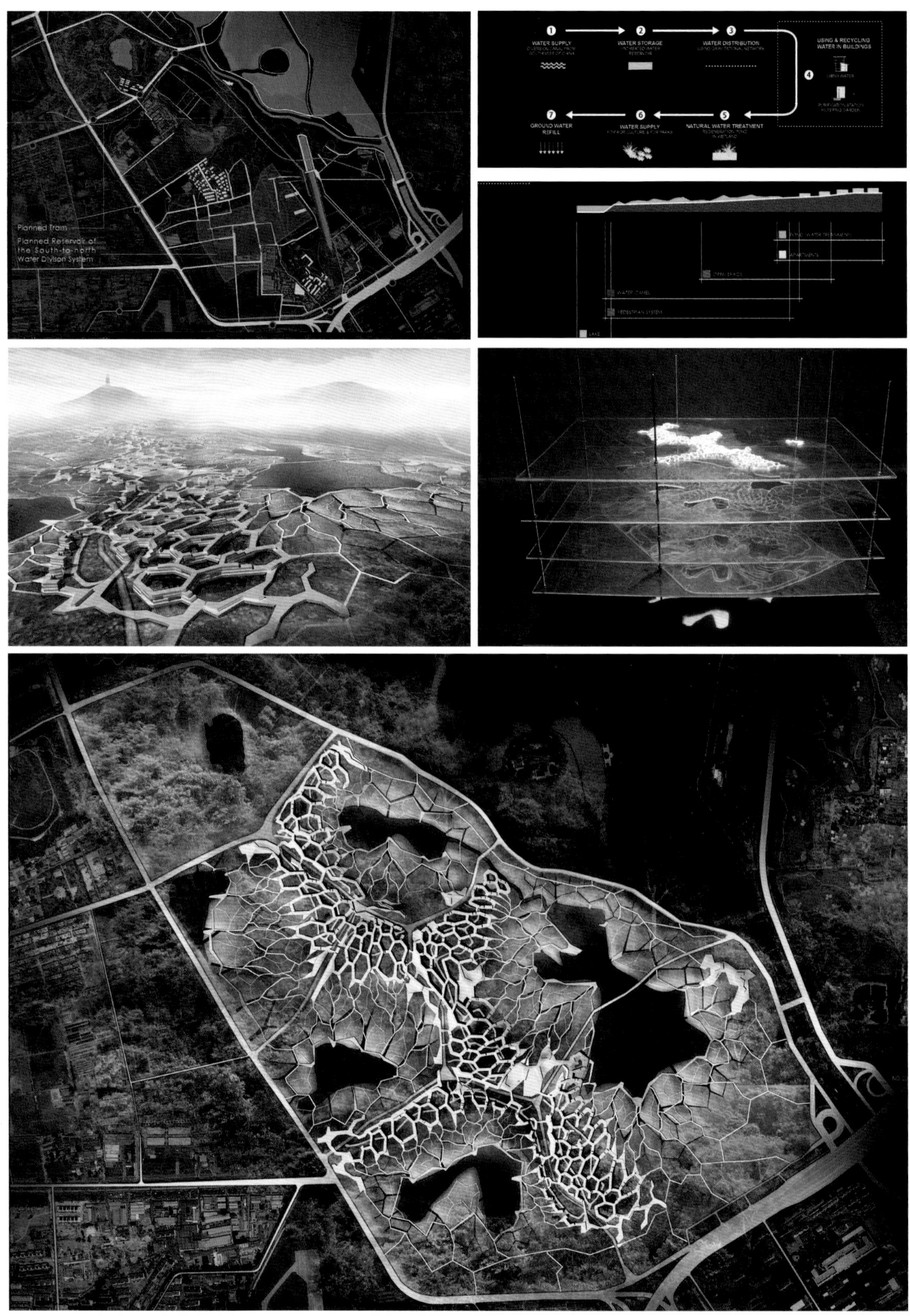

Above: selected work: Regional Landscape Design of Summer Palace southwestern Exterior (Student: Lv Hui).

14) Landscape Planning Studio

This is a core course for the study of Landscape Architecture and the third Studio of the series at the Department of LA. The focus of Landscape Planning Studio is on the allocation of large-scale regional landscape resources. This course lasts one semester (16 weeks), with four class hours each week and a total of four credit points at completion.

Major Goals of the Course:

– Proficiency of skills for large-scale landscape systems including the natural, cultural, and visual perspective, with particular emphasis on the understanding of the "process-structure–function" relationship of regional landscapes;

– Proficiency in the seven steps and approaches for landscape planning: research, analysis, evaluation, planning (including objectives, strategies, space, and action plan), environmental impact analysis, design decision, and implementation;

– To learn the origins of the latest trends in domestic and international landscape planning theories and philosophies, including traditional landscape aesthetics and theories in China; world heritage, global national park, and reserve protection theories; theories on national scenic areas and relevant protective land use systems; modern cities and regional green and open space systems; and tourism and recreation.

– To train students to be proficient and competent at independent thinking, team research, data collection and processing, site analysis, and brainstorming.

2010: Wudalianchi Regional Landscape Planning

Course Time: Spring 2010
Instructors: Yang Rui, Liu Hailong, Zhuang Youbo, Zheng Xiaodi

Course Content:

Wudalianchi is located south of Heihe City in the northwestern part of China's Heilongjiang Province, and falls within the transition zone of Xiaoxing'anling and Songnen Plain. Wudalianchi has five connected border lakes created by volcanic eruptions. Its highest point is 600 meters above sea level, and its lowest point is 248 meters below. It has a temperate, continental monsoon climate with prevailing northwest and westerly winds. The winters are long and cold, with a yearly average low of -24°, and short and cool summers, with a yearly average high of 21.1°; a 45.1° yearly average temperature range. With annual precipitation ranging from 365.3 mm to 781.3 mm, it has rich water resources and mineral springs with medical benefits. Vegetation developing on its lava plateau varies from the low-level lichen communities to advanced coniferous and broad-leaved forests. Overall, Wudalianchi is a rare natural heritage site where unique and intact volcanic landforms, geology, hydrology, and biological resources, as well as distinctive local customs and culture can be found.

Currently the Wudalianchi National Park is applying for inscription in the World Natural Heritage List, which requires some residents to vacate the nominated site and a new town be built to house the relocated residents while providing various services.

This course addresses the needs in the building of a new town for heritage protection purposes and a number of social, economic, and ecological problems that arise, such as balancing the resettlement of residents with social and economic development and heritage protection, creating a harmonious living environment to help alleviate the ecological and climate problems, the proper allocation of land for various purposes, the protection of local culture, and the improvement of local tourist attractions. This course follows a "problem-oriented" approach by exploring the innovative solutions to the above problems by means of regional landscape planning integrated with theoretical methods of other disciplines.

2005, 2006, 2011: Regional Landscape Planning of the Three Mountains and Five Imperial Gardens Area in Beijing

Course Time: Fall 2005, Fall 2006, Spring 2011
Instructors: Yang Rui, Dang Anrong, Liu Hailong, Zhuang Youbo, Zheng Xiaodi

Course Content:

The Three Mountains and Five Imperial Gardens Area, located in the northwestern suburbs of Beijing, is where the most famous Ming and Qing imperial gardens are concentrated. "Three Mountains" refers to the Fragrant Hill, Yuquan Mountain, and Longevity Hill. The "Five Imperial Gardens" include the Jingyi (Providence), Jingming (Light and Tranquility), and Qingyi (Clear Ripples), which make up the Summer Palace on the aforementioned three mountains, but also includes Changchun and Yuanmingyuan Gardens. These are the historic locations of the imperial and private gardens and are important cultural heritage zones.

The area boasts natural landscape elements such as mountains, rivers, wetlands (lakes and paddy fields), woodland, farmland, flora, and fauna and acts as an important natural ecological shelter in the northwest part of Beijing. It is also the fastest-growing urban construction zone in Beijing. Because of rapid urbanization, great changes have taken place in the landscape structure and characteristics: a growing residential, education, transportation, commerce, and high-tech industrial has created a complex mix of diversly functioning spaces. Though some gardens still remain, the cultural heritage systems are no longer intact. Natural processes, including hydrological and biological systems, are being affected by tourism and recreation development. This course requires consideration of the following relations as they effect this area: history and reality; development and protection; imperial (the minority) and general public (the majority); ecology and culture; and urban and rural areas.

The course helps students through the seven steps: research, analysis, evaluation, planning (including objectives, strategies, space, and action plan), environmental impact analysis, design decision, and implementation of landscape planning, to acquire the skills required for the landscape architecture profession through focused investigation, analysis, and research of the "Three Hills and Five Imperial Gardens" area, and examination of deep structural relations between regional landscapes.

2009, 2012: Zhoukoudian Regional Landscape Planning

Course Time: Spring 2009 and 2012
Instructors: Yang Rui, Dang Anrong, Liu Hailong, Zhuang Youbo, Eva Castro, Federico Ruberto, Nicola Saladino

Course Content:

Zhoukoudian is situated about 50 km southwest of Beijing. It used to be an excellent living environment with human and prehistoric settlements dating back approximately 300,000 years. Since the discovery of hominid fossils here in the 1920s and '30s, Zhoukoudian has been known around the world as home of the "Apeman." In 1961, the Peking-Man Site at Zhoukoudian became one of the first Key Cultural Heritage Units under State Protection and was formally added to the UNESCO World Heritage List in 1987. However, this did not put an end to the quarrying and mining activities surrounding the heritage site that had been going on for several hundred years, which not only posed a threat to the stability of rock strata of the mountains within the boundaries of the site but also endangered the ecological environment of the region with sand and dust produced by the outlying barren soil and rock, which in turn hindered the development of tourism. Since the beginning of the 21st century, with Beijing's strategy of "western ecological development zone," a number of cement plants, stone factories, and quarries around the heritage site have been closed. Early in 2007, Beijing issued the "Vegetation Restoration Plan for Abandoned and Shut-Down Mines in the Mountains," in which the Zhoukoudian Peking-Man Site and its periphery were targeted as key restoration areas. Currently, the region faces enormous opportunities and challenges: how to better protect and display the world heritage site of ancient humans at Zhoukoudian; how to reconstruct and restore the ecosystem of the industrial wastelands; how to coordinate the relationship between heritage protection, ecological restoration, and tourism development of the industrial wastelands; and how to sustain community economic development.

2013: Landscape Planning of the Water System of Jiangbei District, Fuzhou City

Course Time: Spring Semester 2013
Instructors: Yang Rui, Liu Hailong, Zhuang Youbo, Elisa Palazzo, Eva Castro, Nicola Saladino, Libny Pacheco

Course Content:

Nowadays, with Fuzhou City's outspread development scale and increasing density, the urban landscape structure has gradually disappeared, the urban water system function has been nearly paralyzed and the urban human settlement environment has deteriorated. The specific phenomenon are as follows: uneven water volume in time and space leading to frequent floods; waste water sewage discharge and garbage deposition resulting in serious water quality pollution problems; spatial isolation causing the separation of activities of surrounding residents and water system; lacking of land use function coordination bringing out the disconnection between water system and adjacent green spaces, communities, and commercial spaces; and traffic barriers sparking the contradiction of residents transportation, surrounding traffic, and water systems. Therefore, this studio looks at the water system of Jiangbei District, Fuzhou City as its case example, leading to the relevant researches on city and landscape with the essential element of water. Through compact integration of the characters, problems, and needs of Fuzhou are taken into consideration based on the "Seven Stages of Education Procedures": investigation, analysis, evaluation, planning, environmental impact analysis, design, and implement. The studio attempts to conduct comprehensive research across disciplines and scales and encourages creative thinking, methods, and design by studying various theories, case studies, technologies, and engineering standards. The design objectives, tasks, content, and methods concern water on multiple scales based on the "Watershed River Site."

Main Lectures:

Yang Rui: Landscape planning theory and method

Liu Hailong: Landscape hydrology, North American landscape urbanism

Zhuang Youbo: Landscape ecology, analysis, and planning

Zhang Jie: 3 lanes & 7 alleys, street landscape renovation in Fuzhou City

Li Junqi: Urban storm water management and planning

Elisa Palazzo: LANDSCAPE IN URBAN DESIGN 1, the landscape tradition in urban design and planning

Elisa Palazzo: LANDSCAPE IN URBAN DESIGN 2, the landscape approach to urban regeneration in Europe part 1

Elisa Palazzo: LANDSCAPE IN URBAN DESIGN 3, the landscape approach to urban regeneration in Europe part 2

Elisa Palazzo: Cultural landscape management and traditional knowledge for community's sustainable development

Eva Castro: Introduction to landscape urbanism

Eva Castro: Landscape urbanism case study

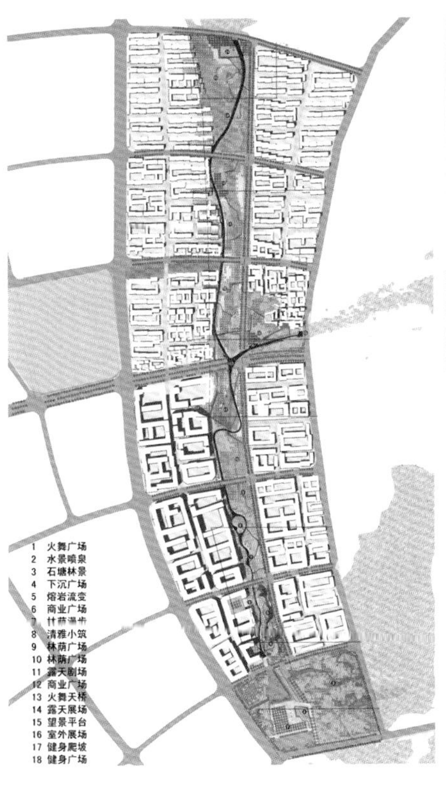

Left: selected work: Concept Planning and Segment Landscape Design of the Wudalianchi New Town (Students: Zhng Jian, Zhang Lei, Zhang Yan, Zhang Juncen).

Left: selected work: Integrating Three Mountains and Five Imperial Gardens Area: From Gardens to Landscapes (Students: Zhao Feifei, Lu Han, Guo Yong).

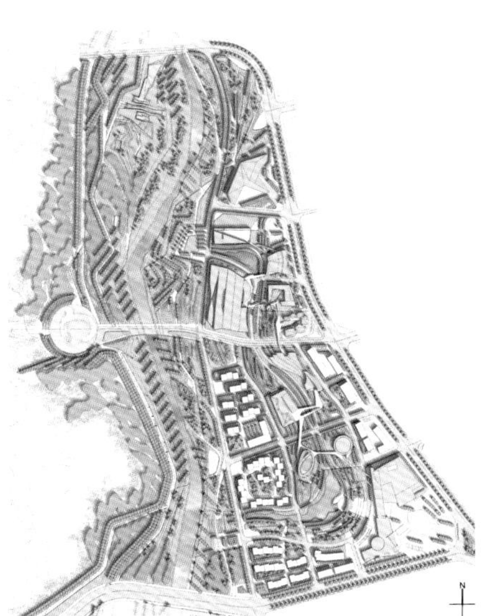

Left: selected work: Essence, Vigor, and Glory: Zhoukoudian Landscape Planning (Students: Liang Shangyu, Ji Wanjing, Zhang Ya).

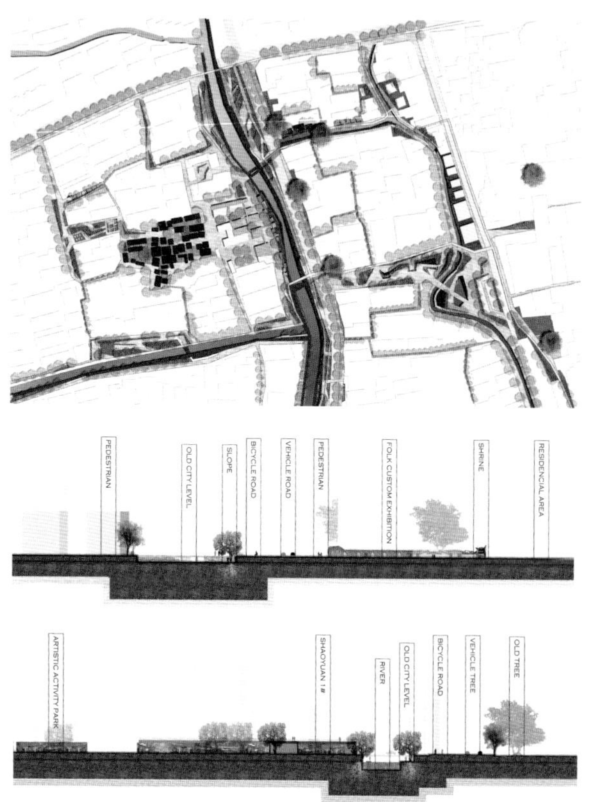

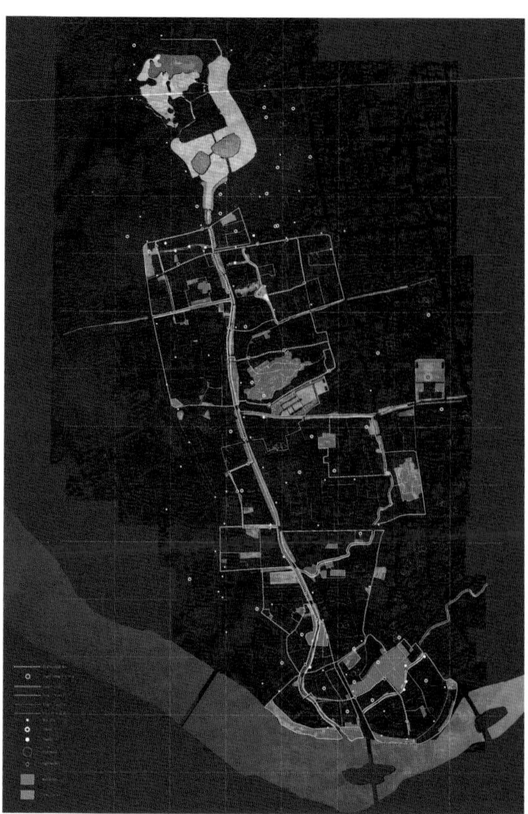

Above: selected work: Growing Capillary: Landscape Planning of Baima River System, Fuzhou (Students: Bian Simin, Ma Xinran, Di Lina, Wu Xin, Lin Ting, Lu Yuyan, Zhang Xiaoya).

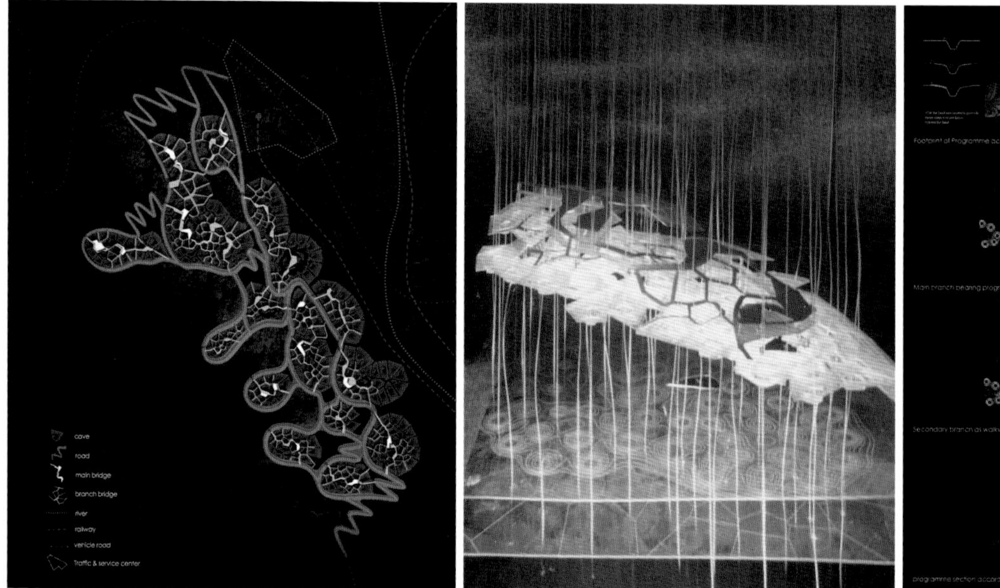

Above: selected work: An open archaeological museum (Students: Wang Chengyu, Zhou Lin, Li Wenling).

14) Final Studio and Graduation Thesis

Students are expected to go through their whole process from topic selection to final report and thesis defense independently under the guidance of the instructor team. The work at this phase is to apply knowledge, methods, and skills acquired in the first year in carrying out independent research while solving practical problems in landscape planning and design so as to achieve a higher level of theory and practice.

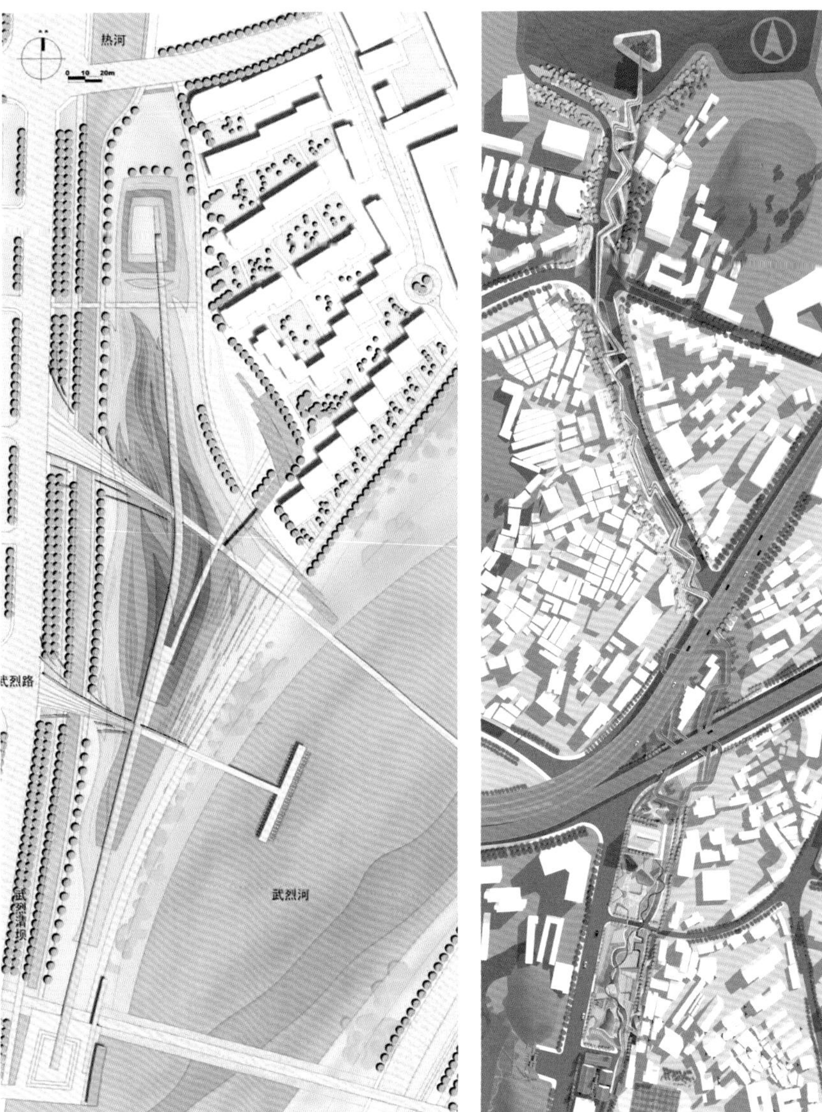

Above: Left from Zhao Feifei; Right from Zhao Chengbin.

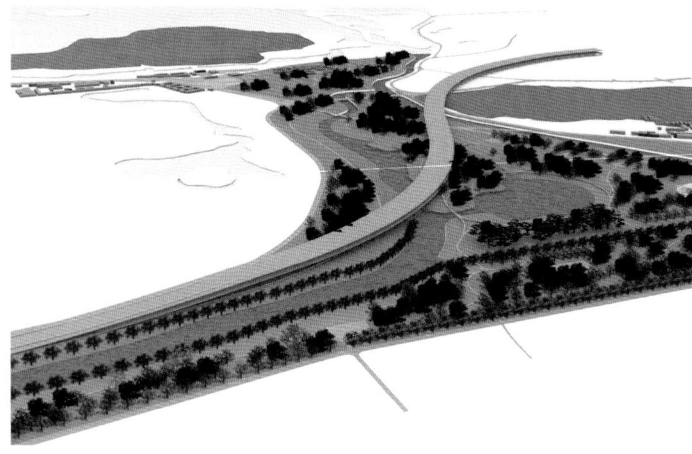

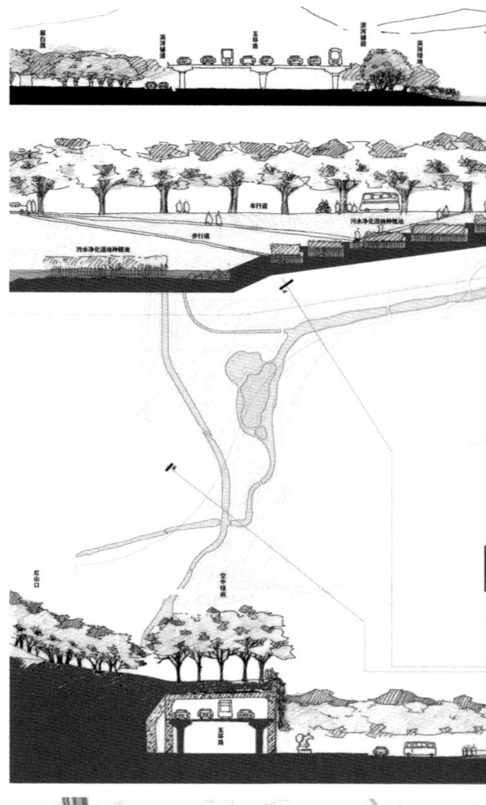

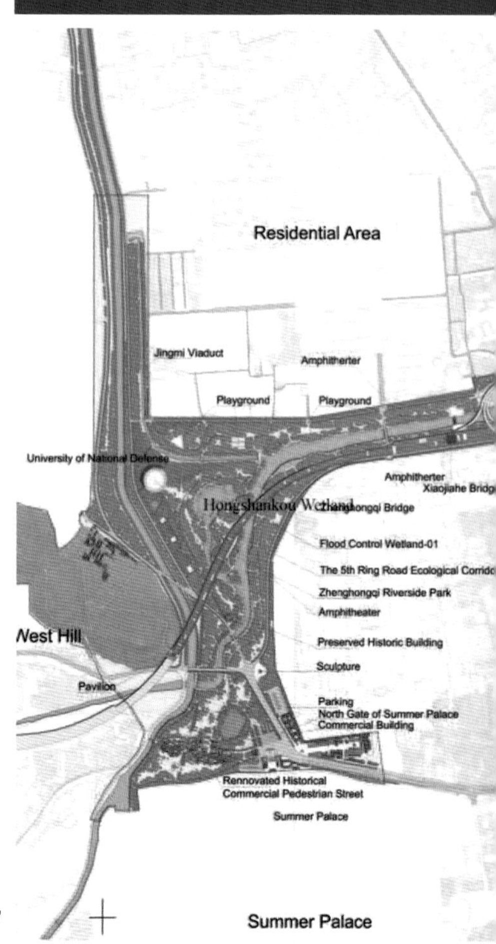

Selected Work from Sewage Canal to Green Corridor: River Bank Landscape Renovation for the Xiaojiahe Section of Qinghe River (Student: Que Zhenqing, Supervisor: Yang Rui).

Note: This project won the honor award in the general design category for the ASLA University Student Design Competition in 2007.

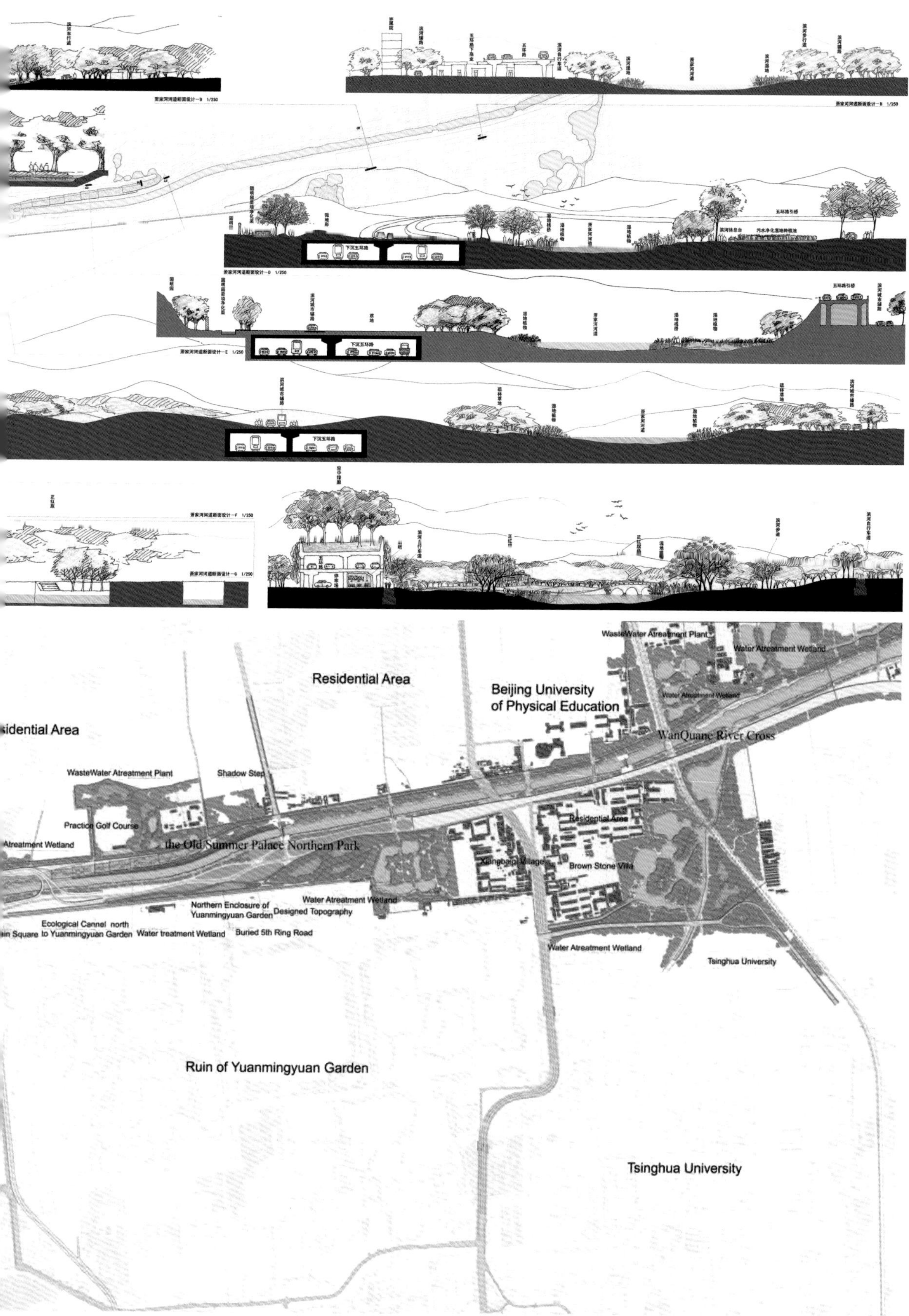
Residential Area
Beijing University
of Physical Education
WasteWater Atreatment Plant
Water Atreatment Wetland
Water Atreatment Wetland
WanQuane River Cross
idential Area
WasteWater Atreatment Plant
Shadow Step
Practice Golf Course
Atreatment Wetland
the Old Summer Palace Northern Park
Residential Area
Xiangbaiqi Village
Brown Stone Villa
Northern Enclosure of
Yuanmingyuan Garden
Designed Topography
Water Atreatment Wetland
Ecological Cannel north
to Yuanmingyuan Garden
in Square
Water treatment Wetland
Buried 5th Ring Road
Water Atreatment Wetland
Tsinghua University
Ruin of Yuanmingyuan Garden
Tsinghua University

Selected Work from A Study of Landscape Design of Gyana Marnyi Stone Mound, Yushu (Student: Xu Yuan, Supervisor: Zhu Yufan).

Note: This project is an outstanding paper, Tsinghua University.

SECTION 3

Crossing Boundaries: Research and Practice

On the basis of extensive data collection, this section compiles the incorporated academic publications, the scientific research projects, and the practice projects, with a general description of major research findings by the Tsinghua University LA department. Six Chapters address findings and overviews of projects organized within the Six Research Directions under the Level-1 discipline of LA: Landscape Architecture History and Theory, Gardens and Landscape Design, Landscape Planning and Ecological Restoration, Landscape Architecture Heritage Protection, Vegetation and Planting Design, and Landscape Architecture Technology and Science. Other papers and practice projects are referenced in the appendices. It is worth pointing out that LA is noted for being trans-disciplinary as is marked by the lack of clear demarcation between the component research directions and the abundance of cross-departmental research findings, so only the most representative research achievements for each direction are noted within the corresponding chapters. In addition, to give a full scope of the accumulation of LA research at Tsinghua since the establishment of the "*Landscape Program*" in 1951, this section covers LA research findings before the establishment of the Department of LA in 2003, however, most of the research and practice projects of the LA faculty in this section will address post-2003 achievements.

This section is intended to offer a fact-based and rigorously objective picture of the research achievements of all LA directions at Tsinghua. This collection, with a focus on mountain and water aesthetics, as well as a down-to-earth exploration of innovation in modern LA theory and techniques highlights the LA department's dedication to Chinese classic gardening. Meanwhile, it is essential to note that we still have a long way to go in the LA academic research.

Left: The process of design (from Chang Xiangqi).

3.1 Landscape Architecture History and Theory

Overview

The Landscape Architecture History and Theory Program at the Tsinghua University is characterized by theoretical research of traditional landscape architecture, scenic areas, cultural heritage, and natural & cultural heritage. It has a profound academic grounding and considerable influence.

A Long History of Fundamental Course Teaching

In 1949 Professor Liang Sicheng envisioned the School of Architecture and Urban Planning at Tsinghua University, consisting of the Departments of Architecture, Urban and Rural Planning, Landscape, Industrial Arts, and Architectural Engineering. Among the courses for the Gardening Department included in the Draft Plan of School System and Education Program for the School of Architecture and Urban Planning at Tsinghua University are Design Theory, Introduction to Landscape Architecture, and other theoretical courses. In 1951, Tsinghua School of Architecture and & Urban Planning and Beijing Agriculture University co-founded the Landscape Program, which marked the beginning of modern landscape architecture education in China. At that time, history and theory related courses for the Landscape Program mainly included: Chinese Landscape History taught by Wang Juyuan and Liu Zhiping, Western Landscape History taught by Hu Yunjing, and Landscape Arts taught by Wang Juyuan and Chen Youmin. The Landscape Program was terminated in 1953, but Wu Liangyong, dean of the Department at that time, set up a teaching and research group of "Urban Planning and Residential Area Landscaping" headed by Master Cheng Yingquan, with Zhu Zixuan serving as secretary. Two of the first graduates from the Landscape Program, Liu Chengxian and Zhu Junzhen served as assistant teachers. In the Urban Landscaping courses taught successively by Liu Chengxian, Yao Tongzhen, and Zhu Junzhen from the early 1950s to the mid-'90s, basic theories of urban landscaping, both home and abroad, were taught. In the Ancient Architectural History of China taught by Zhao Zhengzhi, classical gardens in South China and Beijing were researched. In Architectural History Overseas, Chen Zhihua referred to knowledge of classical gardens overseas. Starting in 1981, Zhou Weiquan offered a course in Chinese Classical Gardens (later known as Chinese Ancient Gardens), which was taken over by Ji Huailu in the mid-1990s. For graduate programs, courses such as Introduction to Landscape Design (by Zhang Junhua) and Introduction to Landscape Architecture (by Yang Rui) were offered starting in 2000, and Introduction to Modern Landscape Architecture in Europe and America (by Zhu Yufan) was added to the growing course list in 2002.

Upon formal establishment of the Department of LA at the School of Architecture in Tsinghua University in 2003, history and theory had become important sections of the curriculum, with a progressive system well in place from the undergraduate to professors and doctorate programs. Currently, courses for undergraduate programs include: Introduction to Landscape Architecture (by Yang Rui) and History of Western Classical Gardens (by Zhu Yufan). Courses for graduate programs include: Outline of Landscape Architecture History (Asia) by Jia Jun, and Outline of Landscape Architecture History (Europe and America) by Zhu Yufan.

Accomplishment through Equal Emphasis on Knowledge and Action

The Landscape Architecture History and Theory Program at Tsinghua University has long been combined with practical projects and is well integrated with the teaching program of thesis design as a forerunner of the learning-research-production 3-in-1 practice.

In human settlement theories, landscape architecture history and theory marks one of the three pillars of human settlement theory put forward by Professor Wu Liangyiong. His *Introduction to the Sciences of Human Settlements* is an important cornerstone for LA theoretical studies at Tsinghua. In many human settlement research and practical projects supervised by Wu Liangyong can be found important components of the landscape architecture theory. For instance, in the "study of the conservation and development of architectural environment during the urbanization of developed areas," a key project supported by National Natural Science Foundation of China he oversaw in 1993, serious problems marking a critical period of China's rapid urbanization were addressed, such as decreasing arable land, resource loss, environmental degradation, and damage of historical and cultural landscapes. In the "study of sustainable development plan for human settlements (including National Parks) in Northwest Yunnan," in 1998, definite conclusions were reached on the relationship between National Parks and development of bio-diversity and cultural diversity on the one hand and construction of human settlements on the other. This led to major challenges, protection and development priorities, and major countermeasures in future landscape projects.

In view of the history and theory of Chinese classical gardens, sustained research on the history of classical gardens, the imperial gardens of the Summer Palace and Yuanmingyuan, and of private gardens has been done. In 1990, Zhou Weiquan published *A History of Classical Chinese Gardens* (1st Edition), which received praise from Jin Bailing as, "the first-ever systematic and complete classic of a book on classical Chinese gardens"; in 1999 the second edition of the book came out and was considered to "carry twice as much weight as the first edition, or should we say that another sword was sharpened in the past 10 years?!" The first and second editions won the Chinese National Excellence Sci-

Tech Book Prize; a third edition was published in 2008. Summer Palace studies have long been good research subjects: survey and mapping of the Summer Palace began in 1951 and continued until the outbreak of the "Cultural Revolution." From 1963, the survey and mapping was no longer undertaken by freshmen but by seniors, with the focal point expanded to the relationship between the buildings and the surroundings and from the survey and mapping of the landscape and architecture to concerns for regional landscape problems. Faculty members and students at that time conducted comprehensive studies of the gardening techniques and arts of the Summer Palace. Supervised by Mo Zongjiang, Zhang Jinqiu finished her thesis "Original State, Gardening Experience, Utilization and Transformation Challenges of the Rear Hill and West Part of the Summer Palace"; Zhou Weiquan, Feng Zhongping, and Lou Qingxi published their monograph *The Summer Palace* (Taiwan Zhaohua Press, 1981; Press of Taiwan Architects Association, Sections I and II, 1990; China Architecture & Building Press, 2000). In the early 1980s Ji Huailu and Yin Yihe directed and produced the TV teaching film *Summer Palace: Her Garden Arts and Architecture.*

In the late 1990s, after her successful application of a research subject of Tsinghua University, Guo Daiheng started her studies of Yuanmingyuan. She finished the Yuanmingyuan Conservation Planning in 2000 and supervised six theses and one dissertation. She published *Yuanmingyuan-The Imperial Work of Emperor Qianlong, The Lost Splendor: Research and Protection of Structures in Yuanmingyuan Garden and Memory of Yuanmingyuan.* In 2009 she began to work on the digital Yuanmingyuan project making 3D virtual simulations of Yuanmingyuan. Other studies of Yuanmingyuan include: *Landscape Arts of Yuanmingyuan* by He Zhongyi and Zeng Zhaofen and the dissertation "*Protection and Rehabilitation of the Landforms, Water System, and Plant Landscapes in Yuanmingyuan Garden*" by Wu Xiangyan, which was supervised by Sun Fengqi. In 1984, Zhu Zixuan, Sun Fengqi, and others started planning design and studies of Shichahai, which ended up with nine undergraduate thesis designs on subjects varying from petty gardens to water landscape, green space, transportation, and commercial streets. This was an early prototype of research studios. In 1981 Feng Zhongping started a posted research project on "Chinese Landscape Architecture" and later published a book on the same (Taiwan Mingwen Press, 1989; Tsinghua University Press, 1988, 2000), which won the second prize of the Scientific and Technological Progress Award of the Ministry of Construction in 1988, prize of honor for the 1988 Chinese Book Award, and was one of the National Best Books of the Year. In 1999 Zhou Weiquan and Lou Qingxi compiled *A Complete Collection of Chinese Architectural Arts 17-Imperial Gardens.* In 2007 Jia Jun conducted a research project on "Historical Origins, Design, and Protection Measures of Private Gardens in Beijing Against the Backdrop of Modern Urban Construction," and published her findings in *A Record of Private Gardens in Beijing.*

In view of history and theory of overseas classical gardens, Chen Zhihua oversaw a project supported by the Tsinghua University Science Foundation titled, "Overseas Classical Gardening Arts and Comparison with Chinese Gardening Arts" from 1988 to 1990 and published the book, *Overseas Gardening Arts* (Taiwan Mingwen Press, 1989; Henan Science and Technology Press, 2001). Besides this, Chen Zhihua also published *Influence of Chinese Gardening Arts in Europe.*

In view of modern landscaping history and theories, *A History of Modern Chinese Gardens* (Part I), compiled under the supervision of Zhu Junzhen, was formally published. It bridged a gap in the research on the history of modern gardens. In the same year, *Modern Gardens in Nanxun*, another book by Zhu Junzhen was published, which incorporates some of the outcomes of the survey and mapping conducted by School of Architecture, Tsinghua University on modern gardens in Nanxun.

As far as scenic and heritage site planning theories are concerned, Zhu Changzhong, Zhu Zixuan, Zhou Weiquan, Xu Yingguang, Zheng Guangzhong, Feng Zhongping, and others started research and planning of Mount Huangshan in the late 1970s. In 1983, under the guidance of Zhu Changzhong and Xu Yingguang, students of the 1978 undergraduate program created the master plan for the Seven-Star Cave, Zhaoqing, Guangdong, and conducted thematic research on the application of master planning, detailed planning, and traditional gardening techniques in large, new-generation parks as thesis design instead of thesis papers. Master plans for the Three Gorges and Lvshan Scenic Area of Liaoning were also built as a result of thesis design. In 1983 Zhu Changzhong finished but did not publish his *Protection, Development, and Management of Scenic Areas (Draft for Discussion).* In 1996 Zhou Weiquan published *Famous Mountain Scenic Spots in China*, a thorough book on the studies of scenic areas in China to the present. Afterwards, Yang Rui, Zhuang Youbo, Wu Dongfan, Zhao Zhicong, and others added to heritage site theories with plans for Mount Taishan, Mount Huangshan, Three Parallel Rivers, Meili Snow Mountain, Laojunshan, Mount Wutai, Mount Huashan, the Temple of Heaven, and Wudalianchi.

In view of landscape design theories, Zhu Junzhen published *Water-Making: Arts of Gardens* and *Hereditary Concepts in Water Landscaping*, two books on water landscape design theory.

Zhu Yufan came up with the Three-Position Design Theory through such practical projects as Reconstruction of No. 13 Courtyard of Beishuncheng Street on the Financial Street in Beijing, Environment Transformation of the Central Area of the Tsinghua Institute of Nuclear and New Energy Technology, and Landscape Design of the National Patriotism Education Base in Qinghai Atomic City.

Since 2003, Yang Rui has been conducting research on the development of the Landscape Architecture discipline and Landscape Architecture education, which ended with the publication of a number of journal papers, including, "Integration, Interaction, Multi-Scale, and Public Concerns: Philosophy of Landscape Architecture Education and Its Practice in Tsinghua University," "Opportunities and Challenges for Landscape Architecture," "Transformation of Civilization and the Mission of Landscape Architecture," "Three Questions About the Academic Community of Landscape Architecture," and "On the Evolution and Characteristics of the Landscape Architecture Discipline: With the Prospect of Chinese Landscape Architecture for the 21st Century." He also drafted the "Demonstration Report on Adding Landscape Architecture as the First Level Discipline" as convener and main author.

This is an overview of the Landscape Architecture History and Theory research for the Landscape Architecture History and Theory Program at Tsinghua University. As theoretical research is based mainly on practice, with particular regard to planning and design theories, some of the theoretical achievements contained in this book may be placed in other corresponding sections. As human settlement theories incorporate three categories—architecture, planning, and landscape architecture—only a limited amount of theories are placed within this section for the sake of clarification.

–Wu Dongfan and Yang Rui

1) Sciences of Human Settlements

Introduction to the Sciences of Human Settlements

Author: Wu Liangyong
Published By: China Architecture & Building Press
Published In: October, 2001

The Sciences of Human Settlements addresses human settlements as the research object and focuses on the relationship between humans and the environment. It stresses that human settlements should be viewed as a whole rather than from a certain part or facet as is the case in urban planning, geography, and sociology. The goal is to understand and master the objective law of the emergence and development of human settlements so as to better construct ideal human settlements. This book, based on years of theoretical consideration and construction practices of academician Wu Liangyong, is composed of two parts: Part I, "Interpretation of the Sciences of Human Settlements" covers the origin of the sciences of human settlements, the composition of human settlements, basic concepts in human settlement building, methodologies of the sciences of human settlements, and case studies in the protection and building of sustainable human settlements; Part II, "Introduction to Doxiadis's EKISTICS" contains systematic research findings on the Greek scholar Doxiadis's theory and practice of human settlements.

Right: *Introduction to Sciences of Human Settlements.*

2) History and Theory of Classical Gardens

Historical Origins, Design and Protection Measures of Private Gardens in Beijing Against the Backdrop of Modern Urban Construction

Project Source: National Natural Science Foundation of China
Project Time: January 2007 to December 2009
Project Leader: Jia Jun
Project Team: Guo Daiheng, Zhu Yufan, Liu Chang, Zhao Xiaomei, Huang Xiao

Private gardens used to exist in Beijing in large numbers with distinctive local characteristics and high artistic merits – characteristics of classical Chinese gardens. Via extensive on-site investigation, survey, and literature research, the Tsinghua School of Architecture project team, headed by Jia Jun, was able to reach conclusions on the historical origin, gardening techniques, garden life, social and cultural connotations, and protection measures of classical gardens based on the first-ever systematic and in-depth analysis on over 300 gardens dating from the Liao Dynasty. The research findings are of great academic value to studies on the history of architecture and landscape architecture, of great relevance to the protection of the ancient city of Beijing, and have certain reference value to the present capital landscape construction.

The project team collected, copied, and scanned a variety sources concerning private gardens in Beijing including local chronicles, poems and articles, notes, diaries, tablet inscriptions, pictures, old photos, interviews, and oral history data. The team conducted site visits to all existent gardens and relics and built a database with the over 20,000 digital photos, general plot plans of 64 classical gardens, as well as plane, elevation, sectional, 3D computer models, and aerial views for some of the gardens generated. The project addressed 36 private gardens of varying scale for case-to-case studies that include site visits, measurement, photography, drawing, and detailed digital image recovery in the case of ruined gardens. For gardens that are destroyed, the team tried all possible means to discover the historical origins of the gardens using literature research in combination with interviews of former owners and first-hand-accounts in order to expound upon and analyze the physical layouts and gardening techniques. In addition, there are also simple analyses of more than 300 private gardens ranging from the Liao, Jin, Yuan, Ming, and Qing Dynasties to the Republic of China Period.

Literature

1. Jia Jun. Tablet and Couplet Art of the Beijing Private Gardens [J]. Chinese Landscape Architecture, 2008(12): 76-78.
2. Jia Jun. Continuous Textual Research of Beijing Shaoyuan Garden in Ming Dynasty [J]. Chinese Landscape Architecture, 2009(5): 76-79.
3. Jia Jun. New Research on Beijing Gongwangfu Garden [J]. Chinese Landscape Architecture, 2009(8): 85-88.
4. Jia Jun. Gunbeizifu Garden in the Xicheng District of Beijing [J]. Chinese Landscape Architecture, 2010(1): 85-87.
5. Jia Jun and Zhu Yufan. Plant Landscape of the Beijing Private Gardens [J]. Chinese Landscape Architecture, 2010(10): 61-69.

3.2 Garden and Landscape Design

Overview

As a subordinate discipline (or direction) to the Level-1 discipline of Landscape Architecture, Garden and Landscape Design, defined as an applied science of constructed medium and small-scale exterior space environments, is core to the landscape architecture discipline. Its objective is to meet people's needs for various spaces for use in outdoor activities. It endeavors to build healthful and beautiful outdoor environments with comprehensive design through site analysis, functional integration, and studies of the social, economic, cultural, and ecological factors to render spiritual and aesthetic pleasure to visitors. Research and practice within its sphere address vegetated parks, roads, residential areas, public facilities as well as courtyards, rooftop gardens, interior gardens, memorial gardens and landscapes, city squares, street and waterside landscapes, landscape park buildings, and landscape structures.

Garden and Landscape Design is important as it is the cornerstone of the larger discipline of Landscape Architecture. Perhaps the advent of landscape design can be dated back to the first time humans linked their fate with natural phenomena and made geographical expression of this. The garden, however, is an exteriorization of humanity's inner yearning for things beautiful, personalized, and diversified. It is in this sense that subject matter of Garden and Landscape Design is considered to have a long history. In ancient Egypt, drawings, records, and scripts of mansions with explicit design were recorded. Garden culture and arts have grown throughout human history gradually into the marrow of various civilizations around the globe, which corresponds with the emergence of changing gardening theories. The profession of garden designer did not appear until le Notre (1613–1700) brought the profession into the forefront in Europe in the 17th century, and Zhang Nanyuan (1587–1671) became a master garden builder in China. After the Industrial Revolution, in the second half of the 19th century, Garden and Landscape Design in Europe and America gradually turned from exclusiveness to universality, with its professional sphere extended to be macro and systematic. In 1900 the first landscape architecture course in the United States was offered and a four-year Bachelor's degree program launched at the Graduate School of Design at Harvard University, marking the formal beginning of the vocational education of a modern profession.

Landscape architecture education in China started in 1951 with the establishment of the Landscape architecture program in the Department of Architecture, Tsinghua University in cooperation with the Department of Horticulture, Beijing Agriculture College. Regrettably, for reasons addressed in books 1 and 2, the LA professional education and practice department failed at first within the Architecture curriculum system at Tsinghua University, however, professional teaching and research achievements, based mainly upon personal interest of the teachers in relation to their areas of interest, landscape architecture practice remained alive. Zhou Weiquan's studies of Chinese classical gardens, Wang Guoyu and Shang Deqi's regionalist architectural design practices, and Wu Liangyong's integration of Landscape Architecture into the academic framework of the general Architecture from a major discipline perspective (1989) are just three examples of these early pioneers work.

Establishment of the Institute of Landscape and Gardening by the School of Architecture, Tsinghua University in 1997 marked the rejuvenation of Landscape Architecture at Tsinghua. With Sun Fengqi (1997) serving as head and Zhang Junhua (1998) and Zhu Yufan (2000) as members, the institute gave Tsinghua a professional landscape team and the School of Architecture expanded to include landscape architecture as a disciplinary program. The team offered theory and design courses in Garden and Landscape Design to students of the professor and doctorate programs while continuing their design practices. By the time the Department of LA was established in 2003, Sun Fengqi had fostered three doctors in the landscape architecture direction while being devoted to explorations of urban public space design theories and practices; Zhang Junhua had turned from improvement on the theoretical system of the investigation and analytic methods in Landscape design to the practice of running a design office and translated several books that advanced the development of the design industry in China; Zhu Yufan had built two of the most important design projects – Reconstruction of No. 13 Courtyard of Beishuncheng Street on the Financial Street in Beijing, and Environment Transformation of the Central Area of the Tsinghua Institute of Nuclear and New Energy Technology. In 2001 the Institute of Natural Resource Preservation and Scenery Tourism was set up at the School of Architecture, which, like other landscape teaching and research institutes, covered the two core fields of landscape planning and design and laid a sound basis for the establishment of the Department.

A new page was turned in October 2003 with the development of the Landscape Architecture discipline at Tsinghua University and the establishment of the Department of LA. Laurie D. Olin, a world-renowned landscape architect in the United States, became first chair of the Department and taught at the school with the international chair professor team he organized. As the first foreign department chair in the Chinese landscape architecture history, he made tremendous contributions to the LA education at Tsinghua and throughout China by putting a brand new educational system in place, which was continued and improved upon by his successor, Professor Yang Rui. Before the establishment of the Department, the LA professors program at Tsinghua was three-years long, with no tailored planning and design courses in the curriculum. To obtain the degree, students were required to submit theses on subjects that were more theoretical and research based than pragmatic. This pedagogical approach features close links between the students and the tutor but cut off horizontal links between the students and other students, particularly students with different tutors. Laurie

D. Olin had previously been chair of the Landscape Architecture Department at the Harvard Graduate School of Design, and a professor of Landscape Architecture at the University of Pennsylvania. Upon heading the Tsinghua Department of LA, he introduced it to the American MLA vocational educational philosophy, a system that catered to professional application. He changed the program to a two-year system, a prevalent form of vocational education worldwide, and instigated the offering of both design-based and research-based programs. This innovation changed the way Tsinghua addressed landscape architecture, which previously had been a research-oriented LA graduate program. The new focuses were popular among students because most of them chose the design-oriented program, with the exception of those seeking to pursue doctoral enrollment via recommendation. The change in focus and enrolment reflected a change in value for Tsinghua LA. The design-based graduate program features a studio-centered curriculum, with the studios ranging from medium and small-scale landscape design to large-scale landscape planning emphasizing cooperation, interaction, and critical thinking. The studios are not closed off but open to natural science, history and theory, and landscape technology sections and influence. The studios also address the current social problems and needs in China, and it follows that research falls upon public, ecological, and brownfield restoration subjects.

It is worth noting that the landscape planning studio, which used to stress large scale projects has adjusted to include small scale research (with the landscape design studio as its testing waters for large scale projects). An analysis of the degree thesis documents consists of six AO design drawings plus the design thesis indicates that all emphasize the necessity of node representation in design regardless of the site area and generality of the subject. Students and faculty started using design practice as evidence of planning concepts and theories they intended to convey.

The revolution in landscape architecture education at Tsinghua caters to the needs and trends of vocational education in China, and the Department of LA experienced a virtually seamless transfer when the School of Architecture also conducted an across-the-board reform moving towards vocational education. To some extent, revolution in landscape architecture education at Tsinghua stresses the fact that garden and landscape design is at the core while design serves as a travelling axle that integrates science, technology, art, and social development using creative means.

For the Garden and Landscape Design discipline, quality and influence of faculty design practices, built works in particular, are an important evaluation index. Laurie D. Olin is an internationally-renowned landscape architect with a half century of professional experiences and diversified design works showing his design philosophy and theory. A mentor both in words and action, he quietly transformed the design philosophy of the young faculty members at the Tsinghua Department of LA.

It is undeniable that the rise of the Department of LA at Tsinghua is closely related to the 2008 Beijing Olympic Games. Faculty of the Department of LA through the cooperation of its stakeholder, the Beijing Tsinghua Tongheng Urban Planning & Design Institute—formerly Beijing Tsinghua Urban Planning and Design Institute—along with the US-based Sasaki Associates, became involved in the landscape planning and design for the Beijing Olympic Park in 2003. Hu Jie's team played a leading role in the construction of the seven-square-km Beijing Olympic Forest Park, which was an unprecedented success that brought fame to the design team. Hu Jie later extended his built design to the scale of cities, and built important design projects such as the Tieling Fanhe New City Landscape Planning and Design and Tangshan Nanhu Eco-City Central Park Overall Planning & Design before making efforts to establish a new concept and connotation for modern Shan-Shui City. These explorations opened a new door for Tsinghua LA with "efficient realization of large-scale landscapes," with emphasis on large scale as opposed to the traditional concept and overall high efficiency. When design reaches a given scale, challenges become complicated, but Hu Jie balanced and filled the gaps between different planning and design scales. The team of the Planning and Design Institute and the technological platform on the basis of integrated trans-disciplinary resources at Tsinghua effectively guaranteed the high-quality of these large-scale planning and design projects and at the same time created more interdisciplinary derivative areas (such as special engineering technologies for large scale) and pushed forward multi-facet development of the LA discipline. Large-scale practice is more noticed – if the overall relationship between the construction of a landscape system and high human settlement generation efficiency of a city or a city district is repeatedly proved or criticized, than this model would be of even greater relevance. Of course, this practice model is full of Chinese characteristics as it caters to the needs of China's current rapid urbanization. It is unique in the world but it has been highly recognized in the LA circle, which is clear from the awards won both home and abroad.

Corresponding to the extension of large-scale landscaping is the development of another tributary of the Garden and Landscape Design discipline at Tsinghua, that is, in-depth exploration into medium and small-scale design. Zhu Yufan started his highly personalized design practice in 2000 through two projects: the Reconstruction of the Courtyard on the Financial Street, and the Environment Transformation of the Central Area of Tsinghua Institute of Nuclear and New Energy Technology. He brought his own modern landscape design language into both projects, and later, with the landscape design of No. 81 Yard on Fragrance Hill (2006) and the planning and design of the Modern Art Park in Beijing CBD (2007). He further improved on this language system with the Landscape Design of National Patriotism Education Base at Qinghai Atomic City (2009), where he made in-depth explorations into critical regionalism landscape design and added new dimensions to his design repertoire. At the same time he also conducted a series of practices in the field of landscape design on modern Chinese-style residential quarters and formed a unique and mature design style with the Quarry Garden in the Chenshan Botanic Garden of Shanghai (2010). These projects won a sustained and extensive influence in the LA circle by means of publication and awards, at home and abroad, and became representations of modern Chinese landscape design works. Zhu Yufan gained worldwide fame from practitioners of landscape architecture for his more recent design practices as well: in 2010 he was invited to the 2010 Venice Architecture Biennale, and his quarry garden won an Excellence Prize in the First China Design Exhibition (2012). His relentless care for design quality and excellence in construction have aided in him receiving strong support from design-theory proponents as well. In his design practices, Zhu Yufan noted that the ways to develop and maintain the genius loci lie with in-depth excavation of the structural relationship between the original position and design by paying close attention to the structural values of original information on the site. He put forward the "Three-Position Theory" in 2007, the "Design Depth of Field Theory" in 2010, and theoretical experimentations of "Research Through Design." These theories respond to the current cultural issues in China as they clash against the prevalence of Western theories in China's landscape design by attempting to find a viable theoretical foundation for design as a whole.

Ron Henderson is another important faculty member of the Tsinghua department of LA who specializes in design teaching. As one of the earliest visiting scholars on Laurie D. Olin's Chair Professor's team, Ron Henderson came to Tsinghua in 2004 and was later recruited as the first full-time foreign faculty member at the Department of LA to teach LA Studio and LA Technology courses. He holds two professor's degrees, one in architecture and the other in landscape design. He is very fond of the Asian culture – Chinese and Japanese in particular. With an acute sense of language and a placid temperament, he easily accommodates qualities of exotic cultures and transforms them into his design, becoming a bridge between the East and the West in its actual sense. Because of his rich professional experience in China and in Japan, he was appointed head of the Landscape Architecture Department, Graduate School of Fine Arts at the University of Pennsylvania. After his departure from Tsinghua, Ron Henderson continued serving as the bridge between the LA departments of the two universities. He is a gifted designer whose works have won various design prizes in the United State. He worked with Renzo Piano on the garden project at the Isabella Stewart Gardner Museum in Boston, and with Wodiczko+Bonder on the project at Mémorial de l'Abolition de l'Esclavage, Nantes, France, which was shortlisted for the 2013 European Union Prize for Contemporary Architecture/Mies van der Rohe Award. Both exhibit a high professional standard. Ron intends to pass on to his students his design style of delicate emotional expression via the Landscape Design Engineering Technology and Design Studio courses.

It is worth mentioning that the Garden and Landscape Design programs at the Department of LA, School of Architecture, Tsinghua University maintain the possibility of full-scale exploration in both teaching and faculty practice. For instance, Liu Hailong heralds ecological design in China with the Reconstruction Design of Shengyinyuan, Tsinghua University where several rain gardens are used to successfully actualize the philosophy of integrating landscape design with the historical and cultural context.

It is also worth noting that Zhang Junhua from the Faculty of Horticulture, Chiba University introduced high-quality design works of famous Japanese designers such as Yoji Sasaki, Toru Mitani, Shunmyo Masuno, and Hiroki Hasegawa to China when teaching at Tsinghua University from 1998 to 2004, which was undoubtedly a stitch in time with far-reaching significance to the Landscape Architecture profession in China. The economic growth at the time was pacing large amounts of practical, modern design guidance and, in a sense, directly driving the growth of the design market in China. Zhang Junhua acted as a human bridge between the landscape architecture circles in China and Japan and was one of the earliest faculty members of the Tsinghua Department of LA to conduct design studio practices who gradually found a unique design language via composite self-positioning to become a contemporary landscape designer with international influence.

Architectural design and creation at Tsinghua University is a continuation of the traditions of being groundbreaking in landscape architecture. Professor Li Xiaodong from the Department of Architecture designed the Yuhu Complete Primary School, Miaolu Mansion, and Liyuan Book Store in Lijiang, Yunnan, and the Qiaoshang Book Store and Primary School in Pinghe County, Fujian, which he won many design prizes for the harmony and cohesion between the buildings and their surroundings. In light of the trend of contemporary architectural design to value landscape planning and active relationship with the environment, the Visitor Center of Yushu New Village designed by Professor Zhang Li, and the landscape design overseen by Professor Wang Lifang of Lover's Slope and other spaces for the Tsinghua Campus Renovation Project are successful examples of a harmonious relationship between architecture, humanity, and environment via the use of design technologies and valuable references for landscape designs.

The teaching, practical, and theoretical development of Tsinghua's garden and landscape design program since 2003 can be concluded as, "continual pursuit of enlightenment through prudent action and a blend of the East and the West." There is no example for China to follow in its development, so it is a viable approach for it to seek enlightenment through prudent action or theoretical findings through practice. Meanwhile, the garden and landscape design program of Tsinghua found it hard to rest upon its disciplinary legacies and made effective disciplinary explorations in both depth and width. The international background and vision of the faculty made it possible for them to render their production with a sense of modernity at a higher level. Of course, with only a 10-year history, the Department of LA is still weak in many aspects, with particular regard to the formation of a design theory system – an area for LA designers to continually work on.

– Zhu Yufan

1) Inheritance of the Chinese Garden

Jiangning Imperial Silk Manufacturing Museum of Nanjing

Project Area: Footprint 18,000 m^2, total floor area 35,000 m^2
First Open In: 2013
Chief Designer: Wu Liangyong
Project Team: Wu Liangyong, Wang Guixiang, He Yuru
Landscape Designer: Zhu Yufan

This museum is near the Mansion of the Imperial Silk Manufacturing Commissioner in the Qing Dynasty, and is the setting of *A Dream of the Red Chamber* by Cao Xueqin. It is meaningful to build a museum at the site where these historical and cultural events took place. Research indicates that the museum is situated where the west garden used to be at the Mansion of the Imperial Silk Manufacturing Commissioner, at the core section of Jiankang, the Capital of the Six Dynasties, or the present-day city of Nanjing. This is indeed a perfect gift to a designer. However, complexities and contingencies of various kinds follow close behind. As a result of changes over time, it was impossible to reconstruct the Mansion of the Imperial Silk Manufacturing Commissioner. At the same time, *A Dream of the Red Chamber* is a multi-faceted work of art. The academic circle has vastly diversified views about research on the novel: even the birth and death of Cao Xueyin is a topic of controversy.

During the design process, the team discussed the proposals for the design before arriving at the concepts of "two models" and "three worlds." The "two models" refers to the "walnut model," which features a traditional kernel within modern shells, and refers to the "potted landscape model," which features natural landscape on top of architectural pallet. The final program is a combination of the two models. Construction for the building was done in urban Nanjing against the backdrop of the natural water and mountain landscape. The main building is constructed in modern style, and is comparable to a pallet upon which layers of traditional gardens are set in formation of a hanging scroll landscape penjing, a miniature of the building from *A Dream of the Red Chamber*. The main building is also a container, at the core of which is a picture of a scroll depicting the "heyday of the Kangxi and Qianlong reign." The scroll is unraveled and surrounds the sculpture of Cao Xueqin in the sinking courtyard. The blended models are created surrounding the 3-in-1 practices of history, art, and architecture in hope of representing the unique artistic conception of the building and unique artistic characteristics of the historical and cultural center of Nanjing.

The museum has a footprint of 18,000-square-meters and a total floor area of 35,000-square-meters. It does not squeeze the urban space with its colossal volume or towering structure but rather adds a stroke of green to the bustling metropolis. From content to form, the museum took root in the local historical and geographical conditions of Nanjing.

The intrinsic cultural is the basis of its form and seeks to be a pertinent reminder of the tradition and world it has come from. New methods and designs were adopted when appropriate (the use of steel structure for the building elevation, modern surface technology, and lighting technologies in representation of brocade mounting approaches). The refrain from using historical architectural symbols when touching upon points of historical interest such as the West Garden, Grand View Garden, and the Mansion of the Imperial Silk Manufacturing Commissioner was important to make the current design feel alive and not dead, traditional, or outdated. The style of the museum remains a regional icon by using historicist understanding with modern architectural implications, technologies, and materials. At a time of globalism and cross-culture movement, international architects have grabbed market in the East. In response, we attempt to push ourselves with this unprecedented new method by blending new-age Chinese elements, with regionalism, historicism, and western modern architectural concepts in the globalized and cross-cultural world.

Left: Constructed photo.

Left: Constructed photo.

2) "New Water and Mountain Landscape City" Practices

Planning and Design of Beijing Olympic Forest Park

Project Area: 680 hectares
Completed In: July 2008
Design Team: Hu Jie, Wu Yixia, Lv Lushan, Zhu Yufan, Yao Yujun, Han Yi, Zhang Jie, Zhang Yan, Liu Hailun, Gao Zhengmin, Su Xinlan, Sun Xiaoming, Guo Zheng, Zhu Hui, Zhao Tingting, Zhao Chunqiu, Zhao Xing

The Beijing Olympic Green, located in the northern part of Beijing's north-central axis, was a centerpiece for the 2008 Olympic Games where most competition venues, including the Olympic Village, the International Broadcasting Center (IBC), and other important facilities, were located. Its southern part was the central area for the Olympics. The most important venues, including the Beijing National Stadium, the Beijing National Aquatics Center, and the Beijing National Indoor Stadium are located there. The northern part is home to the 680-hectare Beijing Olympic Forest Park, which was planned as a sustainable ecological belt nurtured in natural landscape and lush vegetation and a green shelter between the downtown and suburban areas, and is of strategic importance to better urban environment and climate in Beijing. As an important part of the Olympic Green and the largest public park of Beijing, the Olympic Forest Park has been accorded extensive social attention with particular regard to its landscape planning and design.

Different from the sites of previous Olympic Games, the entire Beijing Olympic Green is split by the traditional central axis of Beijing, a city acclaimed as a masterpiece of urban planning and construction. The central axis runs through the Temple of Heaven, Tiananmen Square, and the Forbidden City, all the way to Jingshan, making it among the most impressive and extensive axis in the history of city construction. Historically, the planning layouts of large-scale cities in China are mostly reminiscent of a chessboard, symbolic of the pursuit for order. Gardens in the cities mostly resort to a natural spatial layout, representing the harmony between humanity and nature while indicating respect for the natural land. The master planning of the Beijing Olympic Forest Park, by extending the central axis of the Beijing city to a forest park in the north while meeting the basic function as the Olympic venues, is intended to create a perfect melting away of this matchless urban axis into the woods. In continuation of the concepts of the master plan, this design program is entitled "Axis to Nature." The forest's natural eco-system makes it possible for the central axis, with rich historical connotations, to be lost perfectly into the woods and thus end in a diversified natural landscape.

Beijing Olympic Forest Park is an organic component of the Beijing Olympic Green and an important landscape for the central area of the Olympic Games. It was planned and designed to meet not only the needs of various activities during the Olympics but also the long-term goal of a multi-functional ecological area. During the Olympics, the park was a gift from the city to the athletes and delegations from all countries and IOC officials – a landscape and recreation garden full of Chinese glamour. After the Olympics, this park was opened to the public, becoming a recreational resort for local residents and a rare legacy from the Olympics. The park is of great importance to Beijing in its improvement of the overall ecological environment, urban functions in the northern sectors, qualities of the city, and acceleration of its strides to become an international metropolis, and is, therefore, a natural and cultural legacy in the modern sense.

All in all, the functions of the park are to be a "green lung and ecological shelter of the city, a backyard leisure garden of water and mountain landscape with Chinese glamour, a healthy woodland, and nature's retreat for residents in Beijing."

Awards:

1. First prize of excellence in Landscape Architecture Planning and Design Award from the Chinese Society of Landscape Architecture in October 2011.
2. Green Good Design Award from European Centre for Architecture, Art, Design, and Urban Studies in June 2011.
3. Honor Award at the ASLA Professional Awards-General Design Category in September 2009.
4. President's Award (first prize), 2009 International Federation of Landscape Architects of Asia-Pacific Regional Congress Award in Design Category in August 2009.
5. First prize at the 2007 National Awards for Outstanding Urban/Rural Planning and Design Programs in Urban Planning Category in April 2009.
6. Beijing Olympic Project Outstanding Contribution Award for Implementation of the Concept of "Green Olympics, People's Olympics, and High-tech Olympics" in March 2009.
7. First prize at the Beijing Olympic Project Green Shade Award in March 2009.
8. Beijing Olympic Project Excellence Award for Planning and Design in March 2009.
9. Beijing Olympic Project Special Award for Technology and Innovation with the "Comprehensive Technology and Demonstration Project of Landscape Water Quality Protection in the Beijing Olympic Forest Park" in March 2009.
10. Beijing Olympic Project Excellence Award for Exploration and Design in February 2009.
11. Beijing Olympic Project Comprehensive Achievement Award, Advanced Unit Award and Outstanding Team Award in the Planning Exploration Design and Survey Category in December 2008.
12. President's Award (first prize), 2008 International Federation of Landscape Architects Asia-Pacific Regional Congress Award in Landscape Planning Category in February 2008.
13. First prize, 13th Beijing Excellent Design Project Award in the Planning Category in October 2007.
14. First prize, Torsanlorenzo International Prize in Urban Green Space Section in March 2007.
15. Outstanding prize, International Competition for Beijing Olympic Forest Park and Central Area Master planning in November 2003.

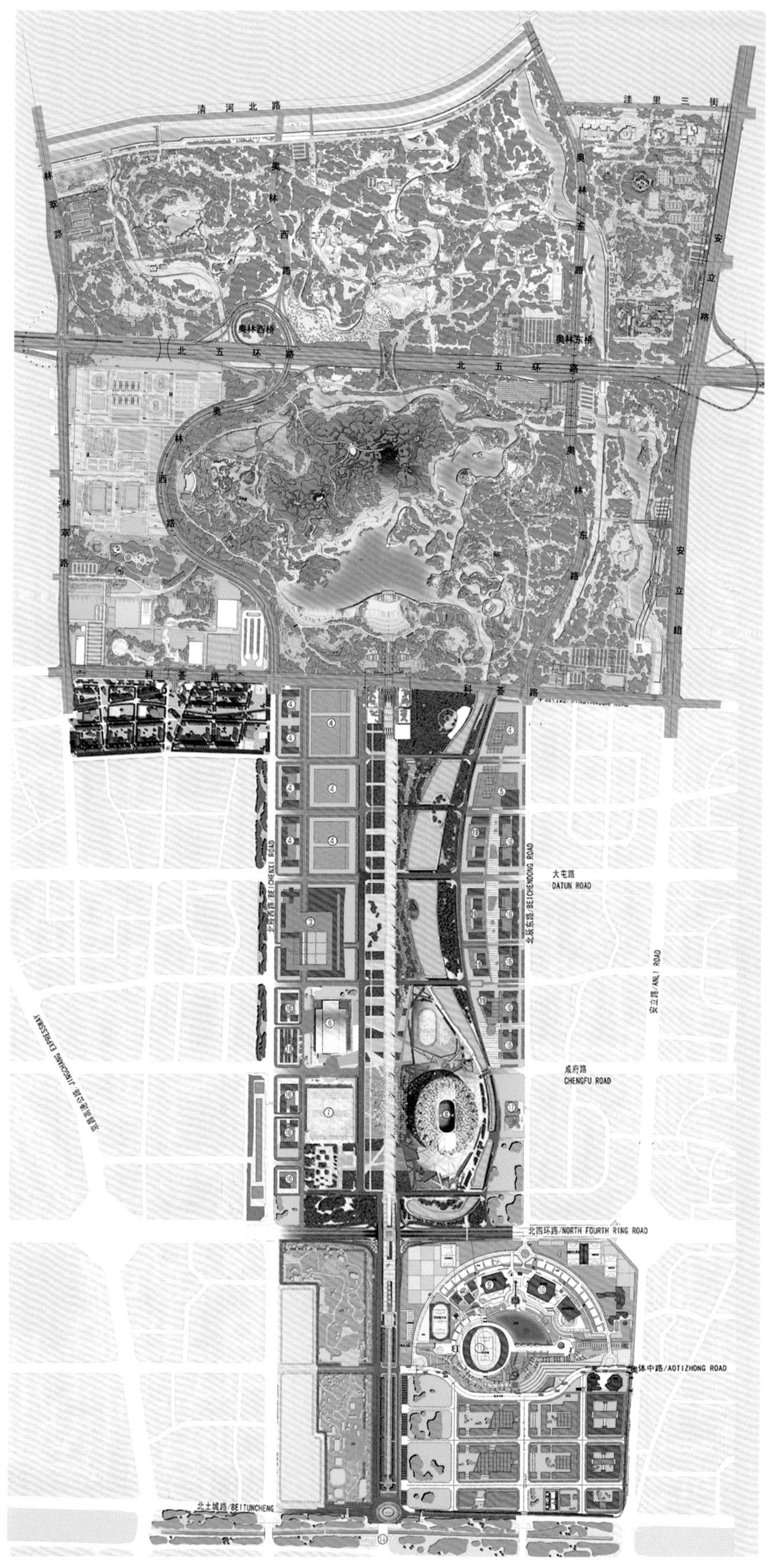

Left: Master plan of Beijing Olympic Park.

Above: Constructed photo.

3) Three-position Theory

Environment Transformation of the Central Area of the Tsinghua Institute of Nuclear and New Energy Technology

Project Area: 0.9 hectare
Completed In: October 2004
Design Team: Zhu Yufan, Yao Yujun, et al.

Tsinghua Institute of Nuclear and New Energy Technology was first built in 1958. The planning setup for its central area exhibits a strong Soviet style: the main building, typical of the Soviet style, is placed in the middle, with the auxiliary buildings lining up on both sides in symmetry. The central axis stands out prominently as the main building 101 reaching out to the South Gate to form a spectacular axial space against the landscape environment.

The environmental transformation of the central area is, in essence, a redesign of the original axial space, and, therefore, all transformative approaches should be based upon understanding of the nature of the axial space. The original setup of the central area of the campus is concise and well grounded, so the key is to sort out and consolidate it systematically on the basis of the structural understanding. The unique historical background of the site and the original juniper enclosure led to the designer's final determination to adopt the Le Notre's axial space as the general blueprint for the environmental transformation while resorting to fundamental strategies of consolidating pool series for enhanced space dramaticism and sequence along the central axle and horizontal axle of the landscape in addition to the original axial space.

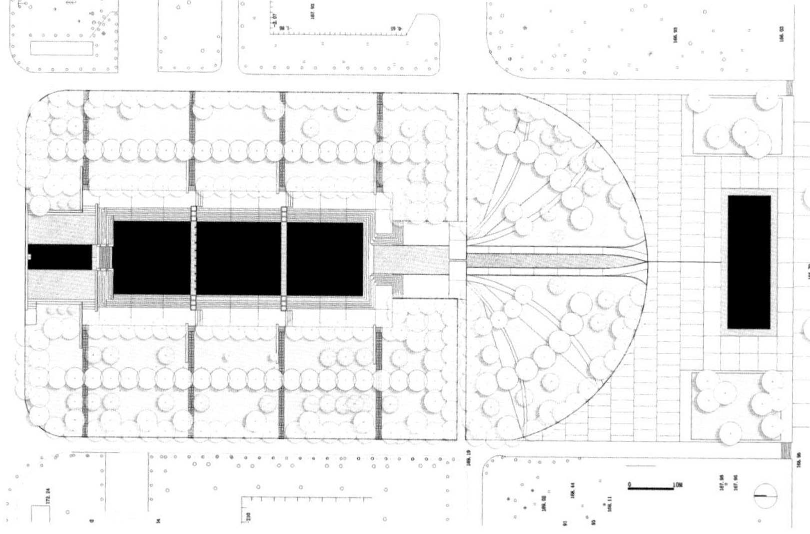

Left: Master plan of the central district of Nuclear Energy and New Energy Technology Institute.

Above: Aerial view of the central district of Nuclear Energy and New Energy Technology Institute.

Above: The autumn leaves were all over the ground.

Above: Mirror surface pool. **Above:** Penetrative relationship of the space of the wooden lands at both sides and the axis.

Landscape Design of National Patriotism Education Base in Qinghai Atomic City

Project Area: 11.16 hectares
Completed In: June 2009
Design Team: Zhu Yufan, Yao Yujun, Guo Yong, Yang Zhanzhan, Liu Jing, Zhang Zhenwei, Wang Dan, Tang Jianren, Li Shuo, Sun Yu, Wang Peibo (sculpture), Du Hongyu (sculpture), Li Fujun (sculpture)

The Memorial Park of the National Patriotism Education Base in Qinghai Atomic City is located in the southeast corner of the center of Xihai Town. Except for the west side, where the Haibei Branch of the Qinghai Provincial Tabacco Corporation is stationed, the park is surrounded by roads on all three sides: the east-west running Yuanzi Road in the north, which used to be the oldest and most important trunk road of the former Factory 211; Menyuan Section of the Provincial Highway 310 in the east; and Tongbao Road leading directly to the Haibei Prefecture Government in the south, approximately 400 meters south were the National Highway 305 links the Qinghai Lake with the provincial capital, Xining. Right upon entering Xihai Town from the National Highway, you will be greeted with the magnificent view of the Memorial Park buildings. In terms of subject matter and siting, the Memorial Park is a landmark. On a land plot 560 meters long on the north and south sides and 200 meters on the east and west sides, the park occupies a total land area of 12 square km. It has a total floor area of 8,400 square meters and a total exterior environment area of 11.16 square-km. The master plan has gone through several revisions. Due to investment budget restrictions, the planned southern boundary was downsized from north National Highway 305 to Tongbao Road, with a corresponding reduction in the total construction area from 20,000-square-meters to 9,615-square-meters. However, no substantive changes were made to the overall layout except the footage and the construction area on different versions of the master plan. The buildings are placed in the south-central area of the site, dividing the entire park space into three sections: Southern Square, Memorial Hall, and Memorial Park.

Above: Pool and "in the remote area."

Above: The "mail box" story statue and the "couple woodland."

Above: Entrance square and memorial sculpture.

By setting a zigzag path, the designer restudied and reorganized the status space and the design space in attempt to protect and use the poplars on site as carriers of the genius loci. The path is an ideal, seamless connection between it and the linear representation of China's independence in developing an atomic and hydrogen bomb.

Another important feature of the pendulum layout of the Memorial Park is the visual relationship between the points along the path and the museum. The path is independent and unique. Walking on the path, the viewer is reminded of the destination as it is looming in the distance. There is no straight shot to the destination though; you must walk the winding path, and only when you finish can you reach the destination. The zigzag is an important metaphor in the case of Atomic City, intended to inform later generations of Path 596 – China's path of independent development of an atomic and hydrogen bomb that began in June 1959, was full of difficulties and hardships, but carried on by the hope and steadfast belief in the cause that kept everyone in line.

Award:
2010 National Landscape Award from the British Association of Landscape Industries (BALI).

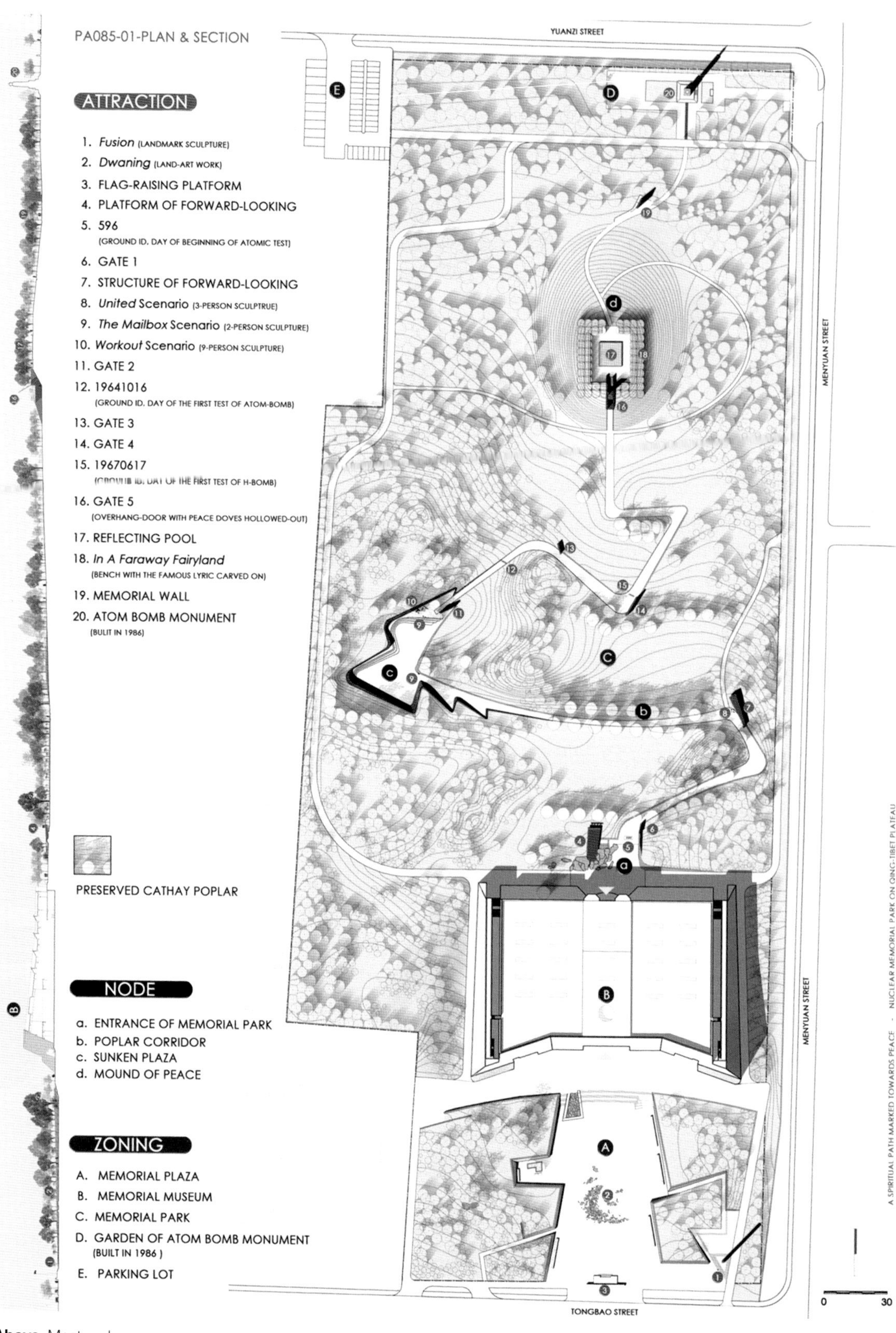

Above: Master plan.

4) The Art of Design

Mémorial de l'Abolition de l'Esclavage (Memorial to the Abolition of Slavery)

Completed In: March 2012
Design Team: Wodiczko+Bonder, Ron Henderson & L+A Landscape Architecture

Mémorial de l'Abolition de l'Esclavage (Memorial to the Abolition of Slavery) is a national memorial park whose design was commissioned by Jean-Marc Ayrault, previously deputy and mayor of Nantes and the 19th Prime Minister of France. Wodiczko+Bonder was awarded the project after winning an international design competition. Ron Henderson and his studio, L+A Landscape Architecture, were the landscape consultants for the competition. This project involved the physical transformation of 350 meters of the coast of the Loire in the center of the city of Nantes. It provides space and means for remembering the slave trade, commemorates the resistance and abolitionist struggle, and reminds visitors of the continued struggle against modern-day slavery. As a political, urban, artistic, landscape, and architectural project, this new public space is intended to become an agent and catalyst for transformative action, human rights activism, and civic engagement. Meanwhile, this project also responds to the Loire embankment space built during the 18th, 19th, and 20th centuries.

Award:

1. Shortlisted for the European Union Prize for Contemporary Architecture, the Mies van der Rohe Award 2013.
2. Special mention in the biennial European Prize for Urban Public Space (Spain) in 2012.
3. Honor Award for Design Excellence, Boston Society of Architects, 2012 (USA).
4. First prize in Architecture and Planning, 2012 Biannual Award of Central Architect Association and Professional Committee (Argentina).

Above: Memorial space, night scene, and memorial crowd.

Gardens at the Isabella Stewart Gardner Museum

Completed In: 2012
Design Team: Ron Henderson & L+A Landscape Architecture, Renzo Piano Building Workshop

Gardens at the Gardner Museum on the Back Bay Fens in Boston cover a total area of 1,100 square meters and are composed of six exquisite gardens of herbal and woody plants: the public entrance on Evans Way, Jordan Garden (outside the Living Room), Achtmeyer Terrace Garden (outside Café G off of Palace Road), Monk's Garden, Lynch Garden, and the new public conservatory, which allow visitors to experience the centrality of gardens arts at the Museum.

When Isabella Gardner opened her doors to the public on New Years' Eve 1903, in the words of Norma Jean Calderwood, the director of the Museum at the time, "she presented a new context for art in America by creating a museum where visitors experienced music, the beauty of gardens, and historic and contemporary art, all in the highly personal setting of her courtyard palace."

The new wing is situated to the west and is connected to the original building by a glass-enclosed corridor. Visitors no longer enter the Museum through the old gate facing the Back Bay Fens but through a new entrance facing Evans Way Park. The design of the Museum's new wing incorporates glass and natural light to create an open and welcoming entrance while alleviating the threat posed by thousands of visitors every year moving across the old building. The colorless glass walls on the ground level include public spaces for people to gather, and offer a transparent reading of the Palace, lined with two groves of gingko trees. The transparency stands in stark contrast with the original heavy brick walls. Strictly selected plant species make marvelous gardens. The design also extends the growing museum from the greenhouse to the gardens. Bamboo poles are placed to help the small upright lacebark elms retain their regular spacing and beautiful vertical form echo perfectly with the linear layout of the Museum designed by Renzo Piano. Two terraced gardens—Café Garden on the north side and the Living Room Garden on the south—abut the museum. In the Monk's Garden on the south side, a high platform was built as the horizontal extension of the museum veranda. There is an east-west meandering path on the sloping bank between the high platform and the high brick walls of the museum. Blueberry bushes were planted on both the platform and the sloping bank, with a total area of 650 square meters, to expand surface area and offer elegant branches, edible jam, red leaves in autumn, and red intricate stems in winter.

Ron Henderson's first collaboration with the museum was 15 years ago when he and the Museum's chief gardener designed the winter exhibition of the Museum gardens.

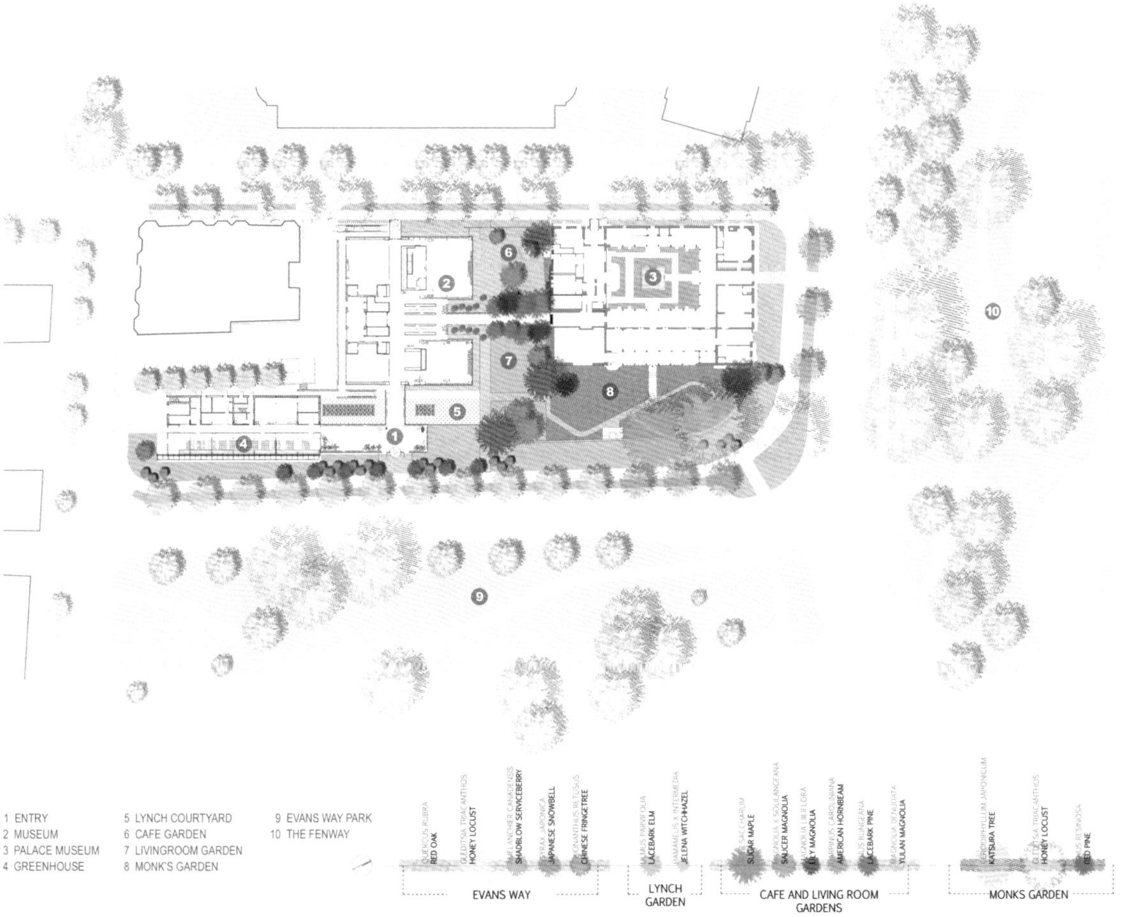

1 ENTRY
2 MUSEUM
3 PALACE MUSEUM
4 GREENHOUSE
5 LYNCH COURTYARD
6 CAFE GARDEN
7 LIVINGROOM GARDEN
8 MONK'S GARDEN
9 EVANS WAY PARK
10 THE FENWAY

QUERCUS RUBRA RED OAK
GLEDITSIA TRIACANTHOS HONEY LOCUST
SHADBLOW SERVICEBERRY
JAPANESE SNOWBELL
CHINESE FRINGETREE
EVANS WAY

LACEBARK ELM
HAMAMELIS X INTERMEDIA JELENA WITCHHAZEL
LYNCH GARDEN

SUGAR MAPLE
SAUCER MAGNOLIA
LILY MAGNOLIA
AMERICAN HORNBEAM
LACEBARK PINE
YULAN MAGNOLIA
CAFE AND LIVING ROOM GARDENS

KATSURA TREE
HONEY LOCUST
RED PINE
MONKS GARDEN

Above: Master plan.

Above: Constructed photo.

5) Design Based on the Water System and Cultural Contexts

Landscape Design for Shengyin Yuan of Tsinghua University

Project Area: 1 hectare
First Opened In: July 2012
Project Team: Liu Hailong, Li Jinchen, Zhang Danming, Xie Henan, Sun Xiaoming, Chen Linlin, et al.

Above: Couple John Mo was at the front of their residence in Shengyin Yuan in the 1950s.

Shengyin Yuan, a residential complex of Tsinghua University, is a historical spot on campus for its rustic, friendly, and vibrant features and for having once been the residence of some of Tsinghua's most distinguished scholars. In recent years, a number of factors have led to the dilapidation of its buildings and environment, and gradual disappearance of its historical ambience and humanistic flavor in large part due to serious waterlogging during heavy rains. After the centennial celebration of Tsinghua University, it was incorporated into the campus planning as the office site of the School of Humanities and Social Sciences, thus embracing an opportunity for protective renovation. The focus of the landscape design of Shengyin Yuan is the excavation of its genius loci, the representation of its history, and a solution to the waterlogging problem. With in-depth research on the history of Shengyin Yuan and the evolution of its environment and comprehensive analyses of the pre-renovation physical conditions, together with feedback collected from the public and experts, the design team proposed that Shengyin Yuan be positioned as a memorial site – a venue for education of school history, a research area with distinctive features, and a living demonstration of Tsinghua's "green university" campaign. With these objectives, the team proposed spatial sequences, functional transformation, cultural symbols, rainwater management, and botanic decoration strategies. They completed systematic landscape design and construction plans, with a focused, in-depth design of the Memorial Square and the Garden on the axial line, the rainwater garden and ecological infiltration system for all the courtyards, and a series of uniform and diverse wooden platforms as small outdoor communication spaces. The new design gave Shengyin Yuan a new spatial structure and sequence, a rainwater management system capable of handling 24-hour rainstorms every two years, a distinctive cultural symbol of its own, and rich and attractive space for the new research office functions and local residents. The design explored the possibility of landscape design oriented towards runoff management through architectural and landscape renovations on historical sites.

Above: Old photo of Shengyin Yuan.

Above: Constructed photo

3.3 Landscape Planning and Ecological Restoration

Theoretical study and practice in the field of Landscape Planning at Tsinghua LA is a continuation and expansion of traditional subjects such as classical gardens, historical sites, and in recent years, world heritage sites.(1) It also breaks ground in areas such as urban-rural water systems and green space planning, brownfield regeneration, resorts design, large city gardens, and bio-diversity preservation. Tsinghua LA responds to the needs of the times, especially those in the field of urbanization, heritage protection, and ecological civilization. A prominent feature of the department is its increased emphasis on natural sciences in teaching, research, and practice, particularly in landscape ecology, landscape hydrology, landscape geoscience, and geographical information courses. Brownfield regeneration of abandoned industrial, mining, and landfill sites, together with the rehabilitation of urban water systems and flood management have become emerging priorities for Tsinghua LA.

Historical Contribution

Although landscape planning has gradually developed into a primary subject in the evolution of modern landscape architecture, it is a subject of learning and practice with a long history in China. For its vast territory, environmental diversity, multiple ethnic origins, and abundant natural resources, China has a long-standing farming, irrigation, domicile, and city construction culture. Taking account of China's rich history, culture, architecture, landscape theories, natural environment and water and mountain aesthetics, Tsinghua LA has worked to create and enrich traditional landscape planning over the years.

Studies in the field of landscape planning at the Tsinghua Department of LA are closely related to cultural tradition and the larger natural context in China. Professor Zhou Weiquan placed the abiding and highly sophisticated Chinese system of classical gardens against the backdrop of vast and varying land in his book *A History of Classical Chinese Gardens* (1990). In another book, *Landscape, Scenery and Architecture* (2006), he stressed that the garden culture, water and mountain culture, and architectural culture of China are inseparable from each other. Professor Lou Qingxi also pointed out in his book *Ten Lectures on Vernacular Landscape* (2012) that vernacular architecture forms a landscape with rich cultural connotation, when combined with the traditional concepts of heaven and earth, water and mountains, and vegetation. Different from the private and imperial gardens and the vernacular cultural landscapes, which are often small-scale, famous mountains and major rivers are a better embodiment of the large-scale characteristics of great landscape.

Among the traditional scenic sites in China, the majority are associated with mountains. "Water and mountain" is often used to refer to natural landscapes, which is reminiscent of the close relations between natural landscapes and mountains. Professor Zhou Weiquan pointed out in his book *Famous Mountain Scenic Spots in China* (1996) that China is the first country in the world to see mountains as scenic resources and as tourism and sightseeing resorts. Many famous mountains are also considered sacred in Buddhism and Taoism, and categorized as both natural and cultural heritage sites. For this reason, the operation and development of famous mountain scenic areas in the past are considered reflections of the great feats of landscape planning in ancient China. Landscape architecture research at Tsinghua has long been conducted under the guiding principle of approaching the landscape from the garden realm, upholding the ancient research methodology of "entirety and association."

Urban Water System and Green Space Planning

Watershed planning, planning and design of water systems, and river courses are important components of landscape planning. This has long been on the development agenda of Tsinghua LA. In 1991, the Tsinghua School of Architecture was entrusted to conduct an urban landscape plan and design for the area covering both sides of the Changhe River and Kunyu Section of the Jingmi Channel by the Capital Planning and Construction Committee. The research, planning, and design were based on an analysis of the history, cultural relics, and waterside activities of the water course and banking areas in combination with the existing urban plan, water conservancy, road, tourism, and garden plans. An evaluation of the Changhe River was also conducted in order to understand the relationship between the city and river in Beijing's water systems.

In 2003, following the establishment of the Department of LA, Landscape Hydrology was added to the curriculum in an attempt to extend the teaching and research scope to water and water-related planning and design from a perspective of landscape as a comprehensive natural and cultural system. In 2006 Tsinghua University set up a multi-disciplinary team to conduct the Architectural Environment Planning for the Central Route of the South-to-North Water Diversion Project, which included in-depth research on the impact of water conservancy projects on human settlement environments. In 2012 a Tsinghua team undertook the water system restoration and human settlement development project for Jiangbei District of Fuzhou City. Based on an integrated research methodology the team reviewed the history and culture of the water systems in Fuzhou, the watershed hydrological process, population and transportation accessibility, water system status quo, and restoration, and integrated various plans related to the water systems before conducting research, planning, and design of the macro watershed, meso sub-watershed, and micro river bank spaces. The emphasis was on providing solutions in flood prevention and drainage; water quality enhancement; blueway, greenway, and slow systems; historical and cultural skeleton; citizen activity space; and public facilities.

The Tsinghua Urban Planning and Design Institute, as the practice platform of Tsinghua LA, undertook many projects in the field of water systems. The areas of focus were twofold. One focus was integrated urban river and lake system projects such as Urban Water System Landscape Planning for Fanhe New City of Tieling (built), Tangshan Nanhu Eco-City Central Park Overall Planning & Design (built), Shijiazhuang Exterior Ring Water System and the Surrounding Area Concept Planning, and Duolunnao'er Urban Water System Landscape Planning. The second focus was maritime waterfront projects such as the Landscape Planning and Design of the Yuelianghe River, the Longwan New District of Huludao (built), and North China drought zone urban river course projects, which included the Xihe River Course Landscape Planning, Yulong New District, Fuxin City (partially built), and Eco-Rehabilitation Landscape Planning of Beidahe River, Jiuquan City, Gansu Province.

Wudalianchi International Low-Carbon Eco-Tourism Demo Town Planning and Design was an active attempt made to approach tourist resort planning and design from a landscape system perspective. The project covers concept planning, detail planning, urban design, demo residential landscape planning, farm, new zone, and old town landscape rehabilitation sites in order to address the volcanic resources, the regional culture, and tourism development. The intact systematic green and open space, and water system planning are among the most prominent features of project.

Tourist Resorts

Tourist resort planning is another new subject for landscape planning in China. Tsinghua LA addressed the issue early on and has gained momentum. In July of 1992, Tsinghua University was commissioned by the Sanya Municipal Government and Urban Planning Bureau in Hainan Province to undertake the Sanya National Tourist Resort Planning with the intention of advancing the protection and development of the Yalong Bay in order to develop Sanya into an international, first-class seaside resort.

In 2007, the Tsinghua team won an International competition for the Longmenshan Mountain Resort, Chengdu, Sichuan and created the strategic planning, concept planning, and planning of the tourism functional areas for the site. The objective was to develop Longmenshan (4,133 square kilometers), with its rich natural and cultural heritage resources, into an international and domestically acclaimed mountain resort. It will have distinctive seasonal features for living and tourism conditions with an eco-economy demo zone at the state level, industrial development zone of Chengdu with balanced urban and rural developments, and conservation and utilization areas.

To meet the development needs of China's tourism industry and provide guidance, the National Tourism Administration called upon the Department of LA at Tsinghua University to develop the service quality of tourist resorts and to promote development and protection of the holiday tourism resources in China. In 2006, Tsinghua LA conducted extensive research on the domestic market and set down the National Criterion of Tourist Resorts Rating to steer and upgrade the development of tourist resorts in China in line with the transition of the tourism industry from being sightseeing-focused to resort-oriented. This criterion was based on written and technical standards both in China and abroad, relevant laws, rules and regulations of tourism administrations, and relevant national standards. The Tsinghua LA team further studied the management and implementation of the criterion. In 2010, again called on by the National Tourism Administration, the Tsinghua team accomplished the compilation of key terms related to tourism for A Dictionary of Chinese Tourism. This is a fundamental project for the science of tourism and a key project used as reference for tourism development practices, the outcome of which have become basic tools for tourism researchers, practitioners, and management authorities, and is a useful reference for tourists and the general public.

Brownfield Regeneration and Ecological Restoration

Brownfield regeneration has become an important subject in the field of landscape architecture in China, and Tsinghua LA has played a leading role in both academic research and practice. Zheng Xiaodi's doctoral dissertation *Landscape Strategies for Brownfield Regeneration based on the Concept of "Brown Earth-Work"* won the First Level Award for Excellent Doctoral Dissertation at Tsinghua University. She has been published in on this subject in both Chinese and English professional journals, including *Topos*, *Chinese Landscape Architecture*, *LA+*, *Architectural Journal*, *Environmental Engineering*, *China City Planning Review*, *Landscape Architecture Frontiers*, and *Beijing Planning Review*. In collaboration with Professor Niall Kirkwood at Harvard University, the first International Conference on Brownfield Regeneration and Ecological Restoration (ICBRER) was held at Tsinghua University in 2016 with the theme of "Brownfield Regeneration and Healthy Cities." It is the first international conference with multi-discipline and multi-professional participation in China's landscape architecture field that considers brownfield regeneration as the main topic. In 2018, the second ICBRER was held in collaboration with China Sustainable Environmental Remediation Conference, making an impact outside of the LA discipline and strengthening the collaboration with the profession of environmental remediation. Zheng Xiaodi's research team has also received two national funds from China's Natural Science Foundation to conduct research on regional strategies of brownfield regeneration.

In practice, Tsinghua LA's faculty members have also worked on award winning brownfield regeneration projects. Chenshan Quarry, in Shanghai, was the relic of an abandoned 100-year-old artificial quarry. From 2000 to 2004, the Municipal Government of Shanghai and the Songjiang District Government made continual renovations on the fencing and risk prevention works and later provided comprehensive geological and environmental rehabilitation to the quarry to turn it into part of the Shanghai Chenshan Botanic Garden. In this Quarry Garden, Zhu Yufan adopted the "subtraction" design strategy of minimum intervention based on analysis of the historical, natural, and spatial conditions of the site, to avoid artificial traces as much as possible by using rusty steel plates and stone walls as a reminder of its industrial history, and by creating an oriental water and mountain landscape.[(2)] This project won the Honor Award of the general design category of the 2012 ASLA Professional Awards.

Tangshan Nanhu Central Park is another exemplary project. The project site is located one kilometer to the south of Tangshan, and has an extensive subsidence area underground as a result of over 100 years of mining and it being a dump and a sewage outlet for Tangshan. Invited by Tangshan Municipal Government, the Landscape Architecture Center of Tsinghua Tongheng Urban Planning and Design Institute designed Nanhu Central Park to clean up the site, to create open space for local residents, and to encourage city development in the surrounding areas. The vision also addressed how to move from the technical side of wetland reutilization and soil reclamation to urban ecosystem and sustainable development so as to use the Nanhu site as a catalyst for future strategy and development of urban space creation in Tangshan. This project provides theoretical and practical reference for resource depleted cities and gives a blueprint for smart and efficient urban development.

Others

Large city parks, as a subject matter of landscape planning within the scope of cities, are also a priority for the Tsinghua landscape architecture programs. Some research is closely related to important events of the country. A good example of this is the Olympic Forest Park planned and designed by the Tsinghua LA team. It is located at the north-end of the Olympic Green, occupying a land area of 680 hectares – an important site of the 2008 Beijing Olympics Games. At the north end of the central south-north axis of Beijing, it is the largest city park in Beijing and a green belt that acts as a shelter between downtown Beijing and its outskirts.

The Tsinghua LA team conducted studies on the bio-diversity protection for perspective landscape plans. In the master plan for the Jianfengling National Rain Forest Park, completed in 1993, there was controversy over the contradiction between the conservation of the rain forest eco-system and the local socio-economic development of the largest existing and most intact virgin rain forest in China. The planning covered scale, structure, land use arrangements, road systems, tourist accommodation facilities, sightseeing routes, and tourist activities. At the basic scientific research aspect, Li Shuhua obtained financial support from the National Natural Science Foundation to conduct studies on urban green island flora and fauna distribution and diversity, and ecological benefits of the urban green belts.

Tsinghua LA closely follows the latest international developments in landscape planning. The department has published a series of translated papers and books, including *Landscape Urbanism,*(3) *Cities and Natural Process,*(4) and *Smart Cities.*

-Liu Hailong and Zheng Xiaodi

1) Township and Water System Planning

Summer Palace-Shichahai & Yuyuantan Water System Planning and Design

Project Area: 24.16 km^2
First Opened In: February 1992
Project Leader: Zhu Zixuan, Zheng Guangzhong, Yang Rui
Project Team: Huang Lei, Zhong Ge, Zhou Dongguang, Lv Xufei, Wei Xiaomei

Entrusted by the Beijing Capital Commission of Urban Planning, the Department of Urban Planning, School of Architecture, Tsinghua University created the landscape planning and design for the Changhe River and the Kunyu Section of the Jingmi Channel in September 1991. The Y-shape river-course runs southward from the southern end of the Kunming Lake inside the Summer Palace to the Zhongmai Bridge where it splits into two tributaries, one heading southeast along the south Changhe River to Shichahai via the Northern Moat and the other south along the Jingmi Channel to the Yuyuantan Lake. It flows from the northwest suburbs directly into the inner city of Beijing. The plan covers 300 to 500 meters on either riverbank.

The planning began with an analysis of the river-course: its history, heritage sites, and riverside activities. Studies further addressed the natural issues that arise from the Changhe River, the relationship between the city and the river, and land use and urban landscape of the existing river systems in Beijing in relation to water conservancy, roads, tourism, and landscape planning. The following areas were targeted based on this research: protection and use of the valuable water surface in support of capital construction; strengthening of the spatial connection between the city and the landscape areas in the northwest suburbs; and provision of recreational resorts for local residents.

Concepts addressed in the planning included: different styles for the two water systems; landscapes with different features; diversified forms of space enclosure; openness; accessibility; and the rhythm of the layout. The land use plans were developed with a specialized urban landscape, road layout, green space, scenic areas, spot plans, and node design.

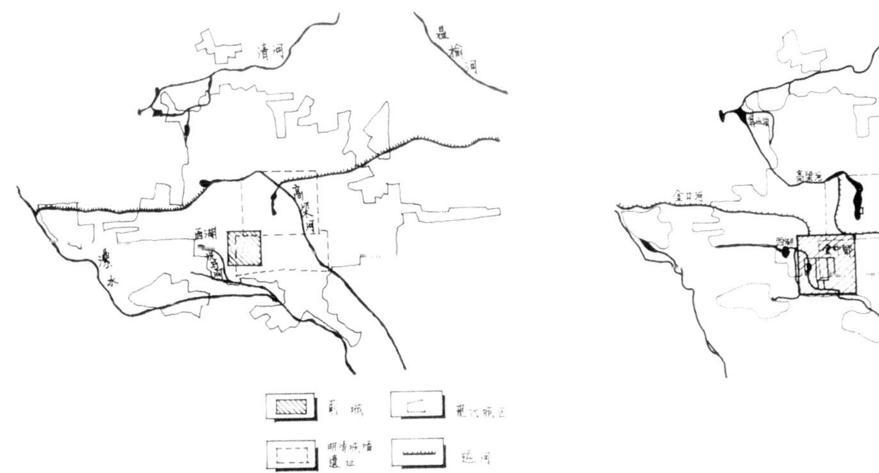

Above: Water system of Ji City in Zhou-Tang Dynasty.

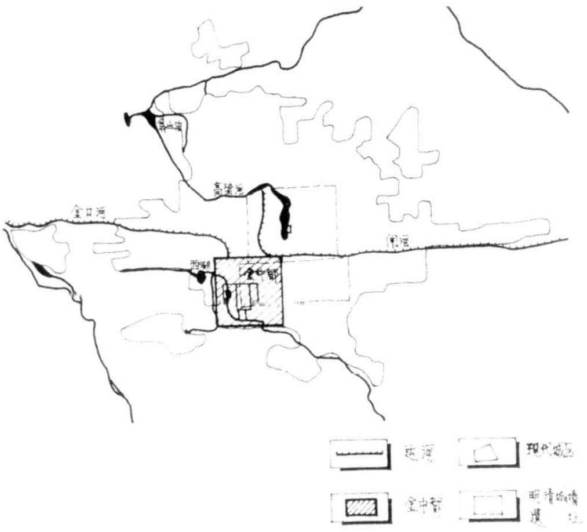

Above: Water system of Jinzhongdu City.

Above: Master plan of the green space system.

Left: Master plan of the land use.

Left: Master plan of the landscape nodes and the view corridors.

Architectural Environment Planning for the Central Route of the South-to-North Water Diversion Project

Project Time: June 2006–August 2008
Project Supervisor: Wu Liangyong
Landscape Supervisor: Zhu Yufan

From June 2006 to August 2008, Tsinghua University conducted the architectural environment planning for the Central Route of the South-to-North Water Diversion Project, which is a world-class mega water diversion project covering a central route 1,432 kilometers in length, costing over 150 billion RMB yuan in investment for the principal part of the project, and involving approximately 2,000 buildings along the route. The land-demanding project features a long route, challenging projects, heavy investment, dense heritage sites, and tremendous impact on urban-rural space development. The architectural environment planning was conducted to coordinate the relationship between design planning, construction, and management, and to improve the conditions between this water conservation project and local ecology, economy, community, and culture. To accomplish this highly complicated planning and design project, Tsinghua University formed a "scientific community" composed of urban planners, architects, landscape, environmentalists, culture and heritage protection experts, and space and information technology. The team conducted field visits along the project route, explored the scientific methodologies of reductionism and holism, made integrated research and design plans from engineering and science-based perspectives, and surveyed individuals living along the route to ensure the desirable usage of the planning outcomes. This project applied the theories of the human settlement science, which laid a firm basis for the actualization of the requirement of the State Council for "harmony between Man and Nature through well-coordinated construction" and "a world-class water diversion project matched with world-class above-ground architectural environment." It provided a typical case for study of the impact of mega projects in China and around the world on human settlements, acting as a demonstration of environmental architecture creation and human settlement construction for the growing number of mega infrastructure projects being undertaken in China.

Awards:
1. First prize in the Beijing Awards for Outstanding Urban/Rural Planning and Design Programs (2011).
2. Third prize in the National Awards for Outstanding Urban/Rural Planning and Design Programs (2011).

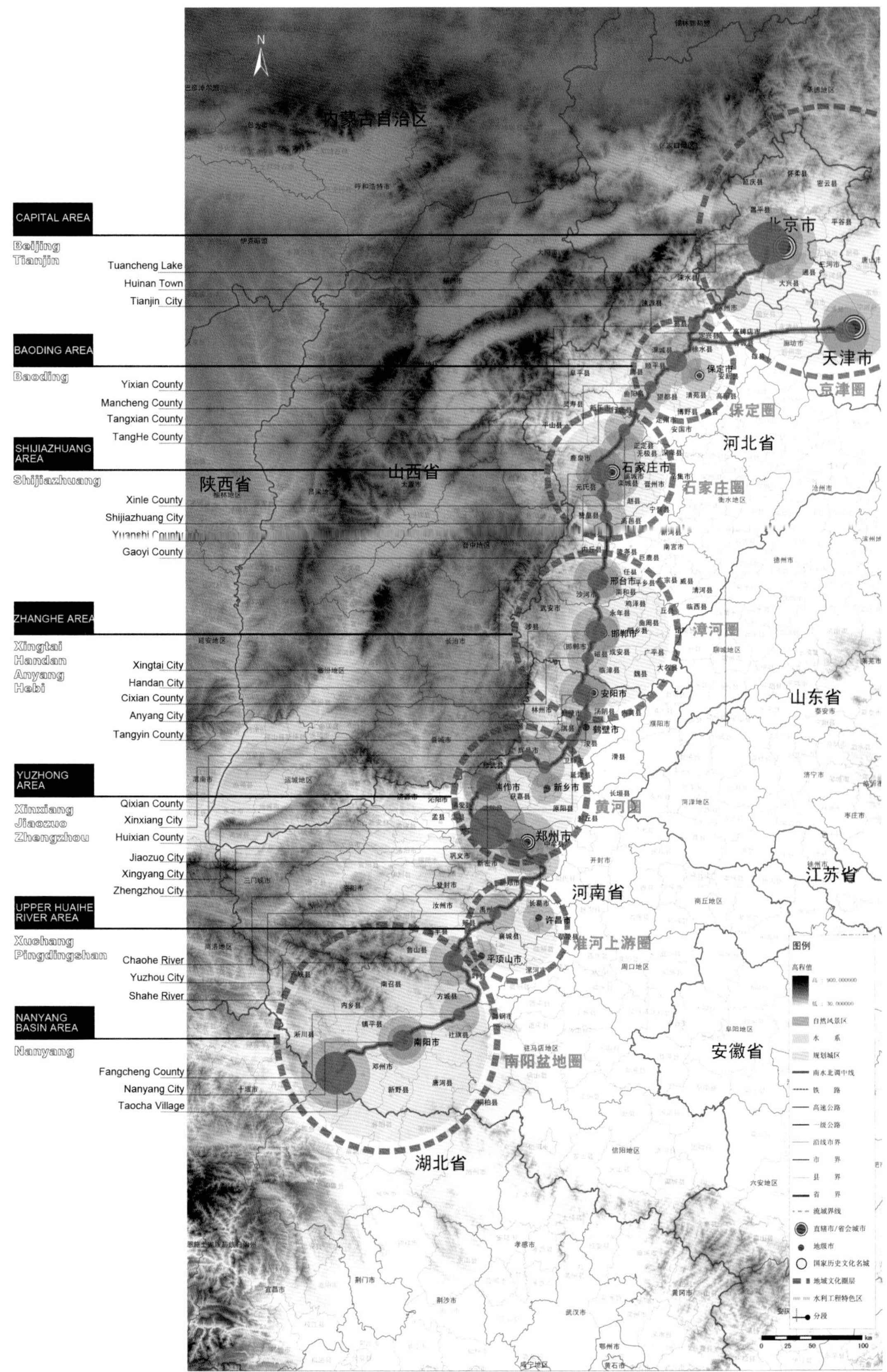

Above: Landscape node construction of the main route of the middle route project of the south to north water diversion.

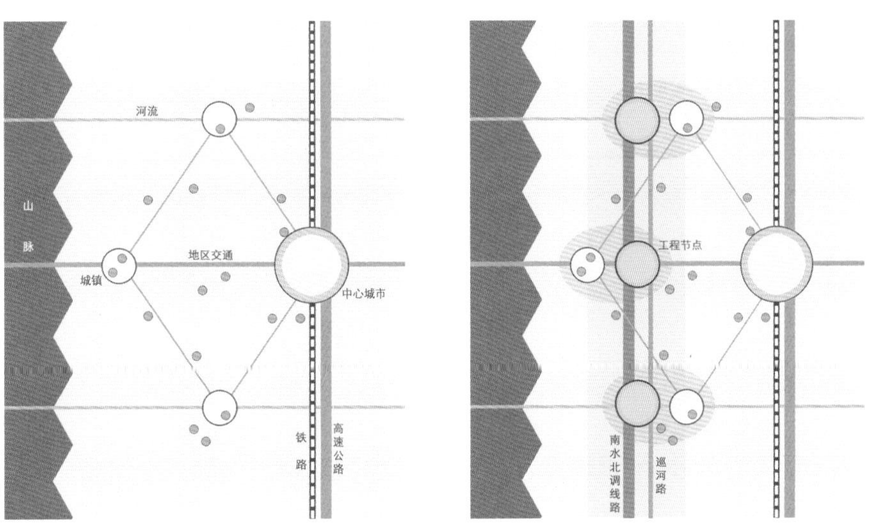

Above: Middle route project of the south to north water diversion and the change of the regional space structure.

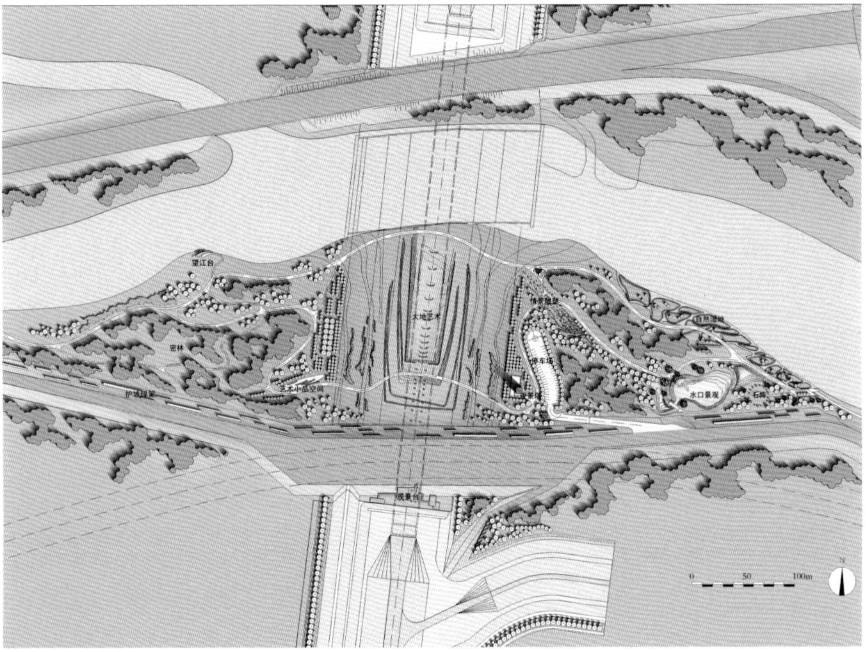

Above: Schematic diagram of the landscape planning and design of Shijiazhuang's old canal hub.

2) Tourist Resorts

Master planning of Yalong Bay National Resort

Project Area: About 18.2 km^2
First Opened In: 1992
Project Team: Zheng Guangzhong, Bian Lanchun, Yang Rui
Project Adviser: Zhu Zixuan

Yalong Bay, located within Sanya City in Hainan Province, is recognized both in China and abroad for its picturesque scenery and unique natural landscape. As one of 11 national tourist resorts in China, it occupies a prominent place in the planning for a major tourism system for the Hainan Island. In July 1992 the Municipal Government of Sanya, through the Sanya Bureau of Urban Planning, entrusted Tsinghua University with the task of planning for this national tourist resort, with the focus on facilitation, protection, and development of Yalong Bay.

According to the Sanya Tourism Regional Planning board, there are 19 scenic areas and natural reserves as well as 115 scenic spots within the 8,100-square-kilometer, fan-shaped area north of Sanya. The multitude of scenic areas forms a competitive edge in terms of scale, effectively pushing tourism development forward in the entire region with Yalong Bay as the flagship. The Yalong Bay National Resort is an first-class winter resort featuring a tropical marine landscape, southern Chinese customs and culture in the 18.2-square-kilometer area enclosed by the coastline in the south, the east Haiyu Highway to the north, the Moon Lake east of the area, and the Hongguang Reservoir to the west.

Through an analysis of the strengths and restriction factors, a landscape resource evaluation and visual space analysis, market demand forecast, and strategic objectives for development, the project team set down the following as guiding principles for the planning of the Yalong Bay National Resort:

(1) Regionalism. It is used to enhance the unique textual atmosphere, architectural style, and sightseeing activities through studied planning of different resort types and styles and an in-depth investigation of the local resources, environment, social, and economic conditions.

(2) Ecology. It is fundamental that development be carried out with the effective protection and conservation of the local natural resources in mind. The planning was done on the basis of investigation of the characteristics and mechanism of the resort area to determine what approaches and measures to implement in order to manage the relationship between conservation and development so as to maintain ecological balance of the resort area and coordinated development of factors within the ecological system.

(3) Elasticity. Planning theories and technologies at a given time are

restricted, so under the condition of limited time and material, there is no once-for-all planning for any resort, however, landscape resources belong to all generations, and once destroyed can hardly be restored, therefore, enough room was left in development to make it possible for future generations to update and alter the design according to the time. China is currently working to reform and open its doors. The socialist market economy is destined to have tremendous impact on the planning of tourist resorts and it is highly probable that unforeseeable contingencies will occur during the development process. It is essential that some elasticity should be maintained with regard to the target and timeframe of the construction.

(4) Sustainability. The current priorities are sustainable and coordinated economic, environmental, and social development of the tourist resorts. It is expected that the planning pay due attention to research in this field as development proceeds. While ensuring sustainable development, stability, and prosperity for the entire planned area, the planner shall carefully study problems related to each stage, and particularly to site selection, development priorities, investment orientation, and the development model and mechanism for the initial stage, so that optimal benefits might be attained for each.

(5) Hierarchy. Hierarchy and integration are factors that cannot be overstressed. The planning target is a system composed of a number of subsystems – scenic spots and the sightseeing systems, environment and the ecosystem, infrastructure, visitor facilities, and resident social and economic structure. To be of practical maneuverability, the planning needs to be seen as a hierarchy of systematic research, planning, and implementation moving from one to the other as procedure.

In accordance with the characteristics of step-by-step development and construction, the planning schemes should resort to the point-line-surface model, that is, taking nodes as the core and the road system as the skeleton and filling the entire resort with relatively independent clusters of villas and holiday houses. The planning concept is to structure the center for public activities as the township, and the holiday house and villa clusters as villages.

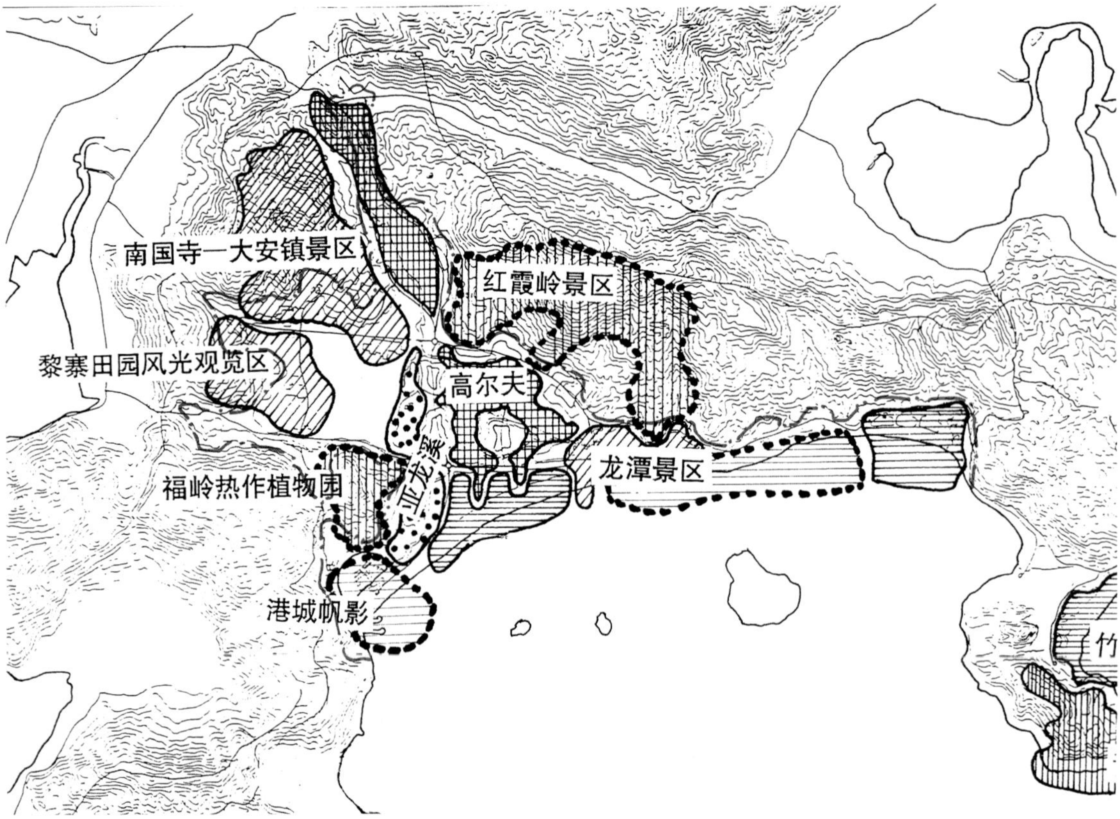

Above: Master plan of the tourism landscape.

Above: Master plan of the transportation system.

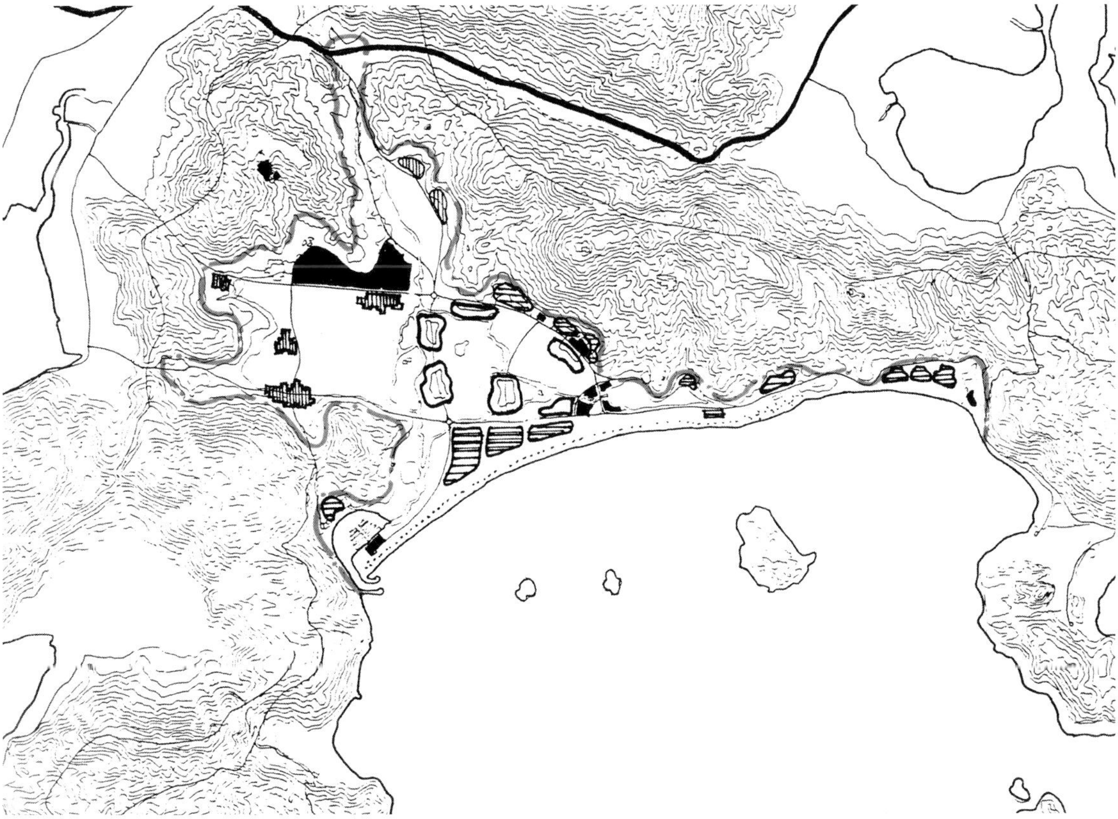

Above: Master plan of the tourism infrastructure.

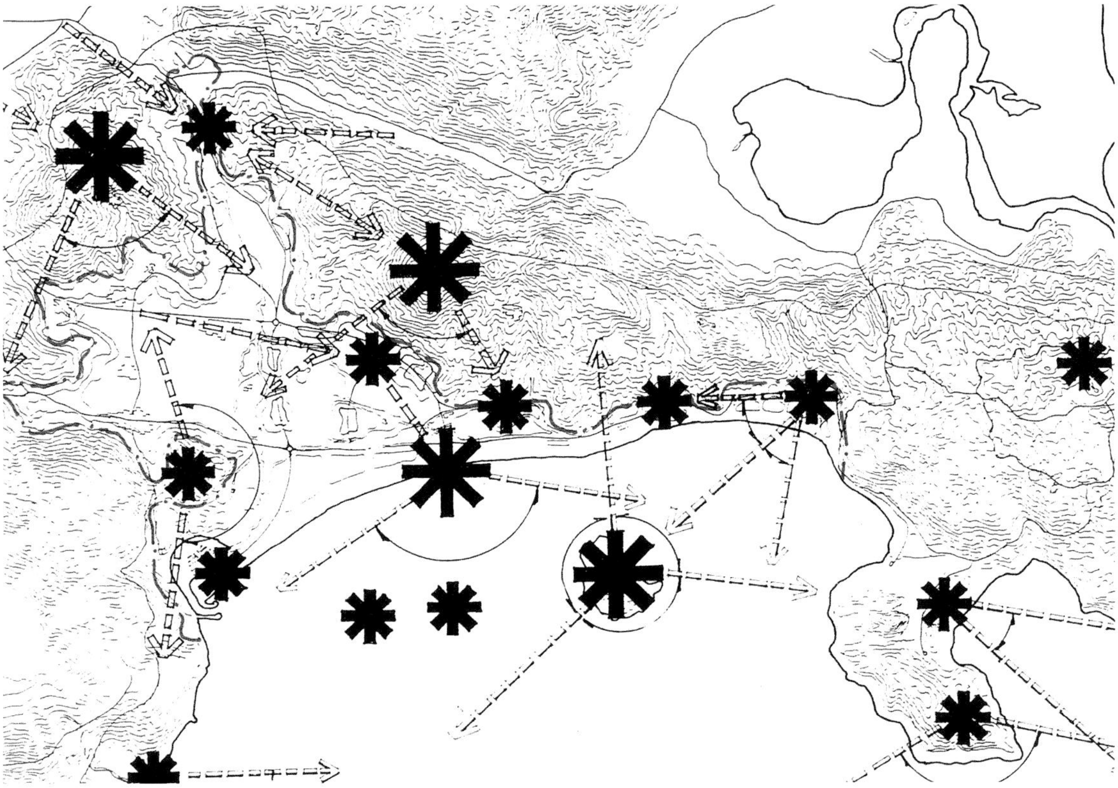

Above: Master plan of the main landscape nodes and the view corridors.

Chengdu Longmen Mountain Resort Planning

Project Area: 4,133 km^2
Project Time: August 2007 to November 2008
Project Supervisor: Yang Rui
Project Member: Liu Hailong
In Cooperation With: The Branch of Landscape Planning and Tourism, Urban Planning and Design Institute of Tsinghua; the Tourism and Leisure Research Institute, HTW Chur University of Applied Sciences; and the Planning and Design Institute of Chengdu

The Longmen Mountain, located in the west of Chengdu in Sichuan Province, has had remarkable achievements in its tourism development since the 1980s. However, it needed a rebranded identity, distinctive products, market appeal, and improved infrastructure. In 2007 Chengdu Municipal Government agreed to allocate tourism resources to integrate and make these updates. In November 2007 the proposal submitted by the Tsinghua team won the bid for the International Tender for Tourism Planning of the Longmen Mountain International Mountainous Region. The Tsinghua team was commissioned to continue, and complete the concept planning, master planning, and functional area planning after a large earthquake hit the planned site on May 12th bringing havoc. After the earthquake, the project team conducted additional investigations of the planned area and conducted a series of studies to address public safety, integrated disaster prevention, and mitigation systems for the resort. Central to the strategic and concept planning was heritage safety through cultural molding; public security as safeguard for development; ecological security for urban-rural harmony; resident enrichment in return for resident-guarded tourism; and urban-rural integration for the high-profile development. "Integration and branding," "fewer road hours for longer sojourn time," "agriculture tourism and industrialized tourism development," "management innovation for increased policy elasticity," and "government-led multi-stakeholder participation" were set forth as strategic approaches to realize the goal of "building a domestic, world-class, best-to-visit, and best-to-live mountain resort with distinctive seasonal landscapes." Planning was done for the overall structure, zoning, transportation, ecological protection, urban systems, and service base. The master planning, as a caption item in the overall planning of Chengdu City, integrates spatial system planning with tourism development planning targeted mainly at regulation and orientation, covering objective, strategy and scale, spatial structure, zoning and management policies, heritage, ecosystem and environment protection, road and transportation systems, regulation of land for construction, regulation of tourism systems, sorted urbanization and village orientation, resort orientation, and infrastructure. The zoning of functional areas addresses the goals of building the Chengdu-Chongqing Pilot Area for Integrated Reform of Urban-Rural Integration while forging a Modern International Garden City in Chengdu. A comprehensive evaluation of the Longmen Mountain's Appeal to Tourists, shows that the natural and cultural heritage resources work together with the sound ecological and agricultural conditions in order to encourage mountain tourism, and the leisure and holiday industry and products, including five systems representing eighteen brands, seventeen key projects, seven tourist industry chains for tourism development.

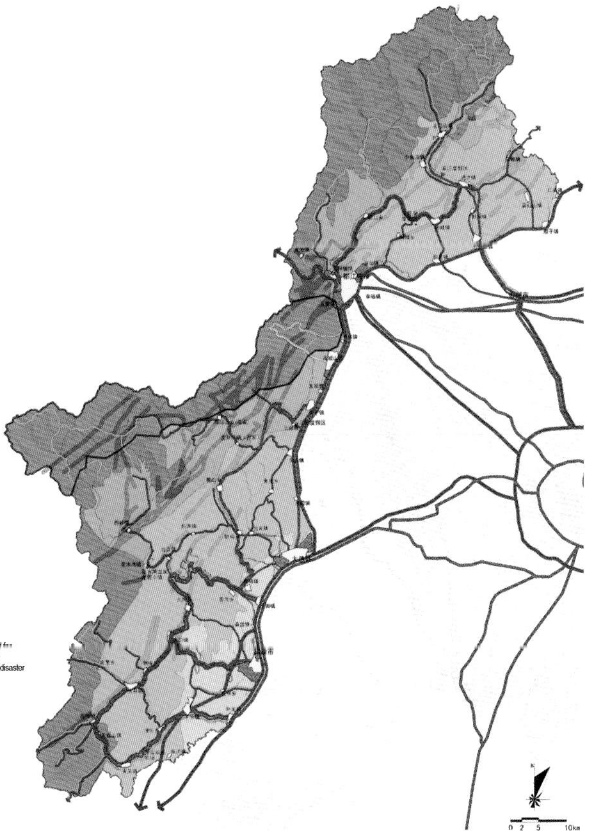

World heritage core zone conservation zone
[illegible] zone buffer zone
Scenic spots.special-first class conservation zone
Geopark core conservation
Water conservation
Ecological corridor
[illegible]
Geologic hazard
World heritage periphery zone
Nature conservation experimental zone
Scenic spots second-third class conservation
[illegible]
Plain landscape
Water zone
Walking route
Biking route
[illegible]
New land for urban construction
New land for tourism infrastructure
New land for railway construction
[illegible] highway construction
Land for rebuild after disaster
Planning area

Right: Master plan of tourism district of Mt. Longmenshan in Chengdu – diagram of the function subdivision.

Lengend

- Ecological core zone
- Ecological conservation zone
- Ecological coordination zone
- Optimized development zone
- Built-up zone

Ecological zoning	area (km²)
Ecological core zone	2166.25
Ecological conservation zone	3587.32
Ecological coordination zone	122.55
Optimized development zone	1084.11
Total	6960.23

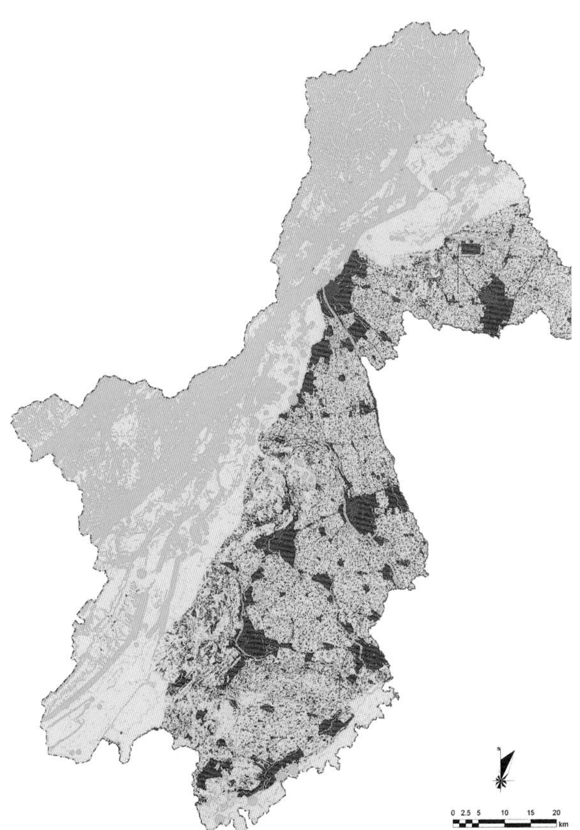

Right: Master plan of eco-tourism integrate function zones of Mt. Longmenshan in Chengdu – analysis diagram of ecological integration zones.

3) Brownfield Regeneration and Ecological Restoration

Landscape Design of the Quarry Garden in Chenshan Botanic Garden of Shanghai

Project Area: 4.3 hectares
Completed In: 2010
Project Team: Zhu Yufan, Yao Yujun, Meng Fanyu, Wang Dan, Yang Zhiguo, Zhai Weiwei, Guo Chang, Meng Yao, Feng Shunni, Zhang Zhenwei, Sun Jianyu, He Xiaohong, Cui Aijun

Chenshan is located about nine kilometers to the northwest of the Songjiang Town of Songjiang District in Shanghai and the Chenshan Quarry of Shanghai. It is a relic of an abandoned 100-year-old artificial quarry. From 2000 to 2004 the Municipal Government of Shanghai and the Songjiang District Government made renovations to the fencing for risk prevention. To protect the relics and speed up ecological restoration and environment beautification construction, a project proposal leveraging the construction of the Chenshan Botanic Garden was submitted to the Ministry of Land Resources and the Ministry of Finance for approval. With matching funding from the local government, the quarry underwent comprehensive environment rehabilitation and was transformed into part of the Botanic Garden, an ideal leisure place for local residents.

The quarry garden is located at the northwest corner of the Shanghai Botanic Garden near the northwest gate. It is linked with other parts of the Garden via the green belt and riverside roads at Chenshan. The master planning of the Botanic Garden was designed to redefine the quarry to become a boutique feature garden, one of preeminence among horticulture gardens in China. The project was a restoration of the garden. Through renovations on the existing deep pond, pit, cut-over land, and cliff top, with some landscape trees, shrubs, and perennial plants as the major building blocks, the quarry was converted into a multi-colored garden with exquisite and diversified landscapes for different seasons over the year.

The following are unique design features:

1. A post-industrial landscape created with minimum intervention

The "subtraction" design strategy was adopted to highlight the texture of the stone, to maintain the original flavor of the place, and to avoid artificial traces as much as possible by using the rusty steel plate and the free stone wall for reminiscence of the appearance of the Industrial Age.

2. An oriental water and mountain natural landscape

The design borrows the utopian ideal of ancient China from the classic literary masterpiece *Peach Blossom Valley* and draws on the existing space to create the waterfall, the natural moat, the plank road, and the water

Above: Aerial view

curtain cave all of which provoke the satori of nature. By leveraging and reinforcing the natural shades and textures of the mountain, the designer adds to it a stroke of artistic form and context typical of a traditional landscape painting. Based on research of the local historical records, the designer intended to bring back to life the 10 most well-known ancient scenes from past writing and tradition: the Spring Cloud at the Cave Entrance; the Moon Above the Mirror Lake; the Sunset at the Sandy Slope; the Sweet Creamy Spring Water; the Rocky Repose for Friends; the Tomb of the Taoist Recluse; the Well of Wisdom and Inspiration; the Bell at the Chongzhen Taoist Monastery; the Tablet for the Charitable Person; and the Former Chrysanthemum Garden.

3. Botanic Landscape

The design was based on the spatial layout (to guarantee overall integrity) and created a texture to the plan, which is actualized by the plants filling the exhibition with education functions that showcase well-balanced spatial structure and elegant colors.

Awards:
The Honor Award under the General Design Category of the 2012 ASLA Professional Awards.

Above: Constructed photo.

Above: Constructed photo.

Left: Constructed photo.

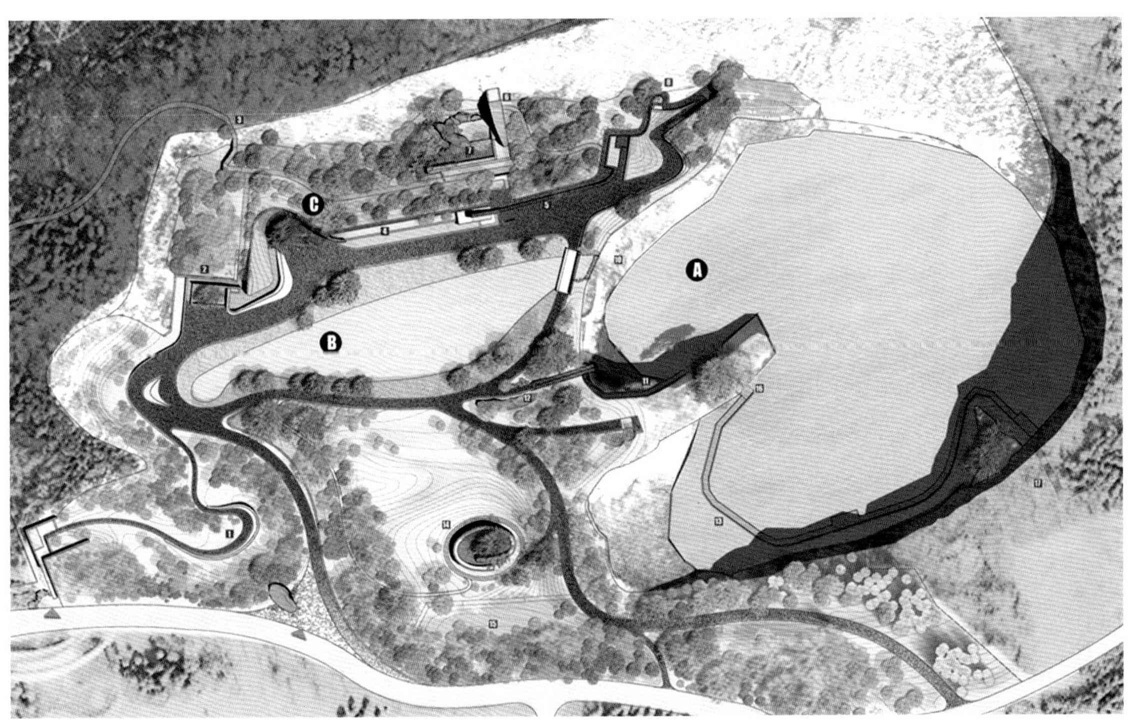

Above. Master plan.

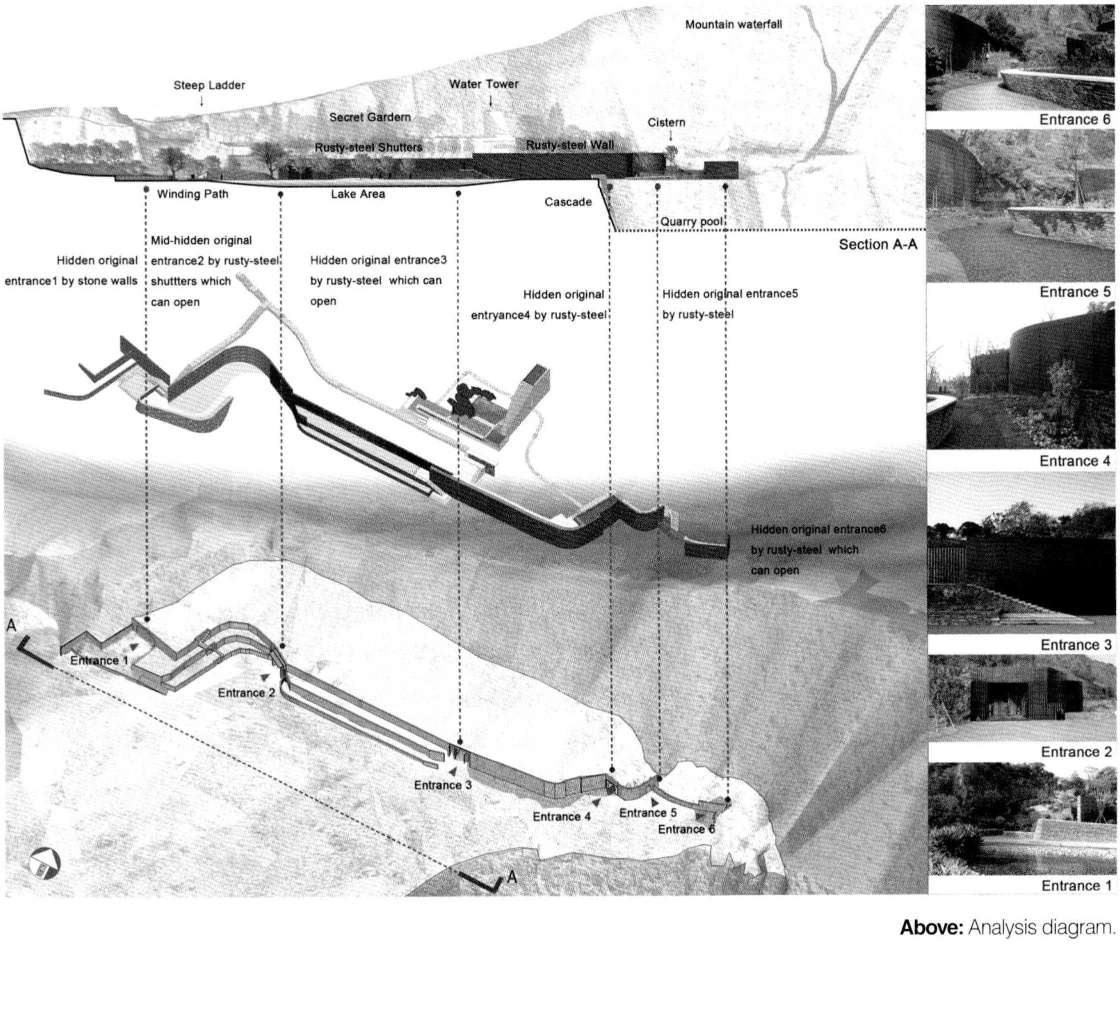

Mountain waterfall
Steep Ladder
Water Tower
Secret Gardern
Cistern
Rusty-steel Shutters
Rusty-steel Wall
Winding Path
Lake Area
Cascade
Quarry pool
Section A-A
Hidden original entrance1 by stone walls
Mid-hidden original entrance2 by rusty-steel shuttters which can open
Hidden original entrance3 by rusty-steel which can open
Hidden original entryance4 by rusty-steel
Hidden original entrance5 by rusty-steel
Hidden original entrance6 by rusty-steel which can open
A
Entrance 1
Entrance 2
Entrance 3
Entrance 4
Entrance 5
Entrance 6
A

Entrance 6
Entrance 5
Entrance 4
Entrance 3
Entrance 2
Entrance 1

Above: Analysis diagram.

Tangshan Nanhu Eco-City Central Park Overall Planning & Design

Project Area: 630 hectares
Completed In: 2010
Project Team: Hu Jie, An Youfeng, Lv Lushan, Wang Xiaoyang, Zhang Lei, Li Chunjiao, Fu Qiong, Zou Mengcheng, Zhang Chuanqi, Mei Juan, Hu Miaomiao, Zhang Fan, Cai Lihong, Liang Sijia, Teng Xiaoyi, Shen Dan, Liu Hui

Above: Citizen activities.

Nanhu, located one kilometer to the south of Tangshan, had extensive hollow areas underground as a result of more than a hundred years of coal mining. These caverns collapsed during the 1976 earthquake and led to a number of surface subsidences. As of 2006, the surface subsidence covered 28 square kilometers and had spread to the neighboring areas.

Because of the extensive surface subsistence and rapid recovery of the underground coal mining after the earthquake, Nanhu was used as a landfill for municipal wastes out of safety considerations. Tangshan went through ups and downs during the past four decades of reconstruction before it surged as the central hub of the Circum-Bohai Sea Economic Circle. Nanhu remained a junkyard for municipal, construction, and industrial wastes, as well as a sewage outlet for Tangshan. It was no exaggeration saying that it was a mountain of garbage, a lake of sewers, a land overgrown with weeds – a dilapidated scene that everyone avoided. Residents in many nearby villages started to move. Eventually, Nanhu became a wasteland discarded by the Tangshan people and a "forbidden zone" for urban development and construction projects. This area is the boundary for Tangshan to expand southward and hindered further growth.

In 2008 the China Seismological Bureau, China Coal Research Institute, and other institutions conducted a prudential analysis and research of the geological structure and potential hazards of the mining subsidence areas of Nanhu, and arrived at the conclusion that most of the area, being under a stable state of surface subsistence, was firm enough for development and construction needs. On the basis of this study, the Tangshan municipal government put forward the strategic vision of "forging Nanhu Central Park," intended to convert the once urban "scar," the mining subsistence, and its surrounding areas into a world-class central ecological park.

After the garbage stacks were disposed of, the design team exchanged views of the mountain landscape with municipal experts to reach the following transformation proposals: collect and stack up the garbage on site; cover the garbage up with low density polyethylene; put layers of soil above the low-density polyethylene; compact the soil layer by layer; construct retaining walls with the leno mesh bags; and develop the waste landfill gas collection system.

Construction of the Tangshan Nanhu Eco-City Central Park not only took care of the ecological security and humanistic needs within the site but also effectively promoted the development of the surrounding area.

Construction of the Central Park has led to:

Above: Cedars and lawn.

(1) a rise of 3–4° in the extreme minimum temperature and a decrease of 3–4° in extreme maximum temperature of Tangshan City;

(2) a forest coverage rate of 44% for Tangshan;

(3) an added land value of at least 100 billion yuan for the Nanhu District;

(4) a residential holding capacity of 400,000, a housing demand of about 480 million yuan, and a newly added retail area with sales of about 80 billion yuan annually as of 2015.

Study of the Nanhu Central Park of Tangshan can provide theoretical and practical reference for resource depleted cities by intensifying urban infrastructure, improving quality of urban open space, and uplifting the urban appearance.

Awards:

1. The Excellence Award, 2011 International Federation of Landscape Architects Asia-Pacific Regional Congress Award in the Design Category in January 2011.
2. Third prize from the 2008 Hebei Provincial Awards for Outstanding Urban/Rural Planning in July 2009.
3. Third prize for the China Architectural Science and Technology Award in the Municipal Engineering Category in December 2012.
4. Green Good Design Award from the European Centre for Architecture Art Design and Urban Studies in June 2012.
5. Gold Medal in international projects from the British National Landscape Association, Landscape Award in December 2011.
6. First prize, the Torsanlorenzo International Prize in the Landscape Design in Transformation of the Territory Section in May 2011.

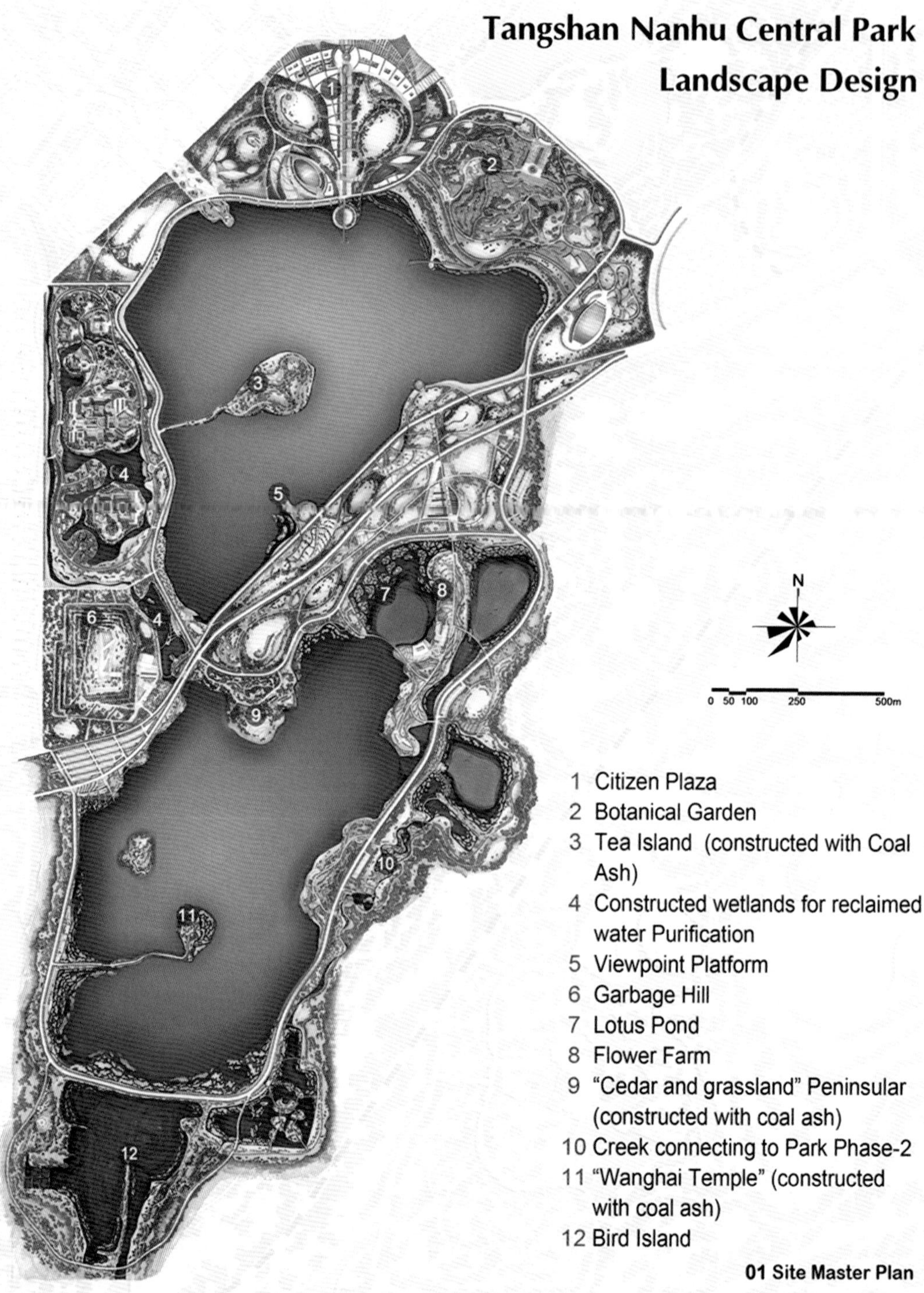

Above: Master plan.

3.4 Landscape Architecture Heritage Protection

Overview

Tsinghua University has a long history of research and practice related to natural and mixed heritage protection. With participation in many local and national research projects, the university has formed a unique method integrating research, practice, and teaching, that addresses the national needs of conservation and construction. Major projects in the 20th century include: Mount Putuo Scenic Area Planning (1979), Mount Huangshan Scenic Area Plannings (1980, 1982), Ziliujin Dinosaur Scenic Area Planning (1985), Dujiangyan Irrigation System Scenic Area Planning (1990), Yalongwan National Tourist Resort Planning and Design of Sanya (1992), Jianfengling National Forest Park Planning and Design of Hainan (1993), the Feasibility Study and Master Planning for Developing Tourism at the Three Gorges Project Area (1994), Construction Planning of Northwest Yunnan National Park and Reserve System (1998), and Master Planning of Mount Taishan Scenic Area (1999).

Since the beginning of the 21st century the research and practice dimensions have been further expanded. With the inception of the Tsinghua Department of Landscape Architecture protection of the natural heritage, mixed natural and cultural heritage, and cultural landscapes have been prioritized for disciplinary construction. In addition to scenic areas' (national parks and reserves) protection and management, scientific research, and practice also cover: protection and management of world natural/mixed heritage sites, multi-scale heritage systems, network construction, cultural landscape protection, and integration of scientific research and teaching.

Scenic Area (National Parks and Protected Areas) Protection and Management

The School of Architecture of Tsinghua University was one of the earliest institutions involved in protection of scenic areas in China. This history of conservation and protection are showcased in academic publications such as *Famous Mountain Scenic Area in China* (1996), and in the sound theoretical and technical basis in scenic area research. Due to the accumulation of achievements in research of scenic area planning and related fields, Tsinghua has received a reputation for excellence.

As head of the discipline, Professor Yang Rui has directed over 20 scientific research and practice projects related to natural and cultural heritage protection, and has been the project overseer for more than 40 academic research papers since 1991. He is currently the chair of the Department of LA, School of Architecture, Tsinghua University; head of the Collegiate Landscape Architecture Discipline Steering Team; deputy secretary general and executive director of the Chinese Society of Landscape Architecture; director of the China Landscape and Historic Site Association; Deputy editor-in-chief of *Chinese Landscape Architecture Journal*; head of the Preparatory Professional Committee for History, Theory, and Heritage Protection at the Chinese Society of Landscape Architecture; a member of the Landscape Architecture Panel for the Ministry of Housing and Urban-Rural Development; a member of the China Forest Landscape Resource Evaluation Committee; and a member of the National Forestry Natural Reserve Assessment Committee.

Based on the practice platforms at the Institute of Resource Protection and Tourism Development of Tsinghua University and the Beijing Tsinghua Urban Planning and Design Institute, Tsinghua University undertook many local and national projects related to scenic areas, including the Mount Taishan master planning (1999 to present), the Jingpo Lake National Park master planning (2000 to 2001), the master planning of the Meili Snow Mountains National Park in the Three Parallel Rivers Scenic Area (1999 to 2002), the master planning of the Laojun Mountain in the Three Parallel Rivers Scenic Area (2003 to 2004), the master planning of the Qianhu Mountain in the Three Parallel Rivers Scenic Area (2004 to 2005), the Mount Huangshan National Park master planning (2002 to 2007), Wuhan East Lake Scenic Area conceptual planning (2007 to 2008), Qinghai Kanbula Tourist Destination conceptual planning (2007 to 2008), detailed planning of Mount Taishan Hongmen Scenic Area (2001), detailed planning of Mount Taishan Tianwaicun Scenic Area (2001), and detailed planning of the core section of the Shaolin Scenic Area at Mount Songshan (2002 to 2003).

Tsinghua University has undertaken many local and national scenic area scientific research projects in recent years, including the "Theoretical and Practical Research on the Protection and Management of Buffer Zones for Scenic Areas" (2010 to 2012, supported by the National Natural Science Foundation), the "Study of Scenic Area Community Planning Based on the Multiple Value Identification" (2012 to 2015, supported by the National Natural Science Foundation), and the "Scenic Area Research for the 2009–2010 Landscape Architecture Development Report" compiled by the China Association for Science and Technology.

In its scientific research and practices, Tsinghua has taken care to integrate international state-of-art theories to address domestic problems in a practical way. Tsinghua has carried out in-depth research on the introduction of international trends and technologies on national parks and reserves in China, analyzing standards, problems, planning procedures, subject matter, approaches and techniques. In the process, the university has accumulated various research achievements, including over 40 published journal papers, 10 doctoral dissertations, and 20 professors' theses.

While acquiring international technologies and theories Tsinghua LA has made four major changes to their protection philosophy of the Worldwide National Parks: parks and reserves are no longer referred to as landscapes but as bio-diverse regions; protection is active instead of passive; multiple stakeholders now govern protection of these areas instead of the government; and spatially, structures are now seen as networks.[1] Focused research on national parks and reserves in the United States have been used to update the planning system, tourist management, and management of park boundaries.[2][3]

Tsinghua analyzed the conditions of natural and cultural heritage sites, including scenic areas and natural reserves in China, and created a list of seven aspects of site upkeep that are affected by poor management: knowledge, legislation, institution, technology, funding, capacity, and environment.[4] In answer to this the university has created four strategies to improve management of the natural and cultural heritage resources in China: science-based across-the-board innovation; multi-stakeholder participation; integration; and different oversight and authority for separate boundaries.[5] Based on this, management of these aspects in China can be monitored through legislation, institutional reform, technical support, social support, planning management, financial resources, and building to capacity, coupled with 41 action recommendations.[6]

In view of these planning procedures, and with reference to the six steps proposed by Carl Steinitz for landscape planning, the entire planning process was divided into seven phases: investigation, analysis, resource assessment, planning, impact evaluation, decision-making, and implementation.[7] This planning procedure differs from the previous one in that it contains two more links—impact evaluation and comparison of different programs—while also incorporating decision-making and implementation into the planning process.

There are improvements on conventional systems that cover the change from physical planning to management planning, from planning with quantitative targets to planning with coordinated targets, from single discipline to blended disciplines, from problem-oriented to problem-and-target-oriented coordination planning: target, strategize, and implement.

Advanced techniques and approaches from abroad were absorbed with a consideration of the scenic areas to generate tailor-made planning approaches and techniques responsive to specific scenic areas. These studies include resource evaluation while targeting visual landscapes, resource evaluation for value and sensitivity, protection of visual landscapes in relation to protection of bio- and cultural-diversity, protective measures, monitoring of holding capacity to assess environmental impact, [8][9][10][11] planning of visitor experience rather than space and facilities,[12] the emphasis of community planning, participation, and buffer zone coordination rather than relocation,[13] zoning for policy rather than function,[14] an understanding of boundaries,[15] and the application of GIS and computer technologies in site planning.[16]

These theoretical studies and practices received recognition both home and abroad. The Mount Taishan Master planning was used as a classic case of Landscape Planning. The Master Guide to Code for a Scenic Area (National

Park of China) Planning and the Master planning for the Meili Snow Mountains National Park in the Three Parallel Rivers Scenic Area were both recognized by the UN World Heritage experts Les Molloy and Jim Thorsell as being key projects to use as a resource for protection evaluation, coordination, management of policy districts, planning maps, interpretation planning, community participation, and community planning. The projects won the 2011 the Excellent Landscape Architecture Planning and Design first prize from the Chinese Society of Landscape Architecture and the 2012 Huaxia Award first prize. The Mount Huangshan National Park Master plan won recognition from the International Union for Conservation of Nature for a redefinition of and adjustment to the boundaries of the buffer zone.

World Natural/Mixed Heritage Value Identification and Management Planning

World natural/mixed heritage research and practices at the Tsinghua University are carried out in close relation to the world heritage work practices in China in coordination with the state governing authorities and the applications. With regard to heritage application, Tsinghua University is very familiar with the process having filed the documents to nominate Mount Wutai to be a world natural and cultural heritage site and handling the planning (2004–2007). Tsinghua also headed up the application for Wudalianchi (2009–2011) and Mount Huashan (2007–2008) to become world natural and cultural heritage sites. Heritage protection management planning and master planning was carried out by Tsinghua for the Meili Snow Mountains National Park in the Three Parallel Rivers Scenic Area, and played a key role in the successful application of the Three Parallel Rivers Scenic Area for recognition as a world heritage site in 2003, and the protection planning of the Jiuzhaigou World Natural Heritage Site was also headed by Tsinghua.

Tsinghua University faculty were commissioned by the Ministry of Housing and Urban-Rural Development to aid in the application process for a number of nominated sites including the Chinese Danxia Landform (2009), Chenjiang of Yunnan (2011), and Mount Tianshan of Xinjiang (2012), acting as domestic and IUCN experts for their field evaluation visits to these nominated sites. With regard to heritage site monitoring, Tsinghua faculty took part in the first (2003) and second (2010 to 2011) cycles of training on and preparation for world heritage periodic reporting as experts representing the Ministry of Housing and Urban-Rural Development, and assisted in heritage site reviewing and modifying. With regard to heritage site protection and management and experience, Tsinghua faculty members have been invited to present at or deliver speeches for domestic and international meetings and events related to world heritage including:

(1) The World Heritage and Sustainable Development Forum, Libo Guizhou (May 2012);

(2) The World Heritage and National Heritage Work Conference (held jointly by the China Association of National Parks and Scenic Sites and the

Urban Development Department of the Ministry of Housing and Urban-Rural Development), Lhasa, China (September 2011);

(3) A Training Workshop during the Second Cycle of the World Heritage Periodic Reporting in Asia and the Pacific, Shanxi (April 2010), Seoul (December 2011);

(4) An International Symposium on China's World Natural and Mixed Heritage Tentative List, Beijing, China (January 17–18, 2009);

(5) An International Expert Meeting on World Heritage and Buffer Zones, Davos, Switzerland (March 11–14, 2008);

(6) An International Conference on Sustainable Tourism Management at World Heritage Sites, Huangshan, China (March 24–27, 2008);

(7) A UNESCO Workshop on Regional Comprehensive Meeting of World Heritage Periodic Monitoring and Reporting, Hanoi, Vietnam (January 20–23, 2003).

The UNESCO Beijing Office and the Urban-Rural Planning Center of the Ministry of Housing and Urban-Rural Development jointly commissioned Tsinghua University to conduct pre-research (2011 to 2014) on codes for protection planning of world natural heritage sites in China. Through an analysis of the current conditions in China and comparison with and reference to international cases, this project addressed the relationship between the protection management planning of world natural heritage sites and existing planning for various protected sites in China in order to determine whether current planning meets the demand for protection and management of the heritage sites, or to see if it is necessary to prepare special protection management planning that is independent of current planning types. If special protection planning is necessary, what would that pertain? If special planning was necessary what would the content framework and draft codes be? All of these would need to be formulated. Periodic achievements from this project were published in *Chinese Landscape Architecture* in September 2013.(17–23)

In recent years, important theoretical work has been carried out in relation to various world heritage projects addressing the following aspects:

(1) Focusing on the identification of universal values of world heritage sites, not only for specific values of the Five Sacred Mountains area as a Heritage site(24) and comparative study.(25) The University has sought to understand international trends such as the IUCN's application of the four criteria and ICOMOS's recommendation of the OUV evaluation framework(26) in order to develop a more complete assessment method.

(2) Mixed heritage concept and tentative lists. The evolution of the mixed heritage concept was reviewed against the research conditions of the mixed heritage concepts and propositions between natural and cultural elements, namely: juxtaposition, mixing, and combination. The relationship between mixed heritage and other heritage sites were studied to understand the significance of the mixed heritage of China, to put forward constructive opinions for the development of mixed heritage areas, and to stress that

China is duty-bound[27] to carry out in-depth research in order to develop its unique, mixed heritage lands. With regard to the tentative list, analysis in China tends to be over-packed, poorly representative, and categorized for insufficient research and inferior mechanism reasons. Possible strategies and action plans were proposed for improvement and perfection of the list. Preliminary research done on potential mixed heritage sites by using the "Gap Analysis" method offer technical road maps for improvement of these tentative mixed heritage lists.[28][29]

(3) Retrospect and prospect of natural and mixed heritage protection and management in China. The year 2012 marked the 40th anniversary of the Convention Concerning the Protection of the World Cultural and Natural Heritage and was the 27th anniversary of world heritage protection in China. Heritage protection and management sites in China were reviewed and categorized as start-up, development, or maturing. Experiences and challenges of natural and mixed heritage protection and management were studied from a legal standpoint to create a set of regulations and management requirements, and from a management planning, scientific research, and local development point of view in order to gain a holistic perspective. International trends were studied and included for future development of world heritage protection and management in China.

Establishment of Multi-Scale Heritage System and Network

Tsinghua University was one of the earliest institutions to study heritage systems. The University has undertaken many national and provincial experimental practice projects, of differing scales, in order address heritage issues. Projects include: the "Construction Planning of Northwest Yunnan National Park and Reserve System," which was a sub-project of the "study of sustainable development plan for human settlements (including national parks) in Northwest Yunnan," and a project Tsinghua was commissioned for by the Yunnan Provincial Association for Promotion of Social Development and the Yunnan Provincial Government (April 1998); the "Planning of the Beijing Municipal Scenic Area System (2004 to 2050)," which was a project commissioned by the Beijing Municipal Planning Committee and the Beijing Municipal Bureau of Landscape Architecture in 2004; the "Study of the 11th Five-Year-Plan Outline for the Protection of National Cultural and Natural Heritage Sites," which was sponsored by the National Development and Reform Commission in collaboration with the Ministries of Finance, Land Resources, Construction, and the Environmental Protection, and with cooperation from the State Administrations of Environmental Protection, Forestry, Tourism, and Cultural Heritage from 2006 to 2007. Professor Yang Rui from Tsinghua University served as the head of the drafting panel for these prestigious projects.

The "Planning of Northwest Yunnan National Park and Reserve System," was a regional practice project, and a study of the integration of scenic areas, natural reserves, and other heritage resources at the regional level. The project addressed environmental factors, construction objectives, spatial structure, management mechanisms, management policies and action plans of different types of protected areas, corresponding with the categories the IUCN protected site management system has in place. The experience created a foundation for the national park and reserve system concerning ontological dimension.(30) The "Planning of the Beijing Municipal Scenic Area System" (2004 to 2050) is one of the earliest studies on the planning of provincial scenic area systems, and was the first initiative by Beijing to conduct scenic area planning research. Findings from the study have been incorporated into the Beijing Overall Urban Plan (2004–2020) and the Beijing Green Space System Planning and serve as references for urban-rural construction management in Beijing. The "Study of the 11th Five-Year-Plan Outline for Protection of National Cultural and Natural Heritage Sites" was the first national-level special protection plan that outlined seeing heritage sites (including natural, cultural, and mixed) as an object since 1949, and coordinated planning of relevant key strategies, measures, projects, and actions for heritage site protection during the 11th Five-Year-Plan period on the basis of in-depth study of conditions of various heritage sites in China that were of significant relevance to the protection of heritage sites in China.

China is still in the early stages of developing a system of guidance over and foundation for macro spatial layout of heritage resource systems, which, together with insufficient evaluation on rational distribution of heritage resources and protected areas, has led to serious resource segmentation at many heritage sites for spatial overlapping and blurred boundaries. In response to this problem, Tsinghua University undertook a number of heritage-related projects funded by the National Natural Science Foundation, including "A Study on the Basis of Spatial Network Theory Methodology on Integrated Protection of Natural and Cultural Heritage Sites in China" (2006 to 2009), and "A Study of the Theories and Practices of Provincial/Regional Heritage Site System Plans in China" (2011 to 2013). The first project, a comparative study of domestic and foreign cases on the basis of the resource features and protection system of the heritage sites in China, set forth the concept of an integrated protection space network, that is, constructing material and physical links by spatial means (such as boundaries, buffer zones, corridors, and patterns) while linking individual heritage sites to continuous and complete spatial system structures. The study also explored protection theories and methodologies suited to the specific conditions of China. The second project included in-depth research on provincial/regional heritage site systems and system planning. The findings resulted in several provincial heritage system plans for empirical study, theoretical support for integrated ontological-scale protection of provincial/regional heritage resources in China, and laid a foundation for standard and scientific planning.

Cultural Landscape Protection

Cultural landscape researches in the context of landscape architecture at the Tsinghua University can be roughly divided into two categories, village/rural cultural landscape research and world heritage cultural landscape research.

Village/rural cultural landscape has included notable projects in recent years including: the "Chinese Village Traditions" project (2005 to 2008), which was supported by the EWI (Earth Watch Institute), based in the United States; and the "Northwest Yunnan Village Cultural Landscape Protection Mode Research Based on Geo-Information Technology" (2012 to 2014), which was financed by the PhD Program's Founder of the Ministry of Education. The first project addressed typical villages in Jiaxian County, Yulin Prefecture, and Shaanxi on the Shaanbei Loess Plateau; the second set included villages in Dali, Lijiang, Diqing, and Nujiang in the northwest Yunnan Province. Both explored the component factors and functioning mechanisms, dynamic evolution patterns, evolutionary models, driving mechanisms, protection methods, and safeguard measures of village cultural landscapes. The evolution of "life activities and their systems" in relation to cultural landscapes[(31)] and village landscapes were also addressed in this study.[(32)] Scenic areas in China cover large tracts of rural areas, but the landscapes of villages are currently not protected. The proposed protection of village cultural landscapes within the scenic areas will help protect the natural and cultural heritage of these villages, protecting the natural resources and minimizing conflict between the communities and management and development organizations. Many master theses designs address the village/rural cultural landscape including: the "Representation of the Disappearing Village Cultural Landscapes in Beiwu" in *Imperial Garden Area in West Suburbs of Beijing* (2006); the "Northern Shanxi Village Cave-Dwelling Cultural Landscape Protection Planning Design-A Case Study of Dangjiashan Village" (2011); and the "Linpan Planning and Design of (Farmhouse Forest) Rural Cultural Landscape on the Front of Mount Longmen" (2010).

Local interest in the value of cultural landscape heritage sites began to rise after the "1992–2002 report on World Heritage Cultural Landscapes" by P. J. Fowler, from 2003. Tsinghua LA's world and cultural heritage landscape research has been conducted in line with the practices outlined by P. J. Fowler, which have been applied to the Mount Wutai project (2004–2007), and preliminary research for Mount Huashan (2007–2008). Tsinghua LA published a series of papers that are held as being some of the earliest study in this field. The focus of these studies was the relationship between cultural landscapes and scenic areas. In terms of concept understanding, scenic areas should correspond to category three of world heritage cultural landscapes, acknowledging the difference between natural value and philosophical conception.[(33)] Through this understanding, scenic and heritage protection sites are to be combined while adding to the intangible cultural elements of the area. This has addition of the human and cultural relationship aspect of landscape architecture has created a new theoretical and methodological framework[34] that integrates the natural with the cultural and the tangible with the intangible.

In recent years, Tsinghua LA has used these learned methods on other studies such as the "Study of Theory and Practice of Cultural Landscape Heritage Protection under the Influence of Imperial Culture" (2011–2013), a project supported by the National Natural Science Foundation. This project addressed the cultural landscape influenced by imperial culture and led to the development of a new protection theory framework designed to address the needs of heritage and imperial cultural landscapes by applying logic to landscape cultural elements and combining this with the poetic wisdom of traditional China in order to break down and reintegrate the cultural elements and protection approaches. "Protection and Management Planning of the Nominated Properties of Mount Wutai," "Master planning of the Imperial Palace," and "Master planning of Beijing Zhongshan Park" offer valuable case studies for this theoretical work.

Integration of Scientific Researches and LA Teaching

Protection and management of the natural heritage sites is a demanding undertaking on professional and cross-disciplinary studies. The understanding of the practitioners is key to the protection and management standards of the heritage sites. At present, a prevalent problem with the natural heritage sites is a lack of well-trained professionals and backup teams. Tsinghua University incorporates philosophy and methodology of protection of natural heritage into its Department of LA curriculum, including the Landscape Planning and Design Studio and Postgraduate Graduation Design Studio, which use natural heritage sites as the course subject in order to lay a solid foundation for talent cultivation. In the Landscape Planning and Design Studio from previous years, heritage protection studies have included: "Landscape Planning of the Three Mountains and Five Imperial Gardens Area," "Landscape Planning of the Zhoukoudian Area," and "Wudalianchi Landscape Planning."

– Zhuang Youbo

1) Scenic Areas

Master planning of Mount Huangshan Scenic Area (1980–1982)

Project Source: Mount Huangshan Administration Bureau, Anhui Province
Project Area: 154 km^2
Project Time: 1980–1982
Tsinghua Team: Zhu Changzhong, Zhu Zixuan, Zheng Guangzhong, Xu Yingguang, Zhou Weiquan, Feng Zhongping
Other Members: Wang Zhiping, Xiao Guoqing (Anhui Department of Construction), Su Wujiu (Mount Huangshan Administration Bureau)

Huangshan Scenic Area was among the first key national scenic areas announced by the State Council in 1982. In June 1980 Tsinghua University began research work on the Huangshan Scenic Area before drafting specialized plans. The planning team consisted of representatives from the Urban Construction Division of the Anhui Provincial Construction Committee, the Forestry Department of Anhui Province, and Hefei Urban Planning and Design Institute. In 1981, Tsinghua University was invited again to participate in the preparation of an "Outline for the Master planning of Mount Huangshan," which received positive feedback at the appraisal meeting in October 1981. After the meeting, Tsinghua University, in conjunction with the Urban Construction Bureau of the Anhui Provincial Construction Committee and the Mount Huangshan Administration Bureau, made modifications on the basis of the amendment proposals and finalized the drawings and specifications of the Master planning of Mount Huangshan.

This was the first comprehensive and integrated plan of its kind in the history of the Mount Huangshan Scenic Area, as well as one of the earliest plans made in the development of scenic areas in China, which broke new ground in planning and methodology for future projects. After review of the conditions and evolution of the scenic area, the planning honed in on analysis of its natural conditions, scenic resources, environmental quality, travel conditions, and major challenges. From this research 10 guiding principles were developed:(1) protection of natural resources;(2) maintainance of landscape features;(3) proper handling of the relationship between development and construction and maintenance of natural landscape;(4) proper handling of the relationship between the immediate and long-term interests;(5) balancing of the need of the tourism industry with that of local communities for economic prosperity;(6) prevention of tourism-related pollution;(7) preservation of local architectural flavor;(8) building tourist infrastructure;(9) strengthening collaboration between the governing authorities;(10) and planning as a prerequisite for development. The planning of this project addressed a variety of issues: landscape protection, overall spatial layout, accessibility, water supply and drainage, power supply, communications, immediate construction projects and investments, and economic returns.

The Mount Huangshan Scenic Area is divided into six sightseeing areas, five protected areas, and one peripheral buffer zone. The six sightseeing areas are the Hot Spring Resort, Yuping Tower, the North Sea, Yungu Temple, Pine Valley Nunnery, and Fishing Bridge Nunnery. These are the main tourist excursion sites and are under graded protection. The five protected areas are Fuxi Stream, Ruozhu, Yanghu Lake, Fugu Temple, and Wuniguan Gateway, all of which are located in the periphery of the sightseeing areas. The mountain slopes act as a buffer zone on both sides of the roads by and leading to the scenic area

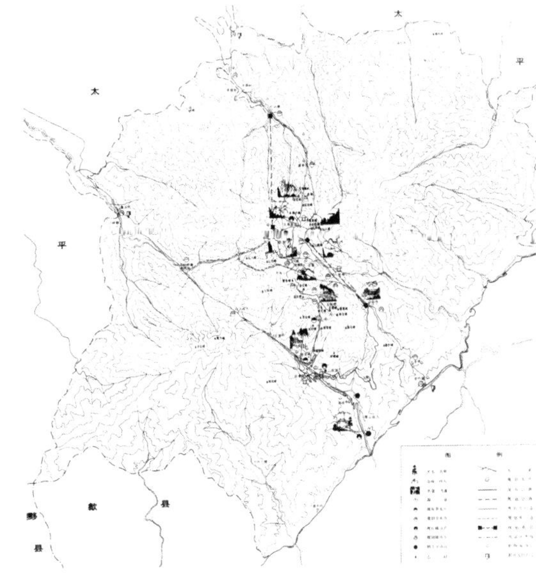

Right: Master plan.

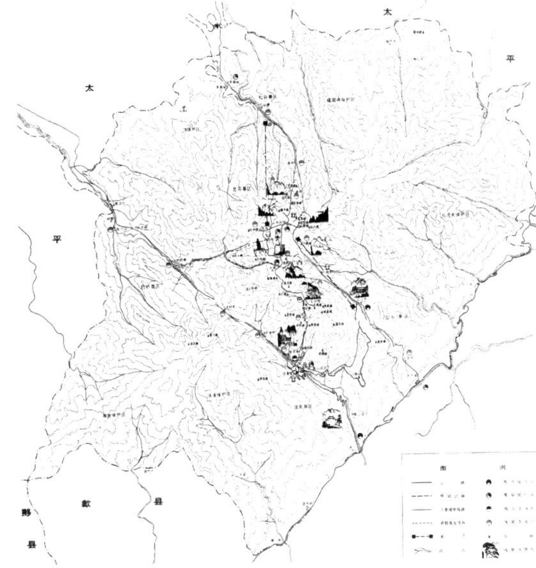

Right: Master plan of the landscape nodes and the tourism routes.

Master planning of Mount Huangshan Scenic Area (2002–2006)

Project Area: 160 km^2 for the scenic area and 490 km^2 for the buffer zone
Project Time: 2002–2006
Project Supervisor: Yin Zhi
Project Leader: Yang Rui
Project Team: Zhuang Youbo, Yuan Nanguo, Luo Tingting, Cui Baoyi, Liu Xiaodong, Qi Huangxiong, Wang Meng, Wang Binshan, Du Pengfei, Lin Jin, Gong Daoxiao, Chen Haiyan

Tsinghua University was once again called upon to work on the master planning for Mount Huangshan in 2002. This time the planning targeted the characteristics of the Mount Huangshan Scenic Area and the problems occurring with the traditional scenic area planning techniques and methods. New studies on the planning content and methodologies for this project include: the target system, zoning, visitor experience management, spatial and temporal distribution model, designated tourism products and marketing for peak days, monitoring systems, and community coordination.

1. Target System: unlike the traditional problem-oriented planning, target-based planning was used. The target system comprises of indefinite, long-term and short-term targets in temporal areas such as resource and environmental protection, visitor management, community management, multi-stakeholder cooperation, and organizational efficiency of planning content. In the target system, a timeline is drawn up for each target, and short-term targets are quantified in order to give guidance to the implementation process.

2. Zoning Management: zoning creates a clear boundary for each functioning zone so that differentiated management and implementation measures may be taken to enhance the viability of the planning. According to resource properties and protection and utilization levels, the scenic area is designated as one of the three categories of protected zoning: a low-use zone, high-use zone, or community-coordination zone. Differentiated policies were adopted for management of the human activities, facility construction, and land use within each zone type. Meanwhile, different indicators were used in the natural and social monitoring and surveillance process within different zones.

3. Visitor Experience Management: visitor experience management is built around the traditional one-sided management mode of scenic areas, and effectively avoids possible disorder upon tourist arrival while alleviating environment impact. By regulating visitor behaviors and excursion patterns as well as interpretation and education, this management mode helps visitors achieve a maximized quality experience while supporting the administrative authority in actualizing the overall management objectives.

4. The Spatial and Temporal Distribution Model: this model is a computer simulation system where computer programs are developed to simulate space factors such as visitor routes, visited sites, and entrances and exits of scenic areas. The system is capable of monitoring visitor distribution within

the entire scenic area in real-time, and effectively predicts and manages the spatial and temporal distribution of the visitors so as to help create order. In this manner, the holding capacity will be greatly increased to reduce negative effects on resources and the environment.

5. Designated Tourism Products and Marketing for Peak Days: designated tourism products refer to the portfolio of entrance and exit points, entry time, visiting routes, boarding and lodging zones, and travelling modes. There are different groups of designated tourism products, from which visitors may select in advance according to their needs. This management pattern leads to a more balanced and orderly distribution of visitors in space and time, increased holding capacity of visitors without adverse effect on the ecological environment of Mount Huangshan, extended visitor residence time triggered by the two-day or multi-day options with designated route and time, and higher quality of visitor experience as a result of matching information and other services of the designated tourism products.

6. Monitoring Systems: this system continuously monitors the implementation progress of the measures. Through real-time, in-depth feedback and evaluation of the current conditions of the scenic area, it is possible to fine-tune the individual experience with the implementation of studied feedback and research gained from successful user experiences. The system enables the managers to constantly adjust measures to changing conditions to ensure effective and orderly implementation of planning.

7. Community Coordination: resource protection is only possible through cooperation with the surrounding community. Cooperation protects resources and renders economic benefits to local communities, encouraging individuals to be more involved in conservation. Community coordination in this planning covers the spatial arrangements of residential points and the management domain including the regulation, coordination, supervision, and management mechanism for low-mountain attractions.

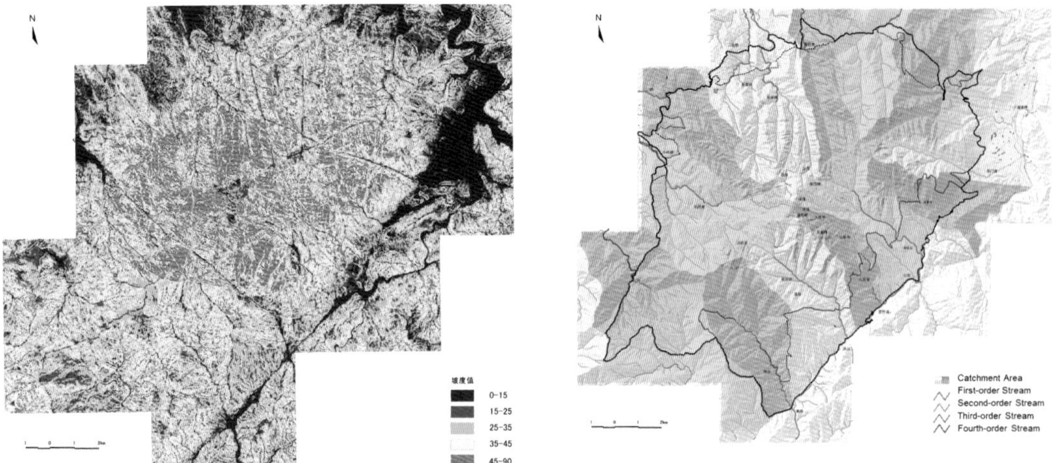

Above: Analysis diagram of the slope.

Above: Analysis diagram of the water system.

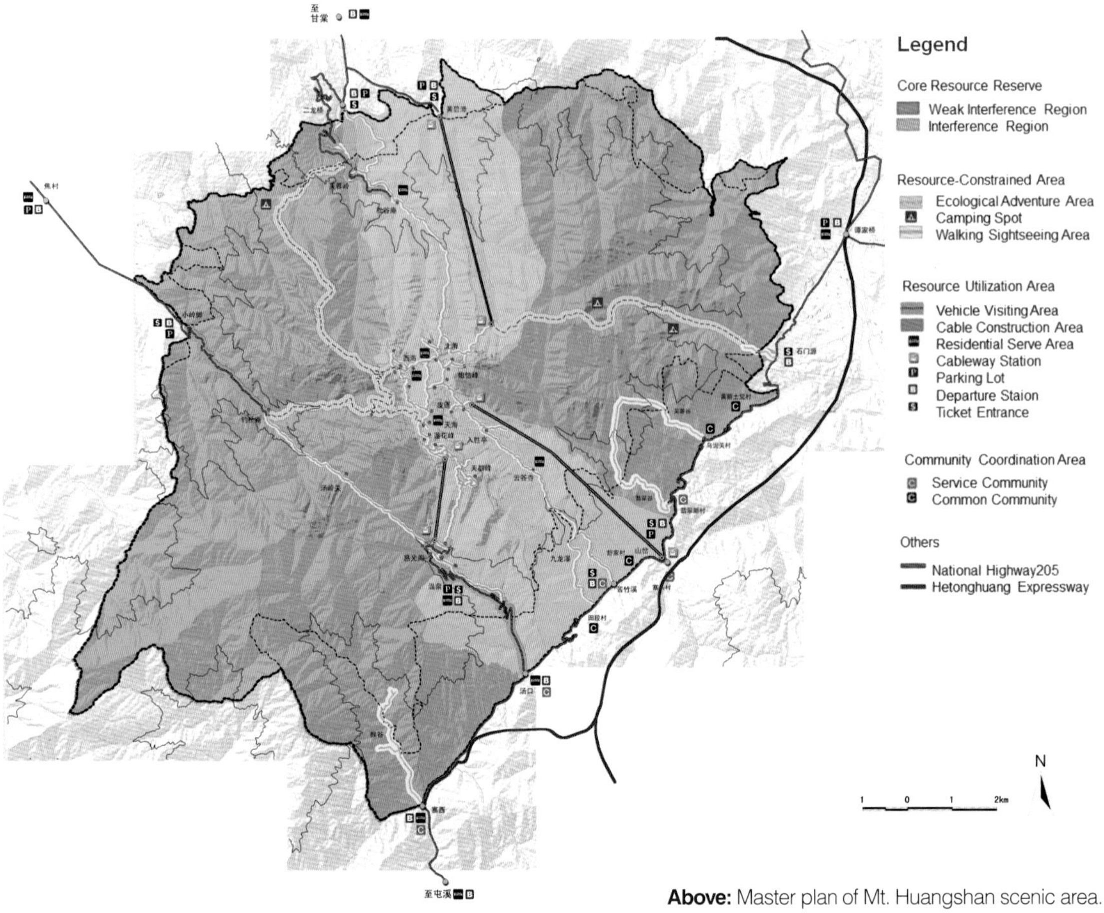

Legend

Core Resource Reserve
Weak Interference Region
Interference Region

Resource-Constrained Area
Ecological Adventure Area
Camping Spot
Walking Sightseeing Area

Resource Utilization Area
Vehicle Visiting Area
Cable Construction Area
Residential Serve Area
Cableway Station
Parking Lot
Departure Staion
Ticket Entrance

Community Coordination Area
Service Community
Common Community

Others
National Highway205
Hetonghuang Expressway

N

1 0 1 2km

至甘棠

至屯溪

Above: Master plan of Mt. Huangshan scenic area.

Master Planning of Jianfengling National Rain Forest Park

Project Area: 633 km^2
Project Time: 1993
Project Team: Zheng Guangzhong, Yang Rui, Cehn Zhijie, Gao Guisheng, Liu Jie, Wang Peng, Wei Dehui, Huang Weihua, Jin Lei, Tan Cheng, Jing Xin, Wang Min, Ouyang Wei, Liu Ying

Jianfengling National Rain Forest Park is located on the west side of the Haiyu West Line Highway on the southwester part of the Hainan Island, some 120 km away from Sanya City.

The Park has the largest and best preserved virgin rain forest found in China, which occupies an important position in the world's tropical primeval forest ecosystem. Jianfengling has vastly diversified biological landscapes – plant landscapes in particular. With six different types of seaside plant landscapes, namely, the thorn scrubs, savanna, tropical semi-deciduous monsoon forest, tropical evergreen monsoon forest, tropical mountain rain forest, and the mossy shrub coppice, Jianfengling boasts the best-preserved plant landscape system on the island.

The tropical rainforest ecosystem of Jianfengling is diversified and rare, and in need of protection, but it is unrealistic to put the entire planning area under absolute protection. Absolute protection requires considerable financial and material resources, and as a national protected forest for years with allowed timber harvesting that was not stopped until January 1, 1993, Jianfengling is occupied by more than 8,000 former forest workers and their families all of who need employment and living spaces. The only solution to the problem lies in economic development of the planned area, but too much development would destroy the balance of the tropical rainforest ecosystem. This is the contradiction between conservation and development. How to properly handle this contradiction was the focal point for the planning, construction, and management of Jianfengling National Forest Park.

Determining the size of the national park is important for developing equilibrium between protection and development.

Jianfengling National Rain Forest Park is located on the west side of the Haiyu West Line Highway on the southwester part of the Hainan Island, some 120 km away from Sanya City.

The Park has the largest and best preserved virgin rain forest found in China, which occupies an important position in the world's tropical primeval forest ecosystem. Jianfengling has vastly diversified biological landscapes – plant landscapes in particular. With six different types of seaside plant landscapes, namely, the thorn scrubs, savanna, tropical semi-deciduous monsoon forest, tropical evergreen monsoon forest, tropical mountain rain forest, and the mossy shrub coppice, Jianfengling boasts the best-preserved plant landscape system on the island.

The tropical rainforest ecosystem of Jianfengling is diversified and rare, and in need of protection, but it is unrealistic to put the entire planning area under absolute protection. Absolute protection requires considerable financial and material resources, and as a national protected forest for years with allowed timber harvesting that was not stopped until January 1, 1993, Jianfengling is occupied by more than 8,000 former forest workers and their families all of who need employment and living spaces. The only solution to the problem lies in economic development of the planned area, but too much development would destroy the balance of the tropical rainforest ecosystem. This is the contradiction between conservation and development. How to properly handle this contradiction was the focal point for the planning, construction, and management of Jianfengling National Forest Park.

Determining the size of the national park is important for developing equilibrium between protection and development.

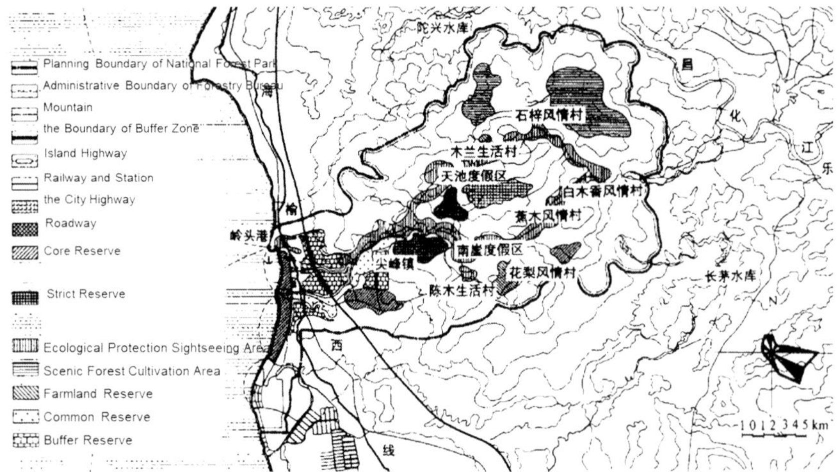

Left: Master plan.

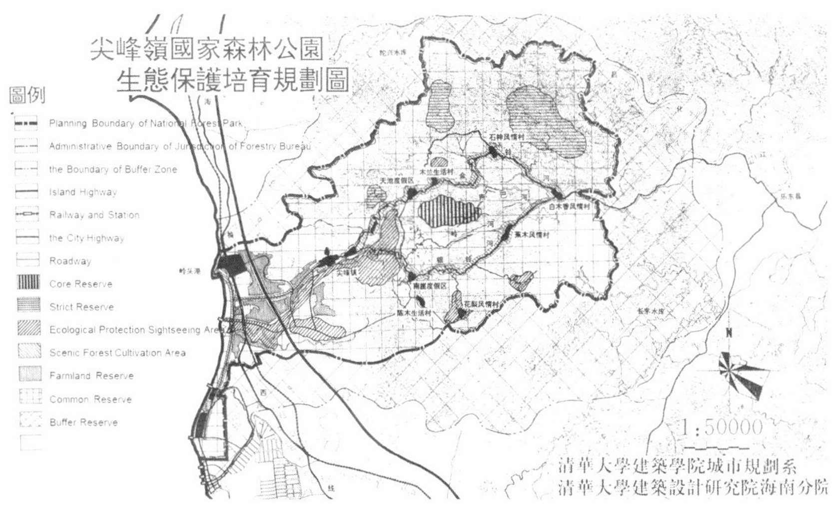

Left: Master plan of the ecological protection and cultivation.

Master Planning of Mount Taishan Scenic Area

Project Area: 202 km^2 for the planned area, 168 km^2 for the core area
Project Time: July 1999
Project Supervisor: Zheng Guangzhong
Project Leader: Yang Rui
Project Team: Wang Binshan, Zhuang Youbo, Deng Wei, Li Shouxu, Zhang Qinghua, Zhang Mingqi, Jiang Gupeng, Yuan Mu, Dang Anrong (surname)

As the most revered of the "Five Sacred Mountains," Mount Taishan is known for its landscape of grandeur, storied history, and numerous heritage sites. It is the epitome of the spiritual and cultural history of China. In 1982, the State Council announced that it would be in the first grouping of national key scenic spots, and in 1987 it was added to the UNESCO World Heritage List. In 2001, around 1.8 million people visited Mount Taishan. The planning area covers 202-square-killometers, including the core section, the paleo-stratigraphic landscape, the Great Wall of Qi, and Yaoxiang Forest Farm. The core section has a total area of 168-square-killometers and eight component scenic spots, with a 1,000-meter planned buffer zone around it.

This plan has the following characteristics:

1. Landscape Resources Survey Report: the plan is based on a full understanding of the current conditions of the scenic area, of which landscape resources are an important part. The landscape resources survey and evaluation not only helps managers and planners to gain a full understanding of the resources within the scenic area but also constitutes one of the main foundations for plan decision-making. The landscape resources survey for planning of the scenic areas used to be incomplete due to the limitation of practices and technologies. For this plan, detailed field surveys here made on every resource, with results carefully recorded and documented covering resource names, categorization (in reference to the "Scenic Area Planning Norms" and partially adjusted in accordance with the actual situation), detailed description of resource properties, grading of the landscape resources (in reference to the "Scenic Area Planning Norms" with clarification that the grading is based not solely on landscape values but rather on a comprehensive evaluation of the landscape values, environmental standards, and level of protection), and photographs.

2. Zoning Techniques: zoning is a technology widely used in urban planning and national park planning, which has not been put to good use in the planning of scenic areas in China. Generally speaking, zoning modes set out in the "Scenic Area Planning Norms" are followed in all scenic area planning practices in China currently. Zoning is done by function in cases of regulation and control needs, by attractions in cases of landscape and excursion organization needs, by reserves in cases of feature identification and cultivation needs, or by a combination of the above for large-scale complex scenic areas. This zoning methodology is still at the stage of physical space planning in terms of cognition and is missing a clear description of space in terms of form and in need of effective control

RESEARCH AND PRACTICE

means for management policy. Although zoning seemingly provides the basis for planning, it can only serve as a guideline (or reference). It cannot exert control over actual plan though, and is not a strong determinant in management.

The Master planning of Mount Taishan Scenic Area, leveraged mature international experiences and took China's scenic area management needs into account to develop zoning control plans for the control of human activities, manual facilities, and land use at the core. Zoning control has the following four advantages: definite land boundaries facilitate sorted and segmented management and phased implementation of the planning, thus enhancing the operability of the planning; protection measures and development intensity for each land plot were expressly identified to coordinate and balance the relationship between protection and utilization; the heritage protection features were highlighted by further classifying the protected land plots according to different objects while implementing corresponding protective measures; and infrastructure building and activity management were tailored to different travelling features of the scenic areas. This planning divides Mount Taishan Scenic Area into 94 zones with 12 groups under four primary categories.

3. Specific Protective Measures: resource protection is the main function of scenic areas and is the top priority for managers of these sites. The master plan is intended to provide adequate guidance for managers in their work so as to ensure smooth operation of protective measures. Therefore, the more specific and science-based the planned resource protection measures are, the greater relevance they are to managerial practices. However, conventional plans tend to contain rather than protect resource conservation measures, and for this reason have no practical use. This master plan provides detailed measures for zoned, sorted, or graded resource protection. In accordance with their respective location, category, and grade, various resources within the scenic area are needed to meet provisions of relevant zoned, sorted, or graded resource protection articles. The scenic area is divided into protected zones, limited utilization zones, and infrastructure construction zones with differentiated protection of the resources. Resources under protection are classified in six groups: heritage buildings, stone inscriptions and tablets, ancient and historical trees, picturesque peaks and rocks, pools and waterfalls, and ecological attractions. They also fall under one of five protection grades: Special, I, II, III, or IV. The resource categorization and protection grades are based on the provisions of the "Scenic Area Planning Norms," which go beyond regular requirements to detailed planning.

4. Recreation Regulation Planning: traditional scenic area planning is generally physical planning, with little concern for management activities and flexibility in plan. With people's increased knowledge of the planning functions, flexible planning content accounts for a greater proportion of overall planning of scenic areas. Recreation regulation planning is flexible planning content that differentiates this planning from traditional physical planning. Uneven, temporal, and spatial visitor distribution has been a

prominent feature of the Mount Taishan Scenic Area. In temporal terms, the site is overloaded with visitors during each May Day Holiday; in spatial terms, the Heaven Scenery Zone accounts for 90% of all visitors to Mount Taishan. The purpose of recreation regulation planning is to regulate the uneven visitor distribution so as to raise and improve the efficiency of recreational resources while keeping the visitor size below the holding capacity. Recreation regulation is actualized on macro-, meso-, and micro-scales. The first two refer to the control of visitor flow through external environments and the relationship between the external environment and the scenic area, emphasizing coordination – specifically in areas where visitor distribution is uneven. The last scale of regulation refers to internal control within the scenic area, covering regulation through physical planning and policy planning. Physical planning is used to regulate land use, roads, and travelling routes whereas policy planning is based mainly on the regulatory tools listed in the planning document such as information services, real-time monitoring, publicity and orientation, ticket spreads, additional use, group coordination, and other managerial issues.

Outcomes of this planning are included in the Landscape Planning: A Manual for the Implementation of the "Scenic Area Planning Norms."

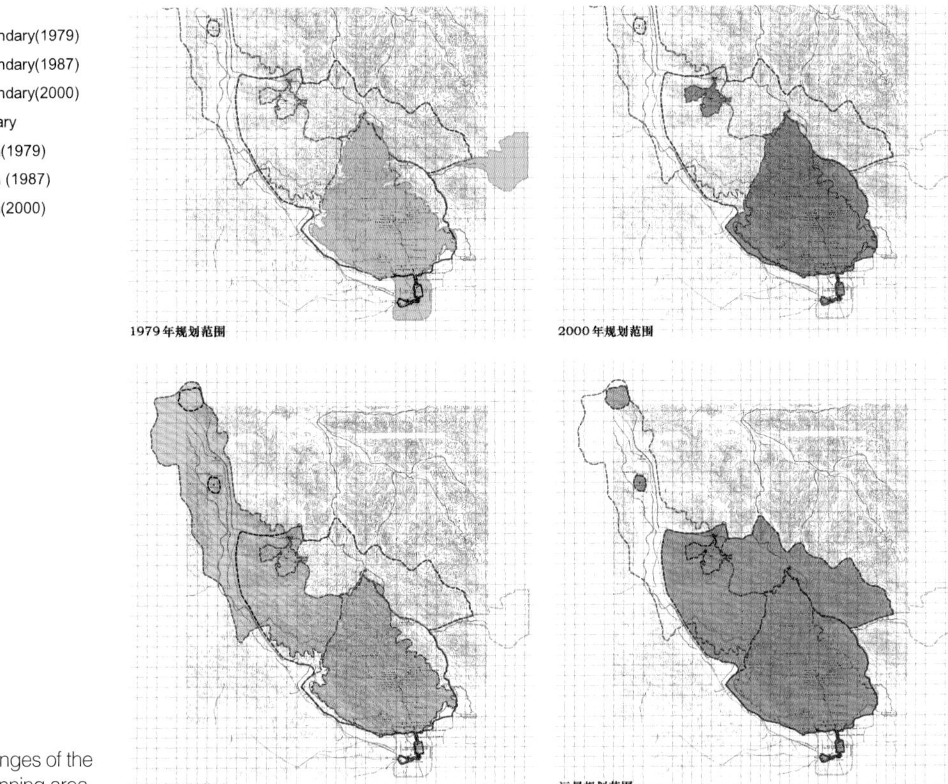

Right: Changes of the planning area.

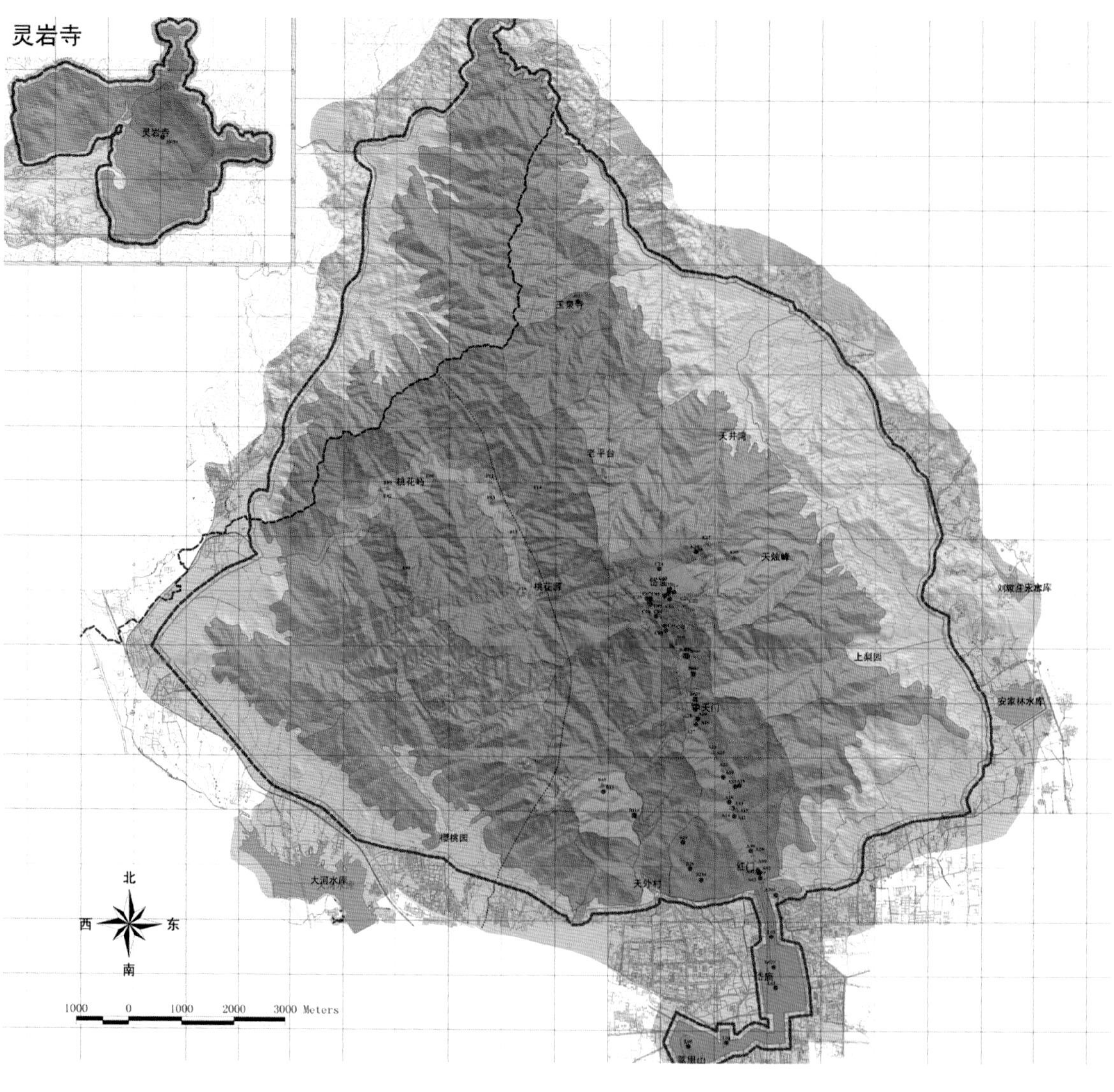

- World Cultural and Natural Heritage Sites (6)
- World Natural Heritage Sites (30)
- World Cultural Heritage Sites (41)

- Cutural Heritage Clusters (square kilometers)
- Natural Heritage Clusters
- Heritage Protection Sensitive Area
- Other Woodland of Scenic Spots
- Other Regions of Scenic Spots

- Planning Boundary
- The City Boundary
- The District Boundary
- Roads
- Water

Above: Master plan of the heritage distribution.

Master Planning of the Meili Snow Mountains National Park in the Three Parallel Rivers Scenic Area

Project Area: 1,587 km^2 for the planned area, 680 km^2 for buffer zone
Project Time: October 2002
Project Leaders: Yang Rui, Dang Anrong
Project Team: Zhuang Youbo, Zuo Chuan, Han Haoying, Li Ran, Chen Xin, Liu Xiaodong

This plan is innovative for a number of techniques and methods used to address resource and community conditions of the Meili Snow Mountains National Park. First, adequate resource evaluations were made and properly associated with the plan. Second, to make the plan more operational, a combination of the goal, strategic, and implementation planning techniques were adopted. The planning area is divided into 245 zones, with a detailed planning atlas prepared and management objectives and policies (governing the management of human activities, artificial facilities, and land use) clarified for each zone. Third, advanced international theories and technologies, such as LAC, VERP, and SCP were used to make conservation and the application of the plan more thorough. Fourth, flexible planning items, such as goals, strategy, interpretation, and management plans were incorporated to help planning outcomes comply with the internationally prevailing practices of "overall management planning." Fifth, a multidisciplinary planning approach was adopted on a trial basis, involving experts in botany, ecology, geology, sociology, and architecture who consulted at different stages of the planning process so incorporate multi-discipline participation.

These planning outcomes constituted an important part of the application documents of the Three Parallel Rivers Scenic Area for recognition on the World Heritage List in 2003, and led to high acclaim from Les Molloy and Jim Thorsell, world heritage assessment experts with the United Nations. The plan has guided the protection, construction, and management practices of the Meili Snow Mountains National Park and offers a foundation for further detailed planning and construction of heritage sites. In 2010, the feasibility report on the project of "Protection Facilities Construction for Meili Snow Mountain National Park" (2010–2011), prepared as result of the planning outcomes, was approved by the National Development and Reform Commission with a 13-million-yuan budget from the second batch of the central budget for investment on national cultural and natural heritage protection. The plan was awarded the First Excellent Landscape Architecture Planning and Design Award first prize from the Chinese Society of Landscape Architecture in 2011 and won the 2012 China Construction Science and Technology Award from the China Construction Science and Technology Awards Committee in January 2013.

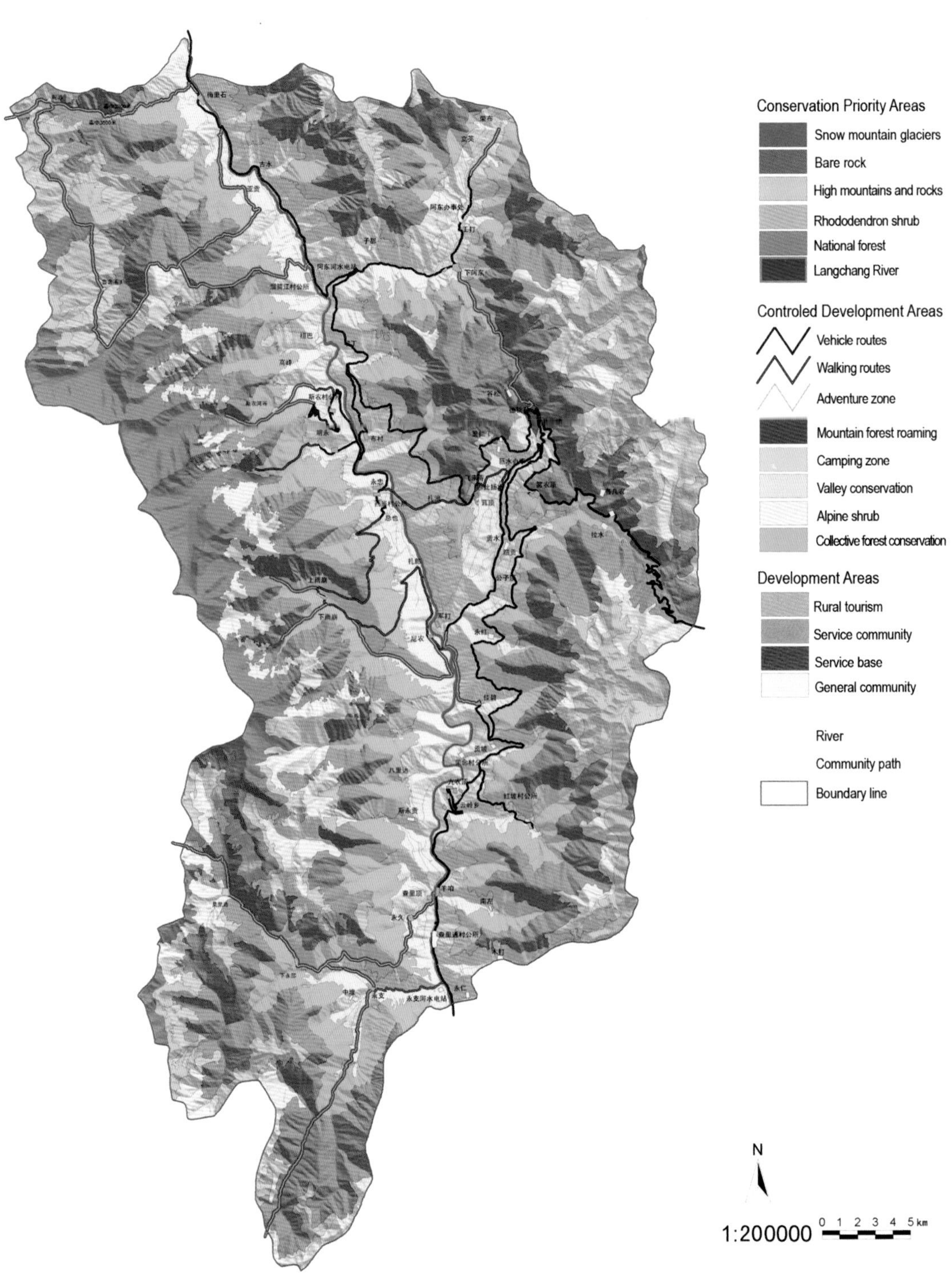

Above: Master plan of Meili Snow Mountains natural reserve in Three Parallel Rivers.

2) Heritage System

Construction Planning of Northwest Yunnan National Park and Reserve System

Project Category: Interschool Scientific and Technology Collaborative Projects of Yunnan Province
Project Source: Provincial Government of Yunnan
Project Time: 1998
Project Supervisor: Wu Liangyong
Sub-Project Leaders: Zuo Chuan, Yang Rui

Northwestern Yunnan, an area with extremely rich resources, a relatively pristine environment, and underdeveloped economic and social conditions, has a unique charm with its ecological, cultural, and landscape diversity. In April 1998 the Yunnan Provincial People's Government commissioned Tsinghua University and the Yunnan Provincial Association for Promotion of Social Development with the project of "Research on the Sustainable Development of Human Settlements (including national parks) in Northwest Yunnan," of which, "Research on the Northwest Yunnan National Park and Reserve System" is a component project. The purpose of this sub-project includes: identification of composition and spatial distribution of the site; the proposal of means to establish and enhance Northwest Yunnan National Park and Reserve System; probing into the mechanisms and policies for effective management of the Northwest Yunnan National Park and Reserve System; and, on the basis of the above, creation of an Action Plan for establishing and enhancing the Northwest Yunnan National Park and Reserve System. As a regional project, the "Construction Planning of Northwest Yunnan National Park and Reserve System" is the first attempt in China to integrating heritage resources of scenic areas and natural reserves at the regional level. Via the study of the environmental factors, development goals, spatial structure, management mechanism, management policies, and action plans for the above system, this project contributes to the accumulation of experiences in building and enhancing the national park and reserve system on the meso scale.

Outline of the 11th FYP for Protection of National Cultural and Natural Heritage Sites

Project Source: National Development and Reform Commission
Project Time: September 2005 to June 2007
Project Supervisor: Yang Rui
Project Team: Liu Hailong, Lv Zhou, Rao Quan, Zhuang Youbo, Wu Dongfan

The "Outline of the 11th FYP for Protection of National Cultural and Natural Heritage Sites" (hereinafter referred to as "National Heritage Protection Plan") is the first of its kind since 1949. As a document for national-level protection it targets heritage sites (including cultural, natural, and mixed heritage), this planning outline developed the basis for various heritage sites' coordinated planning of major strategies, measures, projects, and actions related to the protection of heritage sites during the 11th Five-Year-Plan Period, making it a significant document for the practice of heritage protection. Preparation of this document began in 2005 and continued for more than one year under the coordination of the National Development and Reform Commission with participation from the Ministry of Finance, Ministry of Land Resources, Ministry of Construction, the State Environmental Protection Administration, State Forestry Administration, National Tourism Administration, and the State Administration of Cultural Heritage. The plan was accomplished through "state initiation, expert participation, local coordination, and multi-stakeholder collaboration" by the planning expert panel, headed by Professor Yang Rui of Tsinghua University who conducted special studies on issues related to the planning. The National Development and Reform Commission held several meetings during the planning process to gain feedback from various departments and to engage well-known experts such as Luo Zhewen, Chen Changdu, and Wu Liangyong for draft assessment.

The "National Heritage Protection Plan" was implemented from 2006 to 2010. The goals for it was to ensure that all kinds of heritage resources were properly protected under strengthened protection efforts, with various acts of sabotage effectively curbed; to protect facilities and equipment conditions at heritage sites while improving conservation and management decisions and plans using the most up-to-date scientific research findings, new technologies, and new methods; overall and special plans were made for various heritage sites to offer better guidance and reference for heritage protection and management; heritage sites play an increasingly important role in science education, environmental education, cultural tradition, and patriotism; and to cultivate tourism at the heritage sites under the premise of effective protection.

Planning of Beijing Scenic Area System

Project Area: 16,410 km^2
Project Time: March 2004 to January 2007; revised from September 2010 to July 2011
Project Supervisors: Yang Rui, Dang Anrong
Pplanning Team: Qi Huangxiong, Liu Hailong, Yang Haiming, Wu Lei, Yuan Nangguo, Zhuang Youbo, Zhao Zhicong, Chai Jianghao, Que Zhenqing, Zhai Lin, Wang Meng, Kong Songyan, Cui Baoyi, Luo Tingting
Amendment Team: Zhuang Youbo, Zhao Zhicong, Lin Guangsi, Wang Yinglin, Peng Lin, Li Yihua

"Planning of Beijing Scenic Area System," the first scenic area system planning study carried out in Beijing, and one of the earliest at the provincial/municipality level, and is demonstrative in relevance. The study included: a comprehensive assessment of scenic resources in Beijing in order to generate the target systems, strategic procedures, and action plans for protection and use of these resources; analysis of spatial layouts and structures of the scenic area systems of Beijing (scope, level, and classification as hierarchical structure, size structure, or functional structure); research and implementation of the "Western Ecological Zone" and "National Park Strategy" proposed in the "Strategic Research on Urban Space Development of Beijing"; the establishment of planning implementation that outlines the immediate action steps in order of priority; and the establishment of management as the support platform for the implementation of the "Beijing Scenic Area System Planning." These have been incorporated into the "Beijing City Master plan (2004–2020)" in the scenic area section, which includes the network layout of scenic areas to replace the former island-style layout, updated protection plans for fragmented protection of the Great Wall, and scenic areas accounting for more than one third of Beijing's total land area. These plans have played an important role in guiding the development, positioning, and direction of scenic areas in Beijing and the overall planning of various scenic areas throughout Beijing.

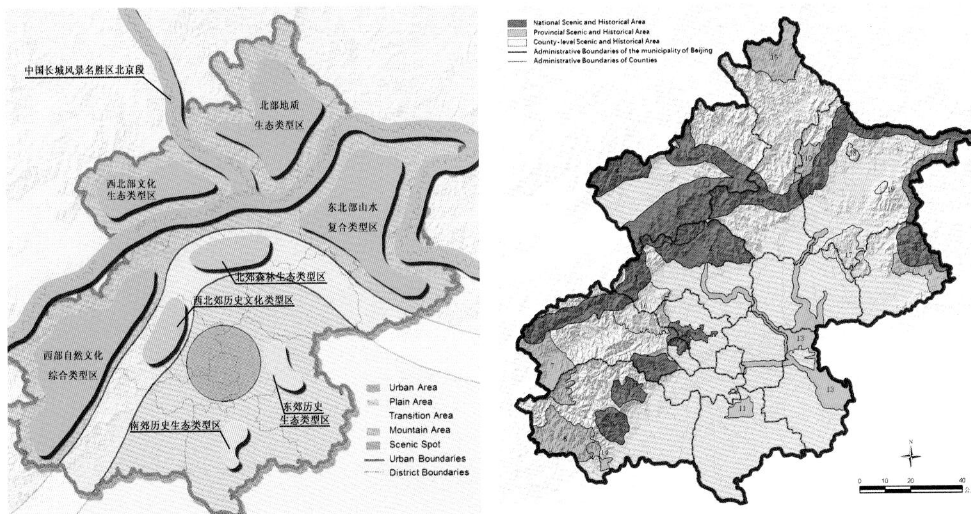

Right: Distribution of the space types.

RESEARCH AND PRACTICE

3) World Heritage

World Heritage Application Documents and Protection and Management Planning of Mount Wutai

Project Area: 607 km^2
Project Time: 2005 to 2008
Project Team: Yang Rui, Wu Dongfan, Zhuang Youbo, Liu Hailong, Jiang Quan, Li Jihong, Yang Haiming, Yang Chunhui, Zhai Lin, Zhao Zhicong

Mt. Wutai is located within the boundaries of Wutai County, Xinzhou Prefecture, in the northeast of the Shanxi Province, the center point of which is 230 kilometers away from the provincial capital Taiyuan and 150 kilometers from the Xinzhou Prefecture. It boasts unique and unspoiled early geological structures and stratigraphic sections of the Earth, rich deposits of animal fossils, Ceonozoic planting surfaces and periglacial landforms which integrally record the geological evolution of the Earth from the Neoarchean to the early Proterozoic Eon and have great significance to the global geological structure, chronostratigraphy and comparative studies, representing an ideal specimen for global comparative studies of crustal evolution, ancient environment and biological evolution. The five mountain tops typical of the ancient planation surfaces result from faults going through orogenic uplifting process to form the nearly flat surfaces; Quaternary glacial erosion transformed the ancient planation surface to form typical periglacial landforms. Mount Wutai, a gem of Chinese Buddhism, retains a large number of Buddhist cultural and architectural heritage properties and is one of the most active contemporary Buddhist ritual practice locations. The fusion of ancient and unique landscapes, the cool alpine climate, and Buddhist culture gave birth to this world Buddhist center of Manjusri worship, with its unique and vibrant mixed cultural landscapes that have lasted for over 1,600 years.

Its inauguration to the World Heritage List will lead to worldwide recognition of the Wutai Buddhist culture, better implementation of environmental rehabilitation measures, and a qualitative leap in the protection and management of Mount Wutai. The nomination process is of great importance as the World Heritage Centre has a high benchmark for the protection, management, planning, and improvement of the nominated property. Due to the disorderly expansion of the modern communities commercial facilities, the cultural atmosphere of the Buddhist building ensemble at the Taihuai core on Mount Wutai has been severely damaged. Surrounded by commercial facilities, the original glory of the hillside monuments is nowhere to be found. Environmental rehabilitation of the core area is imperative, and the nomination offers a good opportunity.

The difficulty of the project lies with the demarcation of the boundaries and core areas of the nominated property, which requires a balance between the maintenance of the heritage representation and the development needs of the local communities.

The project team prepared the application documents and set out the protection and management planning for the nominated site in line with the 2005 Operational Guidelines for the implementation of World Heritage Convention. The application text, core to the whole set of documents, is composed of nine parts, which include the identification, description, justification, conservation status and affecting factors, protection and management, and monitoring of the nominated property, relevant documents, responsible agencies, with the signature by a representative of the State Party. In addition, the document contains special planning for interpretation and education, road transport, service facilities, management office space, infrastructure, disaster prevention, and immediate action plans and safeguard measures for the planning implementation.

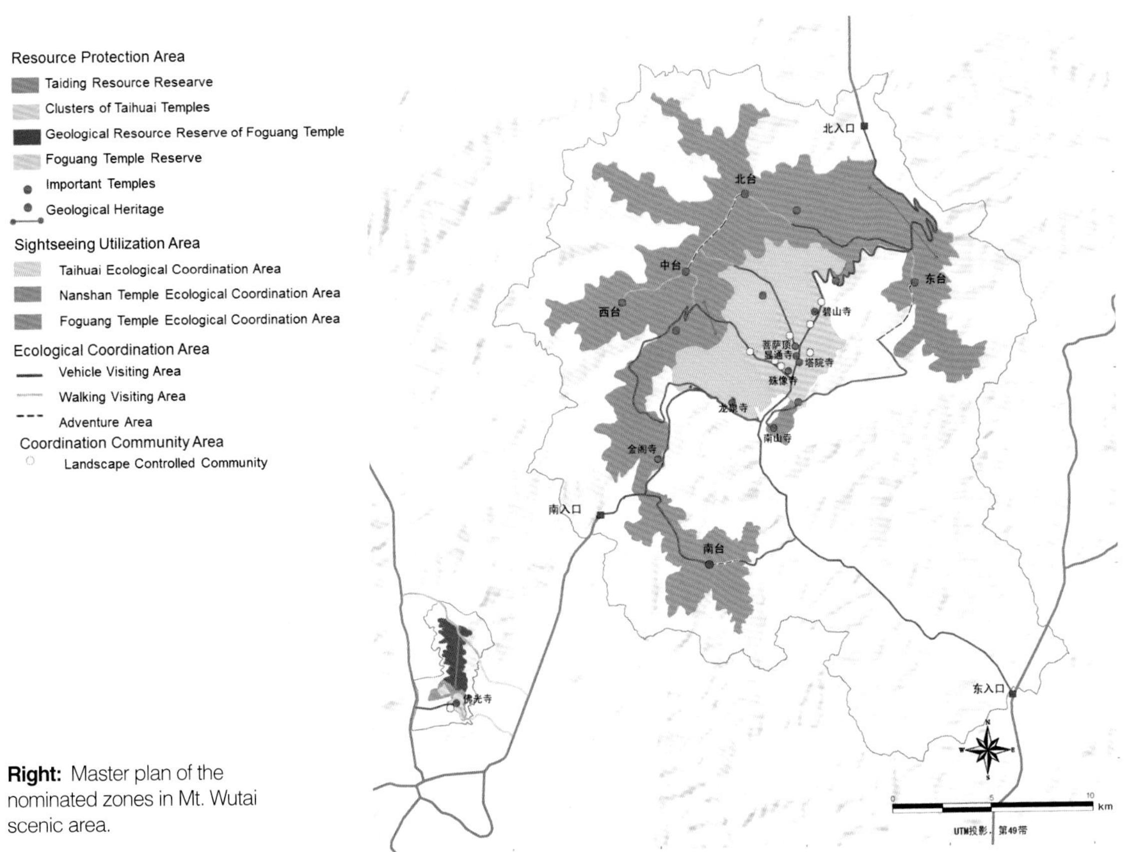

Right: Master plan of the nominated zones in Mt. Wutai scenic area.

Conservation Planning of Jiuzhaigou World Natural Heritage Site

Project Area: 720 km² for the heritage area and 600 km² for the buffer zone
Project Time: July 2011 to present
Project Team: Zhuang Youbo, Yang Rui, Zhao Zhicong, Wang Yinglin, Xu Xiao-qing, Peng Lin, Gao Fei, Jia Chongjun, Jiang Huibin, Cheng Guanhua

Jiuzhaigou, located in the northeast of the Qinghai-Tibet Plateau to the east of the Gaerna Peak in the southern part of the Minshan Mountains, is on the transition belt between the Qinghai-Tibet Plateau and the Sichuan Basin. In 1978, the State Council approved it as a National Nature Reserve. "Master planning of Jiuzhaigou National Nature Reserve (2006–2015)" contains the following appraisal of the values of this nature reserve, "The reserve is a wildlife nature reserve designated for the protection of giant pandas and their habitat. Under protection are: the giant panda and its habitat, karst calc-sinter landforms, and wetland ecosystems." In 1982 the State Council approved Jiuzhaigou as a national scenic area. According to the "Amended Master planning of Jiuzhaigou National Scenic Area (2001–2020)," this scenic area has the following values as appraised, "Jiuzhaigou landscape features can be summarized in five unparalleled wonders, namely, the Jade Sea, cascade waterfalls, colorful forest, snow-capped peaks, and Tibetan customs, but it is the unique waterscapes that raise it above other natural landscapes in China." In 1992, Jiuzhaigou was added to the World Heritage List in line with the World Heritage criteria.

Overall, heritage conservation planning in China is still in its preliminary stages, with their legal status, planning function, positioning, relations with other planning, implementing agencies, and component items waiting to be clarified. At the national level, although special protection and management planning is prepared for nominated sites upon application in recent years, no legislation or technical specifications have been promulgated yet for the protection and management of heritage sites. The Ministry of Housing and Urban-Rural Development is commissioning Tsinghua University with related studies and trying to include the development of the planning norms into the Ministry of Science and Technology's list of research projects for the 12th Five-Year-Plan Period. At the local level, a provincial regulation on world heritage protection has been in effect in Sichuan since 2002 and an Aba Prefecture also approved these regulations in 2007 to provide legal reference for local heritage sites in the compilation of their respective management and protection plans. Meanwhile, the Heritage Office under the Sichuan Provincial Department of Housing and Urban-Rural Development prepared an outline for conservation planning of world heritage sites in Sichuan to provide guidance for the planning. However, it also suggested that the "planning framework" is still at the experimental stage and there is room for discussion and further amendment. This planning is part of the experimentation process.

In terms of planning content, this plan has drawn upon new trends and theories in heritage protection and management from around the world, including: adaptive management, buffer zones as a means of protection and management, highlighted balance between the protection of universal and local values, a focus on cultural landscape, and concern for the impact of climate change and disaster management. The planning framework requires nine component parts: Planning Basis and General Provision, Overview, Outstanding Universal Values, Conservation Status and Environmental Pressure, Management System, Investment Budget and Funding Sources, References, Diagrams, and Annexes. Based on the above trends, the plan continues to evolve with additions in recent years to the Buffer Zone and Regional Coordination and Contingency Planning section, which were combined into one; Management Training and Management Capacity Building sections, which have been combined and renamed as Management System Building; and Publicity and Education for Protection Awareness, which has been amended and renamed Interpretation Education.

With an analysis of the status quo problem and in reference to relevant assessment, this plan proposes three issues of concern: visitor size and holding capacity, community development, and scenery resource protection.

The plan addresses the status quo problems of and potential threats to Jiuzhaigou via a multi-tiered planning system integrating the target system, strategy, zoning, and case-to-case planning. In regard to strategic planning, it is proposed that overall protection should be combined with minimum interference, regional co-ordination with multi-stakeholder participation, spatial measures with management measures, and that strategies of monitor-based adaptive management and incremental changes be adopted.

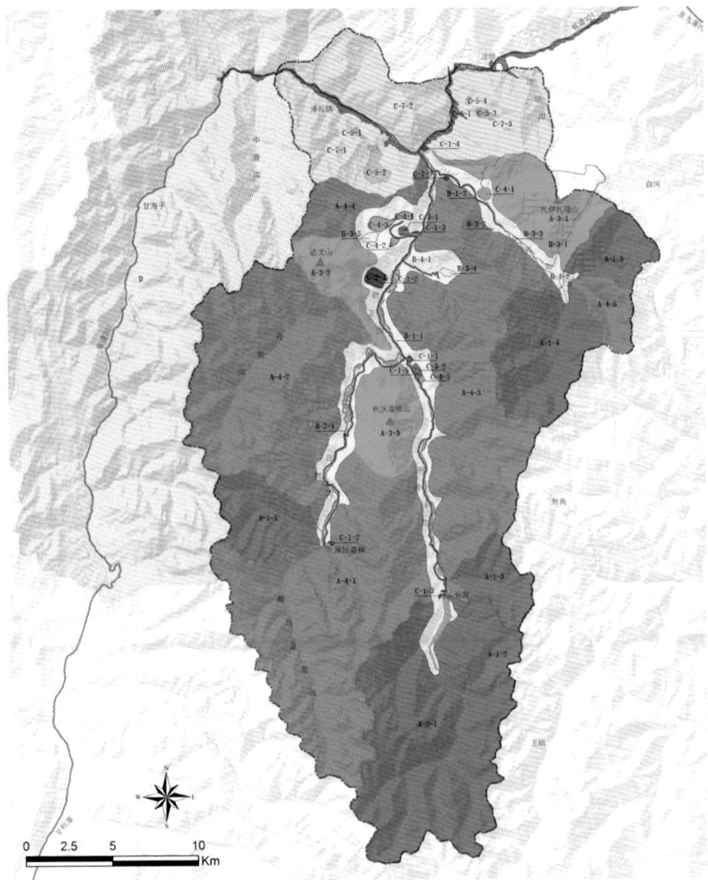

Right: Zoning map of the protection function.

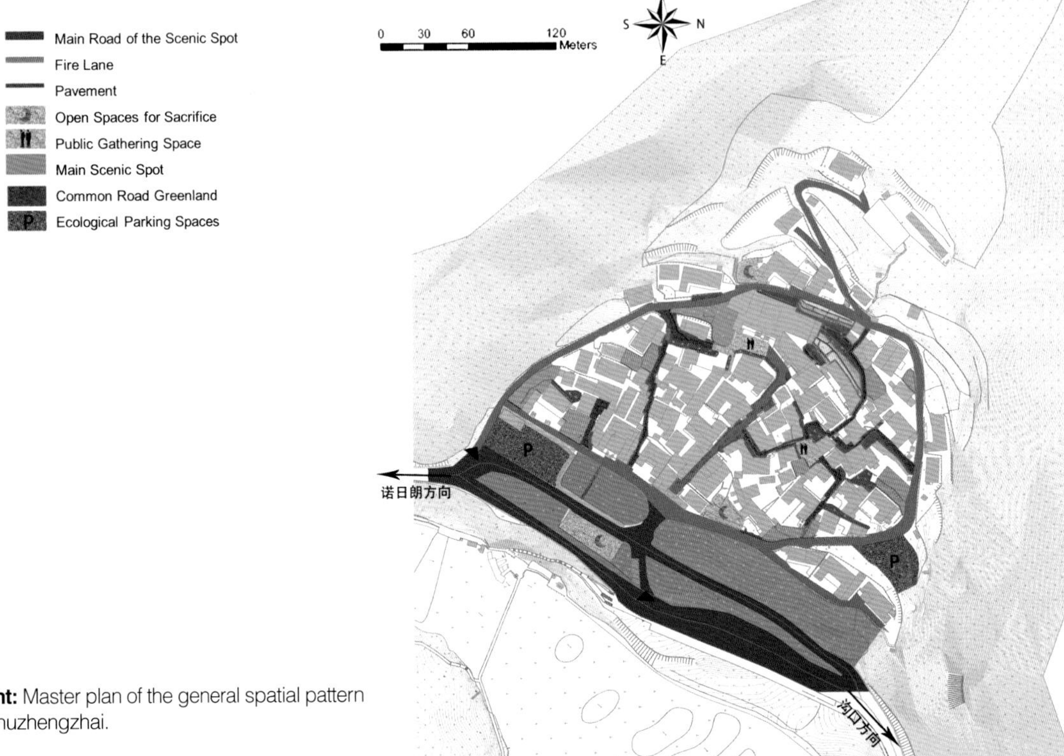

Right: Master plan of the general spatial pattern of Shuzhengzhai.

4) Cultural Landscape

Studies of Chinese Village Traditions

Project Category: International Collaborative Research Project
Project Source: Earthwatch Institute
Project Time: May 2005 to August 2008
Project Supervisors: Dang Anrong, Feng Jin, Lv Jiang
Project Team: Feng Jin, Lv Jiang, Liu Yanfeng, Lang Hongyang, Ma Qiwei, Zhao Jing, Liang Junjian, Zhang Yan, Chen Yang

The Chinese village tradition research project was funded by the Earthwatch Institute (EWI) with Tsinghua University, Lawrence Technological University (USA), and Eastern Michigan University (USA). The Yulin Municipal Government and Jiaxian County Government of the Shaanxi Province gave support to this project, and Yulin City and the Jiaxian County Departments of Cultural Affairs were crucial in the organization and undertaking of the project. The project was supervised by Professors Dang Anrong, Feng Jin, and Lv Jiang, with the participation of professors and graduate students, and visiting individuals from agencies and professional practices in the US, Europe, Australia, and Asia.

The overall objective of the project was to study the development and inheritance of the village cultural traditions, to excavate the features and values of village traditional culture, and to explore the ways that developing village cultural tourism can promote sustained economic development. Field visits were made with reference to historical and cultural backgrounds of the Yulin and Jiaxian counties with Dangjiashan Village as the starting point in a bid to interpret, collect, and analyze in order for the new plans to reflect the past and present culture of the residents and the ecological environment they rely on. The study covered four aspects: the environmental background of the village cultural traditions – the evolution of geographical landscape and ecological environment; the historical background of the cultural traditions including the ruins of the Great Wall, historic buildings, the ancient city, and other monuments; the physical forms of the village culture such as traditional clothing, food, housing, transportation, and products; and the non-material forms of the village traditions such as customs, folklore, religion, music, and legends. The project team conducted this investigation using surveys, visits, measurements, photographs, and videos to record and order first-hand data that reflect the village's traditions in a well-rounded manner. The result provided vivid and accurate scientific material for planning support with the local inhabitants in mind, taking into account their history and heritage in order to protect the area and benefit the locals.

Four years of investigation and study have resulted in the following outcomes with regard to the protection and development of village

Above: Typical village landscape in the northern Loess Plateau and the cave dwelling layout.

Above: Field research photo.

Above: Master plan of the cave village residence and its environmental protection heritage.

traditions: a solution was found for the protection and development of village cultural traditions on the basis of research of the history, culture, ecological environment, and folk traditions of Yulin and Jiaxian counties; a consensus was reached through engagement and exchange with the leadership and government departments of Yulin and Jiaxian on the awareness and importance of the local tradition, which is conducive to their protection and development; the villages received recognition and respect through careful work of project members from the US, UK, Russia, Singapore, New Zealand, Australia, Indonesia, and China.

The project was recognized at the 2007 Annual International Conference of the Earthwatch Institute held in Boston, and Professors Dang Anrong and Feng Jin jointly won the Earthwatch Scientist Award, the only Earthwatch award for that year.

Northwest Yunnan Village Cultural Landscape Protection Mode Research Based on Space Information Technologies

Project Category: Project Funded by the PhD Programs Foundation of Ministry of Education of China
Project Source: Ministry of Education
Project Time: January 2012 to December 2014
Project Supervisor: Dang Anrong
Project Team: Luo Deyin , Zhu Zhanqiang, Yang Yuliang, Zhang Danming, Chen Yang,Zhang Yan, Liu Yanbin

In light of the current challenges to the village cultural landscape, this project adopts integrated space information technology (SIT) in the study of theoretical and technical issues such as the composition and evolution mechanisms of village cultural landscapes to explore effective protection modes. It is of important academic significance to the enrichment of the meso-scale theoretical and technical methods of the Sciences of Human Settlements and of important practical relevance to the transformation and development of the traditional village and the construction of the new countryside.

The research consists of a study of the composition and functional mechanisms of village cultural landscapes based on the case of villages in Northwest Yunnan, a study of the evolution and driving mechanism of the village cultural landscapes, a study of the protection methods and measures based on SIT analyses, and a probe into the protection modes of universal significance on the basis of the case study. Based on the integrated space information technologies of RS, GIS, GPS, and VR, and with reference to the theories and methodologies of architecture, urban planning, rural geography, landscape ecology, and other disciplines, the project addresses the qualitative and quantitative analyses from a coherent multi-disciplinary perspective to generate technology-based methodologies featured by SIT integration advantages.

This research requires an incredible amount of field work, carried out batch by batch. The first batch was done in the Shangrila area in March 2012. The second was done in Nujiang in April 2012. The third was conducted in the Dali and Erhai area in August 2012. The fourth was carried out in the Lancang and Jinsha River Basins in June 2013. With these and continued research the field investigations have been nearly completed.

Currently, the work is focused on data processing and analysis, covering the SIT-based watershed division, constituent factors of village cultural landscape, the relationship between villages and rivers, and a variety of factors affecting the spatial relationship between villages. A series of papers have been written to share the preliminary outcomes. Some of the project outcomes were presented at the "2012 (Taiwan) International Symposium on Digital Cultural Heritage Protection," and were well received.

Above: Villages beside Lancang River.

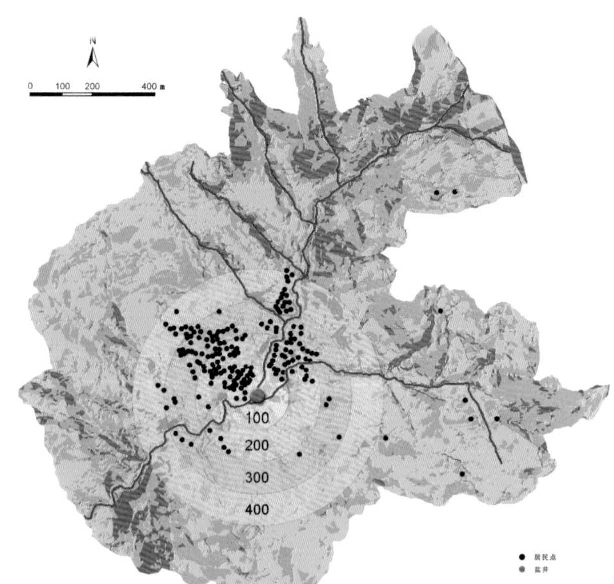

Right: Interactively schematic diagram of the salt wells during the formation of Nuodeng Village.

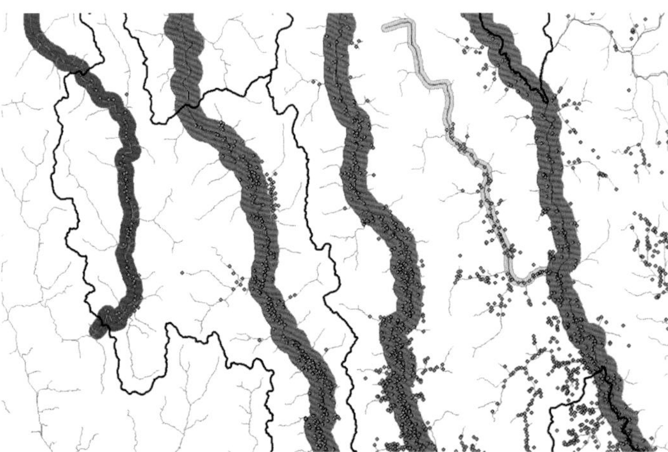

Right: Relatively schematic diagram of the distribution of the rivers and the villages.

Master Planning for the Temple of Heaven

Project Area: 273 hectares
Project Time: March 2007
Project Team: Yang Rui, Wu Dongfan, Zhuang Youbo, Liu Hailong, Zhao Zhicong, Hu Yike, Jia Liqi, Zhang Zhenwei, Liu Wen, Shi Shulin, Guo Yong, Wang Yinglin, Qi Zhengdong, Zhang Yuanling

The Temple of Heaven, a world cultural heritage site under national protection, has great cultural and historical research value. With the growing popularity of tourism and health-promotion exercises, the Temple of Heaven is attracting approximately 20 million people each year for either sightseeing or recreation purposes with unreplicable heritage properties and the ancient cypress trees. Today, this ancient place not only functions as a world heritage site but also as a park.

For various reasons, the Temple of Heaven faces global challenges in protection and management, such as incomplete internal spatial pattern, below average property conservation, dissatisfactory visitor experiences, outdated facilities in need of improvement, a return to local vegetation options, a need for stronger management of surrounding environments, and the need for more careful monitoring and upkeep. Master planning of the protection, and management of the Temple of Heaven have been made in light of the above-noted problems by setting up the target system in the four aspects of heritage protection, tourist and public user management, organizational management, and regional coordination and cooperation; and through the development of seven strategies for overall protection, public support, balanced tourist and recreational needs, appropriate holding capacity, value integration, regional harmony, and science-based management. On this basis, based on size and capacity, the master plan makes clear the planning structure and land use arrangements, zoning, and targeted management policies before incorporating them into the special planning for heritage conservation, landscape plant adjustments, visitor management, interpretation and education, transportation, service facilities, management offices, infrastructure, disaster prevention, and scientific research. The plan provides a step-by-step action plan with safeguard measures proposed for planning implementation.

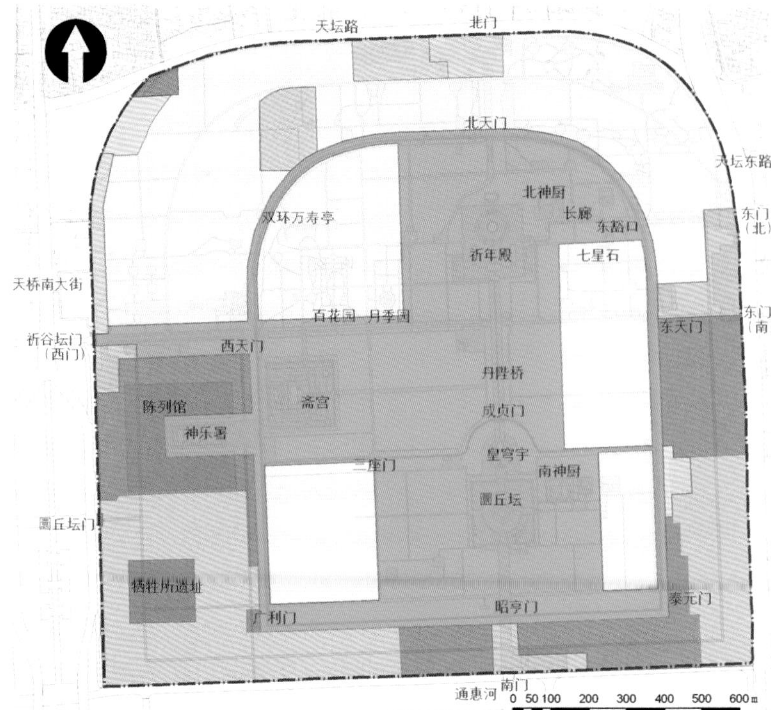

Level1 Reserve
Level2 Reserve
Scientific Exhibition Area
Entrance Service Area
Administration Service Area
Retaking Construction Area
Retaking Coordination Area
Planning Area

Above: General functional zoning map of the Temple of Heaven in the present and future.

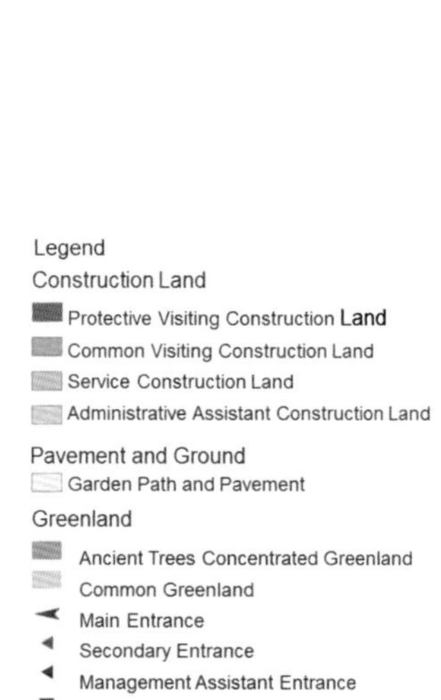

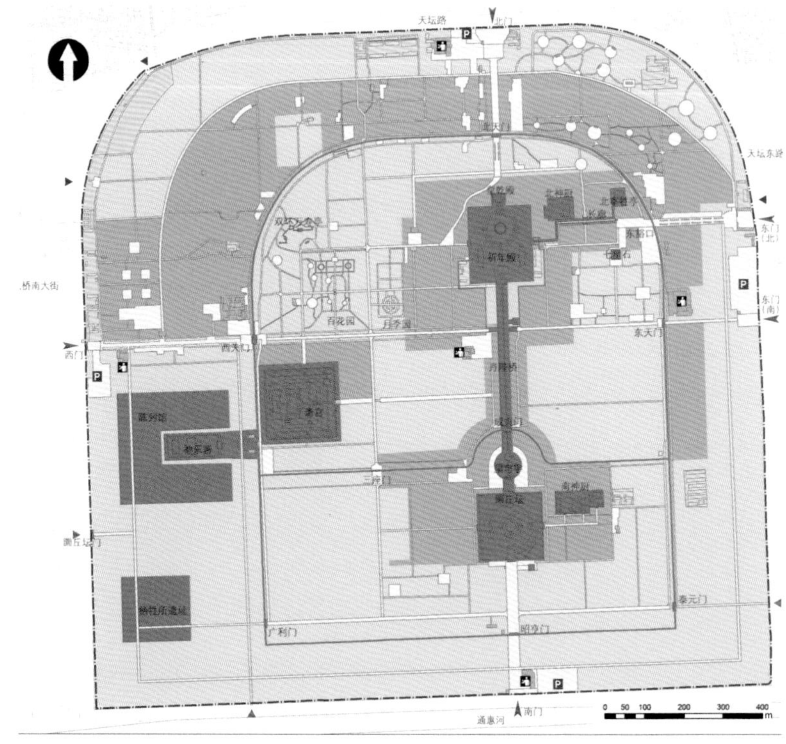

Above: Master plan of the Temple of Heaven.

3.5 Vegetation and Planting Design

Overview

Since the establishment of the first landscape architecture program by the Beijing Agriculture University and Tsinghua University with the joint initiation by Wang Juyuan and Liang Sicheng in 1951, the curriculum of the Landscape architecture program of the Department of Architecture and Urban Planning at Tsinghua University has included a Plant Taxonomy course (taught by Cui Youwen from the Chinese Academy of Science) and the course of Ornamental and Flowering Trees and Shrubs[1] (taught by Wang Juyuan and Chen Youmin). Courses related to landscape plants had a relatively important position in the summer internship programs, visiting practices, graduate practices, and other teaching links within the Landscape architecture program.

Even though the landscape architecture program at Tsinghua University was not its entity, teaching and study of plant and plant application as important component of landscape architecture have never failed to be part of the curriculum. Before the establishment of the Department of LA, Zhou Daoying, from the Beijing Forestry University, was invited to lecture on LA botanic composition, and following the establishment of the Department of LA in 2003, Professor Bao Zhiyi was invited to teach courses in Plant Landscaping Planning and Design. Zhu Junzhen published *The Garden Plant Landscaping Art of China* in 2003, a book reflecting Tsinghua's achievements in LA Plant Application in the past half-century. This section is based on her earlier research findings from the project, "Botanic Composition of Gardens in Hangzhou," with improvements, modifications, and additions during her years of design and teaching. This is therefore a summation of her landscape planning design, teaching, and research practice. With an in-depth study and discussion of the plant landscaping arts with unique traditional characteristics. This section introduces the formation of the plant landscaping styles, plant landscaping of traditional gardens and temple gardens, the spatial, water, road, and architecture aspects of garden planting, and green landscaping for plants in nature.

Since the establishment of the Department of LA, particularly after 2009, the vegetation and planting design program, on the basis of the down-to-earth teaching and scientific research of the project team led by Professor Li Shuhua, has had many momentous achievements. The project team carried out studies on ecological benefits of urban green space, urban bio-diversity distribution features, and basic theories and planning design methodologies related to therapeutic landscapes. Since 2009, the program successfully applied for two projects funded by National Natural Science Foundation, one project by PhD Program Foundation of the Ministry of Education, and two projects by the China

Postdoctoral Science Foundation. The department has also produced several publications including *Planning and Design of Urban Green Space for Emergency and Disaster-Prevention* (China Building Industry Press, 2010), the two textbooks *Garden Planting Design Theories* (China Agriculture Press, 2010) and *Introduction to Therapeutic Gardening* (China Forestry Press, 2011), and the translated edition of *A Handbook of Garden Plant Landscaping: From Planning Design to Construction Management* (China Architecture & Building Press, 2012). Members of the department have published over 60 academic papers in the *Journal of Environmental Management*, *Building Simulation*, *Silva Fennica*, *Acta Ecologica Sinica*, *Chinese Journal of Applied Ecology*, the *Journal of Plant Ecology*, *Chinese Landscape Architecture,* the *Journal of Forestry Science*, and the *Chinese Journal of Ecology.*

Ecological Benefits and Functions of Urban Green Space

Urban linear green space and river corridor green belts are important components of urban green spaces, addressing the needs of the urban ecological corridor while bringing fresh air streams from the suburbs to urban interiors, and insulating and dispersing urban heat. However, due to severe human intervention during the urbanization process, urban linear green space, and urban river corridors in particular, have been intensely affected by human activities and natural processes. The "*Quantitative Study of Ecological Benefits of Urban Green Space,*" by the project team under Professor Li Shuhua's supervision used small-scale quantitative measurements in their three-year study of the relationship between the urban linear green space and urban river corridor green space in Beijing, showing the ecological and environmental benefits. The project was a systematic study of how urban linear green space of different width, interior structure, shade density, and environment types differ in temperature, relative humidity, negative ion concentration, and microbe content factors. With research of urban rivers and riverbank green belts in Beijing, this project led to the analysis of the impact of river width, riverbank green belt width, green belt vertical structure, and shade density on green house effect.

Rapid urbanization has marred the natural eco-system and bio-diversity in the cities. Domestic and overseas research on urban bio-diversity is primarily focused on either plant or animal diversity, however there is a lack of comprehensive systematic research with particular regard to spatial distribution characteristics of urban plant and animal diversity. The team, led by Professor Li Shuhua, performed the study, "*Research on the Plant and Animal Diversity Distribution Characteristics of Urban Green Islands,*" which addressed the urban green islands in Beijing and explored the impact of area, position, shape, and interior structure of urban green islands on plant and animal diversity, and also covered the relationship between plant and animal diversity through field study and data analyses. On the above basis, the project figured results showed the minimum area of the urban green island required for plant and animal diversity stability, revealed the impact of urbanization on the plant and animal species composition and diversity on the urban green island, the difference in plant and animal diversity on green islands of different shapes, and found that different habitats affect plant and animal species composition and diversity. The research findings provided scientific basis for construction of high-quality urban green space, safe urban ecological layout, and rational urban green space system planning so as to create an equilibrium between people and nature in the urban environment and sustainable development of the urban ecological environment.

Basic Theories and Planning Design Approaches of Therapeutic Gardening

Urban landscape green space has therapeutic effects on mental and physical health. With urbanization and the advent of the aging society, urban residents tend to face greater mental pressure. The number of aging and sub-healthy population is rising rapidly. Chronic disease incident rates are up. Medical institutions are reporting growing spending on addressing the aging society. Landscape has health benefits and its effects have been recorded in both eastern and western cultures. Scientific studies have been made, both home and abroad, on the principles, functions, and design of therapeutic gardens. Therapeutic gardening designs will be used increasing as active adjuvant therapies. The study of therapeutic effects urban green space has on human mental and physical health and the corresponding characteristics of green space provide guidance for therapeutic gardening design.

Since 2010, the project team led by Professor Li Shuhua has been studying the basic theories and planning design approaches of therapeutic gardening in an attempt to understand and relate the effects that are gained from landscape and green space characteristics. His research has also addressed how cities of different scales and types use therapeutic landscape design in order to sum up the therapeutic landscape design approaches for urban medical facilities, courtyards of senior care organizations, green spaces in residential areas, and comprehensive parks. Findings could add to the quantitative scientific research on therapeutic landscaping and garden therapy, providing argumentation for extension and popularization of the same. They could further act as a base for therapeutic landscape design and therapeutic landscape-function design, and in turn could provide valuable information for landscape architectural design as a whole. These areas offer a viable way to improve mental and physical health of urban residents while addressing the social problems of an ageing society.

At present the project team has obtained preliminary achievements in the research on the application of "evidence-based design" in therapeutic outdoor space and healing gardens, and empirical research approaches of therapeutic landscape. The research team is experimenting with the biophile design concept and conducting related studies with practical implications. Biophile design, based on human evolution theory, is a design approach that seeks harmonious co-existence of humanity and nature for active influence on the human's mental and physical health. On the basis of the research on "biophila" and biophile design concept and their health promotion functions, the emphasis has been on the analysis of biophile design approach and further empirical study of biophile design of therapeutic landscapes, which have been carried out through the renovation of Beijing Air Force General Hospital.

Prospects

The study of plants, plantings, and design occupy an important position in the curriculum of the discipline of Landscape Architecture at Tsinghua University. In addition to constant exploration of teaching content and teaching methods suited to the characteristics of the students and the disciplinary development of the landscape architecture program at architecture-related schools in the teaching practice of the "*Landscape Plants*" and "*Plant Landscape Planning and Design*" courses, the program has taken the study of quantitative research on ecological benefits of urban green space, research on the distribution characteristics of urban plant and animal diversity, basic theories and planning, and design approaches of therapeutic landscaping to the next level. The next step is to continue to conduct extensive multi-scale, in-depth research on ecological restoration and vegetation restoration by combining the Tsinghua School of Architecture program and integrating its strengths with the other schools at Tsinghua University.

–Li Shuhua, Zhao Yazhou

1) Planting Design

Design of Tsinghua University Centennial Forest

Project Area: 0.52 hectares
Completed In: April 2011
Design Team: Li Shuhua, Liu Jian, Shao Zongbo, Huang Yue, Zhao Yazhou

The Centennial Forest was built in 2011 on the centennial celebration of Tsinghua University at the tree-planting area of the Global Summit of University Presidents (GSUP) and during the 15th Annual President Meeting for Association of Pacific Rim Universities (APRU). In the planning and design of the Centennial Forest, the team kept its function as a Centennial landscape in mind, and, as a venue of the commemorative activities, injected elements of the Tsinghua culture, festive atmosphere, and plantings into the design process. The design fits perfectly into the overall landscape setting, and daily leisure space is included to create this shaded, sloped green space on the campus. The design program intended to address the lack of a pleasant green space for recreation in the eastern part of the campus, and to provide access points to the swimming pool, sports hall, basketball court, and eastern playground by positioning the entrance and making proper use of the space. It is not cut off from the campus though, and echoes with the green space under construction in the northern part of the campus in terms of landform and function. To avoid underground pipelines, and to compact the distribution of the paving and planting areas, the planting positions were organized around the pipeline routes.

The positioning of the Centennial Forest design program is a sustainable landscape design, and a legacy for the next 100 years. It is culturally-sensitive as a continuation of the 100-year tradition of the university, and a diversified landscape design that meets leisure and recreation needs on the campus.

The Centennial Forest design program uses the terrain as the carrier of the 100-year history. The plants symbolize the circle of life, the paving is the spreading branches of exuberance and profusion. Rings of trees, the imprint of life, are used to show the profound history of Tsinghua and how it has blended into the luxuriant foliage of the towering trees. Linking the Tree Ring Square to the repose space is the branch-like path with cracked ice paving symbolizing the continuation of a long history.

2) Ecological Benefits and Functions of Urban Green Space

Quantitative Study of the Ecological Environmental Benefits of Urban Green Belts

Project Source: National Natural Science Foundation of China
Project Time: January 2010 to December 2012
Project Supervisor: Li Shuhua
Project Team: Chang Qing, Zhu Chunyang, Ji Peng, Yang Yuanzhao, Zhang Wenxiu

This project is a systematic study of the urban green belts in Beijing from the relationship between their width to internal structure, canopy density, type of environment, and ecological benefits. Small-scale, quantitative measurements were used in this project for analysis of how different urban linear green spaces differ in temperature, relative humidity, negative ion concentration, and bacterial content. These factors make clear the relationship between the belts and allow for indexing of urban green belts. The research findings are as follows:

1. The Relationship Between Green Belt Width and Ecological Benefits

(A) The relationship between green belt width, temperature, and humidity: the critical width for temperature and humidity benefits is around 34 meters with green coverage of approximately 80% ($P < 0.05$). For maximum benefit the green belt needs to be 42 meters wide where green coverage is approximately 80% ($P < 0.05$). Analyses of the summer data on temperature and humidity benefits indicate that the green space has some cooling and moisturizing effects on the sidewalks nearby but have irregular results overall that are prone to the influence of surrounding environments.

(B) The relationship between green belt width and negative air ion concentration: the critical width for remarkable negative air ion concentration benefits is approximately 42 meters of green coverage at a rate of about 80% ($P < 0.05$). Negative air ion concentration benefits increase gradually with the increase of green belt width in the summer.

(C) The relationship between green belt width and the bacterial content of the air: the critical width for remarkable bacteriostatic benefits is around 34 meters with a green coverage rate of approximately 80% ($P < 0.05$).

2. The Relationship Between the Internal Environment Type and Ecological Benefits Under Similar Width and Canopy Density Conditions:

Green belts containing rivers have remarkably better cooling and moisturizing effects than pure green belts and those containing roads of equal width ($P < 0.05$).

3. The Relationship Between the Internal Structure and Ecological Benefits

(A) The relationship between the internal structure of urban green belts, temperature, and humidity: the temperature and humidity benefits from arbor-grass and arbor-bush-grass on green belts is remarkable ($P < 0.05$).

(B) The relationship between the internal structure of urban green belts and negative air ion concentration: the negative air ion benefits from arbor-grass and arbor-bush-grass on green belts are remarkable ($P < 0.05$).

(C) The relationship between the internal structure of urban green belt and the bacterial content of the air: the bacteriostatic benefits from arbor-grass on green belts are remarkable ($P < 0.05$).

4. The Relationship Between the Canopy Density and Ecological Benefits

(A) The relationship between the canopy density of urban green belts, temperature, and humidity: when the canopy density exceeds 0.44, the temperature and humidity benefits are apparent ($P < 0.05$), and when the canopy density exceeds 0.67, the temperature and humidity benefits reach an exceptional point ($P < 0.05$).

(B) The relationship between the canopy density of urban green belts and negative air ion concentration: when the canopy density exceeds 0.44, negative air ion benefits are exceptional ($P < 0.05$).

Above: Field research photo – the plant community of the arbor and herb structure.

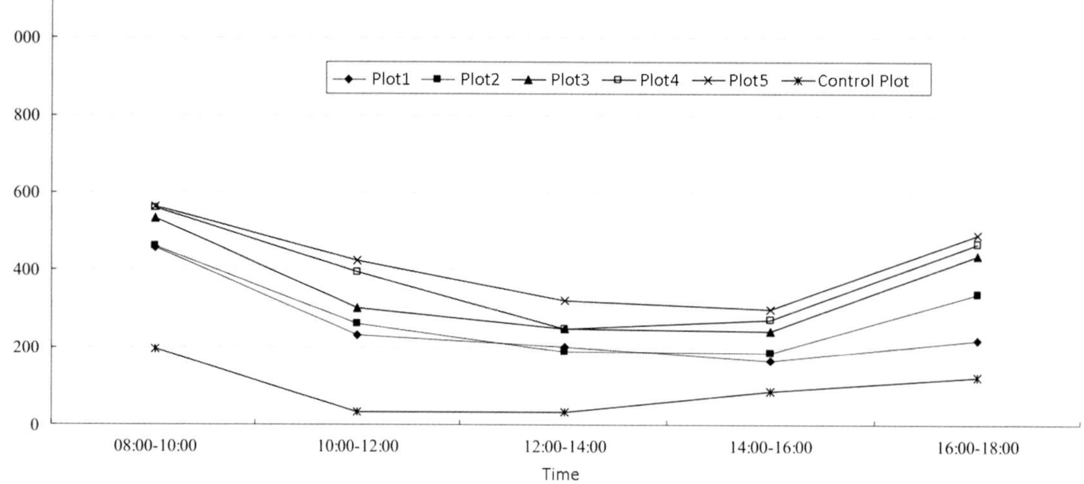

Above: Negative ion concentration change in five periods of one day in the different samples and the control.

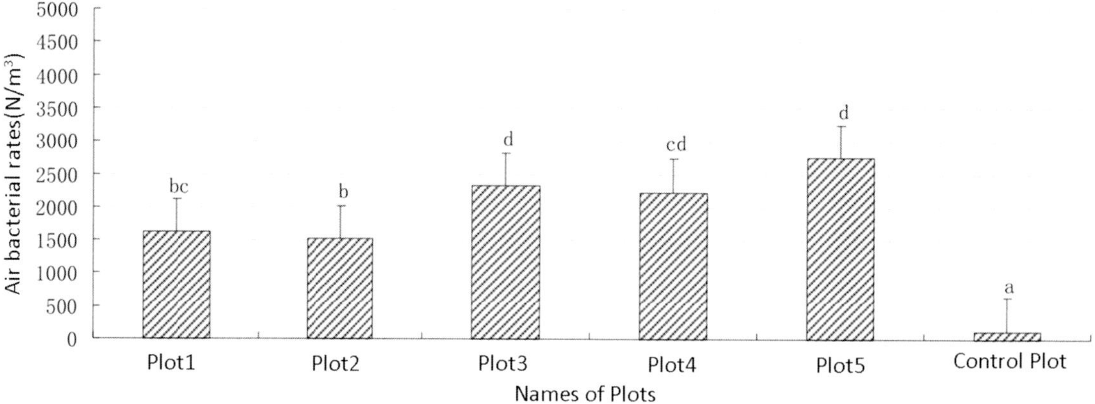

Above: Comparison of average bacteria quantity in the air in three days in the different samples and the control.

Research on Flora and Fauna Diversity Distribution Features of Urban Green Islands

Project Source: National Natural Science Foundation of China
Project Time: January 2012 to December 2015
Project Supervisor: Li Shuhua
Project Team: Zhao Yazhou, Huang Yue, Long Xuan, Liang Daqing, Liu Huanan

Above: Plant survey record.

This project addresses the urban green islands in Beijing in relationship to their impact on surroundings due to area, location, shape, internal structure, flora and fauna, and diversity of plants and animals. This provides a base for calculation of the minimum area of urban green islands to obtain a stable diversity of flora and fauna through excavation and the composition and variance of animal and plant species that are affected by the urbanization process. Analyses of flora and fauna diversity is affected by the shape of the urban green islands, and the above noted study can provide conclusions as to how animal and plant species distribution is affected by habit types.

The following preliminary results have been discovered:

1. Plant Diversity Field Research and Species Identification

Field research on plant diversity has been conducted by sampling during April to August 2012. The sampling consisted of species identification, site identification, and desk research, the latter of which was accomplished from November to December of the same year. Altogether, the survey identified a total of 197 woody plant species (including subspecies and cultivars) and 229 herbal species (including subspecies and cultivars).

2. Insect Diversity Field Research and Species Identification

Three rounds of insect diversity field research were conducted in July 2012. Insect specimens are captured using the net sweeping methods and then preserved in a 70% alcohol solution or by drying. Species identification, conducted in August and September, resulted in the confirmation of 229 insect species (including subspecies and cultivars) in the region.

3. Bird Diversity Field Research and Species Identification

Five rounds of bird diversity field research were conducted from May to November 2012. Species were identified on site using the line transect method, and for some species in question, photos were taken for identification and reference to the illustrations in *A Field Guide to the Birds of China*. Altogether, 126 bird species were confirmed.

Above: Technology Roadmap

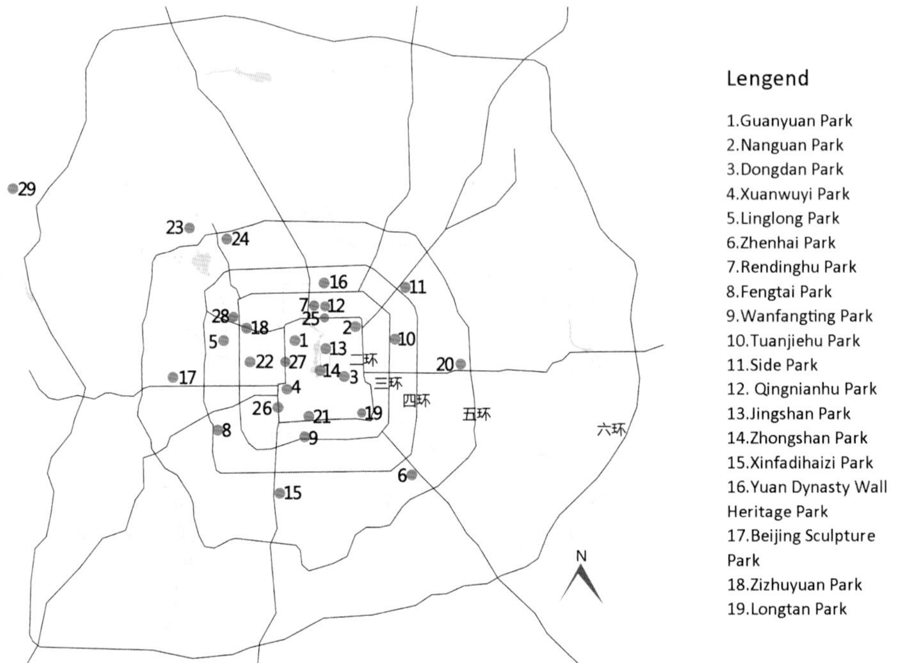

Above: Distribution of the city green islands of the field research in 2012.

3.6 Landscape Architecture Technology and Science

Overview

Historical Overview

Tsinghua LA has a tradition of valuing technology, which is founded on the standing tradition of the university, and has been in existence since the launch of the Landscape architecture program of the Department of Architecture and Urban Planning at Tsinghua University. Upon the establishment of the department, a more independent landscape technology system with more prominent professional features gradually came into being.

In 1951, the curriculum for the Landscape Architecture program included technological courses like gardening, engineering, and surveying. Due to the lack of faculty at that time, the Landscape Architecture program invited teachers from the Tsinghua Department of Civil Engineering to lecture on related courses. In addition, "Architecture" and other technological courses were also open to the students at the time. In the same year, the Landscape Architecture program was devoted to the cultivation of well-rounded, technologically advanced individuals who were said to have "good hands-on and brains-on ability, were savvy in design, construction, maintenance, and management, on the same level as a general engineer."[(1)] This paved the way for a sound platform for the technological tradition of Tsinghua LA.

During the preparatory stage of curriculum planning at the Department of LA, special attention was paid to the teaching of technology, in accordance with its use in the professional practice of landscape architecture. Through a comparison with the architectural, engineering, and planning technologies, Laurie D. Olin suggested in the Proposed Curriculum & Course Outline,[(2)] that there should be technological training for landscape architects and that the teaching should cover technological knowledge of roads, structures, small buildings, bridges, hydropower stations, dams, and canals to the point of mastory of material properties. In the proposal of his curriculum he also stressed the importance of teaching the natural sciences and further suggested offering courses in geographical information systems.

Under this guiding principle, upon the establishment of the Department of LA in 2003, Ron Henderson and Hu Jie jointly offered the "Landscape Technology-Grading and Road Design" course. Meanwhile, Professor Dang Anrong offered, "Introduction to Landscape Geo-Science," and "RS and GIS Technology," while experimenting with landscape planning and design of Geo-Information Technology. Tsinghua LA was able to progress in teaching and scientific research, and expand into sustainable technology combined with engineering projects to gradually develop into the current LA technology system.

Teaching of Landscape Technology Courses

Upon the establishment of the Department of LA at Tsinghua University in 2003, the teaching and research of landscape technology was highly prioritized in order to generate a technological teaching system based on professional skill training and a scientific research systems, which features the application of Geo-Information Technology. This has aided with the expansion into sustainable landscape technology, and helped the integrated development of production, teaching, and research.

"Landscape Technology-Grading and Road Design" is a course primarily for professor's students, and, is intended to train, to mastory, individuals on the basic skills of landscape grading and the integration of technological thinking with operation. It gives special emphasis to experience and practice. Class lectures focus on site grading design, while out of class exercises train students to observe the environment, understand design, identify problems, and accumulate subject matter from the perspective of construction technology through quick sketching. These techniques and observations are used to make analytical models. By the end of the course a student is able to apply theoretical study to site grading design of landforms, roads, squares, banisters, and handrails, and will be familiar with the surveying technology through practical experience.

"Introduction to Landscape Geo-Science" addresses geology, landform, soil, and other natural elements constituting the landscape, and is intended to train students through in-class teaching and field practice activities to know geologic, geomorphologic, pedologic, and other basic geo features of the landscapes, and how to apply these ideas planning and design so as to, "design with nature."

In the "RS and GIS Technology" course, students are required to master the general principles and approaches of RS and GIS technology, in order to apply RS and GIS in landscape planning and design, including data analysis, program evaluation, and decision-making support.

Application of the Geo-Information Technology in Landscape Planning and Design

While teaching landscape technology, the team, represented by Professor Dang Anrong, advanced the application of GIT (Geo-Information Technology) by means of integration. GIT, has developed rapidly since the 1960s, and is used to obtain, manage, process, analyze, and represent space information related to geographic position, including data collected through RS (Remote Sensing), GNSS (Global Navigation Satellite System), GIS (Geographic Information System), and VR (Virtual Reality).

The application of GIT moved from concept (pre-1995), to experimentation (1996–2000), to in-depth application (2001–2005), to digital landscape planning (2006–2010), and now to smart landscape planning (2011 to present). GIT application literature, known for the conceptualization stage before 1995, is very limited and mostly related to discussions of the concept in the field of landscape design, landscape planning, and landscape ecology. During the application experimentation stage (1996–2000), there are some analyses of, and research on, experimental applications of GIS and RS. Among others, Dang Anrong and Yang Rui applied integrated RS and GIS in the data analysis of Mount Taishan National Park Master planning while exploring the technological approaches. During the in-depth application stage (2001–2005), the application depth and width were expanded based on findings during the previous stage, resulting in an increasing number of publications, extended application fields, and quantitative space analyses. Dang Anrong, Yang Rui, and others (2002) applied integrated RS, GIS, and GNSS technologies in the compilation of the master planning of the Meili Snow Mountain Scenic Area, and developed the management information system to meet the planning and management needs. During the afore mentioned stage, great strides were made in integrated GIT application, in projects such as the proposed concept of Digital Earth, and the planning and construction of Digital Cities and Digital National Parks. Digital Earth technology led to GoogleEarth and GoogleMaps. Under the advocacy of the Ministry of Science and Technology and the Ministry of Construction, a number of digital cities were built including: Digital Beijing, Digital Shanghai, and Digital Guangzhou; as well as a number of digital national parks such as Digital Mount Huangshan, Digital Jiuzhaigou, and Digital Mount Putuo. The GIT application in landscape planning and design was pushed into the digital age (2006–2010). During this stage, Dang Anrong and Yang Rui (2005), published their research findings in regards to the digital scenic area master framework.

With the development of the GIT and its application, abundant achievements were made in the development of digital Earth, digital cities, and digital national parks. Meanwhile, with the advent of related new technologies such as the Internet, cloud computing, wireless communication, and mobile terminals, the Smart Earth concept was born (2008). Related concepts including, the Smart City, Smart National Park, and Smart Tourism helped advance the use of GIT. With the evolution of digital cities into smart cities, the digital national parks into smart national parks, digital landscape planning and design were moving into the smart landscape planning and design stage. Smart landscape planning and design was not finished with the construction and development of smart cities and smart national parks though. Dang Anrong and others, concluded the research on connotation and general framework of smart national parks (2011), and explored the general framework of smart cities (2012) thus making an active contribution to the application of the new technology of smart landscape planning and design, subject matter, technologies, and methodologies for future use and practice.

Technological Research Based on Projects

In addition to these teaching and research achievements, Tsinghua LA has been actively involved in research on related technologies. These technologies include surveying and sustainable landscape technologies.

From a historical point of view, landscape architects play a rather limited role, with particular regard to large and complicated development projects. The practice dimensions of landscape architecture has transferred from the design of private gardens in ancient times, to the planning and design of modern public open spaces. The professional dimension of landscape architecture is at the conjunction of architecture, engineering, urban planning, and urban design, with the actual scope continuing to expanded in the practice. Traditionally, to meet the rising needs of the population, civil and urban engineers dominate environmental design, and a lot of natural functions are replaced with artificial objects. However, traditional rain and flood treatment facilities, sewage treatment facilities, and other infrastructures are mostly ugly, costly, and environmentally hostile, and require constant maintenance. With the rising awareness of environmental protection since the 1970s, practitioners of landscape architecture have been showing greater interest in effective water use, aquifer supplements, and other issues, gradually accepting and using pedology, hydrology, and water conservation knowledge in order to build sustainable plant landscapes and wild animal habitats. Landscape architects have begun collecting and analyzing data for sites of different scales to see what would be necessary to support more ecological and systematic planning and design approaches. At present, the relationship between the artificial and natural environment is becoming more and more complicated. Landscape architects have begun to play a leading role in pre-development and ecological restoration projects in a bid to balance development needs with natural conservation, and to establish sustainable development.

Based on the above understanding, the technical team led by Professor Hu Jie has been conducting cross-disciplinary research in large projects. In the Tangshan Nanhu Eco-City Central Park Overall Planning & Design project, the team explored the relationship between the site surveying approach to obtain sufficient data and GIT application. Through experimentation with many engineering projects, they studied the site surveying experience using electronic total station, GPS, unmanned aerial vehicles, simulators, remote data, 3D laser scanning, and photogrammetric technologies for sites of varying scale. Using all technology available, Professor Hu Jie undertook the research and surveying of the rockwork inside the Qianlong Garden in the Forbidden City with the intent of making new contributions to the protection of the imperial garden.

On the basis of planning and design practices by a team led by Professor Yang Rui, the "Research and Development of 3D Real-Time, Rural Eco-Tourism Landscape Simulation Technology" project was conducted to advance the information technology widely used in cities, to build a multi-functional 3D-simulation system targeting rural landscape environments and tourist resources to serve as the IT platform for planning, management, and services related to the rural eco-tourism. This could also be used as a real-time application platform for planners, managers, and tourists.

A team from Tsinghua University collaborated with a team of environmental scientists in study of the Olympic Forest Park titled, "Key Technology Research and Demonstrations for Separation and Reclamation of Domestic Pollution Emitting Sources in the Olympic Forest Park." The project was supported by the National Science and Technology Ministry in 2007, and continued the research begun in 2007 in the "Disposal and Reclamation of Building Wastes in the Olympic Forest Park," which was carried out by the Beijing Municipal Science and Technology Project. The project provided first time analyses on the formation and composition of the building waste sources in the Olympic Forest Park in juxtaposition with population flow. The project used resource reclamation recycling systems on a large scale in the parks, which uses gravity current source separation sanitary ware for sewage discharge. The project included a special yellow water collection as a means of storage and transportation of water, and a resource reclamation system to maintain a friendly environmental footprint. Analyses of the treatment efficiency and economic effects of large-scale use of the current source separation system, as well as the composition of pollution characteristics of the black water from the system have shown positive results.

Outlook and Development

The disciplinary system of Tsinghua LA, with technology and science as important supportive segments will continue to intensify the teaching of vertical design and other professional technologies and applied research of GIT-based landscape architecture while conducting problem-oriented, cross-disciplinary, comprehensive technological studies through large engineering projects. In addition, with current teaching and research, efforts will be made to expand the content of the technological teaching so as to intensify the standardization and specification of the professional technologies. The goal is to compile professional course-books so as to raise the theoretical and systematic standards of the teaching content, and to develop probation and research bases so as to push for further integration of theory and practice through teaching and research.

– Dang Anrong, Hu Jie, Wang Peng, Guo Yong

1) Project-Based Technological Research

Key Technological Research and Demo Projects for Separation and Resource Reclamation of Domestic Pollution Sources in the Olympic Forest Park

Project Category: Project under the 2007 National Science and Technology Support Program
Project Source: Ministry of Science and Technology of the People's Republic of China
Project Time: January 2007 to July 2011
Project Supervisor: Tian Jinxian
Project Team: Hu Jie, Liang Sijia

This project, based on the urban functions positioned in the "Beijing City Master plan (2004–2020)" and the three concepts of the 2008 Beijing Olympic Games, namely, "Green Olympics, People's Olympics, and Hi-Tech Olympics," is a concrete manifestation of the strategies of building a conservation-oriented society through a scientific outlook on development. The overall objective of the project is to put the three concepts into practice via resource recycling, reuse of the sewage and waste discharge, and through the use of water- and energy-efficient economic operations.

Based on the construction projects of the domestic sewage systems, sewage treatment systems, and green waste treatment centers inside the Olympic Forest Park, this project safeguards and supports the energy efficiency, lower energy consumption, and resource utilization initiatives of the park. Research on key technologies and integrated pilot projects for separation and resource reclamation of domestic pollution sources in the park have been used to build a new model of sewage treatment and resource recycling and reuse. The research for this project has been used as a theoretical basis of practical technologies for future construction of similar parks in China. Research findings have led to significant economic, social, and environmental benefits that fully reflect the overall position of China in resource recycling and reuse, integrated environmental management, and urban water environment protection.

The findings from the Olympic Forest Park study will have direct effects on the overall environment of, and landscape inside, the Olympic Forest Park. The cross-the-board application of the domestic waste separation and resource reclamation technologies in the Olympic Forest Park reflects the other Olympic projects' dedication to environmental protection undertakings, which can be viewed as a concrete manifestation of its implementation of and compliance with the "three concepts" outlined within the study. Technological achievements and pilot projects can be used as a platform to showcase to the nation and the world. The achievements from environmental protection and sustainable development have had a remarkable social significance in raising public awareness of environmental protection while enhancing China's image and status in related fields.

Reuse of Building Wastes in the Olympic Forest Park

Project Category: Project under the 2007 Beijing Science and Technology Program
Project Source: Beijing Municipal Science and Technology Commission
Project Time: January 2007 to December 2008
Project Supervisor: Tian Jinxian
Project Team: Hu Jie, Liang Sijia

This project aims to promote, through practical use, and provide publicity for the emerging environmental protection theories of source separation and resource reclamation of household wastes by leveraging the exemplary demonstration functions of Olympic projects. With application for, and development of, environmental protection and resource recycling concepts, this project plays a positive role in the future development of human settlements.

The technological roadmap for the project is to build up the domestic sewage separation system to separate yellow water from the conventional sewage system, store, and then transport it to biological and chemical treatment facilities to generate manure for use in the park with fertilizers from sludge from the septic tanks and green waste in the park that have been treated.

This project targeted the sewage discharged from 49 buildings, of various functions, for the Olympic Games in 2008, using treatment of urine and waste water from stool flushing, hand cleaning, sanitation cleaning, and from catering and bathing sites within the facilities to revitalize the Olympic Forest Park area and to decrease environmental footprint. Material output is intended for park woods and meadows within an area of 456.8 hectares (80%) of the total park area. The experimental area is 3-5-hectare project area within the forest park.

Innovations as a result of the study were implemented for: (1) population flow characteristics, which were studied along with the research and analysis of the formation and composition of the Olympic Forest Park construction waste sources; (2) current source separation sanitary wares that are used on a large scale in large parks for building sewage discharge purposes and for resource reclamation and recycling purposes in light of the garden care and maintenance needs; (3) special yellow water collection, storage, and transportation in resource reclamation systems built inside the park; (4) treatment efficiency and economic effects of large-scale use of the current source separation system, as well as the composition and pollution characteristics of the black water from the system; and (5) soil content inside the park, on which R&D was conducted on integrated, reclaimed organic fertilizer utilization solutions based on local landscape fertilization needs.

Awards:
Special Science and Technology Innovation Award for the Beijing Olympics from the Beijing Municipal People's Government in March 2009.

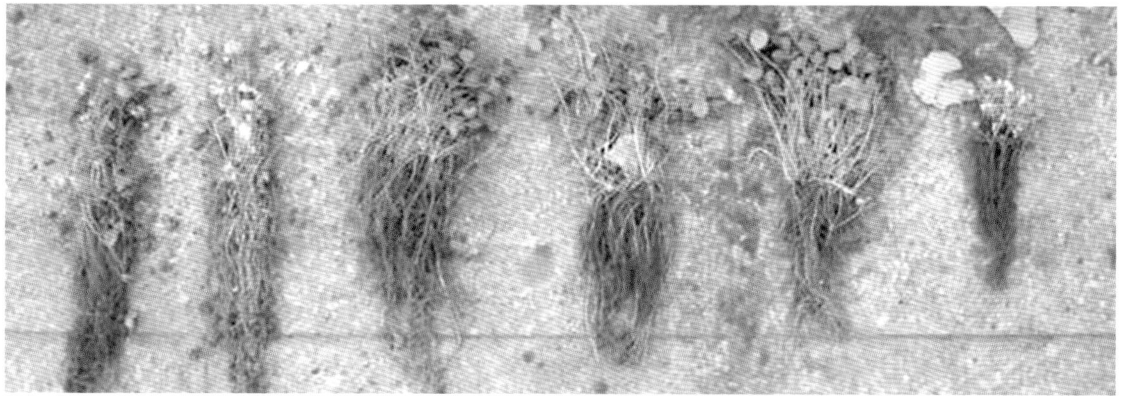

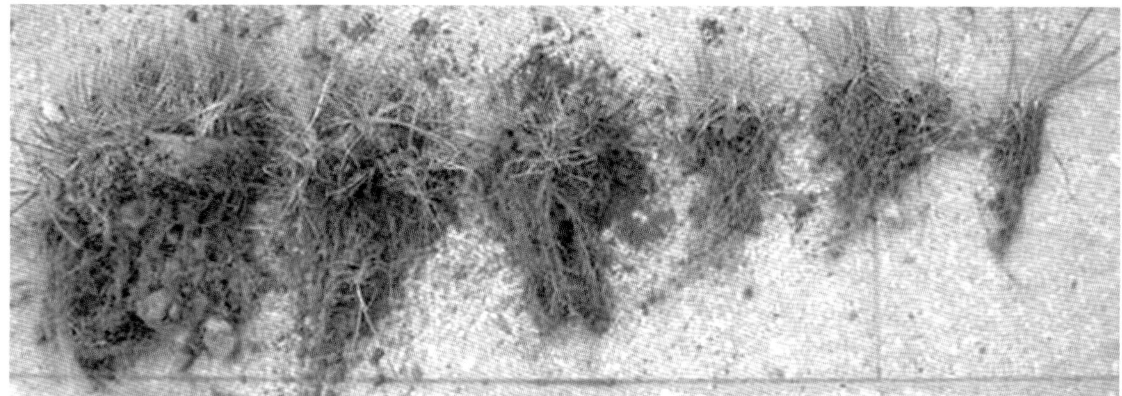

Above: Comparison photo of planting experiment.

Landscape Survey, Photo Library Construction, and Digital Simulation Study of Qianlong Garden, Forbidden City, Beijing

Project Source: National Palace Museum
Project Time: 2009
Project Supervisor: Hu Jie
Project Team: An Youfeng, Li Jiazhong, Wang Peng, Xie Lindong, He Jinlong

In 2009, National Palace Museum commissioned a project team from Tsinghua University that conducted investigations and created drawings, 3D models, and 3D, animated renderings of the rockeries, plants, paving, ornaments, and other elements of the garden inside the Palace of Tranquil Longevity (Qianlong Garden). Along with this site research, the team looked at the history of the garden so as to generate a holistic analysis report of the gardening techniques and garden spaces of the Palace of Tranquil Longevity.

Digital Qianlong Garden was built on the Citymaker platform, which makes it possible to have a panoramic appreciation of the classical garden by breaking through the real-world constraints. The site allows for immersive roaming, and multi-angle and multi-faceted observation of the classical garden. Meanwhile, the digital reconstruction of the Qianlong Garden was completed by using a combination of technology, three-dimensional laser scanning, and close range photogrammetry, to provide a useful reference for the digitized study of classical gardens and a case study with promising prospects for broad extension and application.

Below Left: Short distance photogrammetry.

Below Right: 3D scanning.

References of Overview in Section 3

3.1 landscape architecture history and theory

1. Wang Shaozeng. *A History of Classical Chinese Gardens* (2nd Edition). (Chinese Landscape Architecture, 2000), 87–88.

3.3 landscape planning and ecological restoration

1. Natural and cultural heritage protection is another important subject matter for landscape planning, and is addressed in book 3, section 4.
2. Zhu Yufan, and Meng Fanyu. *Quarry Garden*, 2010: 28–31.
3. Charles Waldheim. *Landscape Urbanism*. Translated by Liu Hailong, Liu Yundong, et al. Beijing: China Architecture & Building Press, 2011.
4. Michael Hough. *Cities and Natural Process*. Translated by Liu Hailong, Jia Liqi, et al. Beijing: China Architecture & Building Press, 2011.

3.4 landscape architecture heritage protection

1.Yang Rui. "Discussion on the Trend of Worldwide National Park Movement." *Chinese Landscape Architecture*, 2003 (7): 10–15.
2. Yang Rui. "Experiences and Lessons from the National Parks and National Park System of the United States." *Chinese Landscape Architecture*, 2001(1): 62–64.
3. Yang Rui. "Comments on the American National Park System Planning System." *Chinese Landscape Architecture*, 2003(1): 44–47.
4. Yang Rui. "Analysis of Current Situations of the Management of Chinese Natural and Cultural Heritage." *Chinese Landscape Architecture*, 2003 (9): 38–43.
5. Yang Rui. "Four Strategies to Improve the Management of Chinese Natural and Cultural Heritage." *Chinese Landscape Architecture*, 2003(10): 39–44.
6. Yang Rui. "Proposed Actions for Improving Management Effectiveness of China's Natural and Cultural Heritage Resources." *Chinese Landscape Architecture*, 2003 (11): 41–43.
7. Yang Rui, Zhuang Youbo, and Dang Anrong. "Process and Techniques in Developing General Management Plan for Meili Snow Mountains National Park of China." *Chinese Landscape Architecture*, 2007 (7):1–6.
8. Zhuang Youbo, and Yang Rui. "The Environmental Impact Assessment Procedure and Indicator System of Scenic Area Master Planning." *Chinese Landscape Architecture*, 2007(1): 49–52.
9. Yang Rui. "A Preliminary Probe into the Environment Carrying Capacity of Scenic Areas." *Urban Planning Forum*, 1996 (6): 12–15.
10. Yang Rui. "LAC Theory: A New Way to Deal with the Environmental Carrying Capacity Problem." *Chinese Landscape Architecture*, 2001(3):19–21.
11. Zhuang Youbo, Xu Ronglin, Yang Rui, and Xu Xiaoqing. "Sustainable Development of Tourism in Jiuzhaigou World Heritage Site." *Landscape Architecture*, 2012 (1): 78–81.
12. Yuan Nanguo, and Yang Rui. "Comparative Study on Current Visitor Management Models for National Parks and Protected Areas." *Chinese Landscape Architecture*, 2005 (7): 9–13.
13. Zhuang Youbo, Yang Rui. "Practices and Trends Analysis of Community Planning for World Natural Heritage Sites in China." *Chinese Landscape Architecture*, 2012 (9): 9–13.
14. Zhuang Youbo, and Yang Rui. "Study of the Zoning Planning of Mount Huangshan Scenic Area." *Chinese Landscape Architecture*, 2006 (12): 32–36.
15. Hu Yike. "Study on Boundary Cognizance of Famous Scenic Areas." Beijing: School of Architecture, Tsinghua University, 2010.
16. Dang Anrong, Yang Rui, and Liu Xiaodong. "Study on the General Framework of Digital National Parks." *Chinese Landscape Architecture*, 2005 (05): 31–34.
17. Zhuang Youbo. "Overview of Management Planning Practices for World Heritage Sites in China." *Chinese Landscape Architecture*, 2013 (09): 6–10.
18. Wang Yinglin, and Yang Rui. "Review on the Management Systems of National Parks in Great Britain." *Chinese Landscape Architecture*, 2013 (09):16–24.
19. Jia Liqi, and Yang Rui. "Study on the Management Framework of World Natural and Mixed Heritage Sites in Australia." *Chinese Landscape Architecture*, 2013 (09): 25–29.
20. Zhao Zhicong, and Zhuang Youbo. "Review on the Management Systems of Protected Areas in New Zealand." *Chinese Landscape Architecture*, 2013 (09): 30–34.
21. Xu Xiaoqing, and Yang Rui. "Introduction to Planning and Management of World Natural and Mixed Heritage Sites in the United States." *Chinese Landscape Architecture*, 2013 (09): 35–40.
22. Zhang Zhenwei, and Yang Rui. "On the Types and Characteristics of Canadian World Natural Heritage Management Plans." *Chinese Landscape Architecture*, 2013(09): 41–45.

23. Peng Lin, Yang Rui. "A Study on the 'Combination' Characteristics and Management Features of Japan's World Natural Heritage Sites." *Chinese Landscape Architecture*, 2013 (09): 46–51.
24. Yang Rui, Zhao Zhicong, and Wu Dongfan. "The Outstanding Universal Value of the Sacred Five Mountains of China." *Chinese Landscape Architecture*, 2007 (12):1–6.
25. Wu Dongfan, Zhuang Youbo, and Yang Rui. "Outstanding Universal Value of Mount Wutai Cultural Landscape Heritage and Its Conservation." *Landscape Architecture*, 2012 (1): 74–77.
26. Yang Rui, and Zhuang Youbo. "A Preliminary Probe into the International Trends and Domestic Practice with Regard to Identification and Assessment of the Outstanding Universal Values." Lhasa: World Heritage and National Heritage Work Conference, 2011.
27. Yang Rui, Zhao Zhicong, and Zhuang Youbo. "Study on the Concept of World Mixed Heritage." *Chinese Landscape Architecture*, 2009 (5):1–8.
28 Yang Rui, Zhao Zhicong, and Wu Dongfan. "Preliminary Study on the National Strategy to Improve the Tentative Mixed Heritage List in China." *Chinese Landscape Architecture*, 2009 (6): 24–29.
29. Yang Rui, Wang Yinglin, and Zhuang Youbo. "Retrospect and Prospect of World Natural and Mixed Heritage Protection and Management in China." *Chinese Landscape Architecture*, 2012 (8): 55–62.
30. Yang Rui. "IUCN Protected Area Categories and Practice in Northwest Yunnan." *Journal of Urban and Regional Planning*, 2009 (1): 83–102.
31. Huang Xinpei. "Cultural Landscape Mechanism Interpretation and Vitality Creation on the Basis of the 'Life and Activities and Their Systems.'" Beijing: School of Architecture, Tsinghua University, 2010.
32. Chen Yingjin. "Conservation and Management of Rural Cultural Landscape in Famous Scenic Sites." *Chinese Landscape Architecture*, 2012 (1):102–104.
33. Zhao Zhicong. "Shades of Meaning between Scenic Areas and World Heritage Cultural Landscapes. Proceedings of the 2009 Annual Meeting of the Chinese Society of Landscape Architecture." Beijing: China Building Industry Press, 2009.
34. Wu Dongfan. "On Cultural Landscape Heritage and Protection of the Landscape and Culture." *Chinese Landscape Architecture*, 2011 (4): 1–3.

3.5 vegetation and planting design

1. Hardback documents contributed by Zhu Junzhen containing the curriculum of the Gardening Program.

3.6 landscape architecture technology and science

1. Remarks made by Mr. Chen Youmin at the "1951 Faculty and Student Roundtable of the Gardening Program."
2. "Landscape Architecture MLA Program: Proposed Curriculum & Course Outline for Masters' Degree in Landscape Architecture for students with prior professional degree in Architecture or Landscape Architecture" by Laurie Olin.

Appendices

Appendix 1:
Profile of Faculty

YANG Rui (male)

Chair of Department of LA

Professor; Supervisor for PhD students

Research and Teaching Interests:

Landscape Planning & Design; Cultural & Natural Heritage Conservation

Education:

PhD in Landscape Architecture, School of Architecture, Tsinghua University, 2003; Master Degree in Urban Planning & Design, School of Architecture, Tsinghua University, 1991 Bachelor Degree in Architecture, School of Architecture, Tsinghua University, 1989

Courses Taught:

Undergraduate: An Introduction of Landscape Architecture; Graduate: Landscape Planning Studio

Main Research Projects:

1998–1999, Action Plan to Build a National Park and Protected Area System in the North-western Region of Yunnan Province, China; 2004–2011, General Plan for the Protected Area System of Beijing, China; 2008, General Management Plan for Mount Wutai National Park.

ZHU Yufan (male)

Vice Chair of Department of LA

Professor; Supervisor for PhD students

Research and Teaching Interests:

History of Chinese Landscape Architecture; Evolvement of Western; Modern Landscape Architecture; Open Space; Campus Planning

Education and Working Experience:

Postdoctoral research and work at the School of Architecture, Tsinghua University, 1999; acknowledged Professor Meng Zhao Zhen as tutor to research history & art of landscape architecture; PhD from the School of Landscape Architecture, Beijing Forestry University, 1997; Bachelor's degree from the Department of Landscape Architecture, Beijing Forestry University, 1992.

Courses Taught:

Undergraduate: History of Western Rraditional Gardens, Site Design Studio. Graduate: History of Landscape Architecture (Europe section); Urban Landscape Design Studio; The Frontiers of Landscape Architecture

Main Research Projects:

2006, Beijing Fragrant Hill no. 81 residential area landscape design; 2009, Qinghai national patriotism education bases Landscape Design; 2010, Landscape Design for Quarry Garden in Shanghai Botanical Garden.

LI Shuhua (male)

Professor; Supervisor for PhD students

Research and Teaching Interests:

Landscape Ecology and Ecological Design in Landscape Architecture, Greenery Technique in Urban Area; The History and Culture of Garden and Landscape Architecture (China, Japan); Horticultural Theory

Education:

PhD from the Department of Landscape Architecture, Kyoto University, Japan, 1997; Master degree from the School of Landscape Architecture, Beijing Forestry University, 1988; Bachelor degree from the Department of Landscape Architecture, Beijing Forestry University, 1985

Courses Taught:

Graduate: Landscape Horticulture, Landscape Planting, Plan, and Design

Main Research Projects:

Tsinghua University Centennial "Century Forest" Park design, Assessment of Ecological Environmental Benefits of Green Belts in Cities Research on the Distribution and Diversity of Plants and Animals on Urban Green Islands.

HU Jie (male)

Senior engineer; deputy dean and chief designer at Beijing Tsinghua Tong Heng Landscape Planning and Design Limited Institute

Research and Teaching Interests:

Theory and practice of urban scale in landscape planning and design

Education:

Master degree in Landscape Architecture from the University of Illinois, USA, 1995; Master degree in Landscape Architecture from Beijing Forestry University,1986; Bachelor degree in Architecture, China Chongqing Architectural and Engineering Institute,1983

Courses Taught:

Graduate: Landscape Techniques

Main Research Projects:

2007, Landscape design of Tieling City Hexin district Lotus Lake National Wetland Park core area; 2008, Beijing Olympic Forest Park Planning and Design; 2010, Tangshan Nanhu Eco-City Comprehensive Planning and Design; 2010, Dalian Lushun Harbor City Landscape Planning, etc.

LIU Hailong (male)

Associate professor; supervisor for PhD students

Research and Teaching Interests:

Landscape Planning and Nature Heritage Conservation; Sustainable Tourism and Recreational Planning and Design; Garden Planting and Ecological Restoration

Education:

PhD in Human Geography from the School of Environment Science from Peking University, 2005; Master in Urban Planning from the School of Architecture, Xi'an University of Architecture and Technology, 2002; Bachelor in Urban Planning from the School of Architecture, Xi'an University of Architecture and Technology, 1999

Courses Taught:

Graduate: Landscape Hydrology, Regional Landscape Planning Studio

Main Research Projects:

2012, Fuzhou Jiangbei District, water remediation and human settlement construction studies; 2011–2013, research studies of theory and practice about China's provincial/regional heritage system planning; 2012, "shengyin yuan" Tsinghua University Landscape Design

WU Dongfan (female)

Associate professor; supervisor for postgraduate students

Research and Teaching Interests:

Landscape Planning and Natural Heritage Conservation; Landscape Design and Theory; Sustainable Tourism & Recreation Planning and Design

Education and Working Experience:

Postdoctoral Researching and Working, School of architecture, Tsinghua University, 2008; PhD in Architecture, School of Architecture, Tianjin University, 2005; Bachelor of Architecture, School of Architecture, Tianjin University, 1999

Courses Taught:

Undergraduate: Site Plan Studio; Graduate: Landscape Design Studio; International Exchange (2006, 2008)

Main Research Projects:

2006–2008, "The grading GB/T 26358-2010 of Tourism and Recreation Zone"(National Standards); 2007–2009, Temple of Heaven Master plan; 2006–2008, Wutai Mountain World Heritage dossiers manuscript and conservation management planning

ZHUANG Youbo (female)

Associate professor; supervisor for PhD students

Research and Teaching Interests:

Landscape Planning and Tourism Development; World Heritage Protection and Management; Landscape Ecology and Restoration Ecology

Education:

PhD in Landscape Architecture from the School of Architecture, Tsinghua University, 2007; Bachelor of Architecture from the School of Architecture, Tsinghua University, 2000

Courses Taught:

Graduate: Landscape Planning Studio; Landscape Ecology

Main Research Projects:

2007–2008,Wuhan East Lake Scenic Area Conceptual master plan; 2010–2012, Research in Conservation and Management of Chinese National Park's Buffer Zones; 2011–present, Conservation Plan for Jiuzhaigou World Natural Heritage Site .

ZHENG Xiaodi (female)

Associate professor; supervisor for PhD students, RLA, ASLA, CHSLA

Research and Teaching Interests:

Brownfield Regeneration; Landscape Architecture Planning and Design; Campus Landscape Design; Landscape Architecture Theories

Education and Working Experience:

Bachelor of Architecture from the School of Architecture, Tsinghua University, 2001; Master in Landscape Architecture from the Graduate School of Design, Harvard University, 2003; PhD from the School of Architecture, Tsinghua University, 2014; Landscape Architect, OLIN, Philadelphia, USA, 2003–2007; Landscape Architect, SWA, San Francisco, USA, 2007–2008

Courses Taught:

Undergraduate: Studio3-1 Between Mountains and Rivers, Landscape

Design Theories, Campus Landscape Design Studio
Graduate: Landscape Design Studio, Theories of Landscape Architecture, Landscape Technology1: Grading and Road Alignment

Main Research Projects:

2017–2019, China's National Natural Science Foundation Young Scholar Research Fund, "Regional Brownfield Cluster's Remote Sensing Information Extraction, Characteristic Identification and Ecological Performance Evaluation," Beijing; 2016–2018, Tsinghua University Independent Research Fund, "Relationship between Campus Landscape and University Culture – Research on Waterfront Landscape at Tsinghua University," Beijing; 2016–2017, Beijing Rural Landscape Planning, Design, Engineering, and Technology Research Center Research Fund, "Research on Environmental Effects of Landfill Ecological Restoration," Beijing.

ZHAO Zhicong (female)

Assistant professor

Research and Teaching Interests:

Landscape Heritage Conservation; National Parks; Landscape Architecture Planning; Cultural Landscape

Education and Working Experience:

Bachelor of Agriculture from the School of Landscape Architecture, Beijing Forestry University, 2005; PhD, Master in Landscape Architecture, Department of Landscape Architecture, School of Architecture, Tsinghua University, 2012; Post-Doctorate, School of Environment, Tsinghua University, 2012–2014

Main Research Projects:

Beijing Municipal Natural Science Foundation Project (youth project): Research on Social Performance of Olympic Forest Park Based on Emotional Cognition Characteristics of User Behavior; China Postdoctoral Science Foundation Project: Research on the Identification and Protection of Cultural Landscape Elements in Jiuzhaigou World Natural Heritage Site; National Natural Science Foundation of China Project: Research on Theory and Practice of National Park Establishment and Development in China (as the primary participant); Planning Projects: Protection and Management Plan of Jiuzhaigou Natural Heritage; master plan of Taishan National Scenic Area.

GUO Yong (male)

assistant professor

Research and Teaching Interests:

Science and Technology of Landscape Architecture; Application Research of Landscape Architectural Information Technology

Education and Working Experience:

Chief Engineer, SSCR Department, Beijing Qinghua Tongheng Urban Planning and Design Institute, 2015; Post-doctorate from Tsinghua University, 2013–2015; PhD of Landscape Architecture from the School of Architecture, Tsinghua University, 2013; visiting scholar for the President Scholarship at TU Berlin, 2009–2011; professor at the School of Architecture, Tsinghua University, 2007; Bachelor of Urban Planning, from the School of Landscape Architecture, Beijing Forestry University, 2005

Courses Taught:

Undergraduate: Site Design Studio; Graduate: Urban Landscape Design Studio, Landscape Architectural Technology: Grading

Main Research Projects:

2013, Planning and Design of the National Archaeological Park of Mausoleum of Emperor Qin Shihuang; 2016, planning research on the Heritage Site of the Ancient City Shugang in Yangzhou; 2017, design of the Park Jade Well in Pingtan, Fujian

Appendix 2:
Profile of First Class of Graduates of Landscape Program

WANG Sui (male)

Wang Sui is a 1953 graduate of the Landscape program who was assigned to a post with the Beijing Municipal Bureau of Parks upon graduation. He went on to work in Baotou in the Inner Mongolia Autonomous Region to support the construction of the border area in June of 1954. He has remained there until the present time, serving as the chief of the Planning Section, the deputy chief and chief of Landscape Division in the Baotou Urban Planning Bureau, the deputy chief engineer of the Chief Engineering Office, and the chief engineer in the Planning Division of the Urban Construction Bureau. He was an acting member of a professional panel of the Urban Planning Office of the Construction in the Inner Mongolia Autonomous Region and made outstanding contributions to the urban construction of Baotou. He is fond of taking photos: the 30,000 photos he has taken of the city since 1955 capture the evolution of the city throughout the years. He was granted a "Productive Aging Elite Award" by the Baotou Municipal Government and a "Green Old Age Award" by the China Association for the Aging. For the past 40 years he has been the chief compiler of Urban Planning of Baotou, he is a scriptwriter and editor, and the producer of the TV documentary *Towards Brilliance*. He is currently working on the compilation of two books, *What History Tells of Future* and *Lens Record and Sensation*.

LIU Shaozong (male)

Liu Shaozong is a 1953 graduate of the Landscape program who has been working in the landscape industry in Beijing serving as deputy chief architect of the Beijing Municipal Bureau of Parks, head and chief architect of the Beijing Institute of Landscape and Traditional Architecture Design and Research, and as the executive director of the Chinese Society of Landscape Architecture. He retired in 1997. His major publications include: *Code for Design of Parks, A Collection of Excellent Works on Chinese Garden Design (1–4), A Collection of Excellent Works on Chinese Garden Design (International Edition), A Collection of Excellent Garden Design Works in Beijing, Plant Landscaping* (Section A), and *On Pavilions*. He has been actively involved in, or a key member of, major design projects including: Taoranting Park, Zizhuyuan Park, Green Landscaping in Tiananting Park, and the Chairman Mao Zizhuyuan Park, and other nationally award-winning projects which include the Garden of Chinese Famous Pavilions in Taoranting Park, Courtyard Green Landscaping at the Fragrant Hill Hotel, and the temporary viewing stand in front of the Tian'anmen Rostrum. His Study of Ecological Benefits of Urban Landscaping and Greening in Beijing earned him the third prize in the National Scientific and Technological Progress Award.

LIU Chengxian (female)

Liu Chengxian was a 1953 graduate of the Landscape program who became an assistant teacher and lecturer at the Tsinghua Department of Architecture upon graduation, teaching a course in allowances in the early 1960s. She was co-translator of the book *Greening Construction* and co-designer of the Yuyuantan Park in Beijing. She later became deputy head of the United Front Work Department of the CPC Committee at Tsinghua University. She passed away in June 1968.

WU Chun (female)

Wu Chun is a 1953 graduate of the Landscape program who was assigned a post in the Urban Planning Institute under the Ministry of Works upon graduation. She then transferred to the Urban-Rural Development Bureau in 1964. She has participated in the master planning and immediate construction planning of Wuhan, the regional planning of Southwest China, the master planning and immediate construction planning of Mianyang of Sichuan, and the master planning of Fuzhou and Quanzhou. She also investigated and filed reports on the landscape greening and management situations of Nanjing, Shanghai, Jilin, Shengyang, Anshan, and of Beihai and Taoranting Parks. In 1972 she was posted to the Xingtai Urban Development Bureau in Hebei Province where she took part in the master planning and immediate construction planning of Xintai, post-earthquake urban planning and development of Tangshan, and the compilation of master planning and immediate construction planning course books for the provincial urban planning training programs. She returned to her workplace (renamed the China Academy of Urban Planning and Design) in 1984 and was engaged as the senior urban planner. She participated in the planning and design of the Hongfeng Lake Scenic Site of Guizhou and served as editing director of the *Urban Planning Overseas* magazine, which she left in 1996 and received an award from the China Academy of Urban Planning and Design.

ZHANG Shouheng (male)

Zhang Shouheng is a 1953 graduate of the Landscape program who became a teacher at the Department of Horticulture at the Beijing Agriculture University upon graduation and later at the Landscape Engineering Program, School of Landscape Architecture at the Beijing Forestry University where he participated in the research and compilation of A Preliminary Study of Qing-Dynasty Mansions in Beijing. He moved to Hong Kong in 1979, and served as landscape architect at the Orient Environment Service Co., Ltd., affiliated with Swire Properties Limited from 1981 to 1995. During this time he built dozens of projects, mainly rooftop gardens of high-rise residential and commercial buildings. He emigrated to the United States in 1997 and was engaged in civil engineering and volunteered to do flower and seeding cultivation at the Huntington Botanical Garden in San Marino and Los Angles from 2000 to 2012.

LI Zhiruo (female)

Li Zhiruo is a 1953 graduate of the Landscape program who became an assistant teacher of the Landscape program in the Department of Horticulture at the Beijing Agriculture University upon graduation. She passed the entrance examination for graduate programs to the Soviet Union in the summer of 1956, studied at the preparatory program for the same at the Beijing, Russian Studies College from the summer of 1956 to the winter 1957, and studied at and obtained her doctorate from the Residential Greening program at the Moscow Forestry College, which she attended from the winter of 1957 until the summer of 1961. Upon her return to China in the summer of 1961, she began teaching at the Department of Gardening at the Beijing Forestry College (now Beijing Forestry University) until her retirement. She taught courses on garden design, garden history, garden art theory, and held the position of deputy dean and dean of the department at the University. She was co-author of *Western Gardens* (with Zhu Jianning), *Chinese Gardens* (with Tang Xueshan), and translator and proofreader of *World Gardens*.

FU Ruihua (male)

Fu Ruihua was a 1953 graduate of the Landscape program who was assigned to a post with the Beijing Municipal Bureau of Parks upon graduation. He has passed away due to his illness.

Appendix 3:

Profile of Architecture Graduates Before the "Cultural Revolution" Who Have Worked in the Field of Landscape Architecture

ZHOU Weiquan (male)

Zhou Weiquan is a 1951 graduate and professor, at the Tsinghua Department of Architecture. He is executive director of the Chinese Society of Landscape Architecture and executive director of the Beijing Society of Landscape Architecture. As professional advisor to the Ministry of Construction on scenic spot issues, he has longterm experience in architectural education and design, and has carried out extensive research on Chinese gardens and architecture. A devoted and diligent practitioner, he played an important role in urban planning, architecture design, and landscape architecture in China. He enjoyed great success within professional circles, and published more than 30 papers on gardening, landscape, ancient buildings, and architectural theory research. He also published important monographs such as *Summer Palace*, *Famous Mountain Scenic Spots in China*, *A History of Chinese Classical Gardens*, and was co-author of *Architectural Design of the Garden*.

ZHU Zixuan (male)

Zhu Zixuan is a 1951 graduate and former head of the Urban Planning Teaching and Research Group and professor at the Tsinghua Department of Architecture. He participated in important projects such as the "Protection and Rehabilitation Planning of Beijing Shichahai Historical and Cultural Scenic District" (starting in 1984) and the "Preservation, Rehabilitation, and Renewal Planning of Tunxi Old Street, Huangshan City" (starting in 1985), and followed up with the implementation of the plans for over 20 years until Shichaihai became a living reminder of Beijing's ancient capital protection efforts and Tunxi Old Street became a demo of the Ministry of Construction's conservation efforts for the historic quarters. His planning of Mount Huangshan Scenic Area (1981) contains valuable explorations into the protection and development of the scenic area. Mr. Zhu has long been devoted to teaching, theoretical research, and practice related to urban planning and urban design; having trained many architects and urban planning professionals, he has made important contribution to China's architecture and urban planning education.

ZHOU Ganzhi (male)

Zhou Ganzhi is a 1952 graduate of the Tsinghua Department of

Architecture and a member of the Chinese Academy of Sciences and the Chinese Academy of Engineering. He later became a guest professor and doctoral supervisor at the Tsinghua School of Architecture. He has had several appointments during his prestigious career including Vice Minister of Construction, chairman of the Chinese Society for Urban Studies, chairman of the Chinese Society of Landscape Architecture, vice chairman of the Urban Planning Society of China, chairman of the China Real Estate and Housing Research Association, and an honorary chair of the International Rooftop Landscaping Association. During his tenure as Vice Minister of Construction he was in charge of landscaping and greening administration and policy-making, and after retirement he continued his research in urban landscaping and greening.

CHEN Zhihua (male)

Chen Zhihua was enrolled in the Department of Sociology at Tsinghua University in 1947 and shifted to the Tsinghua Department of Architecture in 1949. He is a 1952 graduate of the Tsinghua Department of Architecture and later became a professor there teaching History of Western Ancient Architecture, History of Architecture in the Soviet Union, Primary Architecture, Foreign Garden Arts, and the Protection of Heritage Buildings. Since 1989, when he formed the Vernacular Architecture Research Group with Lou Qingxi and Li Qiuxiang, he has been devoted to the research and protection of vernacular buildings in China, making significant contributions to research on rural landscape. He is author of *Foreign Garden Arts* and *Vernacular Architecture in the Upper and Middle Reaches of Nanxi River*.

ZHENG Guangzhong (male)

Zheng Guangzhong is a 1959 graduate and professor of the Tsinghua Department of Architecture. He was once a landscape architecture expert with the Ministry of Construction, and the chair of the Department of Urban Planning that allowed him special government allowances from the State Council. He also served as chief planner of the Beijing, Tsinghua Urban Planning and Design Institute, and as director of the Chinese Society of Landscape Architecture. Considered throughout China as a first-class certified architect and a national certified urban planner, he has taken on several major projects as chief designer including the Protection and Rehabilitation Planning of Beijing Shichahai Historical and Cultural Scenic District, the Planning of Mount Huangshan Scenic Area, the planning of Yalong Bay National Resort District of Sanya, the Three Gorges Dam Scenic Tourism Plan, the tourism planning for the Autonomous Region of Tibet, the plan and design for the Summer Palace-Shichahai-Yuyuan Lake Water System, and master plan for the Tsinghua

Campus. His major publications include Beijing Urban Planning Papers, Past, Present, and Future of Chang'an Street, and The Architecture and Sketches of Zheng Guangzhong. He is also major compiler of the national standards for tourism planning.

FENG Zhongping (male)

Feng Zhongping is a 1960 graduate and teacher at the Tsinghua Department of Architecture. He has served as the department chair and deputy dean of the School of Architecture. Involved mainly in teaching and research related to architecture design and theory, he has published over 30 papers on architecture design, urban design, and landscape architecture while also authoring two garden-related books: *Chinese Garden Architecture* and *Summer Palace*.

GAN Weilin (male)

Gan Weilin is a 1960 graduate from the undergraduate program of the Tsinghua Department of Architecture before studying for his masters in architecture, while also authoring two garden related books. He was on the preparatory committee for the establishment of the Landscape Bureau under the General Administration of Urban Construction in 1978 and became deputy director of the Bureau the following year. His work has largely dealt with urban green space and protection, and the construction of natural scenic areas. He also participated in the drafting of the Temporary Regulation of Scenic Historical Landscape Sites, which was promoted by the State Council in 1985 and played an important role in establishing China's scenic area management system. In 1981 he set up and served as manager of the CSCEC Garden Company to run Chinese Garden construction projects abroad including "Ming Hall" in the Metropolitan Museum of Art in New York, and China Garden at the International Horticultural Exhibition in Munich in 1983. He was a co-founder of the Chinese Society of Landscape Architecture in 1989 and served as its vice chairman from 1998 to 2008 when it joined the IFLA under his initiation.

MA Jiqun (male)

Ma Jiqun is a 1960 graduate of the Tsinghua Department of Architecture. He was former vice chairman of China Landscape and Historic Site and a member of the Landscape Architecture professional panel to the Ministry of Construction. His major publications include: *Landscapers in China* and *A Complete Collection of Scenic Spots in China* (Synthesis Volume).

WANG Bingluo (male)

Wang Bingluo is a 1960 graduate of the Tsinghua Department of Architecture. He has been a devoted administrator of landscape architecture planning and construction with the Ministry of Construction while serving in such positions as chief of the Scenic Sites and Landscape in the Green Space Planning division, vice chairman and secretary general of the Chinese Association of Parks, and is currently a member of the Landscape Architecture Professional Committee of the Ministry of Construction. He also serves as vice chairman of the Chinese Society of Landscape Architecture, and is president and deputy editor-in-chief of the *Chinese Landscape Architecture magazine*. He has published many papers on scenic and natural heritage sites including, "Protecting Scenic Sites for the Well Being of the People," "A Number of Issues Related to Scenic Site Planning," "Protection and Management of Cultural and Natural Heritage Surroundings," and "Value of the Classification of National Cultural and Natural Heritage Sites and Their Surroundings."

ZHANG Jinqiu (female)

Zhang Jinqui is a 1960 graduate of the Tsinghua Department of Architecture. She studied for her masters degree under the supervision of Mo Zongjiang and later became one of the first members of the Chinese Academy of Engineering, and chief architect of the China Northwest Architecture Design and Research Institute. In 2001 she became the vice chair of the Architectural Society of China, steping away from her role as the executive director of the Urban Planning Society of China, which she had held since 1999. Zhang Jinqiu is a guest professor and doctoral supervisor with the School of Architecture, Tsinghua University. Her thesis was entitled "Original State, Gardening Experience, Utilization, and Transformation Challenges of the Rear Hill and West Part of Summer Palace." She has been with the Northwest Architecture Design and Research Institute of China since 1966, which has influenced her design philosophy that can be described as architectural tradition with modernity that results in works with rich vernacular, and blends of planning, architecture, and gardening. Along with extensive practice and academic involvement she has authored the book *Bell and Drum Tower Square, Tang Paradise and South Lake in Xi'an*.

GUO Daiheng (female)

Guo Daiheng is a 1960 graduate of the Tsinghua Department of Architecture and later became a master and doctoral supervisor at the School of Architecture, Tsinghua University. Her graduate program supervisor was Liang Sicheng, the great curator of architectural history. She is a nationally recognized certified architect and author of many major gardening publications including *Yuanmingyuan: The Imperial Work of Emperor Qianlong* and *The Lost Splendor: Research and Protection of Structures in Yuanmingyuan Garden*. As a practician she has participated in the reconstruction design of Liuhe and Leifeng Pagodas in Hangzhou, the design of New Yuan Ming Palace in Zhuhai, the expansion of the Shaolin Temple in Dengfeng, the renovation of Prince Gong's Mansion, and the protection planning for the Historic Monuments of Mount Songshan. Her recent interest has been in the research and creation of the digital representation of Yuanmingyuan.

SUN Fengqi (male)

Sun Fengqi is a 1965 graduate of the Tsinghua Department of Architecture who went on to became a teacher in 1968, and has since served as the deputy department chair and assistant dean of the School of Architecture, Tsinghua University. From 1994 to 1998 he headded the "Study of Redevelopment of Urban Central Squares in China," which was supported by the National Natural Science Foundation of China. He was head of the Tsinghua Institute of Landscape and Gardening, director of the Chinese Society of Landscape Architecture from 2003 to 2009, and executive director of Beijing Society of Landscape Architecture from 2003 to 2010. His major interests are are architecture design theory and urban public space design theory. He teaches courses in Landscape Design and Architecture and Landscape Drawing (graduate level).

ZHAO Baojiang (male)

Zhao Baojiang is a graduate of the Tsinghua Department of Architecture, and has served successively as deputy head, head, and deputy CPC secretary of the Wuhan Architectural Design Institute. He has had a long and fruitful practice serving as deputy director of the Wuhan Municipal Urban-Rural Development Commission, the director of the Wuhan Municipal Planning Bureau, the CPC secretary general and mayor of Wuhan, and the Vice Minister of Construction. He currently is a member of the national committee of CPPCC, chairman of the Urban Planning Society of China, and chairman of the Landscape and Historic Sites Association of China.

Appendix 4:
Requirements of Master and Doctoral Programs

I. Doctor of Philosophy in Engineering – Landscape Architecture

A. Target Discipline/Specialty: Landscape Architecture (Level-1 Discipline, under the Engineering Category, Code: 0834)

B. Program Objectives

1. This program is intended to cultivate innovative academics with international perspective in the field of landscape architecture.
2. The degree recipients are expected:
   a. to be fully aware of the latest academic developments and trends in the discipline;
   b. to have a firm and comprehensive grasp of basic theory and in-depth systematic domain knowledge;
   c. to be able to carry out interdisciplinary research cooperation and innovation;
   d. to be able to work independently as senior scientific researchers, teachers, or designers in Landscape Architecture and related fields.

C. Program Description

Students are taught in the tutorial system. If necessary several faculty fellows will work in collaboration as joint tutors or even better in tutorial groups. In the case of multidisciplinary or interdisciplinary trainings, it is required that qualified teachers from relevant fields be engaged for joint tutorial.

Under the guidance of the tutors, the doctoral candidates are expected to finish all the courses, study related literature, and participate in professional practices and academic exchanges to identify a specific research subject for independent scientific research for creative results.

D. Basic Requirements Regarding Knowledge Structure and Academic Studies

1. Basic Requirements Regarding Knowledge Structure
   a. Basic Theoretical Knowledge
      i. History of Science
      ii. Sustainable Development Theory
      iii. Science, Humanities, and Art Theory
      iv. Contemporary Philosophy and Creative Thinking
   b. Professional Basics
      i. Basic Theories of the Sciences of Human Settlements
      ii. History of the Development of Relations Between Man and Nature
      iii. Urbanization Theory and Practice
      iv. Ecological Civilization and Cluster Culture
      v. Community Development and Community Building

vi. Basic Theories of Ecology and Landscape Ecology
vii. Basic Concepts and Principles of Ecology
viii. Basic Concepts and Principles of Landscape Ecology
ix. Biodiversity and Conservation
x. Materials, Equipment, and Structures
xi. New Materials, New Structures, Techno Aesthetics, and Landscape Architectural Space Creation
xii. Ergonomics

c. Professional Knowledge
i. Landscape Architecture Planning and Design Principles
ii. Chinese and Foreign History of Landscape Architecture
iii. Landscape Ecology
iv. Landscape Hydrology
v. Landscape Geoscience
vi. Landscape Heritage Protection
vii. Landscape Plant Application
viii. Landscape Architecture Technology Application
ix. Applications of Computer and Information Technology in the Planning and Design

d. Frontier Knowledge
i. Landscape Urbanism
ii. Ecological Urbanism
iii. Green Infrastructure
iv. World Heritage Protection
v. Urbanization Theory
vi. Regional Science
vii. Urban Belts and Agglomerations
viii. Contemporary Landscape Architecture, Urban Planning, and Architectural Philosophies
ix. Decision Science and Futurology

2. Cross-Disciplinary Knowledge
a. Architecture and Landscape Architecture
b. Urban and Rural Planning and Landscape Architecture
c. Environmental Science and Landscape Architecture
d. Art Design and Landscape Architecture
e. Ecology and Landscape Architecture
f. Sociology and Landscape Architecture
g. Geography and Landscape Architecture
h. Law and Landscape Architecture

i. Economics and Landscape Architecture
j. Philosophy and Landscape Architecture
k. Information Science and Landscape Architecture

3. Basic Requirements Regarding Academic Studies and Credit Points
   a. Students Enrolled Through Entrance Examinations

      A student who seeks a doctor's degree must earn a minimum of 13 credits through on-campus instruction. Credits for off-campus instruction will be counted separately.

   b. Students Enrolled Upon Recommendation

      A student who seeks a doctor's degree must earn a minimum of 33 credits through on-campus instruction. Credits for off-campus instruction will be counted separately.

E. Degree Dissertation Papers and Requirements

1. Dissertation papers for the doctor's degree is a cumulative reflection of the educational and academic standards of the program and so should be completed by the candidates independently under the guidance of their supervisors.
2. Dissertation papers are expected to be systematic and holistic academic papers and should therefore contain ingenious academic findings in scientific or expertise terms to demonstrate that the candidate have had a solid and extensive mastery of basic theories and systems, and in-depth expertise to enable them to conduct teaching or scientific research work alone.
3. The degree dissertation schedule should be strictly based upon relevant regulations of the Graduate School.

F. Courses and Credit Requirements for Students Enrolled through Entrance Examinations During the study for the PhD degree, the students are required to obtain a minimum of 13 credits, excluding the credits for self-study courses. Courses offered:

1. Public Compulsory Courses (≥4 credits)
   a. Chinese Marxism and Contemporary

      Course ID#: (90680032); 2 credits; (Test-Based)

   b. PhD English or another language

      Course ID#: (90640012); 2 credits; (Test-Based)

2. Course Required for the Discipline (≥4 credits)
   a. Science, Art, and Architecture

      Course ID#: (90000032); 2 credits; (Test-Based)

   b. Landscape Architecture Research Frontier

      Course ID#: (********); 2 credits; (Test-Based)

   c. Relevant Cross-Discipline

      (Level-1) Graduate Courses; 2 credits; (Test-Based)

3. Compulsory Courses (5 credits)

   a. Literature Review and Dissertation Proposal
      Course ID#: (99990041); 1 credit; (Non-Test-Based)
   b. Academic Activities and Reports
      Course ID#: (99990032); 2 credits; (Non-Test-Based)
   c. Qualifying Examination
      Course ID#: (99990061); 1 credit; (Test-Based)
   d. Social Practice
      Course ID#: (69990041); 1 credit; (Non-Test-Based)
4. Self-Study Courses
   Such courses, which can be included in the personal training plan, are for specialized knowledge related to the research area and are defined by the supervisor for systematic self-study.
5. Supplementary Courses
   Students who lack a master's degree background in the discipline (other than those enrolled through recommendation and ahead-of-schedule students) should make up relevant courses under the guidance of the supervisors. Credits for supplementary courses count as non-degree credits.

G. Courses and Credits Requirements for Students Enrolled Upon Recommendations during the study for the PhD degree, the students are required to obtain a minimum of 33 credits, excluding the credits for self-study courses. Courses offered:

1. Public Compulsory Courses (≥5 credits)
   a. Marxist Theories (≥3 credits)
      i. Introduction to Dialectics of Nature
         Course ID#: (60680021); 1 credit; (Test-Based)
      ii. Chinese Marxism and Contemporary
         Course ID#: (90680032); 2 credits; (Test-Based)
2. Foreign Language (≥2 credits)
   a. PhD English or another language
      Course ID#: (90640012); 2 credits; (Test-Based)
3. Course Required for the Discipline (≥23 credits)
   a. Fundamental Theories (≥4 credits)
      i. Introduction to the Sciences of Human Settlements
         Course ID#: (70000212); 2 credits; (Test-Based)
      ii. Landscape Geoscience Fundamentals I: Geology, Geomorphology & Soil Science
         Course ID#: (70000492); 2 credits; (Test-Based)
      iii. Landscape Plants
         Course ID#: (70000551); 1 credit; (Test-Based)
      iv. Landscape Design Theories
         Course ID#: (80000882); 2 credits; (Test-Based)

b. Major Courses (≥ 15 credits)
   i. Compulsory Courses (6 credits)
      (1) Landscape Planning and Design
      Course ID#: (70000474); 4 credits; (Test-Based)
      (2) Landscape Classic Literature
      Course ID#: (80001032); 2 credits; (Non-Test-Based)
      (3) Landscape Architecture Research Frontier
      Course ID#: (********); 2 credits; (Test-Based)
   ii. Optional Courses (≥ 9 credits)
      (1) History of Landscape Architecture I (Asian)
      Course ID#: (80000622); 2 credits; (Test-Based)
      (2) Landscape Ecology
      Course ID#: (80000632); 2 credits; (Test-Based)
      (3) Landscape Techniques I: Vertical and Roads
      Course ID#: (80000652); 2 credits; (Test-Based)
      (4) History of Landscape Architecture II (European)
      Course ID#: (80000662); 2 credits; (Test-Based)
      (5) Landscape Hydrology
      Course ID#: (80000741); 1 credit; (Test-Based)
      (6) Plant Landscape Planning and Design
      Course ID#: (70000542); 2 credits; (Test-Based)

c. Relevant Cross-Discipline (Level-1) Graduate Courses (≥3 credits)
   i. Science, Art, and Architecture
   Course ID#: (90000032); 2 credits; (Test-Based)
   ii. Introduction to Modern Architecture
   Course ID#: (70000012); 2 credits; (Test-Based)
   iii. Urban History and Theory
   Course ID#: (70000142); 2 credits; (Test-Based)
   iv. Environmental and Social Impact Assessment
   Course ID#: (80000131); 1 credit; (Test-Based)
   v. Urban Sociology Research
   Course ID#: (80000491); 1 credit; (Test-Based)
   vi. Introduction to Regional Planning
   Course ID#: (80000471); 1 credit; (Test-Based)
   vii. Urban Geography
   Course ID#: (80000461); 1 credit; (Test-Based)
   viii. Urban Economics
   Course ID#: (70000502); 2 credits; (Test-Based)
   ix. Protection of Cultural Heritage

Course ID#: (80000502); 2 credits; (Test-Based)

x. Introduction to Environmental Behavior

Course ID#: (70000022); 2 credits; (Test-Based)

d. Compulsory Courses (5 credits)

i. Literature Review and Dissertation Proposal

Course ID#: (99990041); 1 credit; (Non-Test-Based)

ii. Academic Activities and Reports

Course ID#: (99990032); 2 credits; (Non-Test-Based)

iii. Qualifying Examination

Course ID#: (99990061); 1 credit; (Test-Based)

iv. Social Practice

Course ID#: (69990041); 1 credit; (Non-Test-Based)

v. Landscape Plants

Course ID#: (70000551); 1 credit; (Test-Based)

vi. Landscape Design Theories

Course ID#: (80000882); 2 credits; (Test-Based)

II. Master of Science in Engineering – Landscape Architecture (Academic)

A. Target Discipline/Specialty: Landscape Architecture (Level-1 Discipline, under the Engineering Category, Code: 0834)

B. Program Objectives

Recipients of the Master of Science in Engineering – Landscape Architecture (Academic) degree should be capable of solving various landscape architecture problems and must be savvy in academic and theoretical terms to enable them to work independently as scientific researchers, teachers, or managers, or to continue studies for higher degrees in the field of landscape architecture.

C. Program Description

Students are taught in the tutorial system. Cross- and inter-disciplinary trainings are encouraged. Under the guidance of the tutors, the master candidates are expected to finish through all the courses, study related literature, and participate in academic exchanges to identify a specific research subject for independent scientific research for creative results to complete the academic degree thesis.

D. Duration of the Program

The duration of this program is two years.

E. Degree Curriculum and Credit Requirements

During the study for the master's degree, students are expected to meet the credit requirements for public compulsory courses and subjective specialized courses and other requirements regarding various program links. A minimum of 30 degree-credits (23 credits from tests) are required. The curriculum for personal training schedules is to be fixed by the candidate and their tutor according to the research interest.

Credits are to be made up of the following parts:

1. 5 credits for public compulsory courses;
2. No less than 23 credits for subjective specialized courses;
3. 2 Credits for compulsory links;
4. A student studying for the Master of Science in Engineering – Landscape Architecture (Academic) degree is required to submit, together with the draft degree thesis, a publishable article that is duly signed by their tutor for approval before being submitted to the Degree Sub-Committee for appraisal.
5. Public Compulsory Courses (5 credits)
    a. Marxist Theories
        i. Introduction to Dialectics of Nature

           Course ID#: (60680021); 1 credit; (Test-Based)
        ii. Theory and Practice of Socialism with Chinese Characteristics

           Course ID#: (60680012); 2 credits; (Test- Based)
    b. First Foreign Language (Fundamentals)

       Course ID#: (60640012); 2 credits; (Test-Based)
6. Course Required for the Discipline (≥23 credits)
    a. Fundamental Theories (≥4 credits)
        i. Introduction to the Sciences of Human Settlements

           Course ID#: (70000212); 2 credits; (Test-Based)
        ii. Landscape Geoscience Fundamentals I: Geology, Geomorphology & Soil Science

           Course ID#: (70000492); 2 credits; (Test-Based)
        iii. Landscape Plants

           Course ID#: (70000551); 1 credit; (Test-Based)
        iv. Landscape Design Theories

           Course ID#: (80000882); 2 credits; (Test-Based)
    b. Optional Cross-Discipline (Level-1) Graduate Courses (≥4 credits)
        i. Introduction to Modern Architecture

           Course ID#: (70000012); 2 credits; (Test-Based)
        ii. Urban History and Theory

           Course ID#: (70000142); 2 credits; (Test-Based)
        iii. Environmental and Social Impact Assessment

           Course ID#: (80000131); 1 credit; (Test-Based)
        iv. Urban Sociology Research

           Course ID#: (80000491); 1 credit; (Test-Based)
        v. Introduction to Regional Planning

           Course ID#: (80000471); 1 credit; (Test-Based)
        vi. Urban Geography

           Course ID#: (80000461); 1 credit; (Test-Based)

vii. Urban Economics
Course ID#: (70000502); 2 credits; (Test-Based)
viii. Protection of Cultural Heritage
Course ID#: (80000502); 2 credits; (Test-Based)
ix. Introduction to Environmental Behavior
Course ID#: (70000022); 2 credits; (Test-Based)

7. Compulsory Courses (2 credits)
   a. Literature Review and Dissertation Proposal
   Course ID#: (69990021); 1 credit; (Non-Test-Based)
   b. Academic Activities (in compliance with the regulations of the Graduate School)
   Course ID#: (99990031); 1 credit; (Non-Test-Based)
8. Academic and Vocational Literacy Course (Optional)
9. Thesis (Academic)

For detailed requirements regarding the compulsory courses, non-degree courses, and thesis, refer to "Regulations of Tsinghua University on Master Programs" and other relevant provisions of the Graduate School.

III. Master of Engineering – Landscape Architecture (Design Studio)

A. Target Discipline/Specialty: Landscape Architecture (Level-1 Discipline, under the Engineering Category, Code: 0834)

B. Program Objectives
Recipients of the Master of Engineering – Landscape Architecture (Design Studio) degree should be capable of solving various landscape planning and design problems and must be savvy with planning and design matters to enable them to work as excellent designers, planners, scientific researchers, teachers, or senior managers in the landscape planning and design industry.

C. Program Description
1. Students are taught in the tutorial system. Cross- and inter-disciplinary trainings are encouraged.
2. Under the guidance of the tutors, the master candidates are expected to finish through all the courses, study related literature, and participate in academic exchanges to complete the design studio.

D. Duration of the Program
The duration of this program is two years.

E. Degree Curriculum and Credit Requirements
During the study for the master's degree students are expected to meet the credit requirements for public compulsory courses and subjective specialized courses and other requirements regarding various program links. A minimum of 35 degree-credits (32 credits from tests and 12 from design studio) is required. Curriculum for the personal training schedule is to be fixed by the candidate and their tutor according to the research interest.

Credits are made up of the following:

1. 5 credits for public compulsory courses;
2. No less than 29 credits for subjective specialized courses;
3. 1 credit for compulsory links;
4. A student studying for the Master of Engineering – Landscape Architecture (Design Studio) degree is required to submit 2 theses.
5. Public Compulsory Courses (5 credits)
   a. Marxist Theories
      i. Introduction to Dialectics of Nature
         Course ID#: (60680021); 1 credit; (Test-Based)
      ii. Theory and Practice of Socialism with Chinese Characteristics
         Course ID#: (60680012); 2 credits; (Test-Based)
   b. First Foreign Language (Fundamentals)
      Course ID#: (60640012); 2 credits; (Test-Based)
6. Course Required for the Discipline (≥29 credits)
   a. Fundamental Theories (≥4 credits)
      i. Introduction to the Sciences of Human Settlements
         Course ID#: (70000212); 2 credits; (Test-Based)
      ii. Landscape Geoscience Fundamentals I: Geology, Geomorphology & Soil Science
         Course ID#: (70000492); 2 credits; (Test-Based)
      iii. Landscape Plants
         Course ID#: (70000551); 1 credit; (Test-Based)
      iv. Landscape Design Theories
         Course ID#: (80000882); 2 credits; (Test-Based)
7. Major Courses (≥22 credits)
   a. Compulsory Courses (14 credits)
      i. Design Studio I
         Course ID#: (70000454); 4 credits; (Test-Based)
      ii. Design Studio II
         Course ID#: (70000464); 4 credits; (Test-Based)
      iii. Final Design Studio I
         Course ID#: (70000444); 4 credits; (Test-Based)
      iv. Landscape Classic Literature
         Course ID#: (80001032); 2 credits; (Non-Test-Based)
   b. Optional Courses (≥8 credits)
      i. History of Landscape Architecture I (Asian)
         Course ID#: (80000622); 2 credits; (Test-Based)
      ii. History of Landscape Architecture II (European)

APPENDICES

Course ID#: (80000662); 2 credits; (Test-Based)

iii. Landscape Techniques I: Vertical and Roads
Course ID#: (80000652); 2 credits; (Test-Based)

iv. Plant Landscape Planning and Design
Course ID#: (70000542); 2 credits; (Test-Based)

v. Landscape Hydrology
Course ID#: (80000741); 1 credit; (Test-Based)

vi. Landscape Ecology
Course ID#: (80000632); 2 credits; (Test-Based)

8. Optional Cross-Discipline (Level-1) Graduate Courses (≥3 credits)
   a. Introduction to Modern Architecture
      Course ID#: (70000012); 2 credits; (Test-Based)
   b. Urban History and Theory
      Course ID#: (70000142); 2 credits; (Test-Based)
   c. Environmental and Social Impact Assessment
      Course ID#: (80000131); 1 credit; (Test-Based)
   d. Urban Sociology Research
      Course ID#: (80000491); 1 credit; (Test-Based)
   e. Introduction to Regional Planning
      Course ID#: (80000471); 1 credit; (Test-Based)
   f. Urban Geography
      Course ID#: (80000461); 1 credit; (Test-Based)
   g. Urban Economics
      Course ID#: (70000502); 2 credits; (Test-Based)
   h. Protection of Cultural Heritage
      Course ID#: (80000502); 2 credits; (Test-Based)
   i. Introduction to Environmental Behavior
      Course ID#: (70000022); 2 credits; (Test-Based)
9. Degree Compulsory Link (1 credit)
   a. Academic Activities (in compliance with the regulations of the Graduate School)
      Course ID#: (99990031); 1 credit; (Non-Test-Based)
10. Academic and Vocational Literacy Courses (Optional)
    This program requires the students to finish two design studios and one final design studio within two years' time. Each studio will continue for 16 weeks under the guidance of the tutors (or tutorial team). The final design studio is to be appraised by the Defense Panel of the Degree Sub-Committee.

IV. Master of Landscape Architecture (MLA)

A. Target Discipline/Specialty: Master of Landscape Architecture, (Code: 0953)

B. Program Objectives

Recipients of the Master of Landscape Architecture degree should be capable of identifying, researching, and solving various landscape architecture problems with savvy in practical and theoretical terms to enable them to provide concrete solutions to problems encountered in reality, and to work as excellent LA planners and designers or senior managers in the landscape architecture industry.

C. Program Description and Program Duration

The program duration is five years at most. Major links such as the laboratory part of the course study, thesis proposal, mid-term report, and thesis writing and defense are to be completed on campus. Thesis research (from the day the thesis proposal is approved to the time the thesis is submitted for appraisal) should run on for no less than one and a half years.

D. Degree Curriculum and Credit Requirements

During the study for the MLA, students are required to obtain more than 28 credits, as is indicated below:

1. 7 credits for public compulsory courses;
2. No less than 20 credits for subjective specialized courses;
3. 1 credit for compulsory link.

E. List of Credits:

1. Public Compulsory Courses (6 credits)
   a. Marxist Theories
      Introduction to Dialectics of Nature
      Course ID#: (60680021); 1 credit; (Test-Based)
   b. First Foreign Language
      Course ID#: (60648003); 3 credits; (Test-Based)
   c. Basic Graduate Courses
      i. Literature Review and Thesis Writing
         Course ID#: (82558001); 1 credit; (Non-Test-Based)
      ii. Landscape Architecture Research Frontier
         Course ID#: (6998012); 2 credits; (Non-Test-Based)
2. Course Required for the Discipline (≥20 credits)
   a. Fundamental Theories (≥4 credits)
      i. Introduction to the Sciences of Human Settlement
         Course ID#: (70000212); 2 credits; (Test-Based)
      ii. Landscape Geoscience Fundamentals I: Geology, Geomorphology & Soil Science
         Course ID#: (70000492); 2 credits; (Test-Based)
      iii. Landscape Plants

APPENDICES

Course ID#: (70000551); 1 credit; (Test-Based)

iv. Landscape Design Theories

Course ID#: (80000882); 2 credits; (Test-Based)

b. Major Courses (≥ 12 credits)

i. Compulsory Courses (6 credits)

(1) Landscape Planning and Design

Course ID#: (70000474); 4 credits; (Test-Based)

(2) Landscape Classic Literature

Course ID#: (80001032); 2 credits; (Non-Test-Based)

ii. Optional Courses (≥6 credits)

(1) History of Landscape Architecture I (Asian)

Course ID#: (80000622); 2 credits; (Test-Based)

(2) History of Landscape Architecture II (European)

Course ID#: (80000662); 2 credits; (Test-Based)

(3) Landscape Techniques I: Vertical and Roads

Course ID#: (80000652); 2 credits; (Test-Based)

(4) Plant Landscape Planning and Design

Course ID#: (70000542); 2 credits; (Test-Based)

(5) Landscape Hydrology

Course ID#: (80000741); 1 credit; (Test-Based)

(6) Landscape Ecology

Course ID#: (80000632); 2 credits; (Test-Based)

3. Optional Cross-Discipline (Level-1) Graduate Courses (≥4 credits)

a. Introduction to Modern Architecture

Course ID#: (70000012); 2 credits; (Test-Based)

b. Urban History and Theory

Course ID#: (70000142); 2 credits; (Test-Based)

c. Environmental and Social Impact Assessment

Course ID#: (80000131); 1 credit; (Test-Based)

d. Urban Sociology Research

Course ID#: (80000491); 1 credit; (Test-Based)

e. Introduction to Regional Planning

Course ID#: (80000471); 1 credit; (Test-Based)

f. Urban Geography

Course ID#: (80000461); 1 credit; (Test-Based)

g. Urban Economics

Course ID#: (70000502); 2 credits; (Test-Based)

h. Protection of Cultural Heritage

Course ID#: (80000502); 2 credits; (Test-Based)

i. Introduction to Environmental Behavior
Course ID#: (70000022); 2 credits; (Test-Based)
j. Urban Infrastructure
Course ID#: (70000271); 1 credit; (Test-Based)
k. Heritage Conservation Technology
Course ID#: (80000511); 1 credit; (Test-Based)
l. Remote Sensing Digital Image Processing and Cartography
Course ID#: (80000342); 2 credits; (Test-Based)
m. Geographic Information System Engineering
Course ID#: (80000382); 2 credits; (Test-Based)
n. Urban Renewal Theory and Practice
Course ID#: (70000261); 1 credit; (Test-Based)
o. Introduction to Digital City
Course ID#: (80000371); 1 credit; (Test-Based)
q. Urban Planning Methodology and Application of Technology
Course ID#: (80000061); 1 credit; (Test-Based)
r. Urban and Rural Land Use Planning
Course ID#: (70000251); 1 credit; (Test-Based)
s. Introduction to Modern Urban Planning
Course ID#: (80000201); 1 credit; (Test-Based)

4. Compulsory Link (1 credit)
   a. Literature Review and Thesis Proposal
   Course ID#: (69990021); 1 credit; (Non-Test-Based)
5. Academic and Vocational Literacy Course (Optional)
6. Supplementary Courses
   Students who lack bachelor's professional backgrounds in the discipline should make up core courses. Credits for supplementary courses are not to be counted as degree credits.

V. Thesis Work Requirements

A. Topics

Thesis topics should be challenging and worth researching. They may come from the following aspects:

1. Actual engineering tasks: Wherein the topics from the actual engineering design tasks call for research design either in accordance with the specific guidelines, requirements, restrictions, and other conditions in the design proposal or following appropriate changes (duly accounted for and demonstrated) to irrational parts in the design proposal.
2. Design tender or competition topics: Wherein the topics from design tenders or competitions call for research design in accordance with specific rules in the bidding documents or competition description without being

restricted by the deadline.

3. Self-selected topics: Wherein the self-selected topics refers to research design projects developed by the author out of practical problems identified from actual investigation on the basis of relevant feasibility studies, whose proposal is to be planned and developed by the author under the guidance of their tutor and involves no party A, but real specific lots, planning, and design conditions that local planning authorities set for the residing location.
4. Research designs in combination with longitudinal research projects: Wherein research designs in combination with longitudinal research projects can be conducted in accordance with the specific requirements.

VI. Full-Time Master of Landscape Architecture Degree (FMLA)

A. Target Discipline/Specialty: Master of Landscape Architecture (Full-Time) (Discipline Code: 0953)

B. Program Objectives

The Full-Time Master of Landscape Architecture Degree (FMLA) is intended to cultivate professional leaders with applied skills and international perspective to meet the needs of the country in the field of landscape architecture.

C. Program Description

In light of the objective of cultivating talents with applied skills, this program collaborates with professional internship bases (practicing landscape architecture institutes) in offering the students the training they need.

D. Students are taught in the tutorial system. Cross- and inter-disciplinary trainings are encouraged.

E. Program Duration

Students study normally two to three years to get the Full-Time Master of Landscape Architecture Degree (FMLA).

F. Degree Credit Requirements

Students studying for the Full-Time Master of Landscape Architecture Degree (FMLA) are expected to meet the credit requirements for public compulsory courses and subjective specialized courses and other requirements regarding various program links. A minimum of 35 degree-credits (21 credits from tests and 12 from design studios) is required. The curriculum for a personal training schedule is to be fixed by the candidate and their tutor or tutorial team according to the research interest.

Credits are to be made up of the following parts:

1. 5 credits for public compulsory courses;
2. No less than 29 credits for subjective specialized courses;
3. 1 credit for compulsory links.

G. List of Credits:

1. Public Compulsory Courses (5 credits)
   a. Marxist Theory Courses

i. Introduction to Dialectics of Nature
Course ID#: (60680021); 1 credit; (Test-Based)
ii. Theory and Practice of Socialism with Chinese Characteristics
Course ID#: (60680012); 2 credits; (Test-Based)
b. First Foreign Language (Fundamentals)
Course ID#: (60640012); 2 credits; (Test-Based)

2. Course Required for the Discipline (≥29 credits)
a. Fundamental Theories (≥4 credits)
i. Introduction to the Sciences of Human Settlements
Course ID#: (70000212); 2 credits; (Test-Based)
ii. Landscape Geoscience Fundamentals I: Geology, Geomorphology & Soil Science
Course ID#: (70000492); 2 credits; (Test-Based)
iii. Landscape Plants
Course ID#: (70000551); 1 credit; (Test-Based)
iv. Landscape Design Theories
Course ID#: (80000882); 2 credits; (Test-Based)
b. Major Courses (≥22 credits)
i. Compulsory Courses (14 credits)
(1) Design Studio I
Course ID#: (70000454); 4 credits; (Test-Based)
(2) Design Studio II
Course ID#: (70000464); 4 credits; (Test-Based)
(3) Final Design Studio I
Course ID#: (70000444); 4 credits; (Test-Based)
(4) Landscape Classic Literature
Course ID#: (80001032); 2 credits; (Non-Test-Based)
c. Optional Courses (≥8 credits)
i. History of Landscape Architecture I (Asian)
Course ID#: (80000622); 2 credits; (Test-Based)
ii. History of Landscape Architecture II (European)
Course ID#: (80000662); 2 credits; (Test-Based)
iii. Landscape Techniques I: Vertical and Roads
Course ID#: (80000652); 2 credits; (Test-Based)
iv. Plant Landscape Planning and Design
Course ID#: (70000542); 2 credits; (Test-Based)
v. Landscape Hydrology
Course ID#: (80000741); 1 credit; (Test-Based)
vi. Landscape Ecology
Course ID#: (80000632); 2 credits; (Test-Based)

This program requires the students to finish two design studios within the first school year. Each studio will continue for 16 weeks under the guidance of the tutors (or tutorial team).

The final design studio is an important link of the Full-Time Master of Landscape Architecture Degree (FMLA) program, where research design is taken as the teaching platform for students to comprehensively apply theories and mythologies taught through the courses in the whole research process of problem identification, clarification, solution, and target fulfillment to get an all-rounded training in scientific research and to accomplish problem-solving skills and planning and design competence in the field of landscape architecture. The final design studio is to be completed during the second school year under the collaborative education and guidance of the Department of LA and relevant professional internship bases. At the design stage, students need to do internship at the relevant professional internship bases. The Degree Sub-Committee is responsible for organizing proposal writing, mid-term review, and final academic report for the final design studio.

3. Optional Courses of Level-1 Architectural Disciplines (≥3 credits)
   a. Introduction to Modern Architecture
      Course ID#: (70000012); 2 credits; (Test-Based)
   b. Urban History and Theory
      Course ID#: (70000142); 2 credits; (Test-Based)
   c. Environmental and Social Impact Assessment
      Course ID#: (80000131); 1 credit; (Test-Based)
   d. Urban Sociology Research
      Course ID#: (80000491); 1 credit; (Test-Based)
   e. Introduction to Regional Planning
      Course ID#: (80000471); 1 credit; (Test-Based)
   f. Urban Geography
      Course ID#: (80000461); 1 credit; (Test-Based)
   g. Urban Economics
      Course ID#: (70000502); 2 credits; (Test-Based)
   h. Protection of Cultural Heritage
      Course ID#: (80000502); 2 credits; (Test-Based)
   i. Introduction to Environmental Behavior
      Course ID#: (70000022); 2 credits; (Test-Based)
4. Compulsory Link (1 credit)
   a. Literature Review and Thesis Proposal
      Course ID#: (69990021); 1 credit; (Non-Test- Based)
   b. (including general graduate quality education courses and lectures)
5. Academic and Vocational Literacy Course (Optional)

VII.Tsinghua-Chiba (Design Studio) Master of Landscape Architecture

A. Target Discipline/Specialty: Landscape Architecture (Level-1 Discipline, under the Engineering Category, Code: 0834)

B. Program Description

1. This is a program run jointly by School of Architecture, Tsinghua University and Faculty of Horticulture, Chiba University. Cross- and inter-disciplinary trainings are encouraged.
2. Students will be supervised by two tutors: one designated by Chiba University and on by Tsinghua University.
3. Students are expected to finish all the courses, study related literature, participate in academic exchanges, and finish off all program links required to obtain the degree under the guidance of the tutors.
4. Program Duration
   Students study normally two to three years for the master's degree.
5. Program Objectives
   Recipients of the (Tsinghua-Chiba Design Studio) Master of Landscape Architecture degree should be capable of solving various landscape planning and design problems, should be savvy in planning and design, and promising of becoming excellent designers, planners, scientific researchers, teachers, or senior managers in the landscape planning and design industry.
6. Degree Credit Requirements:
   a. Students from Tsinghua University Studying with the Program
      i. During the study for the master's degree, students are expected to meet the credit requirements for public compulsory courses and subjective specialized courses and other requirements regarding various program links. A minimum of 35 degree-credits (22 credits from tests and 12 from design studios) are required. The curriculum for a personal training schedule is to be fixed by the candidate and their tutor according to research interest.
      ii. During the study at Tsinghua University, students are required to get 18 credits, of which there are 5 credits for public compulsory courses, at least 12 credits for the courses required by the discipline (8 major credits and 4 fundamental theory credits), and 1 credit for the degree compulsory link.
      iii. During the study at Tsinghua University, students are required to get 17 credits (at most 17 credits recognized by both sides).
      iv. During the study with the program students are required to submit two articles.
   b. Students from Chiba University Studying with the Program
      i. During the study for the master's degree, students are expected to meet the credit requirements for public compulsory courses and subjective specialized courses and other requirements regarding various program links. A minimum of 35 degree-credits are required.

ii. The curriculum for a personal training schedule is to be fixed by the candidate and their tutor according to research interest.

iii. During the study at Tsinghua University, students are required to get 18 credits, of which there are 4 credits for public compulsory courses, at least 13 credits for the courses required by the discipline (8 major credits and 5 fundamental theory credits), and 1 credit for the degree compulsory link.

iv. During the study at Tsinghua University, students are required to get 17 credits (at most 17 credits recognized by both sides).

v. During the study with the program students are required to submit two articles.

C. Curriculum

1. Public Compulsory Courses

a. Students from Tsinghua University Studying with the Program (5 credits)

Marxist Theory Courses

i. Introduction to Dialectics of Nature

Course ID#: (60680021); 1 credit; (Test-Based)

ii. Theory and Practice of Socialism with Chinese Characteristics

Course ID#: (60680012); 2 credits; (Test-Based)

iii. Japanese

2 credits (Test-Based)

b. Students from Chiba University Studying with the Program (4 credits)

Chinese Culture Courses

i. Chinese Society and Culture

Course ID#: (60610082); 2 credits; (Test-Based)

ii. Chinese

2 credits (Test-Based)

2. Courses Required for the Discipline for Students from Tsinghua University Studying with the Program (≥29 credits)

a. Fundamental Theory Courses (≥11 credits)

i. Fundamental Theory Courses Offered by Tsinghua University (≥4 credits)

(1) Introduction to the Sciences of Human Settlements

Course ID#: (70000212); 2 credits; (Test-Based)

(2) Landscape Ecology

Course ID#: (80000632); 2 credits; (Test-Based)

(3) History of Landscape Architecture I (Asian)

Course ID#: (80000622); 2 credits; (Test-Based)

(4) History of Landscape Architecture II (European)
Course ID#: (80000662); 2 credits; (Test-Based)

(5) Landscape Techniques I: Vertical and Roads
Course ID#: (80000652); 2 credits; (Test-Based)

(6) Plant and Plant Landscape Planning and Design
Course ID#: (80000781); 1 credit; (Test-Based)

(7) Landscape Geoscience Fundamentals I: Geology, Geomorphology & Soil Science
Course ID#: (70000492); 2 credits; (Test-Based)

(8) Landscape Hydrology
Course ID#: (80000741); 1 credit; (Test-Based)

(9) Planning and Design of Scenic Spots
Course ID#: (80000571); 1 credit; (Test-Based)

(10) Protection of Cultural Heritage
Course ID#: (80000502); 2 credits; (Test-Based)

ii. Fundamental Theory Courses Offered by Chiba University (≥7 credits)

(1) Urban Space Planning
2 credits (Test-Based)

(2) Living Area Space
2 credits (Test-Based)

(3) Impression of Natural Scenery
2 credits (Test-Based)

(4) Garden Environmental Design
2 credits (Test-Based)

(5) Natural Landscape Planning
2 credits (Test-Based)

(6) Green Space Environment Creation
2 credits (Test-Based)

(7) Wide Area Green Space Planning
2 credits (Test-Based)

(8) Ecological Design
2 credits (Test-Based)

(9) Green Space Environment Assessment
2 credits (Test-Based)

(10) Environmental Planting Design
2 credits (Test-Based)

(11) Planting Management
2 credits (Test-Based)

(12) Land Use Management
2 credits (Test-Based)
(13) Environmental Gardening Planning Workshop
1 credit (Test-Based)
(14) Environmental Gardening Design Workshop
1 credit (Test-Based)
(15) Environmental Gardening Management Workshop
1 credit (Test-Based)
(16) Care Design
2 credits (Test-Based)
(17) Environmental Health
2 credits (Test-Based)
(18) Naturopathy
2 credits (Test-Based)
(19) International Landscape Architecture Special Topics I
2 credits (Test-Based)
(20) International Landscape Architecture Special Topics II
2 credits (Test-Based)
(21) International Landscape Architecture Extended Topics I
2 credits (Test-Based)
(22) International Landscape Architecture Extended Topics II
2 credits (Test-Based)
(23) Introduction to Japanese Gardening
2 credits (Test-Based)

b. Major Courses 18 (credits)

i. Compulsory Courses Offered by Tsinghua University (8 credits)

(1) Design Studio I
Course ID#: (70000454); 4 credits; (Test-Based)
(2) Design Studio II
Course ID#: (70000464); 4 credits; (Test-Based)
(3) Final Design Studio (Offered by Tsinghua, guided by both)
Course ID#: (70000444); 4 credits; (Test-Based)

ii. Compulsory Courses Offered by Chiba University Recognized by Both (4 credits)

(1) Special Rehearsal (Offered by Chiba University)
4 credits (Test-Based)

iii. Optional Courses (6 credits)

(1) Internship I
2 credits (Test-Based)

(2) Internship II
2 credits (Test-Based)

(3) Asian Environmental Gardening Studio and Internship
2 credits (Test-Based)

(4) Enterprise Internship
2 credits (Test-Based)

(5) Professional Japanese I
2 credits (Test-Based)

(6) Professional Japanese II
2 credits (Test-Based)

3. Students from Chiba University Studying with the Program (≥30 credits)

a. Compulsory Courses (16 credits)

i. Compulsory Courses Offered by Tsinghua University (8 credits)

(1) Design Studio I
Course ID#: (70000454); 4 credits; (Test-Based)

(2) Design Studio II
Course ID#: (70000464); 4 credits; (Test-Based)

ii. Compulsory Courses Offered by Chiba University Recognized by Both (8 credits)

(1) Special Rehearsal
4 credits (Test-Based)

(2) Special Research + Final Design Studio
(Offered by Tsinghua, Guided by Both)
4 credits (Non-Test-Based)

b. Optional Courses (≥14 credits)

i. Fundamental Theory Courses Offered by Tsinghua University (≥ 5 credits)

(1) Introduction to the Sciences of Human Settlements
Course ID#: (70000212); 2 credits; (Test-Based)

(2) Landscape Ecology
Course ID#: (80000632); 2 credits; (Test-Based)

(3) History of Landscape Architecture I (Asian)
Course ID#: (80000622); 2 credits; (Test-Based)

(4) History of Landscape Architecture II (European)
Course ID#: (80000662); 2 credits; (Test-Based)

(5) Landscape Techniques I: Vertical and Roads
Course ID#: (80000652); 2 credits; (Test-Based)

(6) Plant and Plant Landscape Planning and Design
Course ID#: (80000781); 1 credit; (Test-Based)

(7) Landscape Geoscience Fundamentals I: Geology, Geomorphology & Soil Science
Course ID#: (70000492); 2 credits; (Test-Based)

(8) Landscape Hydrology
Course ID#: (80000741); 1 credit; (Test-Based)

(9) Planning and Design of Scenic Spots
(80000571); 1 credit; (Test-Based)

(10) Protection of Cultural Heritage
Course ID#: (80000502); 2 credits; (Test-Based)

ii. Fundamental Theory Courses Offered by Chiba University Recognized by Both (≥ 9 credits)

(1) Internship I
2 credits (Test-Based)

(2) Internship II
2 credits (Test-Based)

(3) Urban Space Planning
2 credits (Test-Based)

(4) Living Area Space
2 credits (Test-Based)

(5) Impression of Natural Scenery
2 credits (Test-Based)

(6) Garden Environmental Design
2 credits (Test-Based)

(7) Natural Landscape Planning
2 credits (Test-Based)

(8) Green Space Environment Creation
2 credits (Test-Based)

(9) Wide Area Green Space Planning
2 credits (Test-Based)

(10) Ecological Design
2 credits (Test-Based)

(11) Green Space Environment Assessment
2 credits (Test-Based)

(12) Environmental Planting Design
2 credits (Test-Based)

(13) Planting Management
2 credits (Test-Based)

(14) Land Use Management
2 credits (Test-Based)

(15) Environmental Gardening Planning Workshop
1 credit (Test-Based)
(16) Environmental Gardening Design Workshop
1 credit (Test-Based)
(17) Environmental Gardening Management Workshop
1 credit (Test-Based)
(18) Green Space Hydrological Engineering
2 credits (Test-Based)
(19) Greening Information Science
2 credits (Test-Based)
(20) Green Space Micrometeorology
2 credits (Test-Based)
(21) Green Space Sciences Special Lecture I
1 credit (Test-Based)
(22) Plant Growing Geography
2 credits (Test-Based)
(23) Plant Growing History
2 credits (Test-Based)
(24) Diversity-Preservation Biological
2 credits (Test-Based)
(25) Greening Technology
2 credits (Test-Based)
(26) Eco-Management Regeneration Science
2 credits (Test-Based)
(27) Green Space Science Project Internship I
2 credits (Test-Based)
(28) Green Space Science Project Internship II
2 credits (Test-Based)
(29) Water Environment Science
2 credits (Test-Based)
(30) Green Space Science Special Lecture 2
1 credit (Test-Based)
(31) Ecological Engineering
1 credit (Test-Based)
(32) Care Design
2 credits (Test-Based)

4. Cross-Disciplinary Courses
   a. Natural Environment Conservation Workshop
   2 credits (Test-Based)

   b. Enterprise Internship I
      2 credits (Test-Based)
   c. Enterprise Internship II
      2 credits (Test-Based)
   d. Enterprise Internship I
      2 credits (Test-Based)
   e. Enterprise Internship I
      2 credits (Test-Based)
   f. Plant-Human Relations
      2 credits (Test-Based)
   g. Environmental Health Science
      2 credits (Test-Based)
   h. Naturopathy
      2 credits (Test-Based)
   i. Security Management and Field First Aid
      2 credits (Test-Based)
   j. Environmental Nursing
      2 credits (Test-Based)
   k. Green-Space Health Workshop I
      1 credit (Test-Based)
   l. Green-Space Health Workshop II
      1 credit (Test-Based)
   m. Environmental Health Internship I
      2 credits (Test-Based)
   n. Environmental Health Internship II
      2 credits (Test-Based)
5. Basic Courses
   a. Enterprise Internship I
      2 credits (Test-Based)
   b. Life and Environmental Ethics
      2 credits (Test-Based)
   c. International Corresponding Courses I
      2 credits (Test-Based)
   d. SME Business
      2 credits (Test-Based)
6. Asian Environmental Gardening Courses
   a. International Landscape Architecture Special Topics I
      2 credits (Test-Based)
   b. International Landscape Architecture Special Topics II

2 credits (Test-Based)

c. International Landscape Architecture Extended Topics III
2 credits (Test-Based)

d. International Landscape Architecture Extended Topics IV
2 credits (Test-Based)

e. Asian Environmental Gardening Rehearsal and Internship
2 credits (Test-Based)

7. Degree Compulsory Link

a. Students from Tsinghua University Studying with the Program (1 credit)

i. Academic Activities (Tsinghua-Chiba, in compliance with the regulations of the Graduate School)
Course ID#: (99990031); 1 credit; (Non-Test-Based)

ii. (Including general graduate quality education courses and lectures)

b. Students from Chiba University Studying with the Program (1 credit)

i. Academic Activities (Tsinghua-Chiba, in compliance with the regulations of the Graduate School)
Course ID#: (99990031); 1 credit; (Non-Test-Based)

ii. (Including general graduate quality education courses and lectures)

8. Academic and Vocational Literacy Course (Optional)
Course ID#: (99990031); 1 credit; (Non-Test-Based)

Appendix 5:

List of Doctoral Dissertations in Landscape Architecture (by 2017)

Year	Title	Author	Supervisor
1997	Study on the Planning of Eco-Green Space System and Human Settlements Construction	Li Min	Wu Liangyong
2000	The Ecological Approach to the Sustainable Development of Human Settlements	Lin Wenqi	Wu Liangyong
2000	Heritage Development and Cultural Tourism in the Tourist-historic city Quanzhou	Johan M.Nilsson	Lu Junhua and Sun Fengqi
2002	A comparative Study on the Urban Structure Evolution and Historical Urbanscape Protection for the Historic City in Korea and China: A caase Study on Xi'an and Kyongju City	Kang Taiho	Wu Liangyong and Zhou Weiquan
2003	Integration and Harmony of Complexity – A Study on the Practice of Plan and Architectural Design in Mt. Huang Scenic Spot	Lu Qiang	Shan Deqi and Wang Lu
2003	Improving the National Park and Protected Area System of China: Theories and Practice	Yang Rui	Zhao Bingshi
2004	Soundscape Study and Soundscape Design	Li Guoqi	Qin Youguo
2004	Preservation and Rehabilitation of Yuan Ming Yuan Ruins' Mountain and Water System as Well as Plants	Wu Xiangyan	Sun Fengqi and Wang Yuanping
2004	Studies of Greening's Effects on Outdoor Thermal Environment	Lin Borong	Zhu Yingxin
2006	Research on the Recreation Theories and Integrated Strategies From Human Settlements Perspective	Wang Yu	Wu Liangyong
2006	Ecological Security and Human Settlement – Based on the Research in Northwest Yunnan	Ou Xiaokun	Wu Liangyong
2006	Cultural Landscape Studies: The conservation and Development of City Landscape in the 21st Century	Huang Wenshan	Sun Fengqi
2006	Study of the Evolution of Beijing Urban Parks	Hsu Wenhuay	Sun Fengqi
2007	Environmental Impact Assessment of General Management Plan for the Chinese National Parks	Zhuang Youbo	Yang Rui
2008	Research of Beijing's Greenbelt Policy: History Review, Implementation, and Problems	Yang Xiaopeng	Mao Qizhi
2009	Research of Eco-planning Theory and Methods of Urban and Rural Planning	Rao Rong	Yin Zhi
2009	Research on the Private-Use of Public Eco-space: A Case Study of Golf Course Construction in Beijing	Peng Jianbo	Li Qiang
2009	Traditional "Shan-Shui-City" Pattern: A Case Study of Beijing-Tianjin- North-Hebei Region	Chen Yulin	Wu Liangyong
2010	The Optimization of Eco-benefit of Green Space in the Residential District at Shenzhen	Huang Yixiang	Li Dexiang
2010	Urban Landscape Lighting Planning	Rong Haolei	Qin Youguo
2010	Small Tourist Town Planning in West Sichuan Minority Areas	Wang Binshan	Laurie Olin

Year	Title	Author	Supervisor
2010	The Functions of the Wetland System on Human Settlements Under the Impact of Global Climate Change with Applicaton to the Jingjinji Area	Li Mengying	Wu Liangyong
2010	Boundary Cognizance and Marking for Chinese National Parks	Hu Yike	Yang Rui
2010	Mechanism-Interpreting and Dynamic-Building for Cultural Landscapes Based on Daily Activities with Their Systems	Huang Xinpei	Yang Rui
2011	Planning Strategies of Beijing's Greenbelt: Oriented to the Mitigation of Surface Thermal Effect	Gan Lin	Wang Guangtao
2011	Perception and Conservation of Chinese National Parks as Cultural Landscapes	Zhao Zhicong	Yang Rui
2012	Character Assessment and Planning of Rural Landscape	Chen Yingjin	Yang Rui
2013	Designerly Research into the Landscape Conversion of Irregular Landfills Surrounding Beijing City	Guo Yong	Zhu Yufan
2013	Research on Public Interests of Landscape and its Protection	Zhang Zhenwei	Yang Rui
2014	Landscape Stratergies for Brownfiled Regeneration based on the Concept of "Brown Earth-Work"	Zheng Xiaodi	Yang Rui
2014	Multiple Values Identification Based Research on the Community Planning in the National Parks of China	Wang Yinglin	Yang Rui
2015	Research on the Planning and Implementation Mechanism of the World Heritage Buffer Zone from the Perspective of the Scenic Area in China	Jia Liqi	Yang Rui
2015	The Methodology of Bird Habitats' Making and Planning at Beijing Urban Green Spaces	Huang Yue	Li Shuhua
2015	Aesthetic Value Identification and Conservation in Chinese Mountain Scenic Areas	Xu Xiaoqing	Yang Rui
2015	Aesthetical Value Identification Based Research on the Landscape Architectural Reclamation & Reuse of Discarded Quarries	Cui Qinwei	Zhu Yufan
2015	The Evidence-based Design of Healing Landscapes for Elderly People in China	Liu Boxing	Li Shuhua
2016	Beijing Center Area Water Corridors as Provider of Urban Ecosystem Services	Xue Fei	Yang Rui
2016	The Rural Cultural Landscape Driven by Land System Around the Boundary Between Guangzhou and Huizhou, During 1690s–1930s	Yang Xi	Zhu Yufan
2016	Beijing Center Area Water Corridors as Provider of Urban Ecosystem Services	Cao Kaizhong	Zhu Yufan
2016	Research on Identification of the Holistic Value and the Corresponding Protection strategies of National Scenic and Historic Areas in China	Peng Lin	Yang Rui
2016	The Conservation and Development Strategies of a Multicultural Community in George Town, Malaysia	Lin Tiancai	Li Shuhua
2017	The Rural, Cultural Landscape Driven by Land System Around the Boundary Between Guangzhou and Huizhou	Xu Yuan	Zhu Yufan

Appendix 6:
List of Postdoctoral Final Report in Landscape Architecture (by 2017)

Year	Title	Author	Supervisor
	Tourism Development Of Greater-Beijing Region	Dou Qun	Wu LiangYong, Zheng Guangzhong, Zuo Chuan
2005	Comprehend to Respect: Research on the Planning of Sustainable Landscape Development – The Theory of Protected Land-system Planning within Beijing	Qi Huangxiong	Zuo Chuan, Yang Rui
	A Study on the Development of Campus Space within Chinese Universities – From the Late 19th Century to 2005	Zhang Xuhong	Hu Zhaoxue, Yuan Ying
	The Natural And Cultural Courses of Historical Lanscape	Zhao Xia	Wu Liang Yong
2007	Connections and Cooperations: The Study of the Spatial Network for the Integrated Conservation of Natural and Cultural Heritage	Liu Hailong	Yang Rui
2008	Criterion of Tourist Resort Destination Rating	Wu Dongfan	Yang Rui
2011	A Study about Regulations on Urban and Rural Landscaping and Greening	Lin Guangsi	Yang Rui
2012	Optimizing Landscape Design of the Metropolitan Viaduct and Adjunctive Spaces	Gao Jie	Zhu Yufan
2012	Planning and Design Practice of Green Space Under New Trends for Urban Development	Liu Jian	Li Shuhua
	Water Supply and Water Security Pattern Analysis of World Class Cities and the Water Secutity Pattern Action Plan for Beijing	Li Mengying	Wang Zhongjing, Wu Liangyong
2010	An Evaluation of the Lack of Landscape Eco-construction Technology in Beijing	Lan Siren	Yang Rui
2014	The Study of Conservation and Use of Old and Valueable Trees in the Summer Palace, Beijing	Zhao Yazhou	Li Shuhua
2013	The Study of Environmental Benefit and Risk Prevention Function of Green Space in Urban Parks	Pan Jianbin	Li Shuhua
2012	The Study of Green Space Planning and Design under the New Trend of Urban Development.	Liu Jian	Li Shuhua
2012	The Study of Landscape Optimization of Urban Viaduct Adjunct Space	Gao Jie	Zhu Yufan
2013	The Study of Modern Urban Park Heritage	Zhang An	Zhu Yufan
2016	Research and Practical Application of Landscape and Planting Design in Summer Palace	Shao Dangjin	Li Shuhua
2015	The Study on Landscape Planning of Ecological Forest Protection in Jinchang City, Gansu Province	Shen Jie	Zhu Yufan
2015	The Study of Management Measures of Stormwater and the Construction of Ecological Water Systems Under the Perspective of Landscape Hydrology.	Yang Dongdong	Liu Hailong
2015	Construction of Landscape Information Models: A Case Study on the Landscape Planning of National Archeological Parks for the First Qin Emperor Mausoleum	Guo Yong	Wu Tinhai
2015	The Language of Landscape and Healthy Places	Yuan Lin	Yang Rui
2015	The Study of Landscape Planning and Design on Urban Water Systems and Stormwater Management	Sun Yuan	Liu Hailong
2015	The Study on Vegetation Resources and Characteristics of the Old Summer Palace	Kang Ning	Li Shuhua

Appendix 7:

Published Papers under the Discipline of Landscape Architecture at Tsinghua University (by 2013)

Landscape Architecture History and Theory

1. WU Liangyong. *Habitat Environment and Aesthetic Culture*—Keynote Presentation for the 2012 Annual Conference of the Architectural Society of China [J]. Architectural Journal, 2012 (12): 2–6.

2. WU Liangyong. *Reflections upon Classification of Architecture, Urban Planning and Landscape Architecture as Level-1 Discipline* [J]. Chinese Landscape Architecture, 2011 (5): 11–12.

3. WU Liangyong.*On Development Trend of the Sciences of human Settlements* [J]. Urban and Regional Planning, 2010 (7): 1–14.

4. WU Liangyong.*Thinking about Landscape Architecture Restructuring and Professional Education* [J]. Chinese Landscape Architecture, 2010 (1): 27–33.

5. WU Liangyong.*The Necessity of Establishing the Discipline of Human Settlements Science* [J]. Bulletin of Chinese Academy of Sciences, 2006 (6): 442–43.

6. WU Liangyong.*Sciences of Human Settlements and Landscape Architecture Education* [J]. Chinese Landscape Architecture, 2004 (1): 7–10.

7. WU Liangyong. *A Probe into the Sciences of human Settlements* [J]. Planners, 2001 (6): 5–8.

8. WU Liangyong.*Enlightenment of Traditional Chinese Philosophies of Human Settlements upon Contemporary Urban Design* [J]. World Architecture, 2000 (1): 82–85.

9. WU Liangyong.*Evolution of Environment Creation and Traditional Environment Concepts from the Perspective of the Development of the Shaoxing City* [J]. City Planning Review, 1985 (2): 6–17.

10. WU Liangyong.*"To Guild the Refined Gold" or "To Give a Timely Shot"?—Some Brief Thoughts about Landscape Construction* [J]. City Planning Review, 1982 (5): 16–17.

11. ZHU Changzhong. *Exploration into the "Water and Mountain Landscape City"* [J]. Huazhong Architecture, 1998 (3): 11.

12. ZHU Changzhong.*Landscape Environment and Construction* [J]. Urban and Rural Development, 1998 (2): 16–17.

13. ZHU Changzhong.*Sculpture and Natural Landscape Environment* [J]. Sculpture, 1997 (3): 17.

14. ZHU Changzhong. *Planning and Design of Water and Mountain*

Landscape City (Summary of Planning and Design of Tongshi City, Hainan) [J]. Planner, 1994 (4): 4–5.

15. ZHU Changzhong. *Landscape Environment and "Landscape City"* [J]. Planner, 1994 (3): 17–18, 86.

16. ZHU Changzhong.*Landscape Environment and Tourist Hotel—Comments on the Planning and Design of the Fragrant Hill Hotel* [J]. Architectural Journal, 1983 (4): 59–60.

17. ZHU Junzhen.*In Commemoration of the 10th Anniversary of Death of Professor Wang Juyuan* [J]. Chinese Landscape Architecture, 2006 (3): 6–8.

18. ZHU Junzhen.*Kowloon Walled City Park in Hong Kong* [J]. Forum for Advancement, 1997 (6): 30.

19. ZHU Zixuan.*Cherished Memories of Professor Wang Juyuan* [J]. Chinese Landscape Architecture, 2006 (3): 4.

20. ZHU Zixuan.*Preliminary Probe into the Planning of Yuanmingyuan Imperial Garden* [J]. Architectural Journal, 1981 (2): 51–59.

21. ZHENG Guangzhong, ZHANG Min, and YUAN Mu. *Ecological City, Eco-Farming and Eco-Tourism—A Case Study of the Planning of the West Coast Ecological Agriculture Tourism Zone of Shenzhen* [J]. Architectural Journal, 2000 (5): 4–7.

22. ZHENG Guangzhong, ZHANG Min. *Tourism Planning for Beijing Shichahai Historical and Cultural Scenic District—On Historical Properties and Tourism Development* [J]. Beijing Planning Review, 1999 (2): 11–15.

23. LOU Qingxi. *A Glimpse of Chinese Architectural Culture (IV) Love for Local Landscape* [J]. Chinese Painting and Calligraphy, 2003 (6): 116–117.

24. LOU Qingxi. *A Glimpse of Chinese Architectural Culture (III) Suzhou Gardens* [J]. Chinese Painting and Calligraphy, 2003 (5): 110-111.

25. LOU Qingxi. *A Glimpse of Chinese Architectural Culture (II) Imperial Gardens* [J]. Chinese Painting and Calligraphy, 2003 (4): 120–121.

26. SUN Fengqi. *Landscape and Environment Construction Problems with Urban Residential Areas in China* [J]. Urban Architecture, 2007 (5): 9–10.

27. SUN Fengqi. *Creating Modern Urban Landscape with More Local Characteristics* [J]. Architectural Creation, 2003 (7): 26–27.

28. SUN Fengqi. *Developing Historical and Cultural Heritage while Keeping the Characteristic Architectural Style Intact—In the Case of the Design of the Yongning Ancient Acropolis Ruins Park* [J]. Chinese Landscape Architecture, 2003 (2): 12–17

29. SUN Fengqi. *Human-Centered Design of City Square with Good Space*

Quality [J]. Architectural Journal, 2003 (5): 31–33.

30. SUN Fengqi. *Modern Urban Landscape Architecture* [J]. Development of Small Cities and Towns, 2001 (7): 24–25

31. SUN Fengqi. *Research on the Reconstruction and Redevelopment of City Central Square in China* [J]. Architectural Journal, 1999 (8): 22–25.

32. SUN Fengqi. *Careful Casualness and Deliberate Pursuit—On the Creation of Urban Landscapes* [C]. Landscape Architecture, Human Settlements and Well-Off Society—Proceedings of the Fourth National Congress of China Society of Landscape Architecture (Book I) 2008: 125–126.

33. SUN Fengqi. *Developing Historical and Cultural Heritage while Keeping the Characteristic Architectural Style Intact—Draft Design of the Yongning Ancient Acropolis Ruins Park* [M] Accession to the WTO, China's Science and Technology and Sustainable Development—Challenges and Opportunity, Responsibility, and Countermeasures (Book II). Beijing: China Science and Technology Press, 2002: 1174.

34. LIU Jing and SUN Fengqi. *Analysis on Problems Related to Urban Public Space Landscape Design, Regulations and Planning* [J]. Chinese Landscape Architecture, 2004 (6): 21–23.

35. GUO Daiheng. *Historic Gardens in the Metropolis of Beijing* [J] Zhongguancun, 2012 (11): 34–36.

36. GUO Daiheng. *Reproduction of Yuanmingyuan Imperial Garden* [J]. Zhongguancun, 2012 (11): 40–43.

37. GUO Daiheng. *Yuanmingyuan and Yangshi Lei*[J]. Forbidden City, 2011 (4): 8–19.

38. GUO Daiheng. *Architectural Space of the Lingering Garden in Suzhou* [J]. Architectural Journal, 1963 (3): 19–23.

39. GUO Daiheng. *Zhuhai New Yuanming Palace and Yuanmingyuan* [M] "Proceedings of the History of Architecture" (11th Edition) Beijing: Tsinghua University Press, 1999: 262–83, 312.

40. HE Yan, GUO Daiheng, and XIAO Jinliang. *Bridge Relics Protection Design for Jiuzhouqingyan Hall in Yuanmingyuan*[M] "Urban and Rural Planning from an Ecological Civilization—Proceedings of the 2008 Annual Meeting of the Urban Planning Society of China." Dalian: Dalian Press, 2008: 3319-320.

41. WANG Lifang, TAN Zhaoxia.*Essay on the Landscape Design of the Jingyuan Garden on the Northern Campus of Tsinghua University* [J]. Chinese Landscape Architecture, 2001 (2): 23–25.

42. WANG Lifang.*Basic Relationship between Architecture and Landscape Environment in Scenic Areas*[J]. Chinese Landscape Architecture, 1990 (2): 24–26.

43. WANG Lifang.*Human Factors of Traditional Scenic Areas* [J]. Chinese Landscape Architecture, 1988 (3): 41–42.

44. WANG Lifang.*Landscape Painting Theory and Traditional Landscape Architecture* [J]. Chinese Landscape Architecture, 1988 (2): 28–29.

45. JIA Jun. *A Probe into the Temples and Other Sacrificial Buildings in the Three Gardens of Yuanmingyuan*[J]. Palace Museum Journal, 2012 (5): 109–128.

46. JIA Jun.*A Probe into the Governance Space in Yuanmingyuan* [J]. Architectural Journal, 2011 (5): 100–106.

47. JIA Jun. *A Probe into the Imitation Calligraphies in the Imperial Gardens of Qing Dynasty* [J]. Decoration, 2010 (2): 16–21.

48. JIA Jun. *Lion Forest Garden inside the Garden of Eternal Spring and Lion Forest Garden of Suzhou* [M] "Proceedings of the History of Architecture" (Edition 26). Beijing: Tsinghua University Press, 2010: 109–21.

49. JIA Jun. *A Probe into the Private Gardens in Hexia Town, Huai'an Administration in Ming and Qing Dynasties* [M] "Journal of Chinese Architecture History" (Edition 3). Beijing: Tsinghua University Press, 2010: 409–36.

50. JIA Jun. *The Art of Signboard Inscriptions of Private Gardens in Beijing* [J]. Chinese Landscape Architecture, 2008 (12): 76–78.

51. JIA Jun. *Continued Verification of Shaoyuan Garden of Beijing in Ming Dynasty* [J]. Chinese Landscape Architecture, 2009 (5): 76–79.

52. JIA Jun. *A New Probe into the Garden inside Prince Gong's Residence in Beijing* [J]. Chinese Landscape Architecture, 2009 (8): 85–88.

53. JIA Jun. *Study on the Garden of Prince Gunbeizi in Beijing.* [J]. Chinese Landscape Architecture, 2010 (1): 85–87.

54. JIA Jun and ZHU Yufan. *Plant Landscapes inside Private Gardens in Beijing* [J]. Chinese Landscape Architecture, 2010 (10): 61–69.

55. ZHU Yufan. *Discussion on Some Issues in the Study of Genyue Royal Garden of the Northern Song Dynasty* [J]. Chinese Landscape Architecture, 2007 (6): 10–14.

56. ZHU Yufan.*Cultural Heritage and "Three Set Theory"—the Landscape Architectural Design Methodology of Respecting Tradition and Facing Future* [J]. Chinese Landscape Architecture, 2010 (1): 37–40.

57. WU Dongfan and ZHUANG Yue. *Chinese Classic Garden Culture from the Perspective of Cultural Commonality*[J]. Chinese Landscape Architecture, 2010 (1): 37–40.

58. WU Dongfan and CHEN Yang. *Poetic Dwelling: Spiritual Connotation of Chinese Classic Gardens*[J]. Chinese Landscape

Architecture, 2008 (4): 51–56.

59. WU Dongfan and CHEN Yang. *Two Kinds of Sceneries of Traditional Chinese Gardens* [J]. Chinese Landscape Architecture, 2007 (11): 89–92.

60. WU Dongfan. *Scenery for the Heart, Words for the Essential—Chinese Words and the Traditional Garden Practice* [J]. Chinese Landscape Architecture, 2005 (4): 39–42.

61. WU Dongfan.*Verification of the Yiyuan Garden in Nanxun—Study of Excellent Cases of Modern Chinese Gardens.* The 2011 Annual Meeting of the Chinese Society of Landscape Architecture.

62. WU Dongfan. *Poetic Imagery and Picturesque Concept of Traditional Chinese Literary Gardens* [C], 2010 International Symposium: Identity of Traditional Asian Landscapes, Korea: IFLA APR Cultural Landscape Committee, 2010: 31–40.

63. WU Dongfan. *A Preliminary Probe into the Reconstruction of Poetic Dwellings* [M] "Proceedings of 2010 Annual Meeting of the Chinese Society of Landscape Architecture," Beijing: China Building Industry Press, 2010: 356.

64. LIU Hailong. *Landscape Practice Against the Myriad Contemporary Eco-Concepts* [J]. Architectural Journal, 2010 (4): 90–94.

65. LIU Hailong. *Review on "Landscape Urbanism Reader"* [J]. Regional and Urban Planning, 2008 (3): 206–09.

66. LIU Hailong. *An Overview of the LA Professional Evaluation System in the US and Its Relevance to China*[J]. Chinese Landscape Architecture, 2007 (2): 66–70.

67. HU Yike and LIU Hailong. *A Discussion of the Landscape Urbanism Concept* [J]. Chinese Landscape Architecture, 2009 (10): 64–68.

68. *Ecological City, Eco-Farming and Eco-Tourism—A Case Study of the Planning of the West Coast Ecological Agriculture Tourism Zone of Shenzhen* [J]. Architectural Journal, 2000 (5): 4–7.

69. HUANG Xinpei.*A Discussion of the Concept of "Landscape Ecology"* [J]. Chinese Landscape Architecture, 2011 (01): 33–36.

70. HUANG Xinpei.*On the Essence of Landscape—From Disrupt Concepts to Unified Connotation*[J]. Chinese Landscape Architecture, 2009 (04): 26–29.

71. HUANG Xinpei.*On Vernacular Landscape—"Discovering Vernacular Landscape" and the Concept of Vernacular Landscape* [J]. Chinese Landscape Architecture, 2008 (07): 87–91.

72. HU Yike, YANG Rui, and WANG Jintao. *Synthetic Analysis and Comparison of Chinese Classical Gardens and British Landscape Gardens* [J]. Huazhong Architecture, 2009 (01): 202–07.

73. *A Study of Rockery Design of Imperial Gardens in China* [D]. Beijing: Tsinghua University, 2009.

74. WANG Jintao. *On Specialization of Rockery Design in Chinese Classical Gardens* [J]. Chinese Landscape Architecture, 2008 (01): 91–94.

75. WANG Jintao. *On the Relationship between Garden Rockery Design and Painting in the Ming and Qing Dynasties* [J]. Huazhong Architecture, 2008 (02): 170–72.

76. WANG Jintao. *Evolution of Rockery Design for Chinese Classical Gardens and Underlying Reasons* [J]. Huazhong Architecture, 2007 (08): 188–190.

77. WANG Jintao.*On Gardening Techniques and Concepts Reflected in Yuanye (the Classic Chinese Text on Garden Design)* [J]. Huazhong Architecture, 2007 (12): 100–101.

78. PENG Lin and WANG Qianna. *Aesthetic Characteristics of Modern Gardens in Kyoto, Japan in the Context of "Heritage and Innovation"* [J]. Agricultural Science and Technology and Information (Modern Landscape Architecture), 2012 (03): 4–8.

79. PENG Lin. *Rural Landscapes in Yuanmingyuan: Identification and Classification* [C]. The 2013 Annual Meeting of the Chinese Society of Landscape Architecture.

80. SUN Tianzheng. *Changing the Viewing Angle—Discovering the Beauty of the 15th–19th Century European Landscape Gardens*[J]. Chinese Landscape Architecture, 2012 (03): 42–48.

81. SUN Tianzheng. *From Scenery to Landscape, From Building to Architecture—Discussions of the Theoretic Names from the Ontological Perspective of Landscape Architecture* [J]. Huazhong Architecture, 2011 (07): 110–12.

82. ZHANG Zhenwei. *A Discussion of Urban Greening Technologies in China* [C]. "Academic Committee of the Doctoral Forum of China Architecture. Human Settlement Development in the Context of Scientific Outlook on Development: Proceedings of the 2009 Doctoral Forum of China Architecture." Beijing: China Building Industry Press, 2009: 463–66.

83. ZHANG Zhenwei. *Analysis of CHEN Zhihua's Historical Thought of Garden* [J]. Chinese Landscape Architecture, 2010, 26 (10): 29–32.

84. ZHANG Zhenwei. *Research on Landscape Architects Licensure Law of United States of America* [J]. Chinese Landscape Architecture, 2012, 28 (5): 38–41.

85. YANG Rui and WANG Yinglin. *A Text Research of "Feng Jing (Landscape)" through Si Bu Cong Kan* [J]. Chinese Landscape Architecture, 2012 (03).

86. ZHAO Zhicong and YANG Rui. *Review of the "Landscape Planning and Design" Graduate Program Tsinghua University* [J]. Landscape Architecture, 2006 (05).

87. DONG Libing and ZHAO Zhicong. *The Construction of NRW Landscape Law and Enlightenment on Chinese Legislation*[A]. The 47th International Federation of Landscape Architects (IFLA) World Congress. London Science Publishing Limited, 2010 (11).

88. CUI Qingwei. *Review on "Designerly Ways of Knowing"* [J]. Landscape Architecture, 2011 (2): 78–80.

89. GUO Yong. *Overview of Current Design Research Methodology* [J]. Landscape Architecture, 2011 (2): 68–71.

90. YONG Guo. *Research Report "Ute Frank EKLAT: Entwerfen und Konstruieren in Lehre, and Anwendung und Theorie."* Berlin, Teknische Universitaet Berlin, 2011.

Garden and Landscape Design

1. WU Liangyong and ZHU Yufan. *Environmental Design Based on Confucian Aesthetic Thoughts—A Case Study of the External Environmental Planning and Desgin of Qufu Confucius Research Institute* [J]. Chinese Landscape Architecture, 1999 (6): 10–14.

2. HU Jie, ZHANG Kun, and HAN Yi. *Cracked Ice Paving on the Diamond Plaza in the Core Area of Tieling Fanhe New Town* [J]. Chinese Landscape Architecture, 2010 (6): 119–22.

3. HU Jie, HAN Yi, and WU Yixia. *Welcoming Music with Mountain and Water Landscape—Tieling New City Planning and Design* [J]. Chinese Landscape Architecture, 2007 (3): 3–8.

4. HU Jie, WU Yixia, and Ron Henderson. *Fuzhou University New Campus Landscape Design* [J]. Chinese Landscape Architecture, 2006 (9): 21–26.

5. HU Jie, WU Yixia, LV Lushan.*General Introduction to Beijing Olympic Forest Park Landscape Plan* [J]. Chinese Landscape Architecture, 2006 (6): 1–7.

6. HU Jie. *From Regional Planning to Site Design—Practice of the "Landscape City" Concept in Multi-Scale Landscape Planning* [C]. "Proceedings of the 2011 Annual Meeting of the Chinese Society of Landscape Architecture (Book 1)." Beijing: China Building Industry Press, 2011: 258–63.

7. HU Jie. *"Landscape City"—Eco-City with Chinese Characteristics* [C]. "Harmony and Prosperity—Inheritance of Tradition and Sustainable Development: Proceedings of the 2010 Annual Meeting of the Chinese Society of Landscape Architecture (Book 1)." Beijing: China Building Industry Press, 2010: 253–59.

8. HU Jie, WU Yixia, LV Lushan, ZHANG Yan, LI Wei, and LIU Hui. *Beijing Olympic Forest Park Eco-Water Technology* [J]. Construction Science and Technology, 2008 (13): 72.

9. HU Jie, WU Yixia, LV Lushan, and LIU Hui. *Beijing Olympic Forest Park Landscape Planning and Design* [J]. Architectural Journal, 2008 (9): 27–31.

10. HU Jie, WU Yixia, and LV Lushan. B*eijing Olympic Forest Park Vertical Planning and Design* [J]. Chinese Landscape Architecture, 2006 (6): 8–13.

11. HU Jie, WU Yixia, and LV Lushan. *Beijing Olympic Forest Park Water System Plan* [J]. Chinese Landscape Architecture, 2006 (6): 14–19.

12. HU Jie, WU Yixia, DUAN Jinyu. *Beijing Olympic Forest Park Traffic System Plan* [J]. Chinese Landscape Architecture, 2006 (6): 20–24.

13. HU Jie, WU Yixia, Andreas Luka, and ZHAO Chunqiu. *Beijing Olympic Forest Park Children's Playground Planning and Design* [J]. Chinese Landscape Architecture, 2006 (3): 58–63.

14. HU Jie, WU Yixia, and LV Lushan. *Creation of Mountain and Water Landscape for Beijing Olympic Forest Park* [J]. Chinese Landscape Architecture, 2006 (3): 49–57.

15. HU Jie, WU Yixia, and ZHANG Yan. *Beijing Olympic Forest Park Planting Planning and Design* [J]. Chinese Landscape Architecture, 2006 (6).

16. HU Jie and YANG Yizhao. *Jesse Rodenbiker. The Concept of Mountain and Water Landscape City—Lvshun New Harbor City Landscape Planning and Design* [C]. "Proceedings of the International Federation of Landscape Architects (IFLA) Asia-Pacific Conference and the 2012 Annual Meeting of the Chinese Society of Landscape Architecture (Book 1)." Beijing: China Building Industry Press, 2012: 259–62.

17. HU Jie. *Planning Attitudes and Methods in the Development of New Urban Areas—A Case Study of the Landscape Planning and Design for the Longwan CBD of Huludao* [C]. Proceedings of the 2011 Annual Meeting of the Chinese Society of Landscape Architecture (Book 1). Beijing: China Building Industry Press, 2011: 166–71.

18. HAN Yi, HU Jie, LV Lushan, LU Han, LV Xiaofang, and HU Miaomiao. *Landscape Planning Based on the Existing Natural Context and Shanshui Culture—A Case Study of Lvshun New Harbor City Landscape Planning* [C]. "Proceedings of the 2011 Annual Meeting of the Chinese Society of Landscape Architecture (Book 1)." Beijing: China Building Industry Press, 2011: 239–44.

19. WU Yixia, LV Lushan, HU Jie, and LIU Hui. *Application of Architectural and Ecological and Energy-Saving Building Technologies in the Beijing Olympic Forest Park* [J]. Architectural Journal, 2008 (9): 32–35.

20. ZHU Yufan. *Who to Sit With?—Analysis on the Experimental Reconstruction Design of the Courtyard at No. 13 Beishuncheng Street, Financial Street, Beijing* [J]. Chinese Landscape Architecture, 2005 (8): 11–22.

21. ZHU Yufan. *Who to Sit With?—A Case Study of the Transformation of the Courtyard at No. 13 Beishuncheng Street, Financial Street, Beijing* [J]. World Architecture, 2004 (11): 104–07.

22. ZHU Yufan and YAO Yujun. *Axis of Eternity—Environment Transformation of the Central Area of the Tsinghua Institute of Nuclear and New Energy Technology* [J]. Chinese Landscape Architecture, 2007 (2): 5–11.

23. ZHU Yufan and YAO Yujun. *"Urban Eden"—Planning and Design of the Modern Art Park in Beijing CBD* [J]. Chinese Landscape Architecture, 2007 (11): 50–56.

24. ZHU Yufan and YAO Yujun. *New Poetic Mountain Residence—the External Environment Design of Fragrant Hill No. 81 Yard (Phase II of Banshan Fenglin)* [J]. Chinese Landscape Architecture, 2007 (5): 66–70.

25. ZHU Yufan and YAO Yujun. *External Environment Design of Fragrant Hill No. 81 Yard (Phase II of Banshan Fenglin)* [J]. Urban Environmental Design, 2008 (11): 37–40.

26. ZHU Yufan and YAO Yujun. *For the Poplars Over There (1)—Landscape Design of the Memorial Park of National Patriotism Education Base in Qinghai Atomic City* [J]. Chinese Landscape Architecture, 2011 (9): 1–9.

27. ZHU Yufan and YAO Yujun. *For the Poplars Over There (2)—Landscape Design of the Memorial Park of National Patriotism Education Base in Qinghai Atomic City* [J]. Chinese Landscape Architecture, 2011 (10): 21–29.

28. ZHU Yufan and YAO Yujun. *For the Poplars Over There (3)—Landscape Design of the Memorial Park of National Patriotism Education Base in Qinghai Atomic City* [J]. Chinese Landscape Architecture, 2011 (11): 18–25.

29. ZHU Yufan. *The Power of Mix and Match—Landscape Design for the Ruyuan Exhibition Area in Beijing Wukuang Vanke Residential Area* [J]. Landscape Architecture, 2012 (8): 140–45.

30. HU Yike, GUO Yong, and WANG Yinglin. *Mobile Green vs. Lingering Green—An Integration of Traffic and Green through the Transformation of Bus Stops into Garden* [J]. Landscape Architecture, 2009 (05): 30–31.

31. HU Yike and SONG Ruiqi. *Song Ruiqi. Munich Olympic Park Planning and Urban Life* [J] Architects, 2008 (03): 52–59.

32. CHEN Yingjin. *Reuniting Man and Nature—Recreating Nature*

Theme of New York's Central Park [J]. World Architecture, 2003 (4).

33. YANG Mi and ZHANG Zhenwei. *Mud vs. Drug: Political and Landscape Mosaic in Wa Area: Reconstruct a Utopia with Transformation of Salween River* [J]. Chinese Landscape Architecture, 2008, 24 (10): 31–35.

34. LIU Boxin. *The Application of Evidence-Based Design in Healing Landscape Environments* [M]. "Urban Landscapes in the Perspective of Level-1 Discipline of Landscape Architecture compiled by School of Architecture and Urban Planning, Huazhong University of Science and Technology. Wuhan: Huazhong University of Science and Technology Press, 2013 (1): 91–101.

35. LIU Boxin and HE Xiaojun. *Landscape Design of Roots Resort, Hangzhou* [J]. Modern Landscape Architecture, 2013 (4): 9–14.

36. WANG Chuan, CUI Qingwei, XU Xiaoqing, and ZHUANG Yongwen. *From Tomb to Home—Green Infrastructure to Stop Desert Expansion* [J]. Chinese Landscape Architecture, 2009 (12): 40–44.

37. CUI Qingwei. *Application of Surface Corroded Steel Plate Material in Landscape Architecture Design Practice* [C]. "Proceedings of the 2010 Annual Meeting of the Chinese Society of Landscape Architecture." Beijing: China Construction Industry Press, 2010. 227–231.

38. XU Xiaoqing and ZHAO Zhicong. *Study of Waterfront Space Development for Yangzhou—A Case Study of Small Qinhuai River* [C]. "Proceedings of the 2011 Annual Meeting of the Chinese Society of Landscape Architecture (Book 2)." Beijing: China Building Industry Press, 2011.

39. GUO Yong and ZHANG Yang. *Seeking the Mutualized Eden of Nature, City and Human Beings: An Introduction to the Jury Award Winners' Work in the 2007 IFLA International Student Design Competition* [J]. Chinese Landscape Architecture, 2007 (09): 11–13.

40. GUO Yong and ZHANG Yang. *Eye on the Faces of One Waste Dump—Seeking the Mutualized Eden of Nature, City and Human Beings: An Introduction to the Jury Award Winners' Work in the 2007 IFLA International Student Design Competition* [J]. Chinese Landscape Architecture, 2007 (09).

41. GUO Yong and ZHANG Yang. *Research into the Design Principles for German Citizens' Garden* [J]. Landscape Architecture, 2011 (2): 72–77.

42. GUO Yong. *Special Art Inheriting the History of Garden Life—Park Andre Citroen Review* [J]. Landscape Architecture, 2010 (4): 113–18.

43. LIANG Shangyu. *Response to Life—A Probe into the Transposition of Event Memory in Landscape Design*. Proceedings of the 2010 Annual Meeting of the Chinese Society of Landscape Architecture, 2010.

44. LIANG Shangyu. *Designerly Thinking in the Perspective of Critical*

Regionalism (Landscape). 2011 International Conference on Social Sciences and Society, 2011.

45. LIANG Shangyu. *Revive the Fading Memory of Urban Ecology: An Eco-Landscape Planning and Design Method Fused with Cultural Ecology.* 2011 National Doctoral Forum (Architecture, Planning, and Landscape Architecture), 2011.

Landscape Planning and Ecological Restoration

1. WU Liangyong. *Borrowing the Brilliance of the Famous Painting to Bring Out the Splendid Landscape—A Rustic Opinion on the Que and Hua Mountains' Historical and Cultural Park in Jinan* [J]. Chinese Landscape Architecture, 2006 (1): 2–5.

2. WU Liangyong. *Thoughts on Methodology of the Research on Sustainable Development in Rough Subsistence Conditions—A Case Study of Human Settlement Planning for Northwest Yunnan* [J]. Science & Technology Review, 2000 (8): 37–38.

3. WU Liangyong and ZHAO Wanmin. *Three Gorges Project and Human Settlement Construction* [J]. City Planning Review, 1995 (4): 5–10, 64.

4. WU Liangyong. *On "Landscape City" and China's Urban Development in the 21st Century—On the Occasion of Shanshui City Seminar* [J]. Architectural Journal, 1993 (6): 4–8.

5. WU Liangyong. *Guilin City Style and Protected Targets* [J]. City Planning Review, 1988 (5): 3–8.

6. ZHU Yufan, GUO Yong, and WANG Di. *From Engineering to Ecology and Art—Yangfushan Landfill Sealing Disposal and Ecological Restoration Project in Wenzhou* [J]. Chinese Landscape and Architecture, 2007 (12): 41–45.

7. YANG Yuanchao, LI Shuhua, REN Binbin, ZHANG Wenxiu, and GAO Yufu. *GIS-Based Analysis on Protection of Biological Resources in Mountainous Regions in the Huancui District of Weihai [J].* Journal of Beijing University of Agriculture, 2011, 26 (3): 73–77.

8. WU Dongfan and LIU Hongbin. *Slow Traffic System Planning and Design for Tourist Towns* [J]. South Architecture, 2011 (3): 45–47.

9. WU Dongfan, YANG Rui, and LIU Hailong. *Minneapolis Park System and Its Water Space* [J]. Chinese Landscape Architecture, 2007 (3): 24–30.

10. ZHANG Shumin and WU Dongfan. *Study on the Development and Tendency of Chinese Tourism Resorts* [J]. China Population, Resources, and Environment, 2013 (1): 170–176.

11. LIU Hailong, YU Kongjian, and ZHAN Xuemei. *Flood-Control Planning Following Natural Hydrological Process—A Case Study of Yongningjiang River, Taizhou, Zhejiang* [J]. Urban Environment Design,

2008, 4 (25): 29–33.

12. WANG Binshan. *Theoretical Review on the Authenticity of the Planning of Small Tourist Towns in Minority Areas* [J]. Landscape Architecture, 2010 (04): 98–101.

13. WANG Binshan. *Neo-Vernacular Design in the Minority Areas: Making a Kind of Reconciled and Developing Local Landscape* [J]. Chinese Landscape Architecture, 2009 (12): 84–87.

14. WANG Binshan. *Research on Small Tourist Town Planning in Minority Areas—A Case Study of Shangri-La Town* [J]. Landscape Architecture, 2009 (06): 84–87.

15. LI Mengying and HU Yike. *Amphibious Life—A Case Study of Coastal Lowlands Environment Renovation* [J]. Chinese Landscape Architecture, 2009 (02): 68–72.

16. QIANNA Wang, LIN Peng, Martin Mwirigi M'Ikiugu, Isami Kinoshitai, ZHICONG Zhao. *Key factors for renewable energy promotion and its sustainability values in rural areas: findings from Japanese and Chinese case studies* [C]. 2013 Spatial Planning and Sustainable Development.

17. WANG Yinglin, YANG Mi, YOU Cong, and ZHANG Lu. *Landscape Planning and Design in the Restoration of the Industrial Wasteland—Research on Renewal and Restoration of Ertong in Beijing* [A]. "Proceeding of the 10th Annual Meeting of China Association for Science and Technology" (II) [C], 2008.

18. CUI Qingwei and MENG Fanyu. *From Cavern Pool to Arcadia—Renaissance of the Quarrying Industry Relics Landscape of the Mine Park of Shanghai Chenshan Botanical Garden* [J]. Landscape Design, 2013 (1): 26–33.

19. GUO Yong. *Exploration on Contaminated Urban Manufactured Sites' Remediation Management Strategies in Beijing* [C]. The 4th International Conference of the International Forum on Urbanism, 2009. 10.

20. ZHU Yufan and GUO Yong. *From Engineering to Ecology and Art –Yangfushan Landfill Sealing Disposal and Ecological Restoration Project in Wenzhou* [J]. Chinese Landscape Architecture, 2007 (11): 41–45.

21. ZHU Yufan and MENG Fanyu. *Quarry Garden* [J]. Garden, 2010 (5): 28–31.

22. Dr. Christine Haaland, Dr. Anders Larsson, Dr. Anna Peterson, and Dr. Mats Gyllin (Sweden). Translated by GUO Yong and TIAN Tian. *Implementing Multifunction Greenways in Sweden: Challenges and Opportunities* [J]. Landscape Architecture, 2010 (6): 30–33.

23. ZHENG Xiaodi. *People-Oriented for What Purpose?—Reflections on Beijing's Urban Landscape* [M]. "Li Xianjun Thinking City." Wuhan: Huazhong University of Science and Technology Press, 2010.

24. ZHENG Xiaodi. *Three Distinctive German Industrial Heritage Sites* [J]. Beijing City Planning & Construction Review, 2011 (01): 140–153.

25. ZHENG Xiaodi. *On the Relationship between Brownfield Redevelopment with Industrial Architectural Heritage Protection* [J]. Beijing City Planning & Construction Review, 2011 (01): 82–85.

26. ZHENG Xiaodi. *Review of English Dissertation and Publications on the Subject of Brownfield Regeneration* [J]. Chinese Landscape Architecture, 2013 (02): 5–10.

27. ZHENG Xiaodi. *Three Distinctive German Industrial Heritage Sites* [J]. Beijing City Planning & Construction Review, 2011 (01): 140–53.

28. ZHENG Xiaodi. *On the Relationship between Brownfield Redevelopment with Industrial Architectural Heritage Protection* [J]. Beijing City Planning & Construction Review, 2011 (01): 82–85.

29. ZHENG Xiaodi. *Review of English Dissertation and Publications on the Subject of Brownfield Regeneration* [J]. Chinese Landscape Architecture, 2013 (02): 5–10.

30. ZHENG Xiaodi. *What Makes the New York Brookfield Landfill Transformation Conspicuous* [J]. Worldscape, 2013 (01): 136–145.

31. ZHENG Xiaodi. *Three Approaches to Teach Brownfield Studios in Landscape Architecture Department* [J]. Landscape Architecture, 2009 (09), 24–27.

Landscape architecture Heritage Protection

1. ZHU Changzhong. *Issues Regarding Management of Scenic Areas* [J]. City Planning Review, 1982 (5): 5–9.

2. ZHU Changzhong. *Planning and Construction of Natural Scenic Landscape and Landscape Protection* [J]. City Planning Review, 1982 (1): 34–40.

3. *Discussion of Huangshan Scenic Area Planning* [M]. Yuanmingyuan Journal (III). Beijing: China Building Industry Press, 1984: 184–85.

4. YANG Rui, WANG Yinglin, and ZHUANG Youbo. *Review and Prospect of China's Natural and Mixed World Heritage Management* [J]. Chinese Landscape Architecture, 2012 (8): 55–62.

5. YANG Rui, WANG Yinglin, and ZHUANG Youbo. *Study on the Concept of World Mixed Heritage* [J]. Chinese Landscape Architecture, 2009 (5): 1–8.

6. YANG Rui, ZHAO Zhicong, and WU Dongfan. *Preliminary Study on the Strategy to Improve on the Tentative List of Chinese Mixed World Heritage* [J]. Chinese Landscape Architecture, 2009 (06).

7. YANG Rui, ZHAO Zhicong, and WU Dongfan. *Preliminary Study*

on the Strategy to Improve on the Tentative List of Chinese Mixed World Heritage [J]. Chinese Landscape Architecture, 2009 (06): 24–29.

8. YANG Rui. *"IUCN Protected Area Management Categories" and Its Practice in the Northwestern Region of Yunnan Province, China* [J]. Urban and Regional Planning, 2009 (01): 83–102.

9. YANG Rui and ZHAO Zhicong. *The Outstanding Universal Values of "The Sacred Five Mountains of China"* [J]. Chinese Landscape Architecture, 2007 (12).

10. YANG Rui, ZHAO Zhicong, and WU Dongfan. *The Outstanding Universal Values of "The Sacred Five Mountains of China* [J]." Chinese Landscape Architecture, 2007 (12): 1–6.

11. YANG Rui. *Discussion on the Trend of Worldwide National Park Movement* [J]. Chinese Landscape Architecture, 2003 (7): 10–15.

12. YANG Rui. *Comments on the National Park Planning Systems of the USA* [J]. Chinese Landscape Architecture, 2003 (1): 44–47.

13. YANG Rui. *Analysis of Current Situation of the Management of Chinese Natural and Cultural Heritage* [J]. Chinese Landscape Architecture, 2003 (9): 38–43.

14. YANG Rui. *Strategies to Improve the Management of Chinese Natural and Cultural Heritage Sites* [J]. Chinese Landscape Architecture, 2003 (10): 39–44.

15. YANG Rui. *Proposed Actions for Improving the Management Effectiveness of China's Natural and Cultural Heritage Resources* [J]. Chinese Landscape Architecture, 2003 (11): 41–43.

16. YANG Rui. *Lessons and Experiences from the National Parks and the National Park System of the United States* [J]. Chinese Landscape Architecture, 2001 (01): 62–64.

17. YANG Rui. *LAC Theory: A New Way to Solve the Problems of Environmental Capacity* [J]. Chinese Landscape Architecture, 2001 (3): 19–21.

18. YANG Rui. *Preliminary Study of the Concept of Environmental Capacity for Scenic Areas* [J]. Urban Planning Forum, 1996 (6): 12–15.

19. YANG Rui. *Finding a Balance Between Protection and Development–Master plan of Jianfengling National Forest Park* [J]. City Planning Review, 1997 (2): 23–25.

20. YANG Rui. *A Study of the Master planning Techniques and Methods for the Meili Snow Mountain Scenic Area* [J]. Chinese Landscape Architecture, 2007 (4): 1–6.

21. YANG Rui and ZHUANG Youbo. *Mountains and Buddhas in the Clouds* [J]. World Heritage Review, 2004,1 (36): 28–37.

22. YANG Rui and ZHUANG Youbo. *From Mt. Tai To Mt. Huang: Case Studies of GMPs for Chinese WHs* [R]. Huangshan, China: Proceedings of International Conference on Sustainable Tourism Management at World Heritage Sites, 2008.

23. YANG Rui, ZHUANG Youbo, and LUO Tingting. *Buffer Zone and Community Issues of Mount Huangshan World Heritage Site, China* [R]. Davos, Switzerland: Proceedings of the International Expert Meeting on World Heritage and Buffer Zones, 2008.

24. YANG Rui and ZHUANG Youbo. *Challenges and Strategies for Management of the Three Parallel Rivers World Heritage Site* [R]. Kunming: International Workshop on China World Heritage Biodiversity Program (Kunming), 2004.

25. YANG Rui and ZHUANG Youbo. *Problems and Solutions to Visitor Congestionat Yellow Mountain National Park of China* [J]. Parks, Vol 16 No.2 (the visitor experience challenge), 2006: 47–52.

26. YANG Rui, ZHUANG Youbo, and LUO Tingting. *Buffer Zone and Community Issues of Mount Huangshan World Heritage Site, China* [R]. Davos, Switzerland: Proceedings of the International Expert Meeting on World Heritage and Buffer Zones, 2008.

27. WU Dongfan, ZHUANG Youbo, and YANG Rui. *A Study of the Outstanding Universal Value and Its Conservation for the Cultural Landscapes of the Mount Wutai World Heritage Site* [J]. Landscape Architecture, 2012 (1): 74–77.

28. WU Dongfan and YANG Rui. *Problems and Suggestions for the Conservation and Tourism Development of World Heritage Sites—The Great Wall of China* [J]. Chinese Landscape Architecture, 2008 (5): 60–64.

29. WU Dongfan. *Conference Culture and Heritage Cultural Landscape* [J]. Chinese Landscape Architecture, 2011 (4): 1–3.

30. ZHUANG Youbo and YANG Rui. *Practices and Trend Analysis of Community Planning for Chinese World Heritage Properties* [J]. Chinese Landscape Architecture, 2012. 28 (9): 9–13.

31. ZHUANG Youbo and YANG Rui. *The Procedure and Indicator System of the Scenic Area Master plan Environmental Impact Assessment of the General Management Plan for Chinese Scenic Areas* [J]. Chinese Landscape Architecture, 2007 (1): 49–52.

32. ZHUANG Youbo, YANG Rui, ZHAO Zhicong, HU Yike, and LIN Guangsi. *2009-2010 Report on Advances in Landscape Architecture—Research on Development of the Landscape Architecture Discipline Focusing on the Subject of Scenic Areas* [M]. Beijing: China Science and Technology Press, 2010.

33. ZHUANG Youbo. *A Preliminary Probe into the Current Status and Conceptual Models of Buffer Zone of Scenic Areas* [M]. "Harmony and

Prosperity—Inheritance of Tradition and Sustainable Development: Proceedings of the 2010 Annual Meeting of the Chinese Society of Landscape Architecture (Book 1)." Beijing: China Building Industry Press, 2010: 309–13.

34. ZHUANG Youbo and YANG Rui. *Research on Value Identification and Protection of Beijing Sheji Temple. 2010 IFLA APR Cultural Landscape Committee International Symposium* [C]. International Federation of Landscape Architects Asia and the Pacific Region International Symposium (Conference Reports and Papers).

35. ZHUANG Youbo. *Overview of the Training Session on the 2nd Cycle of the APR World Heritage Periodic Reporting* [R]. Taiyuan: China, World Heritage Protection and Management Workshop sponsored by the Ministry of Housing and Urban and Rural Development, 2010.

36. ZHUANG Youbo. *Research and Implication of US National Park Management* [C]. "Proceedings of the 2009 Annual Meeting of the Chinese Society of Landscape Architecture." Beijing: China Building Industry Press, 2009: 199–203.

37. ZHUANG Youbo. *Tourism Management of World Heritage Sites in China: A Case Study of Mount Huangshan* [R]. Montana, USA: 2009 International Seminar of Protected Area Management sponsored by USDA Forest Service, 2009.

38. ZHUANG Youbo. *Overview of the Management Planning Practice for World Natural Heritage Sites in China* [J]. Chinese Landscape Architecture, 2013 (08): 6–10.

39. ZHUANG Youbo and YANG Rui. *Study of the Zoning Planning of Huangshan Scenic Area* [J]. Chinese Landscape Architecture, 2006 (12): 32–36.

40. ZHUANG Youbo. *Research and Implication of US National Park Management* [M]. Proceedings of the 2009 Annual Meeting of the Chinese Society of Landscape Architecture. Beijing: China Building Industry Press, 2009: 199–203.

41. ZHUANG Youbo and Yang Rui. *Practices and Trends Analysis of Community Planning for World Natural Heritage Sites in China* [J]. Chinese Landscape Architecture, 2012.28 (9): 9–13.

42. ZHUANG Youbo and LI Yihua. *Increase Protected Landscape's Connectivity with Other Protected Areas in Regional Urbanization Background: Case Study on Huangshan National Park of China* [R]. Beijing: Eighth International Conference of Landscape Ecology, 2011.

43. ZHUANG Youbo, XU Ronglin, YANG Rui, and XU Xiaoqing. *A Discussion of Sustainable Development of Tourism in Jiuzhaigou World Heritage Site* [J]. Landscape Architecture, 2012 (1): 78–81.

44. ZHUANG Youbo. *Preliminary Comments on the 2nd Cycle of the APR*

World Heritage Periodic Reporting [J]. Chinese Landscape Architecture, 2012 (7): 97–100.

45. ZHUANG Youbo and YANG Rui. *Research on Value Identification and Protection and Management of Beijing Sheji Temple (Zhongshan Park)* [J]. Chinese Landscape Architecture, 2011 (4): 26–30.

46. ZHUANG Youbo and YANG Rui. *Minimize Negative Tourism Impact in Chinese National Parks: Case Study on Mt. Huangshan National Park.* IUCN/WCPA 5th Conference on Protected Areas of East Asia (Hong Kong). 2005, 6.

47. ZHUANG Youbo and YANG Rui. *Mount Huangshan: Site of Legendary Beauty* [J]. World Heritage Review, 2012 (5): 30–37.

48. ZHUANG Youbo and YANG Rui. *Minimize Negative Tourism Impact in Chinese National Parks: Case Study on Mt. Huangshan National Park* [J]. IUCN/WCPA 5th Conference on Protected Areas of East Asia (Hong Kong) 2005, 6.

49. ZHUANG Youbo. *Current Situations and a Concept Model of Buffer Zones of Chinese National Parks* [C]. 47th International Federation of Landscape Architects (IFLA) World Congress. Suzhou, P. R. CHINA, 2010: 121–25.

50. ZHUANG Youbo and YANG Rui. *Mount Huangshan: Site of Legendary Beauty* [J]. World Heritage Review. 2012 (5): 30–37.

51. DANG Anrong, MA Qiwei, and ZHAO Jing. *A Study of the Village Traditional Culture Protection from the Perspective of Spatial Information Technology* [J]. Urban Flux, 2012 (1): 26–29.

52. DANG Anrong, LV Jiang, and ZHAO Jing. T*he Development and Conservation of Cave Dwellings* [J]. China Homes, 2009 (2): 12–15.

53. DANG Anrong, LANG Hongyang, and FENG Jin. *Variation and Conservation of Cave Dwelling Architecture in Northern Loess Plateau* [J]. World Architecture, 2008 (9): 90–93.

54. LIU Hailong.*Biological Conservation Planning in Urban Areas from the Process Perspective: A Case Study of Taizhou, Zhejiang* [J]. Chinese Journal of Ecology, 2010 (1): 8–15.

55. LIU Hailong and YANG Rui.*Thinking of Establishing the Integrated Conservation Network for Natural and Cultural Heritage Sites in China* [J]. Chinese Landscape Architecture, 2009 (1): 24–28.

56. LIU Hailong and PAN Yunwei. *The Spatial Distribution of Geoparks of China and Suggestions on Geological Conservation Network* [J]. Journal of Natural Resources, 2009, 9 (25): 1480–88.

57. *Connection and Cooperation: The Ecological Network Planning Based on Experiences in Europe and the Netherlands* [J]. Chinese Landscape Architecture, 2009 (9): 31–35.

58. LIU Hailong. *On Key Problems Related to Spatial Network of the Heritage System in China.* "Proceedings of 2010 Annual Meeting of the Chinese Society of Landscape Architecture." Beijing: China Building Industry Press, 2010: 75–78.

59. LIU Hailong. *Analysis and Comparison of Two Military Heritages in China and the Netherlands* [J]. South Architecture, 2009 (4): 84–88.

60. LIU Hailong. *Biological Conservation Planning in Urban Areas from the Process Perspective: A Case Study of Taizhou, Zhejiang* [J]. Chinese Journal of Ecology, 2010, 29 (1): 8–15.

61. LIU Hailong. *The Breakout of Cultural Heritage Sites: the Protection of the Surrounding Cultural Environment and the Creation of the Pedestrian Zone of Cologne Cathedral* [J]. Urban Planning International, 2009, 24 (5): 100–05.

62. LIU Hailong and WANG Yiyao. *Study on the US National Park System Planning and Assessment—A Case Study of National Parks of Natural History Categories* [J]. Chinese Landscape Architecture, 2013 (9).

63. YANG Yuliang, ZHANG Danming, and DANG Anrong. *Spatial and Time Characteristics of the Formation Mechanism of Villages Cultural Landscape—A Case Study of Nuodeng Village* [J]. Chinese Landscape Architecture, 2013 (3): 60–65.

64. YANG Yuliang and DANG Anrong. *Cross-Disciplinary Research Methods for Village Cultural Landscapes—A Case Study of Nuodeng Village* [J]. Urban Flux, 2012 (1): 18–22.

65. WANG Binshan, YANG Rui, and ZHENG Guangzhong. *Tarzan landscape protection and utilization of resources* [J]. City Planning, 2001 (4): 76–80.

66. WANG Binshan, YANG Rui, and ZHENG Guangzhong. *T arzan landscape protection and utilization of resources* [J]. City Planning, 2001 (4): 76–80.

67. WANG Binshan. *Research on the Protection of the Mountain World Heritage Site in China—The Protection and Use of Landscape Resources in the Taishan Mountain* [D]. Beijing: School of Architecture of Tsinghua University, 2001.

68. YANG YuLiang and DANG Anrong. *Cross-Disciplinary Research Methods for Village Cultural Landscapes—A Case Study of Nuodeng Village* [J]. Urban Flux, 2012 (1): 18–22.

69. YANG YuLiang, ZHANG Danming, DANG Anrong, and XIE Haoyun. *Spatial and Time Characteristics of the Formation Mechanism of Villages Cultural Landscape—A Case Study of Nuodeng Village* [J]. Chinese Landscape Architecture, 2013 (3): 60–65.

70. YANG YuLiang, ZHANG Danming, DANG Anrong, and XIE Haoyun. *The Visible and Invisible Hand: Village Cultural Landscape*

Formation Mechanism from a Multi-Disciplinary Perspective [J]. Planner, 2012. 28 (z2): 253–57.

71. MA Qiwei, DANG Anrong, and ZHAO Jing. *Village Cultural Landscape Planning and Design* [J]. Urban Flux, 2012 (1): 37–42.

72. CHEN Yingjin. *Protection and Management of Scenic Areas under the Category of Village Cultural Landscape* [J]. Chinese Landscape Architecture, 2012 (01): 102–04.

73. CHEN Yingjin. *Conservation and Management of UK and French National Parks* [J]. Chinese Landscape Architecture, 2011 (06): 61–65.

74. PENG Lin and YANG Rui. *A Study on the "Combination" Characteristics and Management Features of Japan's World Natural Heritage* [J]. Chinese Landscape Architecture, 2013 (09): 37–42.

75. ZHANG Zhenwei. *On Scenic Area Legislation* [M]. "Proceedings of the 2009 Annual Conference of the Chinese Society of Landscape Architecture: Integration and Growth." Beijing: China Building Industry Press, 2009: 431–36.

76. ZHANG Zhenwei, and YANG Rui. *On the Types and Characteristics of Canadian World Natural Heritage Management Plans* [J]. Chinese Landscape Architecture, 2013, 29 (9): 37–41.

77. ZHAO Zhicong and PENG Lin. *Five Questions Regarding The Wolf Teeth Mountain* [J]. Landscape Architecture, 2012 (05): 154–55.

78. ZHAO Zhicong. *"Literally" or "Tailored"—the Concepts of Chinese Scenic Spots and World Heritage Cultural Landscapes* [A] "Proceedings of the 2009 Annual Meeting of the Chinese Society of Landscape Architecture," 2009 (09).

79. ZHAO Zhicong. *On Characteristics and Historical Limitations of China's Scenic Spot System upon Its Start-Up* [A] "Proceedings of the 2009 Annual Meeting of the Chinese Society of Landscape Architecture," 2009 (09).

80. ZHAO Zhicong. *Trends of "Lanscape Approaches" for Conservation and Management of World Heritage Forests and Its Implications for China* [A] "Proceedings of the 2009 Doctoral Forum of China Architecture," 2009 (10).

81. ZHAO Zhicong and ZHUANG Youbo. *Review of "Landscape Planning in New Zealand"* [J]. Chinese Landscape Architecture, 2013 (08): 30–34.

82. XU Xiaoqing and YANG Rui. *Introduction to World Natural and Mixed Heritage Planning and Management in the US* [J]. Chinese Landscape Architecture, 2013 (08): 35–40.

83. JIA Liqi.*On the National Scenic Trail Management System of US—A Case Study of the Appalachian Trail* [C]. "Proceedings of 2009 Annual

Meeting of the Chinese Society of Landscape Architecture." Beijing: China Building Industry Press, 2009: 218-221.

84. JIA Liqi and YANG Rui. *Research on the Management Framework of World Natural and Mixed Heritage in Australia* [J]. Chinese Landscape Architecture, 2013 (08): 25–29.

85. JIA Liqi. *Interpretation of Alterations to "Buffer Zone" in the 2005 Edition of the "Implementation of the World Heritage Convention Operational Guidelines"* [R]. Beijing: 2011 Doctoral Forum of the School of Architecture of Tsinghua University, 2011.

86. WANG Yinglin and YANG Rui. *Lange. Review of the UK National Park Management System (Chinese and English)* [J]. Chinese Landscape Architecture, 2013 (08): 16–24.

87. WANG Yinglin. *Research on the National Park Buffer Zone Management in Nepal and Its Implications* [R]. Beijing: 2011 Doctoral Forum of the School of Architecture of Tsinghua University, 2010.

88. WANG Yinglin. *Preliminary Study about Generation and Development of World Heritage Integrity Concept* [J]. Suzhou: 47th International Federation of Landscape Architecture (IFLA) World Congress, 2010.

89. YUAN Nanguo and YANG Rui. *Comparative Study of the Existing National Park Visitor Management Models* [J]. Chinese Landscape Architecture, 2005 (07): 9–13.

90. HU Yike and YANG Rui. *Study on Boundary Cognizance of Famous Scenic Sites* [J]. Chinese Landscape Architecture, 2011, 27 (6): 56–60.

91. DANG Anrong, YANG Rui, and LIU Xiaodong. *Research on the Framework of Digital National Parks* [J]. Chinese Landscape Architecture, 2005 (05): 31–34.

92. CHEN Yingjin. *Protection and Management of Scenic Areas under the Category of Village Cultural Landscape* [J]. Chinese Landscape Architecture, 2012 (01): 102–10.

93. PAN Yunwei and YANG Ming. *Research on Spatial and Temporal Distribution and Evolution Characteristics of World Heritage in Danger* [J]. Geography and Geo-Information Science, 2012(7): 88–110.

94. DU Jianmei, LI Shuhua, and WU Dongfan. *Characteristics of Plant Landscapes of the Altar Outside the Temple of Heaven in Beijing During Ming and Qing Dynasties* [J]. Chinese Landscape Architecture, 2012 (1): 102–04.

Vegetation and planning design

1. ZHU Junzhen. *Artistic Means of Disposition of Landscape Plants* [N]. China Flower and Gardening News, 2010-03-04.

2. ZHU Junzhen. *The Formation of the Chinese Landscape Style of Garden*

Plants [J]. Chinese Landscape Architecture, 2003 (9): 37–41.

3. ZHU Junzhen. *On Universal Greening* [J]. Chinese Landscape Architecture, 1985 (1): 7–9.

4. LI Shuhua. *Su Shi's Love for Stone and Related Poems in the Northern Song Dynasty* [J]. Agricultural Science and Technology and Information (Modern Landscape Architecture), 2012 (1): 4–7.

5. LI Shuhua. *Trying to Explain the Directive Function of the Theory on Tian, Di and Ren in the Practice of Landscape Architecture Construction [J]. Chinese Landscape Architecture (I)* [J]. Chinese Landscape Architecture, 2011, 27 (6): 33–37.

6. LI Shuhua. *Trying to Explain the Directive Function of the Theory on Tian, Di and Ren in the Practice of Landscape Architecture Construction [J]. Chinese Landscape Architecture (II)* [J]. Chinese Landscape Architecture, 2011, 27 (7): 51–56.

7. LI Shuhua. *Symbiosis and Circulation—The Basic Thought of Urban Green Space Construction in the Low-Carbon Economic and Social Context* [J]. Chinese Landscape Architecture, 2010, 26 (22): 19–22.

8. LI Shuhua. *Historical Development, Subject and Target of City Park Green Space Construction in Tokyo* [M] "2010 New Starting Point for Urban Gardening and Greening in Beijing." Beijing: China Forestry Press, 2010: 28–36.

9. LI Shuhua and ZHANG Wenxiu. *Progress in the Scientific Research of Horticultural Therapy* [J]. Chinese Landscape Architecture, 2009, 25 (8): 19–23.

10. LI Shuhua and MA Xin. *The Concept and Application of Landscape Planting Design Units* [C]. "Harmony and Prosperity—Inheritance of Tradition and Sustainable Development: Proceedings of the 2010 Annual Meeting of the Chinese Society of Landscape Architecture (Book 1)." Beijing: China Building Industry Press, 2010: 888–91.

11. PAN Jianbin and LI Shuhua. *Re-Interpretation of the Theory "Matching Species with the Site" Based on the Planning and Design of Landscape Plants* [J]. Chinese Landscape Architecture, 2013, 29 (4): 5–7.

12. LIU Boxin and LI Shuhua. *Analysis on Healing Landscape Design Based on Neuroscience Research* [J]. Chinese Landscape Architecture, 2012, 2 (11): 47–51.

13. LIU Boxin and LI Shuhua. *The Horticultural Therapy Garden Design in China Discipline Inspection & Supervision Institute* [J]. Agricultural Science and Technology and Information (Modern Landscape Architecture), 2012 (1): 31–34.

14. LIU Jian, HU Lihui, and LI Shuhua. *Analysis of the Landscape Historical Transition of "Three Hills and Five Gardens" Region in Beijing* [J]. Chinese Landscape Architecture, 2011, 27 (2): 54–58.

15. REN Binbin, FENG Jiuying, and LI Shuhua. *Plant Landscape Design in Imitation of the Natural Plant Communities in Handan* [J]. Journal of Zhejiang Agriculture and Forestry University, 2011, 28 (6): 870–77.

16. HONG Bo, LIU Shu, and LI Shu-hua. *Ecological Landscape Planning and Design of an Urban Landscape Fringe Area: A Case Study of Yang's District of Jiande City* [J]. Procedia Engineering, 2011, 21: 414–20.

17. REN Binbin, LI Shuhua, YIN Lifeng, and ZHU Chunyang. *Village Ecological Plant Landscape Creation in Southern Jiangsu* [J]. Chinese Journal of Ecology, 2010, 29 (8): 1655–61.

18. WANG Zhijing, HU Lihui, and LI Shuhua. *Investigation on the Influence of Prototype Landscape on People's Environmental Perceptions* [J]. Chinese Landscape Architecture, 2010, 26 (7): 46–48.

19. REN Binbin, LI Shuhua. *Research on Plant Landscape Design in imitation of the Natural Plant Communities inYan'an* [J]. Chinese Landscape Architecture, 2010, 26 (5): 87–90.

20. REN Binbin, LI Shuhua, ZHU Chunyang, and ZHANG Xiaotong. *Numerical Classification and Ordination of Forest Vegetation Communities in Yushan Mountain, Changshu* [J]. Journal of Nanjing Forestry University (Natural Science Edition), 2010, 34 (3): 45–50.

21. PAN Jianbin, LI Shuhua, and DONG Li. The correlation between negative air ion and plant community-Case study of Beijing Olympic Forest Park. IFLA Asia Pacific Region Conference, 2012. (oral presentation).

22. LIU Boxin, YAN Lei, and ZHENG Jinghong. *The Site and Practice of Horticultural Therapy* [J]. Modern Landscape Architecture, 2012 (2): 5–13.

23. JI Peng, ZHU Chunyang, and LI Shuhua. *Effects of Urban River Width on the Temperature and Humidity of Nearby Green Belts in Summer* [J]. Chinese Journal of Applied Ecology, 2012, 23 (3): 679–84.

24. JI Peng, ZHU Chunyang, and LI Shuhua. *Effects of Different Structures of Green Belts on the Temperature and Humidity in River Corridors* [J]. Scientia Silvae Sinicae, 2012, 48 (3): 58–65.

25. JI Peng, ZHU Chunyang, and LI Shuhua. *Selected Vertical Structures of Green Belts Along Urban Rivers Affect Seasonal Temperature and Humidity* [J]. Acta Agrectir Sinica, 2012, 20 (3): 456–63.

26. ZHU Chunyang, LI Shuhua, and LI Xiaoyan.*Effects of the Different Canopy Density of Urban Green Belts on the Air Ion Concentration and Bacteria Rate* [J]. Chinese Landscape Architecture, 2012, 28 (9): 72–77.

27. JI Peng, ZHU Chunyang, GAO Yufu, and LI Shuhua. *Effects of Different Green Belt Widths on the Temperature and Humidity in River Corridors* [J]. Scientia Silvae Sinicae, 2012, 28 (5): 109–12.

28. JI Peng, ZHU Chunyang, and LI Shuhua. *Effects of Greenbelt Widths on Air Temperature and Humidity in Urban River Corridors* [J]. Chinese Journal of Plant Ecology, 2013, 37 (1): 37–44.

29. GAO Yufu, LI Shuhua, and ZHU Chunyang. *Effects of the Forest Type of Urban Green Belts on Temperature and Humidity* [J]. Chinese Landscape Architecture, 2012, 28 (5): 109–12.

30. ZHU Chunyang, LI Shuhua, and LI Xiaoyan. *Air Ion Concentration and Affecting Factors in Urban Green Belt* [J]. Urban Environment & Urban Ecology, 2012, 25 (2): 34–37.

31. ZHU Chunyang, LI Shuhua, and LI Xiaoyan. *Research on Comprehensive Evaluation Indicators of Urban Green Belts.* The 2011 Annual Meeting of the Chinese Society of Landscape Architecture. Nanjing, Jiangsu, P.R. China. 2011: 724–33.

32. ZHU Chunyang, LI Shuhua, and JI Peng. *Relationship between the Urban Green Belt Widths and Temperature and Humidity* [J]. Chinese Journal of Ecology, 2011, 31 (2): 383–94.

33. ZHU Chunyang, LI Shuhua, and JI Peng. *Relationship between the Urban Green Belt Structures and Temperature and Humidity* [J]. Chinese Journal of Applied Ecology, 22011, 22 (5): 1255–60.

34. ZHU Chunyang, LI Shuhua, and JI Peng. *Impacts of Urban Green Belt Widths on Air Quality* [J]. Chinese Landscape Architecture, 2010, 26 (12): 20–24.

35. ZHU Chunyang, JI Peng, and LI Shuhua. *Impacts of Urban Green Belt Structures on Air Quality* [J]. Journal of Nanjing Forestry University (Natural Science Edition), 2013, 37 (1): 18–24.

36. ZHU C.Y., LI S H, and REN B.B. *Effects of Different Green Belt Widths on the Temperature, Humidity, and Inhibiting Bacteria. Urban Biodiversity and Design*, 2010.

37. HUANG Yue and LI Shuhua. *Urban Wildlife Habitat Creation Theory and Practices* [C]. "New Cities and Architecture in the Process of Rapid Urbanization—Proceedings of the 2011 National Doctoral Forum (Architecture, Planning, and Landscape Architecture)." Beijing: China Building Industry Press, 2012: 286–90.

Landscape Architecture Technology and Science

1. DANG Anrong, ZHANG Danming, and CHEN Yang. *Study on the Essential Concept and General Framework of Smart Famous Scenic Sites* [J]. Chinese Landscape Architecture, 2011 (9): 15–21.

2. DANG Anrong, LI Gongli, and CHANG Shaohui. *Research on Cultural Landscape Monitoring for the IoT-Based Smart Summer Palace* [R]. The Seventh China City Construction Technology Seminar, 2012.

3. CHANG Shaohui, LI Gongli, and HUANG Tianhang. *Information Infrastructure Programs for the IoT-Based Smart Summer Palace* [J]. Chinese Landscape Architecture, 2011 (9): 22–25.

4. PENG Xia, ZHU Zhanqiang, and ZHANG Yan. *Research on the Smart Huangshan Famous Scenic Site Decision Support System* [J]. Chinese Landscape Architecture, 2011 (9): 36–39.

Appendix 8:
Selected Projects (by 2013)

1. Protection and Construction Planning of Yuanmingyuan
   Planning Time: 1978
   Participants: WU Liangyong, ZHU Zixuan, ZHENG Guangzhong, Xu Yingguang, etc.
2. Master plan of the Seven Star Crags Scenic Area in Zhaoqing, Guangdong
   Planning Time: 1983
   Participants: ZHU Changzhong, Xu Yingguang, WANG Menghui, MENG Weikang, LI Yong, etc.
3. Landscape Architecture Plan of Muyunge, Yantai
   Design Time: 1983
   Designer: FENG Zhongping
4. Design of Juyuan Garden, Kaifeng, Henan
   Design Time: 1984
   Designer: XU Boan
5. Mount Putuo Scenic Area Planning
   Planning Time: 1984
   Participants: ZHOU Weiquan, ZHENG Guangzhong, JIN Bolin, LIAO Huinong, SHEN Huisheng, and ZHU Junzhen
6. Planning of the Shichahai Historical and Cultural Tourist Resort in Beijing
   Planning Time: 1984 to 2004
   Participants: Y1984–2004 students and postgraduates
   Consultant: WU Liangyong, etc.
   Supervisors: ZHU Zixuan, ZHENG Guangzhong, ZHU Junzhen, and HUANG Changshan
7. Planning of the Square in Front of the Baoding Railway Station
   Design Time: 1985
   Designers: ZHENG Guangzhong and ZHUANG Ning
8. Planning of Bailongtan (White Dragon Pool) Scenic Area in Beijing
   Planning Time: 1985
   Participants: ZHENG Guangzhong, HU Baozhe, etc.
9. Planning of the Jinci Temple—Tianlong Mountain Scenic Area in Taiyuan
   Planning time: 1986
   Supervisors: ZHENG Guangzhong and ZHUANG Ning
   Participants: LIN Shufeng, Qiu Xiaoxiang, LIU Erming, LI Yue, and SONG Chao bin
10. Planning and Design of the Central Square of Longkou City, Shandong
    Design Time: 1986
    Designers: ZHENG Guangzhong and ZHUANG Ning

11. Design of the Central Square of Dujiangyan City
    Design Time: 1990
    Participants: ZHENG Guangzhong, YUAN Mu, DENG Wei, etc.
12. Planning of the Fragrance Hill Disctrict in Beijing
    Planning Time: 1991
    Supervisors: ZHU Zixuan and ZHENG Guangzhong
    Participants: students
13. Design of Nanning National Plaza
    Design Time: 1991
    Designer: SUN Fengqi
14. Haikou Rinpoche Resort Planning
    Planning Time: 1992
    Supervisors: ZHENG Guangzhong and YANG Rui
15. Regulatory and Detailed Planning for Sanya Bay Resort District
    Planning Time: May 1992
    Supervisors: ZHENG Guangzhong and ZHUANG Ning
    Participants: LU Weidong, LU Yi, SUN Yan, WU Qinghua, YUAN Mu, CAO Chun, JING Xin, and LUO Xiaofang
16. Master planning of Yalong Bay National Resort
    Planning Time: March 1993
    Supervisors: ZHENG Guangzhong, BIAN Lanchun, and YANG Rui
    Participants: LIU Yihong, LIN Yougan, MO Lisheng, CHEN Zhijie, LIANG Wei, ZHU Chunhang, XU Yang, GAO Guasheng, LIANG Jian, ZHONG Ge, and HAN Linfei
    Coopeator: XIE Wenhui and DENG Wei
17. Master planning of Jianfengling National Rain Forest Park
    Planning Time: 1993
    Supervisors: ZHENG Guangzhong and YANG Rui
    Participants: CHEN Zhijie, GAO Guisheng, LIU Jie, WANG Peng, WEI Dehui, HUANG Weihua, JIN Lei, TAN Cheng, JING Xin, WANG Min, OUYANG Wei, and LIU Ying
18. Regulatory and Detailed Planning for Sanya Bay Resort District
    Planning Time: 1994
    Supervisors: ZHENG Guangzhong, BIAN Lanchun, and YANG Rui
    Participants: LIANG Wei, ZHU Chunhang, XU Yang, LIANG Jian, HAN Linfei, LIU Jie, CHEN Zhijie, and GAO Guisheng
19. Master planning of Wuzhishan Baihualing Scenic Area
    Planning Time: January 1994
    Supervisors: ZHENG Guangzhong and YANG Rui
    Participants: MO Lisheng, HAN Linfei, CHEN Zhijie, and GAO Guisheng
20. Master planning of Shandong Rushan Silver Beach Resort
    Planning Time: March 1994
    Supervisors: ZHENG Guangzhong and YANG Rui
    Participants: LIU Jie, JIN Lei, WEI Dehui, HUANG Weihua, and WANG Peng
21. Master planning of Three Gorges Dam Scenic Area

Planning Time: 1994–1996
Supervisors: ZHENG Guangzhong and YANG Rui
Participants: ZHANG Yonggang, LIU Jie, WANG Peng, DONG Ke, FENG Ke, BU Bing, CHEN Changqing, HE Xin, LI Benhuan, and HE Tiancheng

22. Master planning of Shandong Rushan Silver Beach Resort
Planning Time: March 1994
Supervisors: ZHENG Guangzhong and YANG Rui
Participants: LIU Jie, WEI Dehui, HUANG Weihua, JIN Lei, WANG Peng, CHEN Zhijie, QIAN Gennan, and YANG Zhengmao
23. Master planning of Shandong Rushan Silver Beach Resort City
Planning Time: 1994
24. Master planning of Three Gorges Dam Scenic Area
Planning Time: 1994–1996
25. Feasibility Study and Master planning for Developing Tourism at the Three Gorges Project Area
Planning Time: 1994–1996
Supervisors: ZHENG Guangzhong, YANG Rui, and ZHANG Min
Participants: ZHANG Yonggang, LIU Jie, WANG Peng, CHEN Changqing, HE Xin, LI Benhuan,HE Tiancheng, DONG Ke, FENG Ke, and BU Bing,
26. Yichang City Tourism Development Plan
Planning Time: 1997–1998
Participants: ZHENG Guangzhong, YANG Rui, and DENG Wei
27. Zhuhai New Yuanmingyuan Garden Design
Completion Time: 1997
Designers: GUO Daiheng, LV Zhou, LIAO Huinong, MA Lidong
28. Planning and Design the Shali River Scenic Area of Luohe
Design Time: February 1998
Supervisors: ZHENG Guangzhong, LI Yunian, DENG Wei
Participants: WANG Zhaobin, ZHANG Xiaoguang, HUANG He, ZHAO Jingfang, and JIN Li
29. Detailed Planning of the Hulun Tourist Resort, Manzhouli, Inner Mongolia
Planning Time: August 1998
Supervisors: ZHENG Guangzhong and ZHANG Min
Participants: WANG Binshan, ZHANG Jungang, HUO Xiaowei, and GAO Lidong
30. Planning and Design of the Shenzhen Waterlands Resort
Design Time: October 1998
Supervisors: ZHENG Guangzhong, ZHANG Min, and YUAN Mu
Participants: WANG Binshan, CAO Yujun, ZHAO Jingfang, YUN Shuang, XU Yang, and WANG Xiaoou
31. Detailed Planning of Daihai Tourist Resort and of Zhongshuitang Hot Spring Resort in Inner Mongolia
Planning Time: April 1999
Supervisors: ZHENG Guangzhong and ZHANG Min

Participants: WANG Binshan, FAN Sibin, SONG Yang, and XIONG Jie

32. Yuanmingyuan Conservation Planning
    Planning Time: 2000
    Participants: GUO Daiheng, etc.
33. Planning of the Yantian Eco-Tourism Resort in Shennongjia
    Planning Time: 2000
    Participants:ZHENG Guangzhong, DENG Wei, YANG Rui, LI Bosheng, etc.
34. Master planning of Mount Taishan Scenic Area and Detailed Planning of Daiding Scenic Spot
    Planning Time: January 2000
    Supervisors: ZHENG Guangzhong, YANG Rui, DENG Wei, and YUAN Mu
    Participants: WANG Binshan, ZHAO Jingfang, SONG Yang, LI Shouxu, BAI Yang, ZHU Quancheng, ZHANG Qinghua, ZHUANG Youbo, JIANG Gupeng, and WANG Zhenming
35. Master plan of Jingpohu National Scenic Area (2000–2001)
    Planning Time: September 2000–December 2001
    Participants: ZHAO Bingshi, YU Xuewen, YANG Rui, TAN Zongbo, DANG Anrong, ZHUANG Youbo, HAN Haoying, SHI Huizhen, ZHANG Qinghua, YANG Di, PAN Fang, YU Wei, LIU Jianfeng, LI Li, and WANG Xu
36. Detailed Planning of the Dujiangyan Outer River Waterfront
    Planning Time: December 2001
    Supervisors: ZHENG Guangzhong and YUAN Mu
    Participants: LIU Jie, ZHANG Qinghua, XING Guoxu, JI Haibin, and LI Shouxu
37. Detailed Planning of Mount Taishan Tianwaicun Scenic Area
    Planning Time: 2002
    Participants: ZHENG Guangzhong, YUAN Mu, YANG Rui, YE Kai, LIU Jie, WANG Binshan, ZHAO Jingfang, and DU Guowu
38. Detailed Planning of Lijiang Chama Park
    Planning Time: January 2002
    Supervisors: ZHENG Guangzhong and YUAN Mu
    Participants: ZHANG Qinghua, WANG Xiaoou, CAO Yujun, JI Haibin, and XING Guoxu
39. Detailed Planning of Songshan Shaolin Temple Scenic Area
    Planning Time: April 2002
    Supervisors: ZHENG Guangzhong and YANG Rui
    Participants: ZHANG Qinghua, JIANG Quan, LUO Tingting, CUI Baoyi, JI Haibin, YUAN Nanguo, ZHANG Rong, and YANG Haiming
40. Tibet Tourism Development Master plan (2005–2020)
    Planning Time: 2003 to 2006
    Participants: YIN Zhi, ZHENG Guangzhong, YUAN Mu, LI Bosheng, WANG Xingbin, etc.
41. Landscape Design for the Core Zone of the National Wetland Park of

Lianhua Lake, Fanhe New District, Tieling City
Completion Time: 2007
Participants: HU Jie, LV Lushan, HAN Yi, TONG Qingyuan, etc.

42. Reconstruction Planning and Design of the Daming Lake Scenic Area of Jinan
Design Time: April 2007–December 2007
Designers: ZHANG Jie, HUO Xiaowei, JIANG Ying, XU Biying, LU Liuying, etc.

43. Master plan of Zhongshan Park in Beijing
Planning Time: June 2007–May 2010
Participants: YANG Rui, ZHUANG Youbo, WU Dongfan, ZHAO Zhicong, HU Yike, WANG Yinglin, SHI Shulin, SHEN Xue, LV Qi, and ZHANG Siyuan

44. Landscape Planning and Design for the Core Zone of Tieling New City
Completion Time: 2008
Designers: HU Jie, HAN Yi, etc.

45. Master plan Longquan Mountain Resort of Chengdu
Planning Time: July 2008–November 2009
Participants: YANG Rui, LIU Hailong, DENG Bing, WU Dongfan, WANG Jingtao, CHEN Yingjin, XUE Fei, WANG Chuan, WANG Yinglin, and KONG Songyan

46. Wudalianchi Application Documents for Inscription onto the World Natural Heritage List and Conservation and Management Plan of the Nominated Property
Planning Time: August 2009–June 2011
Participants: YANG Rui, ZHUANG Youbo, LIN Guangsi, ZHAO Zhicong, ZHANG Zhenwei, WANG Yinglin, JI Wanjing, SHEN Xue, HU Yike, and XU Tingyun

47. Concept Planning of the Wudalianchi International Low-Carbon Eco-Tourism Demo Town
Planning Time: November 2009–February 2010
Participants: YANG Rui, WU Dongfan, LIU Hailong, LIN Guangsi, LIN Borong, ZHANG Zhenwei, WANG Yinglin, LIU Jiagen, JI Wanjing, SHEN Xue, ZHUANG Yongwen, and YU Qiong

48. Professor, Regulatory, and Detailed Plannings of the Wudalianchi Tourism Town
Planning Time: February 2010–September 2010
Participants: YANG Rui, WU Dongfan, LIU Hailong, LIN Guangsi, LIN Borong, ZHANG Zhenwei, WANG Yinglin, LIU Jiagen, JI Wanjing, SHEN Xue, ZHUANG Yongwen, and YU Qiong

49. Professor, Regulatory, and Detailed Plannings of the Farm New Zone of the Wudalianchi Tourism Town
Planning Time: July 2010–October 2010
Participants: YANG Rui, WU Dongfan, LIU Hailong, LIN Guangsi, ZHANG Zhenwei, YU Yang, XU Diandian, and PENG Fei

50. Urban Design of the Wudalianchi Tourism Town

Design Time: October 2010–Present
Designers: YANG Rui, WU Dongfan, YU Yang, PENG Fei, and XU Xiaoqing

51. Detailed Plan and Feasibility Study of Environmental Renovation for Outer Altar of Temple of Heaven Landscape
    Planning Time: November 2009–Present
    Participants: YANG Rui, WU Dongfan, WANG Chuan, XU Diandian, PENG Fei, and YU Yang
52. Landscape and Gardening Planning and Design of the Ningxia Sandy Dunes Park
    Completion Time: 2009
    Designers: HU Jie, WU Yixia, LV Lushan, AN Youfeng, GUO Zheng, etc.
53. Landscape Planning and Design of Tangshan Fengnan Zone in Xicheng Ward
    Completion Time: 2010
    Designers: HU Jie, AN Youfeng, LV Lushan, WU Yixia, SHEN Dan, etc.
54. Core Area Landscape Planning for Dalian Lushun New Harbor City
    Completion Time: 2010
    Designers: HU Jie, PAN Furong, etc.
55. Core Area Landscape Planning and Design for Fuxin Yulong New City
    Completion Time: 2010
    Designers: HU Jie, MA Yu, LU Bihan, ZOU Yubo, David Clough, Bruno Pelucca, etc.
56. Bronze Art Plaza Design in Ordos City
    Completion Time: 2010
    Designers: HU Jie, WU Yixia, LV Lushan, HAN Yi, etc.
57. Hoelun Park Design in Ordos City
    Completion Time: 2010
    Designers: HU Jie, LV Lushan, HAN Yi, etc.
58. Conceptual Master Plan of Wuhan East Lake Scenic Area
    Design Time: 2007–2008
    Designers: YANG Rui, ZHUANG Youbo, WU Dongfan, WANG Jingtao, HU Yike, ZHAO Zhicong, LV Qi, ZHANG Siyuan, YAN Xida, and MENG Yujing
59. Conceptual Master planning for Kanbula Resorts in Qinghai Province
    Design Time: 2007–2008
    Designers: YANG Rui, ZHUANG Youbo, ZHOU Jingfeng, LIU Huan, ZHAO Zhicong, HU Yike, YAN Keyu, and NIU Mujing
60. Mount Hua Application Documents for Inscription onto the World Natural and Cultural Heritage List and Preliminary Studies for the Conservation and Management Plan of the Nominated Property
    Planning Time: 2008–2009
    Participants: YANG Rui, WU Dongfan, ZHUANG Youbo, ZHAO Zhicong, HU Yike, LV Qi, ZHANG Siyuan, WANG Yinglin, CHENG

Guanhua, and MENG Yujing

61. Landscape Planning and Design of Chongqing Longhu Wisdom City
    Planning Time: December, 2009
    Designers: ZHU Yufan, YAO Yujun, QI Ling, TIAN Ying, WANG Danqing, JIA Jing, CAO Ran, YANG Zhanzhan, Tang Jianren, SUN Tianzheng, LIANG Shangyu, HOU Fang, and WEI Fang
62. "Water Seal" at Venice Biennale
    Exhibition Time: September to November, 2010
    Designers: ZHU Yufan, TIAN Ying, BAO Ruiqing, MENG Fanyu, YANG Zhanzhan, and YANG Mi
63. Landscape Design for Liaoyang Yanxiu Park, Liaoning Province
    Completion Time: 2012
    Designers: HU Jie, AN Yongfeng, LV Lushan, etc.
64. Outdoor Environment Design of Shanghai International Trade Center
    Completion Time: 2012
    Designers: ZHU Yufan, YAO Yujun, WANG Dan, QI Ling, YAN Zhiguo, MENG Fanyu, LIU Wenao, ZHAI Weiwei, DONG Shunfang, CUI Shiyao, CHANG Yulin, LV Hui, and YANG Xi.
65. Landscape Planning and Design of the Greening System and Waterfront Forest Park of Future Science City in Beijing
    Completion Time: 2013
    Designers: HU Jie, LV Lushan, WANG Xiaoyang, MA Yu, CUI Yanan, etc.
66. Landscape Design of West Hill Base of Creation Industry in Beijing
    Completion Time: 2013
    Designers: ZHU Yufan, YAO Yujun, YANG Zhanzhan, TIAN Ying, MENG Yao, GONG Qinchun, WEI Fang, CUI Qingwei, HU Hao, etc.